DEFINING JUDAISM

Critical Categories in the Study of Religion

Series Editor: Russell T. McCutcheon, Professor, Department of Religious Studies, University of Alabama

Critical Categories in the Study of Religion aims to present the pivotal articles that best represent the most important trends in how scholars have gone about the task of describing, interpreting, and explaining the place of religion in human life. The series focuses on the development of categories and the terminology of scholarship that make possible knowledge about human beliefs, behaviors, and institutions. Each volume in the series is intended as both an introductory survey of the issues that surround the use of various key terms as well as an opportunity for a thorough retooling of the concept under study, making clear to readers that the cognitive categories of scholarship are themselves historical artefacts that change over time.

Published:

Syncretism in Religion
A Reader
Edited by Anita M. Leopold and Jeppe Sinding Jensen

Ritual and Religious Belief
A Reader
Edited by Graham Harvey

Defining Hinduism
A Reader
Edited by J.E. Llewellyn

Religion and Cognition
A Reader
Edited by D. Jason Slone

Mircea Eliade
A Critical Reader
Edited by Bryan Rennie

Defining Buddhism(s)
A Reader
Edited by Karen Derris and Natalie Gummer

Defining Islam
A Reader
Edited by Andrew Rippin

Myths and Mythologies
A Reader
Edited by Jeppe Sinding Jensen

Readings in the Theory of Religion
Map, Text, Body
Edited by Scott S. Elliott and
Matthew Waggoner

Forthcoming:

Defining Religion
A Reader
Edited by Tim Murphy

Religious Experience
A Reader
Edited by Russell T. McCutcheon and
Leslie Smith

Missions, Management and Effects
A Reader in Religion and Colonialism
Edited by Mark Elmore and Caleb Elfenbein

What is Religious Studies?
A Reader in Disciplinary Formation
Edited by Steven J. Sutcliffe

Defining Shinto
A Reader
Edited by Okuyama Michiaki and
Mark MacWilliams

DEFINING JUDAISM

A READER

Edited by

Aaron W. Hughes

LONDON   OAKVILLE

Published by

UK: Equinox Publishing Ltd., Unit 6, The Village, 101 Amies St., London SW11 2JW
USA: DBBC, 28 Main Street, Oakville, CT 06779

www.equinoxpub.com

First published 2010

British Library Cataloguing-in-Publication Data
A catalogue record for this book is available from the British Library.

ISBN-13   978 1 84553 608 4 (hardback)
           978 1 84553 609 1 (paperback)

Library of Congress Cataloging-in-Publication Data

Defining Judaism : a reader / edited by Aaron W. Hughes.
       p. cm. — (Critical categories in the study of religion)
    Includes bibliographical references and index.
    ISBN 978-1-84553-608-4 (hb) —
    ISBN 978-1-84553-609-1 (pb) 1.
  Judaism. I. Hughes, Aaron W., 1968-
  BM40.D44 2009
  296—dc22
                                    2009022376

Typeset by S.J.I. Services, New Delhi
Printed and bound in Great Britain by Antony Rowe, Chippenham, Wiltshire

CONTENTS

ACKNOWLEDGEMENTS

Chapter 1: Saadya Gaon. *The Book of Beliefs and Opinions.* Translated by Samuel Rosenblatt. Pp. 14–37. © 1948, Yale University Press. Used by permission of the publisher.

Chapter 2: Maimonides, Moses. "Thirteen Articles of Faith." In J. Abelson, "Maimonides on the Jewish Creed." In *The Jewish Quarterly Review* 19/1, pp. 47–58. October, 1906. In public domain.

Chapter 3: *Transactions of the Parisian Sanhedrin, Or, Acts of the Assembly of the Israelitish Deputies of France and Italy, Convoked at Paris by an Imperial and Royal Decree dated May 30, 1806.* Collected by Diogene Tama and translated by F. D. Kirwan. Pp. 149–57, 176–83, 193–207. London, 1807. In public domain.

Chapter 4: Geiger, Abraham. *Judaism and Its History.* Pp. 230–46. Lanham: University Press of America, 1911. In public domain.

Chapter 5: Plaskow, Judith. "Setting the Problem, Laying the Ground." In *Standing Again at Sinai.* Pp. 1–24. © 1990 by Judith Plaskow. Used by permission of HarperCollins.

Chapter 6: Boyarin, Daniel. "Apartheid Comparative Religion in the Second Century: Some Theory and a Case Study." In *Journal of Medieval and Early Modern Studies* 36/1, pp. 3–34. © 2006, Duke University Press. All rights reserved. Used by permission of the publisher.

Chapter 7: Wasserstrom, Steven. "Who Were the Jews? Problems in Profiling the Jewish Community Under Early Islam." In *Between Muslim and Jew: The Problem of*

Introduction:
Judaism, Judaisms, Jewish: Toward Redefining
Traditional *Taxa*

Aaron W. Hughes

Defining Judaism, like defining any phenomenon, is fraught with problems. Whose Judaism? What counts as valid data, or not? Who decides on the parameters of inclusion and exclusion? Definition is a politically- and ideologically-charged activity, something imposed, both retroactively and from the outside, on a complex and often unwieldy set of data. Definition often forces order when there is no such thing. This imposition of order on chaos is reflected in the very act of defining something: we must first isolate that which is to be defined, the *definiendum*, from its immediate contexts, subsequently dislodge it by removing all that had hitherto connected it to these contexts, and then analyze it by comparing and contrasting it to other *definienda*. Such analysis can either signal the object's uniqueness (for a critique of this approach, see Smith 1990, 36–53) or attempt to point out the resemblances, familial or otherwise, with other phenomena that have been ascertained using similar methods. Definition, like so many of our academic activities, is a fragile, highly fractured, and ultimately artificial process.

Despite this fragility or artificiality, persist we must. The way we define the objects of our definitions, and the reasons behind our willingness or desire to engage in the activity in the first place, demand transparency. According to the now famous and oft-quoted formulation by J. Z. Smith:

> Religion is solely the creation of the scholar's study. It is created for the scholar's analytic purposes by his imaginative acts of comparison and generalization. Religion has no independent existence apart from the academy. For this reason, the student of religion, and most particularly the historian of religion, must be relentlessly self-conscious. Indeed this self-consciousness constitutes his primary expertise, his foremost object of study. (Smith 1982, xi)

Without such self-consciousness and self-reflection we risk further reifying the reifications implicit in our definitions and further essentializing their often-bland essentialisms. Definitions, and an understanding of this principle is crucial to our enterprise, level the topography of our interaction with and in the world, simplify the complex, and sully an accurate representation of an imagined reality that paradoxically we construct and by which we are alternatively constructed. Definitions, by definition, constrict. We must attempt to pry them open by means of constant scrutiny and the realization that phenomena are not stable and eternal, but undergo constant change and fluctuation in response to a variety of other related and often non-related variables.

Definition must, at least in theory, do the impossible. It must both tell us what some "thing" is and subsequently provide an account of this thing's temporal, geographic, and gendered difference. This is surely an impossible task and involves giving with one hand and then taking away with the other. How one defined Judaism[1] in the second century CE differs radically from how it was defined in the twelfth century, and both of these definitions would, in turn, seem strange to someone doing the defining now. For example, a lesbian Reform Jew would have a radically different understanding of the meaning of Judaism than, say, most Orthodox males. Likewise, a Conservative Jew living in Buffalo would likely define the parameters of Judaism differently than a Hasidic Jew in Jerusalem. From the outside looking in, we certainly would not hesitate to define them all as "Jewish," even though the people we are defining as Jews would probably chafe at our definition and all of them would differ on many basic issues, not the least of which is who even gets to count as a Jew in the first place (see, e.g., Freedman 2000). In all of these cases, it is often assumed—both by the individual actors and those doing the analysis—that to be Jewish is an objective reality, when in point of fact Jewish identity, like any type of identity, is a state of consciousness that is constructed based on a host of temporal, spatial, and geographical forces (Bourdieu 1984, 466–70; Bayart 2005, 22). And as such, Jewish identity is as empty and as fictive as any other identity-formation.

To be human is to define. Without definitions we would have chaos and thus even more uncertainty. What makes defining anything possible and necessary, however, also makes it problematic from an analytical perspective. If we lock the world and all of the phenomena in it into a series of rigid categories and terms of our own invention, we risk seeing the world (and indeed the word) monochromatically. Defining Judaism comes at a cost—a cost of distortion, a cost of exclusion, a cost of misrepresentation— unless we keep our sense of definition and our task of defining open. Towards this end, I have collected together the following chapters that all deal in one way or another with defining or understanding Judaism. These chapters present contradictory accounts of Judaism; some want to define the tradition very narrowly; others open it to the surrounding milieux in ways that frequently blur the distinctions between "Jew" and "non-Jew." Taken as a whole and not just as the sum of its parts, however, this collection reveals something of the manifold ways that scholars have interpreted, explained, and understood Judaism, both synchronically and diachronically.

Defining Definitions

Definitions seek to understand their *definiendum*—claiming, for example, that it is "a" and "b," but not "c" and "d"—both as an analytical category and as a real human phenomenon. Largely interested in locating and ascertaining essence, definitions rarely want to tell us about the permutations their objects undergo historically in relation to a series of other such objects. How can a pithy few sentences define, describe, analyze, and celebrate at the same time? They cannot and this difficulty is exacerbated whenever we attempt to make definitions, as we inevitably do, a central component of bringing order—deciding what is in and what is out—to unwieldy "traditions" that span over centuries or millennia. David Chidester has argued that the modern study of religion works on an "apartheid" model. According to him, we are determined to "identify and reify the many languages, cultures, peoples, and religions of the world as if they were separate and distinct regions" (1996, 4). We are then able to compare and contrast "religions" as if they were stable entities that move unchanged throughout history and in all those places—temporally and geographically—in which they have existed and indeed where they continue to exist. Definition plays a central role in this activity and this activity is largely responsible for precisely the sort of hermetically sealed containers by which we subsequently compare and contrast various human beings and their systems and ideologies (including religion). This is a model that is also perpetuated in classrooms, in textbooks, and very often in our own writing about "religion." This approach, again to quote Chidester, is responsible for organizing "human diversity into rigid, static categories [as] one strategy for simplifying, and thereby achieving some cognitive control over, the bewildering complexity of a frontier zone" (1996, 22–23).[2]

The chapters that follow seek to define something of the nature or quiddity of Judaism. My goal in putting them in counterpoint with one another is to show that attempts to define Judaism are always conditioned by historical circumstances, the politics of identity, and various ideologies informing constructions of some perceived authenticity. This is especially true for the first section of the book, which presents a series of historical and chronological vignettes of what Judaism is or should be. In the two final sections the concern is less with defining Judaism *per se* than with various attempts to demonstrate something of the permeability and the flexibility necessary to understanding Judaism (or Judaisms) in relationship to other traditions, using the familiar categories associated with critical discourses in the academic study of religion and cognate disciplines.

The following chapters attempt to show some of the myriad contexts wherein Judaism has been understood, explained, interpreted and re-interpreted, configured and re-configured. I am less interested in the history of Judaism as a civilization or as a world religion than I am in how various individuals—living in different times and places—have successively labeled and defined something as "Jewish" and how this category has been subsequently deployed in ways that seek to make sense of a series of overlapping human beliefs, behaviors, and institutions. Taken as a whole, these chapters show the paradoxes, the contradictions, and the confusions that emerge when "Judaism" has been, often all too neatly, differentiated from a variety of cognate beliefs, behaviors, and institutions within the non-Jewish cultures in which Jews frequently found themselves.

Defining Judaism: A Subset of Defining Religion

It is important to contextualize the problem of defining Judaism as a subset of the larger species of defining religion. The terms we use, the cognitive categories we manufacture, and the various issues that we deem important are never completely innocent and are often implicated in all sorts of ideological, xenophobic, and racist genealogies. These genealogies have contributed to the manifold ways that we continue to describe, interpret, and explain the various beliefs, institutions, and customs that are regarded as constituent elements of something lazily dubbed as "religion" or "religious." When students are introduced to religion in general or a religion in particular, they often hear claims of "transcendence" or "sacrality." Such claims are in many ways endemic to the discipline (see the comments in McCutcheon 1997; Fitzgerald 2000), thereby unnecessarily and artificially separating that which is deemed "religious" from other cultural, political, ideological, and social phenomena. As far as I am concerned, whenever we define Judaism simply in terms of its commitment to monotheism we echo virtually the only positive element that philosophers highly critical of Judaism, a tradition that Kant did not even want to label a religion (see the comments in Bland 2000, 15–22; Mack 2003, 23–41), were willing to assent to.

Instead of invoking reified claims to transcendence or monotheism, the chapters that comprise the final two-thirds of this volume rarely attempt to define Judaism by appeals to such essences. Instead they provide tremendous insight into the porous nature of the boundaries separating "Judaism" from, for lack of a better term, "non-Judaism." In so doing, these essays are cognizant of the artificiality of the entire project devoted to the act of defining. On this latter point more generally, I quote from the work of Tim Murphy:

> Modern linguistics has shown that "definition" is not a natural, inevitable, activity, but it is a *specific* trope or operation, a very particular manner for dealing with words, one which tends to reduce language to the meaning of *individual* words. (Murphy 2007, 5; his italics)

The danger is that a naïve understanding of definition will lead us to the assumption that because there exists a single word (e.g., religion, Judaism) then there must also exist some essence that the word itself names or signifies. This nominalist view of language

> efface[s] "real history" because it claims—perhaps only very implicitly, by the very manner of its definitional act—that there is an unchanging, constant, meaning to the *definiendum* which is there, irregardless of context, time or place. (Murphy 2007, 5)

Here we need to be cautious that our categories are precisely that, a series of attempts to fit, or—perhaps better—force, the world we encounter into a set of conceptual boxes that we have created for it. In so doing, we establish what will count as facts and, subsequently, the disciplinary fields in which these facts become objects of analysis (cf. Hughes 2007, 33–40). What follows then is meant to look at the history of the discourse or set of discourses within which "Judaism" has been variously signified and from which it has taken on its various meanings. Following Clifford Geertz, it is essential to acknowledge that

> cultural analysis is (or should be) guessing at meanings, assessing the guesses and drawing explanatory conclusions from the better guesses, not discovering the Continent of Meaning and mapping out its bodiless landscape. (Geertz 1973, 20)

Defining a complex and multifaceted tradition like Judaism cannot be about making a series of neat incisions to safely remove its "religious" essence from other historical and cultural contexts. On the contrary, it is necessary to be aware of the difficulty of the enterprise and to realize our obsession with essences and the concomitant notion of artificiality that arises whenever we try to isolate a series of features under the guise of defining Judaism.

Attempts to Define Judaism

Since the following chapters attempt to locate and define something as "Judaism" from within, it is also important to be aware that many attempts to define this religion (or, as it came to be known in the nineteenth and twentieth centuries, "race") came from the outside. It is, thus, important to be aware of the dialectics of Jews defining the tradition and non-Jews doing the same, especially how the former often play off the latter. Regardless of their point of origin, all of these definitions take complexity and turn it into the simple; take the richness of polyphony and put it into the staccato of mono-rhythm.

Defining a Jew, of course, is always a political or an ideological act. Consider, for example, the following two examples. In paragraph 17 of the "Law Regarding the Restoration of Professional Service" (April 7, 1933) we read that

> A person is to be regarded as non-Aryan, who is descended from non-Aryans, especially Jewish parents or grandparents. This holds true even if only one parent or grandparent is of non-Aryan descent. This premise especially obtains if one parent or grandparent was of Jewish faith... If Aryan descent is doubtful, an opinion must be obtained from the expert on racial research commissioned by the Reich minister of the Interior. (Mendes-Flohr and Reinharz 1995, 642)

In this decree, the first step on the path to depriving Jews of their civil rights, non-Aryans (the term used in legal documents as a circumlocution for Jews) are defined as any individual having at least one grandparent who was non-Aryan. This definition, imposed from without, is meant to create an ontological division between Jew and non-Jew. It draws its potency from contemporaneous racial theory and romantic notions of Volkishness (cf. Lincoln 1999, 47–75) and seeks to define some stable core of Jewishness that can be neatly differentiated from non-Jewishness. Here we see the obsession for essences and definitions as a way to control, master, and ultimately to exterminate.

Example number two comes from an amendment (1970) to the Law of Return to the State of Israel (1950). Like the previous attempt at definition, we once again see the contours of Jewishness emerge through genealogy:

> 4A. (a) The rights of a Jew under this Law and the rights of an [immigrant] under the Nationality Law, 5712-1952, as well as the rights of an [immigrant] under any other enactment, are also vested in a child and a grandchild of a Jew, the spouse of a Jew, the spouse of a child of a Jew and the spouse of a grandchild of a Jew, except for a person who has been a Jew and has voluntarily changed his religion.

> Definition:

> 4B. For the purposes of this Law, "Jew" means a person who was born of a Jewish mother or has become converted to Judaism and who is not a member of another religion. (Israel Ministry of Foreign Affairs)

Here we see the imposition of who is a Jew or who gets to call oneself a Jew based on political expediency, this time to resettle the land of Israel in the aftermath of the Shoah (Holocaust). It is more inclusive than the previous definition because one can become Jewish based on conversion;[3] yet it is also a definition that too easily masks the political struggles of who gets to define Jewishness and the various contestations that occur along these fault-lines.[4]

Although these two examples are extreme in their appeals to a complex web of political, ethnic, and religious claims, nevertheless they both reveal that definitions are never arbitrary nor completely innocent, but often serve the agenda of those who propose them. To juxtapose these two definitions with more contemporary understandings, it might be worth, Hegelian-like, to introduce a third understanding of Judaism into the picture, that of Madonna Louise Veronica Ciccone:

I'm never going to be Jewish, and I hate the phrase. And I've not converted to Judaism, and I'm not a member of any religion. It just makes me sick when people say that all the time, because nobody ever bothers to do the research to find out what it actually is. [Kabbalah] is not a religion. It's a belief system, a philosophy... Religion fragments people, and Kabbalah unifies people. (qtd. in Myers 2007, 121–22)

Here, Madonna is quite happy to partake of the "philosophy" of Jewish mysticism without buying into the "religious" practices of Judaism. Without wanting to get into her (or the Kabbalah Center's) misreading of classical kabbalah, it should suffice to point out that this definition emerges from a particular New Age critique of religion and fondness for spirituality. On her reading, then, Judaism—like all religions—is a highly politicized entity that prevents people from realizing their spiritual potential. For Madonna, religion in general and Judaism in particular are inherently divisive and this divisiveness is ultimately responsible for the problems we face.

Without wanting to give Madonna, especially her definition of Judaism, the final word in this section, I think it important to reiterate that definitions of religions are never innocent and that such definitions often have genealogies, whether implicit or explicit, that need unpacking and further analysis.

Defining Judaism in the Classroom

The major question facing anyone who teaches religious studies is how to employ critical categories in the classroom. Many of the textbooks that we employ work on the twin assumptions that religion neatly exists in the world and that it can be easily defined (e.g., as human's encounter with the transcendent or with ultimate reality). These assumptions are usually informed by liberal Protestant assumptions that religion is something internal and that it is timeless and eternal (for a critique, see McCutcheon 2005, 52–60). But religion, if it in fact exists, does so in history, in culture, and can only be studied in those contexts. Moreover, assuming that religions exist, for no other reason than that practitioners say they do, it is important not to assume that they do so as hermetically sealed entities that move effortlessly throughout the historical record. Religions morph, change, absorb, and respond to changing ideological and historical circumstances. All of this should signal that we must be very careful when speaking of religion in general and specific religions in particular.

Unfortunately, it is precisely in such a manner that religion is introduced in the classroom. Consider, for example, several of the dozens of introductory textbooks or websites that seek to introduce students to Western religions. According to these, Judaism is "a monotheistic religion based on principles and ethics embodied in the Hebrew Bible, as further explored and explained in the Talmud and other texts. Judaism is among the oldest religious traditions still being practiced today" (Wikipedia); "the commitment to monotheism" (Ludwig 2006, 115); "a belief in the oneness of God who works in and through historical events and who has in some manner chosen the Jewish people as agents" (Hopfe and Woodward 2007, 233); or as having "its historical origins in an act of obedience" (Jaffee 1998, 3).

All of these definitions may well tell us something of what we, or the people doing the defining, imagine Judaism to be. However, they also tell us surprisingly little about the complexity of both Judaism and Jewishness. A commitment to monotheism does little to differentiate Judaism from either Christianity or Islam. An emphasis on peoplehood does little to clarify this concept and the various permutations that it has undergone both temporally and geographically (witness the chapters in Part II below). The reality is often much more complex than textbook presentations imply. Yet we continue to subject students to these neat and tidy formulations so that they may better *understand* something of Judaism in ways that coincide with their existing assumptions about the nature of religion and how it works, or should work, in people's lives.

While definitions such as the above may well provide something of an overview of Judaism, they do little to address the complexities and nuances within the tradition. As in so many other traditions, it is perhaps easier and probably much more accurate to speak of *Judaisms* in the plural as opposed to the monovocality suggested by the singular. One of the greatest desiderata of modern Jewish Studies scholarship, in this regard, is to try and trace the anatomical contours of Judaism/s from the late antique period to the present. To quote Steven Wasserstrom, for example,

> Trajectories of Judaism into early Islam remain a vexed area of research. We know very little in any detail concerning the varieties of Judaism from the destruction of the Temple in 70 C.E. until the efflorescence of datable Jewish sources in the ninth and tenth centuries. Until we know more concerning the physiognomy of Judaism during the rise and development of Islam, we can draw few serious conclusions concerning the relation between the two communities. (1995, 13)

Here Wasserstrom correctly notes that our understanding of Judaism is only as good as the historical record. What we know about Judaism in any given historical period necessarily determines what we can say about its contours and the various ways in which the symbols associated with this tradition are utilized and manipulated by a variety of groups that we today label as "Jewish." Having said this, however, we cannot assume that the anatomy of Judaism in late antiquity or the middle ages was what it is today. The borderlines separating Judaism from all that is not-Judaism are often not nearly as clear, especially on the margins, as we would like them to be. The tendency is to assume that these borders are airtight when, in fact, they are anything but.

Defining Judaism as a "Religion"

There is a clichéd observation that "the rabbis didn't do theology" in any way that could be called a sustained treatment. This is both significant and disappointing. It is disappointing because it is often very difficult to isolate a topic that we today deem important and subsequently derive a neat and tidy answer in rabbinic sources. It is, however, also significant because it clearly reveals that the rabbis of late antiquity and of the middle ages were not nearly as interested in clearly defining "Judaism" as we are today. In other words, they were quite unwilling to excise a particular set of phenomena as religious in such a manner that differentiated this set neatly or sharply with other related cultural, legal, and social phenomena. This is certainly not to say that there do not exist many highly technical halakhic or legal questions and discussions about determining Jewish pedigrees (e.g., *Talmud Kiddushin*) or the procedures for conversion (*Yevamot*). However, these discussions rarely provide the types of answers to the types of questions deemed significant by the discipline of religious studies.

It is only in the medieval period that we begin to catch glimpses of what we would today consider to be more appropriate definitions of Jewishness (witness the first two selections in Part I). These discussions, however, only emerge in response to a series of internal threats by groups who questioned the authority of the Oral Torah (e.g., the Talmud) and instead emphasized the Hebrew Bible without all of the subsequent rabbinic commentary. The result was the need to respond to such internal attacks and thereby establish the parameters of true belief. In the case of Saadya Gaon (our first selection, below), the person who was most responsible for formulating the rabbinic response to Karaism,[5] this meant defining Jews as a people by virtue of the written and oral Torahs. Maimonides, a twelfth-century figure and the author of our second selection, attempts to define Judaism by articulating a series of principles to which true believers must attest. Less concerned with sectarian polemics than Saadya, Maimonides main concern is to raise the level of what he considers to be proper worship (Lerner 2000, 3–13).

In the modern period, beginning in late-eighteenth-century France and Germany, there emerge a series of full-blown attempts to define Judaism in ways that we would today recognize as a religion in the modern sense of the term. These definitions, certainly not coincidentally, develop out of non-Jewish attempts to carve out a space for Christianity in the face of encroaching Enlightenment ideals and all of the scientific and industrial repercussions that followed in their wake (e.g., Hertzberg 1990 [1968]; Meyer 1967, 29–56). If Jews are to be at home in Europe, the main question that concerned both Jews and non-Jews was how could the former be successfully integrated into mainstream society. Perhaps Moses Mendelssohn (1729–1986), the first Jewish philosopher of the modern period, best summarizes this sentiment in his own definition of Judaism:

> I recognize no eternal truths other than those that are not merely comprehensible to human reason but can also be demonstrated *and verified by human powers*... I believe that Judaism knows of no revealed religion in the sense in which Christians understand this term. The Israelites possess a divine *legislation*— laws, commandments, ordinances, rules of life...but no doctrinal opinions, no saving truths, no universal propositions of reason. These the Eternal reveals to

us and to all other men, at all times, through *nature* and *thing*, but never through *word* and *script*. (1983 [1783], 89–90; his italics)

As this passage by Mendelssohn—and the third and fourth selections below—reveals, making Judaism into a religion involved transforming it into something internal to the individual, making it an inner experience or set of experiences that would enable the individual to function as a regular member of society. Many of these discussions centered on the role of the *mitzvot* ("commandments"): If Judaism was now a religion, based on inner experience, did one really have to perform all of the onerous *mitzvot*, anchored as they were in action as opposed to belief, that threatened to alienate Jews from their non-Jewish neighbors? It is in their differing responses to this and related questions that the main forms of modern Judaism (i.e., Reform, Conservative, and Orthodoxy) came into existence. Unlike earlier formulations, all of these modern conceptions of Judaism worked on the European model of binaries that included religious/political, sacred/profane, inner experience/outer observance, etc. We can read, for example, Abraham Geiger (1810–1874), the author of Chapter 4 below, and one of the founding fathers of Reform Judaism, claim:

> Religion is not an invention of idle priests; it existed and exists in mankind, and every good and noble aspiration—when man, putting aside his seclusive selfishness, lovingly and fervently attaches himself to his country and gives to it his own life and welfare and gladly labors for all and is filled with the desire to strive toward the Highest—is the work of religion. Though religion may present itself according to its rise in various outward forms, religion, as such, is a necessity, the noblest feature within man. If Judaism did and still does work such an effect as religion, it is one of the noblest animating forces among mankind. (Geiger 1985 [1911], 22–23)

Geiger here makes religious sentiment internal to the individual, thereby encouraging Jews not to set themselves apart from their fellow citizens, but rather to "attach themselves to their country," to be nothing other than Germans whose religion happens to be that of Judaism. Many would certainly follow Geiger's advice, but once they entered mainstream German (or other European) society *en masse*, they were quickly labeled or defined as Jews again, only this time from the outside, and the consequences, as the horrors of the twentieth century well attest, were anything but academic. Defining Judaism and individual Jews now became invested in the activity of extermination and genocide.

The Contours of Judaism: Centers and Margins

Too often, scholars working in the areas of religious studies fall into the trap of writing as though communities constitute themselves through a simple recuperation of a true essence, thereby ignoring the task of communal invention and reinvention, and the multiform challenges posed by enforcing the bounds of community. Communities, as Benedict Anderson reminds us, are after all imagined (2006 [1983]) and, as such, we should focus more on the contents and ideologies associated with such imaginings. This, in turn, will enable us to understand something of the strategies associated with the discourses both producing and governing cultural identities and perceived authenticities (Bayart 2005, 7–15).

A focus on boundaries, especially the collaborations and clashes that take place on or around them, should force us to question not only their perceived given nature, but also the so-called "centers." It is for this reason that I have chosen the essays in Part II below. One of the most interesting and unique aspects of Judaism is that, from roughly the first century CE, Jewish existence has largely been diasporic. As a consequence, Judaism has always developed, morphed, and changed in the midst of other—for lack of a better term—"civilizations." Although many contemporaneous sources are quick to posit hard and fast lines between Jews and non-Jews, these lines were often much more porous than these sources might let on because their goal—as the chapters by D. Boyarin, Wasserstrom, and Bodian make clear—was both the construction and maintenance of such boundaries.

However, the diasporic existence of Judaism makes necessary the exploration and interrogation of borderlines with the ultimate aim of calling into question their ideological positioning and assumed naturalness. This, it seems to me, begins to decenter the entire enterprise that neatly separates phenomena and is ultimately responsible for their traditional categorization. This shift toward boundaries, toward the idea that the real action is at the margins and not at the center, destabilizes our notions of or attachments to identity, whether collective or otherwise. As the chapters in this section demonstrate, the attachment to some positive projection of a *sui generis* core of group identity is often precisely that, a projection. In particular, how is it possible to think about the borderlines separating "Christians" from "Jews" in the third century or "Muslims" from "Jews" in the eleventh century or Jews and (ex-)conversos in Amsterdam in the seventeenth century from the vantage point of today where the lines separating such identities are often firmly entrenched in the given order? How, for example, does the current and seemingly intractable impasse between Jew and Arab, or Jew and Muslim, refract the ways in which we think about pre-modern boundaries between such groups? Are we forced to inscribe modern conceptions of "Jewishness" and "Arabness" or "Muslimness," which are often defined using hard and fast essentialisms, onto the historical record? Or, perhaps do we realize the political and ideological implications of such definitions, as we glimpse at various regimes of truth that skirmish with one other around highly contested concepts and terms?

Future Prospects

The essays in the final section of this volume also represent recent trends in thinking about Judaism as a category in the discipline of religious studies. Building upon the work being done in Jewish margins and how this, in turn, impacts centers, has many important and exhilarating repercussions. The chapter by Eilberg-Schwartz presents an attempt to bridge the often-disparate studies of Judaism and critical discourses that emerge from the field of religious studies, especially the anthropology of religion. He does this by deconstructing the traditional boundaries separating "Judaism" from so-called "savage" religions, and by analyzing the symbolic language and social practices that inform Jewish practices of, for example, circumcision and menstruation.

Eilberg-Schwartz's emphasis on structural anthropology naturally leads into Jonathan Boyarin's postmodern anthropology. His suggestive piece explores the intersecting set of ideas associated with ethnicity, personhood, and contemporary Jewish identity. In an essay not included here, entitled "Death and the Minyan," Boyarin explains that

> it remains tempting to write nostalgically of (Jewish) community (especially) as a survival. And yet it remains important to guard against the rhetoric of "survivals" today, because the word presumes the existence of the past of authentic community, when such an assumption in our own present is precisely what we are trying to interrogate. (1996, 65–66)

Here he is interested in what it means to think in a Jewish body, situated within a Jewish milieu, the constructed nature of both, and how all of this ultimately grounds and limits one's thoughts.

The final chapter, my own, takes us out of the realm of Jewish cultural studies and into that of Jewish thought and philosophy. Now the focus is on some of the traditional texts of Judaism, but this time filtered through a new hermeneutical prism. My interest here is the series of relationships that open up between Jewish philosophy and its relationship both to "traditional" Judaism and the various non-Jewish cultures in which Jews found themselves. In particular, I suggest, using certain trajectories within modern literary theory, that we need to focus on genre as opposed to just ideas, on the polemical tenor of philosophy, and on philosophy's social, cultural, and religious embodiedness.

Notes

1. Being well aware that the term "Judaism" is an English-language term and would not have been employed by any second-century Jew, or twelfth-century Jew either for that matter.
2. On the uses to which this model can be applied for thinking about Judaism, see the chapter by Daniel Boyarin—entitled "Apartheid Comparative Religion in the Second Century: Some Theory and a Case Study"—below.
3. Although this is now no longer as tidy as it may seem, since only certain conversions (i.e., Orthodox) and not others (e.g. Reform, Conservative) have been traditionally acknowledged or sanctioned by the Ministry of Religious Affairs.

4. For example, in the state of Israel there are at least 250,000 immigrants from the former Soviet Union who, according to the Orthodox rabbinate, are not recognized as Jews, but who themselves may be very happy and contented to label themselves as such.
5. Karaism was a Jewish sectarian movement that rejected the Oral Torah and rabbinic readings of scripture for a form of Judaism that stressed the literal level of the Bible without rabbinic interpretation (see, e.g., Nemoy 1952; Frank 2004).

References

Anderson, Benedict. 2006 [1983]. *Imagined Communities: Reflections on the Origin and Spread of Nationalism*. Rev. ed. London: Verso.

Bayart, Jean-François. 2005. *The Illusion of Cultural Identity*. Chicago: University of Chicago Press.

Bland, Kalman P. 2000. *The Artless Jew: Medieval and Modern Affirmations and Denials of the Visual*. Princeton: Princeton University Press.

Bourdieu, Pierre. 1984. *Distinction: A Social Critique of the Judgement of Taste*. Translated by Richard Nice. Cambridge, MA: Harvard University Press.

Boyarin, Jonathan. 1996. "Death and the Minyan." In Jonathan Boyarin, *Thinking in Jewish*, 63–86. Chicago: University of Chicago Press.

Chidester, David. 1996. *Savage Systems: Colonialism and Comparative Religion in Southern Africa*. Charlottesville: University Press of Virginia.

Fitzgerald, Timothy. 2000. *The Ideology of Religious Studies*. New York: Oxford University Press.

Frank, Daniel. 2004. *Search Scripture Well: Karaite Exegesis and the Origins of the Jewish Bible Commentary in the Islamic East*. Leiden: Brill.

Freedman, Samuel. 2000. *Jew vs. Jew: The Struggle for the Soul of American Jewry*. New York: Simon and Schuster.

Geertz, Clifford. 1973. *The Interpretation of Cultures*. New York: Basic Books.

Geiger, Abraham. 1985 [1911]. *Judaism and its History in Two Parts*. Lanham, MD: University Press of America.

Hertzberg, Arthur. 1990 [1968]. *The French Enlightenment and the Jews: The Origins of Modern Anti-Semitism*. New York: Columbia University Press.

Hopfe, Lewis M., and Mark R. Woodward. 2007. *Religions of the World*. 10th ed. Upper Saddle River, NJ: Prentice Hall.

Hughes, Aaron W. 2007. *Situating Islam: The Past and Future of an Academic Discipline*. London: Equinox.

Israel Ministry of Foreign Affairs. 5710-1970. *The Law of Return*. Online at http://www.mfa.gov.il/MFA/MFAArchive/1950_1959/Law+of+Return+5710-1950.htm.

Jaffee, Martin S. 1998. "Scripture and Tradition in Judaism." In *Jewish, Christians, Muslims: A Comparative Introduction to Monotheistic Religions*, ed. John Corrigan, Frederick M. Denny, Carlos M. N. Eire, and Martin S. Jaffee, 3–25. Upper Saddle River, NJ: Prentice Hall.

Lerner, Ralph. 2000. *Maimonides' Empire of Light: Popular Enlightenment in an Age of Belief*. Chicago: University of Chicago Press.

Lincoln, Bruce. 1999. *Theorizing Myth: Narrative, Ideology, and Scholarship*. Chicago: University of Chicago Press.

Ludwig, Theodore M. 2006. *The Sacred Paths of the West*. 3rd ed. Upper Saddle River, NJ: Prentice Hall.

Mack, Michael. 2003. *German Idealism and the Jew: The Inner Anti-Semitism of Philosophy and German-Jewish Responses*. Chicago: University of Chicago Press.

McCutcheon, Russell T. 1997. *Manufacturing Religion: The Discourse on Sui Generis Religion and the Politics of Nostalgia*. New York: Oxford University Press.

_____2005. *Religion and the Domestication of Dissent: Or, How to Live in a Less than Perfect Nation*. London: Equinox.

Mendelssohn, Moses. 1983 [1783]. *Jerusalem, Or, On Religious Power and Judaism*. Trans. Allan Arkush, introduction and commentary by Alexander Altmann. Hanover: University Press of New England for Brandeis University Press.

Mendes-Flohr, Paul, and Jehuda Reinharz, eds. 1995. *The Jew in the Modern World: A Documentary History*. 2nd ed. New York: Oxford University Press.

Meyer, Michael A. 1967. *The Origins of the Modern Jew: Jewish Identity and European Culture in Germany, 1749–1824*. Detroit: Wayne State University Press.

Murphy, Tim. 2007. *Representing Religion: Essays in History, Theory and Crisis*. London: Equinox.

Myers, Jody. 2007. *Kabbalah and the Spiritual Quest: The Kabbalah Centre in America*. Westport, CT: Praeger.

Nemoy, Leon. 1952. *Karaite Anthology: Excerpts from the Early Literature*. New Haven: Yale University Press.

Smith, Jonathan Z. 1982. *Imagining Religion: From Babylon to Jonestown*. Chicago: University of Chicago Press.

_____1990. *Drudgery Divine: On the Comparison of Early Christianities and the Religions of Late Antiquity*. Chicago: University of Chicago Press.

Wasserstrom, Steven M. 1995. *Between Muslim and Jew: The Problem of Symbiosis Under Early Islam*. Princeton, NJ: Princeton University Press.

PART I

HISTORICAL AND CHRONOLOGICAL DEFINITIONS

ORIENTATION

Judaism, like any collective or even individual, maintains a certain degree of flexibility while at the same time a sufficient measure of coherence. As a result, it is important to think about Jewish identity as a series of constant reimaginings and reinventions (Boyarin 2008, 19). By way of introduction to the chapters in this section, I provide something of the historical, cultural, and intellectual contexts of the authors in question. These contexts, more often than not, dictated and determined the nature of how Judaism was defined. This was the case because Jews, like virtually every other group, tended to define themselves by what they were not, something that occurred in their encounters with others (i.e., non-Jews). Although, as the selections in Part II will reveal, the terms "Jewish" and "non-Jewish" are certainly not hermetically sealed containers or markers of identity, they nevertheless functioned, for the authors considered here, as precisely such containers. Although most of these authors grappled with and ultimately pushed the boundaries of what terms like "Jew" or "Judaism" consisted of, these definitions are certainly historically situated.

As mentioned in the introduction, rabbinic Judaism, despite its voluminous writings, was not necessarily interested in issues that we would today call theological. The first person really interested in defining who counted as a "Jew" and what beliefs defined "Judaism" was Saadya ben Joseph (882–942), the head rabbi (*gaon*) of the main rabbinical academy located in Sura (modern-day Iraq). Influenced by the rational school of Islamic theology, known as *kalām*, he emphasized the importance of reason for understanding religious belief. It is probably worth pointing out that the influence of Islamic theology may be witnessed in Saadya's composition of his main work, *Kitāb al-amānāt wal-ʾiʿtiqādāt* ("The Book of Beliefs and Opinions") in Arabic, using Arabic theological terms to define and describe what he considered to be Jewish beliefs.

In the passage included here, we witness Saadya's definition of what constitutes true belief (*īmān*) and how this is to be distinguished from improper belief. True belief, according to him, is that which is contingent upon four roots of knowledge: direct observation (e.g., based on the five senses), intuition (e.g., the true is better than the false), logical necessity (e.g., where there is smoke there is fire), in addition to what he calls *authentic tradition*. This latter category is composed of all that is contained in the biblical and rabbinical traditions. Here we have to remember that Saadya was very critical of the Karaite tradition within Judaism that upheld the Bible but ridiculed rabbinical texts such as the *Talmud*s. Saadya's definition of what counts as rational belief, for him the only kind of belief, is that supplied by the rabbinical Jewish tradition, something that upholds the tenets of reason. He is also quick to juxtapose this with a taxonomy of what constitutes heretical belief.

Maimonides (1137–1204) is generally considered to be the most important philosopher and thinker in the Jewish tradition. His two greatest works are the *Guide of the Perplexed*, written in Arabic, which attempts to harmonize the points of discrepancy between faith and reason by reading the former allegorically. His *Mishneh Torah*, written in Hebrew, presents a rational synthesis of the entire rabbinical corpus. The selection reproduced here, his Thirteen Articles of Faith, comes from another work, his *Commentary to the Mishnah*. These principles, coming at the end of the commentary, are meant to establish the beliefs to which all Jews must assent to be assured a "place in the world to come." This systematic formulation, the first in the history of Judaism, would prove the point of departure for subsequent attempts—often acrimonious—to articulate the dogmas of Judaism (see the comments in Kellner 1986, 1–9).

Yet, if Jews tried to define the quiddity of Judaism, often in response to non-Jews, the latter also did not hesitate to define what Judaism was or was not. (Witness, for example, Church law from the medieval period or, more recently, the Nuremberg Laws.) In this respect, the third selection, that from the Assembly of Jewish Notables, provides evidence for this. In 1789, the French National Assembly began the ambiguous process of granting Jews, as individuals and not as a nation or collectivity, citizenship (Hertzberg 1990, 1–12). Although Jews might well have received legal emancipation, their basic acceptance into French society was not nearly as swift or as smooth. In order to try and address this, Napolean, the self-styled custodian of the French Revolution, called 112 Jewish Notables to the Hôtel de Ville in Paris on July 29, 1806. There he put to them a series of questions meant to ensure that Judaism did not violate the civic and moral statutes of the French Republic.

Living in both the aftermath of the emancipation brought about by the French Revolution and the continued ambiguity of Jews living in Europe was Abraham Geiger (1810–1874). As both a well-respected scholar of Islam and one of the founding fathers of Reform Judaism, Geiger's methodology was based on the necessity of understanding religious texts within their immediate historical, intellectual, and social contexts. Motivated largely by ideological concerns, he sought to show that the aridity of rabbinic Judaism was but one stage in the evolutionary development of Judaism. This, of course, would pave the way for arguing that the normative sources of rabbinic texts could be either revised or jettisoned because they were not an integral part of the religion.

The final chapter, from *Standing Again at Sinai* by Judith Plaskow, is the only modern piece in this section. She argues that many of the Jewish religious sources—and, by extension, definitions of Judaism—have been penned by men and, thus, uphold the categories of patriarchy. Her project, in contrast, is one of reclamation: to redefine Judaism in such a manner that is inclusive of women and women's experiences.

References

Boyarin, Jonathan. 2008. *Jewishness and the Human Dimension*. New York: Fordham University Press.

Hertzberg, Arthur. 1990. *The French Enlightenment and the Jews: The Origins of Modern Anti-Semitism*. New York: Columbia University Press, 1990.

Kellner, Menachem. 1986. *Dogma in Medieval Jewish Thought: From Maimonides to Abravanel*. Oxford: Oxford University Press for the Littman Library.

Selection from Book One of
The Book of Beliefs and Opinions

Saadya Gaon

A nd now that we have finished expounding, as much as we felt it desirable, the matter of resolving uncertainties and doubts, it behooves us to explain what is meant by belief. We say that it is a notion that arises in the soul in regard to the actual character of anything that is apprehended. When the cream of investigation emerges, [and] is embraced and enfolded by the minds and, through them acquired and digested by the souls, then the person becomes convinced of the truth of the notion he has thus acquired. He then deposits it in his soul for a future occasion or for future occasions, in accordance with the statement of Scripture: "Wise men lay up knowledge; but the mouth of the foolish is an imminent ruin" (Prov. 10:14); and it says also: "Receive, I pray thee, instruction from His mouth" (Job 22:22).

Now beliefs fall into two categories: true and false. A true belief consists in believing a thing to be as it really is; namely, that much is much, and little is little, and black is black, and white is white, and that what exists exists, and what is nonexistent is nonexistent. A false belief, on the other hand, consists in believing a thing to be the opposite of what it actually is, such as that much is little, and little is much, and white is black, and black is white, and that what exists is nonexistent, and what is nonexistent exists.

The praiseworthy wise man is he who makes reality his guiding principle and bases his belief thereon. Notwithstanding his wisdom, he relies only on what is deserving of trust and is wary wherever caution is in order. The reprehensible fool, on the other hand, is he who sets up his personal conviction as his guiding principle, assuming that reality is patterned after[1] his belief. Notwithstanding his ignorance, he trusts in what should be shunned and shuns what is deserving of trust. All this is borne out by Scripture, which says:[2] "A wise man feareth, and departeth from evil; but the fool behaveth overbearingly, and is confident" (Prov. 14:16).

To this [last] observation I must append the expression of my amazement at [the view of] certain people who, being slaves, yet believe that they have no master, and who are confident that any object the existence of which they deny must be nonexistent and whatever they declare to be in existence is so. These individuals are so sunken in folly as to have reached the very nadir of mental deterioration.[3] For if they be right, then let him among them who has no money take it into his head that his coffers and chests are filled with money, and see what it would profit him. Or let him believe he is seventy years old, when he is only forty years of age, and see what good it would do him. Or let him assume that he is sated when he is hungry, or that his thirst is quenched when he is thirsty, or that he is covered up when he is naked, and see what would happen to him. Or let him among them who has a vicious enemy believe that his enemy has died, aye perished, with the result that he no longer takes precautions against the latter. But, oh, quickly will he [in such a case] be overcome by the misfortune[4] of which he was not [sufficiently] apprehensive.

Now it is sheer folly on the part of people to imagine that their [mere] refusal to acknowledge the sovereignty of the Lord exempts them from [heeding] His commandments and prohibitions and from [being subject to] His promise of reward and threat of punishment and other such things. It is such individuals that Scripture quotes [as saying]: "Let us break their bands asunder" (Ps. 2:3).

Thus there are certain Hindus who have hardened themselves against fire, although it burns them whenever they come in contact with it. Again there are individuals who, affecting youthfulness, have hardened themselves to endure the blows of the cane and the scourge, although they smart from them whenever they are struck by them. How much more should this apply in the case of those who in this wise embolden themselves against the Creator of the universe! Their [mere] ignorance [of it] will not cause them to escape the lot that His wisdom has decreed for them, as Scripture has indeed said: "He is wise in heart, and mighty in strength"; "who has hardened himself against Him, and prospered?" (Job 9:4).

*

Having concluded now what we thought fit[5] to append to our first statement, it behooves us to give an account of the bases of truth and the vouchers of certainty which are the source of all knowledge and the mainspring of all cognition. Discoursing about them in keeping with the aim[6] of this book, we declare that there are three [such] bases. The first consists of the knowledge gained by [direct] observation. The second is composed of the intuition of the intellect. The third comprises that knowledge which is inferred by logical necessity.

Following up [this] enumeration with an explanation of each of these roots of knowledge, we say that we understand by the knowledge of observation whatever a person perceives by means of one of the five senses; that is, by means of sight or hearing or smell or taste or touch. By the intuition of the intellect, we mean such notions as spring up solely in the mind of a human being, such as approbation of truthfulness and disapproval of mendacity. By the knowledge derived from logical necessity, again, is meant conclusions, which, unless they are accepted by the individual as true, would compel his denial of the validity of his rational intuitions or the perception of his senses. Since, however, he cannot very well negate either of these two, he must regard the said inference as being correct. Thus we are forced to affirm, although we have never seen it, that man possesses a soul, in order not to deny its manifest activity. [We must] also [agree], although we have never seen it, that every soul is endowed with reason, [merely] in order not to deny the latter's manifest activity.

Now we find that there are many people who deny [the reliability of] these three sources [of knowledge]. A small minority of them reject the first source. Of these we shall give an account in the first treatise of this book, together with a refutation of their view. By rejecting the first source, they have automatically rejected the second and the third, since the latter two are based upon the first. More numerous than this group are those that acknowledge the validity of the first but reject the second and the third [sources]. Of their thesis, too, we shall make mention in the first treatise and refute it. Most numerous of all, however, are those who acknowledge the validity of the first two sources [of knowledge] and reject the third. The reason for the difference in their rating of these [various sources of knowledge] lies in the fact that the second [type of] knowledge is more recondite than the first, and likewise the third more so than the second, and that whatever is invisible can more readily be denied than what is visible.

Again there are people who reject the validity of this [last type of] knowledge in certain instances[7] and recognize[8] it in others, each group among them affirming what its opponent negates. Their argument [in each case] is that logical necessity led them to the particular conclusion. Thus there is he who affirms that all things are at rest. He consequently denies the reality of motion. Another, again, affirms that all things move, and by virtue thereof denies the reality of rest. Each one declares the evidence adduced by his opponent dubious and unconvincing.

As for ourselves, the community of monotheists, we hold these three sources of knowledge to be genuine. To them, however, we add a fourth source, which we have derived by means of the [other] three, and which has thus become for us a further principle. That is [to say, we believe in] the validity of authentic tradition, by reason of the fact that it is based upon the knowledge of the senses as well as that of reason, as we shall explain in the third treatise of this book.

At this point, however, we remark that this type of knowledge (I mean that which is furnished by authentic tradition and the books of prophetic revelation), corroborates for us the validity of the first three sources of knowledge. Thus it enumerates the senses in connection with the denial of their functioning in the case of the idols, making them a total of five with two more added to them. It says, namely: "They have mouths but they speak not; eyes have they but they see not ... neither speak they with their throat" (Ps. 115:57).

The first five [organs] mentioned refer to the senses themselves, whilst of the two [functions] that are added to them, one is motion. This is implied in the statement: "Feet have they but walk not" (Ps. 115:7). By means of this faculty [incidentally] there is also obtained consciousness of heaviness and lightness. Thus a person may be prevented from moving about [freely] by reason of his weight, whereas he would not thus be hindered if he were light. On this account, indeed, certain people were minded to add to the number of the senses, for they asked [themselves]: "How [else] can the sensation of lightness and heaviness be experienced?" Our answer is: "By means of the sense[9] of motion, according to whether the latter is found to be easy or difficult."

The other one [of the added faculties] is [that of] speech. It is implied in the statement: Neither speak they with their throat. [By] that [of course] is [meant] speech in general, [whether it consists] of individual nouns or combinations [of words], or premises, or proofs, as we have previously explained.

Furthermore [authentic tradition] verifies for us the validity of the intuition of reason. It enjoins us, namely, to speak the truth and not to lie. Thus it says: "For my mouth shall utter truth, and wickedness is an abomination to my lips. All the words of my mouth are in righteousness, there is nothing perverse or crooked in them" (Prov. 8:7, 8).

Besides that it confirms for us the validity of knowledge inferred by logical necessity, [that is, to say] that whatever leads to the rejection of the perception of the senses or rational intuition is false. The untenability of any [theory] that rejects the perception of the senses is affirmed by such Scripture statements as: "Thou that tearest thyself in thine anger; shall the earth be forsaken for thee, or shall the rock be removed out of its place?" (Job 18:4). Again, apropos of the untenability of any theory that rejects rational intuitions concerning the falseness or truth [of propositions], it remarks: "And if it be not so, now, who will prove me a liar, and make my speech nothing worth? (Job 24:25).

Next [tradition] informs us that all sciences are [ultimately] based on what we grasp with our aforementioned senses, from which they are deduced and derived. Thus it says: "Hear my words, ye wise men; and give ear unto me, ye that have knowledge. For the ear trieth words, as the palate tasteth food" (Job 34:2, 3). Moreover this last source of knowledge also confirms for us the validity of trustworthy reports. That is the import of its statement: "I will tell thee, hear thou me; and that which I have seen will I declare which wise men have told from their fathers, and have not hid it; unto whom alone the land was given, and no stranger passed among them" (Job 15:17–19). The [reliability of the] types [of knowledge] referred to depends, of course, on conditions which we have explained in the interpretation of these verses in their [respective] places.

Having given an account of these four sources of knowledge, it behooves us [now] to explain how they are to be used for purposes of evidence. We say, then, that as far as the knowledge [derived] from sensation is concerned, whatever is correctly perceived with our senses, by virtue of the connection existing between us and the object in question, must be acknowledged by us to be in truth as it has been perceived by us, without [the admission of] a doubt. [This is, of course] posited on the assumption that we are [sufficiently] experienced in detecting illusions so as not to be led astray by them. [We should not, for example, act] like those people who believe that the image which they see in the mirror is an image that has really been created there, when in fact it is only a property of polished bodies to reflect the outline of objects facing them. Nor [should we be deceived] like those people who regard the figure, which appears reversed in the water, as possessing a reality which was created at that [particular] time, not knowing that the cause of that [illusion] resides in the fact that the water is deeper in measurement than the length of the figure. So long, then, as we beware of such illusions and the like, our cognition of what is perceived with the senses will be correct, and we will not be led astray by such fancies as the one referred to by Scripture in its statement: "And the Moabites saw the water way off as red as blood" (2 Kings 3:22).

Now as for the intuitions of the intellect, anything that is conceived in our mind in complete freedom from accidents [of any sort] is to be regarded as true knowledge about which no doubt [is to be entertained]. [This, too, is] posited on the assumption that we know how to reason and carry the reasoning process to its conclusion, being wary [at the same time] of fancy and dreams. There are, namely, people who definitely consider these dreams to be realities created in the forms seen by a person. They feel compelled to abide by this view, so they maintain, in order not to reject what they have seen with their eyes, not realizing that [what they believe they have seen] may be due partly to the previous day's affairs that flitted through the mind, of which Scripture says: "For a dream cometh through a multitude of business" (Eccles. 5:2).

Some [of these musings] again may be the result of the victuals consumed, according to whether they were hot or cold, or great or small in quantity. Hereof Scripture says: "And it shall be as when a hungry man dreameth and, behold, he eateth" (Isa. 29:8). Others may be brought on by the fact that the humor has exceeded its proportion in the mixture [of the elements of which the body is composed], with the consequence that the resulting heat and moisture produce the generation of [uncalled-for] mirth and gaiety. On the other hand, excessive dryness would cause the generation of [unwarranted] sadness and sorrow. In regard to this matter the pain-racked invalid said: "When I say: 'My bed shall comfort me, my couch shall ease my complaint'; then thou scarest me with dreams, and terrifiest me through visions" (Job 7:13, 14). Of course there is also apt to be mingled with these dreams a glimmer of heavenly light in the form of a hint or a parable, as Job intimates in his statement: "In a dream, in a vision of the night, when deep sleep falleth upon men, in slumberings upon the bed; then He openeth the ears of men" (Job 33:15, 16).

As for the knowledge which is inferred by logical necessity, whenever our senses perceive anything the existence of which has been verified, and [the belief in the reality of] that thing can be upheld in our minds only by virtue of the simultaneous acknowledgment [of the reality] of other things, then we must acknowledge [the existence of] all of them, be they few or many in number, since the validity of the sense percept in question is maintained only by them. Now these [necessary postulates] may be one, or they may be two or three or four or more than that. But whatever [figure] they may reach [really makes no difference, for], since there is no negating of the sense percept in question, there is no negating any of them either.

As an illustration of a single [concomitant] let it be supposed that we see smoke, but do not see the fire from which that smoke originates. We must [in that case] assume the existence of the fire because of the existence of the smoke since the one can be effected only by means of the other. Likewise if we hear the voice of a human being from behind a wall, we must assume the existence of that human being, since a human voice can emanate only from an existing human being.

As an example, again, of more than one [concomitant phenomenon that must be postulated, the following might be cited.] When, for instance, we see food go down in bulk in the belly of an animate being, and its refuse come out from it, then, unless we assume [that] four operations [were involved in the process], what has been perceived by our senses could not possibly have been carried out. That is [to say] that there must be in the belly of that being a force that draws the food into the interior, and a force that holds it until it has been digested, and a force that furthers its digestion and disintegration, and a force that expels the refuse that is in it as it goes out. Now inasmuch as what has been perceived by the senses could be effected only by means of these four [operations], we must assume that these four [forces] are a reality.

Sometimes, too, our acknowledgment of the reality of what we observe becomes possible only by the invention of a science that verifies it for us. We may even be compelled to resort to many such sciences. Once, however, it is realized that the sense percept in question is dependent [for its corroboration] on the said [sciences], it follows of necessity that we must acknowledge all of the latter as valid so that the reality of the sense percept in question may be upheld.

Thus, for example, we see the moon rise upon the earth and set again at different moments of the night and the day. It does this by following either a long or a short route, according to whether it consumes less time than is required for reaching one of the twenty-eight stations that we have distinguished and designated by name or it consumes more time and so passes the latter. We note, furthermore, that at one time it travels to the south [of the sphere of the constellations][10] and at another to the north. From this we infer that, if it had only one motion, there could have been no variation in either the speed[11] of its course or its extent. The fact, therefore, that we see these two [factors] vary leads to the inevitable conclusion that the moon has many motions and that these multiple motions can be due only to a multiple number of bodies, since one body cannot be endowed with two different motions at one and the same time, let alone three or four motions. Furthermore [we know] that, when a multiple number of bodies equal in form intercept each other, they thereby diminish or increase the speeds of their respective motions.

[All] this is demonstrable only by means of the science of geometry, which shows us synthetically how one figure enters into the other. [That is to say] we must first master the science of plane geometry. Having acquainted ourselves with [the properties of] points and lines, we begin with the study [of the properties] of plane figures, such as the triangle, the square, the circle, the concentric, the tangent, and the secant, until we get to know the properties of the intercepting [spherical] figure,[12] and which of its segments is impossible and which is tenable. This finally enables us to recognize that the figures of the heavenly bodies are spherical or circular, and that some are concentric with others.

Once these sciences have been thoroughly mastered, it becomes clear to us that the moon's course is a composite of five distinct motions. We must, therefore, acknowledge [the theorems of] all these sciences as being correct, since it is only by means of them that our hypothesis of the variation of the moon's course by natural law can be upheld.

And now that we have explained the character of knowledge obtained by logical inference, we must note how it may be preserved against defect, for most of the controversies of men and the variation of their evidence center about it or are due to it. We say, then, that when someone declares: "I believe such and such a thing to be true in order not to negate a percept of the senses," we must inquire whether that percept might not be sustained by some other hypothesis than the one he puts forth. For in the latter event his assumption would fall to the ground.

Thus, for example, there are those who believe, because of its whiteness which they observe, that the Milky Way had formerly been circled by the sphere of the sun. However, when we test their hypothesis, we find that another [explanation] is equally possible. This whiteness might, for instance, be an ascending mist, or a permanent particle of fire, or a conglomerate of little stars, or some other such thing. Their allegation, therefore, falls to the ground.

Again, if someone were to say: "I believe such and such a thing to be true in order not to negate a rational concept," we must make inquiry [into the matter]. [For] if that concept could be upheld by a hypothesis other than the one propounded by him, that assumption of his becomes null and void. Thus, for example, there are those who maintain that there exists another earth aside from this one in which we live. Their argument [in support of this view] is that thereby the fire would be located in the center [of the world], it being acknowledged that whatever is highly prized is kept in the center. However, such [a position of distinction] is already accorded by us to man, who dwells on the earth, which is the center of the universe. Their conclusion, therefore, falls to the ground so far as we are concerned.

Suppose, again, that someone were to say: "I believe such and such a thing to be true by way of analogy with what is perceived with the senses." It so happens, however, that that assumption on his part would invalidate another sense percept. In that case one must decide in favor of the more important of the two percepts, and of the arguments that support it. Thus, for example, there are those who maintain that all things were created from water, because animals originate from the humid element. They fail to consider, however, the water's visible tendency to percolate and flow over. It is, therefore, impossible that it should be the origin of all things, since it does not stand up by itself. When, then, in the search for explanatory hypotheses, two such [contradictory phenomena] are encountered, the more important of the two is the more deserving of being accepted as such.

Again, if someone were to say: "I believe such and such a thing to be true by way of analogy with a certain sense percept," but one part of his theory contradicts another, then his theory is null and void. Thus there are those who maintain that the good is that which gives us pleasure, because that is how they feel it to be. They do not recall, however, that the killing of them would please their enemies just as much as the killing of their enemies would please them. The act would consequently be good and evil at one and the same time, [which is, of course,] a contradiction.

Suppose, furthermore, that someone were to say: "I believe such and such a thing to be true for such and such a reason," but upon a thorough investigation of that reason, we find that it leads to a conclusion other than that which he believes to be true. That reason would then be voided. Thus, for example, there is the theory of the proponents of the eternity of the world who declare: "We believe that all things have existed since eternity because we do not regard as real anything except what our senses perceive." However, the fact that they do not regard anything as real except what their senses perceive would prevent them from believing that all things exist since eternity, because it is impossible that they should have perceived in its prime what exists since eternity.

Again someone may say: "I reject such and such a thesis for such and such a reason." Yet thou findest that he ventured into [a theory] more difficult [of entertainment] than the one he had sought to avoid. Thus, for example, certain monotheists shunned the view that God was unable to bring back yesterday in order not to ascribe to Him impotence. They thereby, however, let themselves into something worse by ascribing to God an absurdity, as we shall note in part of the second treatise of this book, if God, exalted be He, is willing.

So, then, if we seek to establish the truth in the domain of knowledge obtained by logical inference, we must guard it against the above-mentioned five types of vitiating factors. [We must,] namely, [make certain] (a) that there is no other [means than the theory in question] of sustaining the truth of what is perceived [with the senses], nor (b) any other [method] of upholding what is [intuitively] apprehended [by reason]. Furthermore (c) it must not invalidate any other [accepted] fact, nor (d) must one part of it contradict another, let alone (e) that a theory be adopted that is worse than the one that has been rejected.

[All] these [precautions are to be taken] in addition to exercising, in the determination of the sense percepts and the rational concepts, such expert care as we have outlined before. Add to these the quality of perseverance until the process of reasoning has been completed, and we have a total of seven points that must be observed to make possible for us the accurate emergence of the truth. Should, therefore, someone come to us with an allegation in the realm of inferential knowledge, we would test his thesis by means of these seven [criteria]. If, upon being rubbed by their touchstone and weighed by their balance, it turns out to be correct as well as acceptable, we shall make use of it. Similarly also must we proceed with the subject matters of authentic tradition—I mean the books of prophecy. However, this is not the place for explaining the properties of these books, something that I have already done for an extensive portion of this subject in the introduction to my commentary on the Torah.

*

Now someone might, of course, ask: "But how can we take it upon ourselves to indulge in speculation about the objects of knowledge and their investigation to the point where these would be established as convictions according to the laws of geometry and become firmly fixed in the mind, when there are people who disapprove of such an occupation, being of the opinion that speculation leads to unbelief and is conducive to heresy?" Our reply thereto, however, is that such an opinion is held only by the uneducated among them. Thus thou seest the masses of this country labor under the impression that whoever goes to India becomes rich. It has likewise been reported about certain uneducated people of our own nation that they labor under the illusion that something resembling a whale swallows the moon as a result of which it becomes eclipsed. [It is] also [related] about certain uneducated Arabs that they are under the impression that whoever does not have a she-camel slaughtered on his grave is brought to the last judgment on foot. And many other such ridiculous [stories are circulated].

Should one say, however: "But did not the foremost of the sages of the children of Israel forbid this sort of occupation, and especially speculation about the beginning of time and place, saying: Whoever speculates about the following four matters would have been better had he not been born; namely, 'What is below and what is above, what was before and what will be behind?'" (Hagh. 11b), we would reply—and we ask the Merciful One to stand by us—that it is inconceivable that they should have prohibited us from [engaging in genuine speculation]. For did not our Creator Himself enjoin us to do this very thing apropos of authentic tradition, as it is evident from the declaration [of the prophet]: "Know ye not? Hear ye not? Hath it not been told you from the beginning? Have ye not understood the foundations of the earth?" (Isa. 40:21). Furthermore there is the remark made by the saints to each other: "Let us choose for us that which is right; let us know among ourselves what is good" (Job 34:4). Extensive statements of a similar nature on this subject were moreover made by the five persons figuring in the Book of Job—I mean, Job, Eliphaz, Bildad, Zophar, and Elihu.

What the sages forbade was only to lay the books of the prophets aside and accept any private notion that might occur to an individual about the beginning of place and time. For whoever speculates in this wise may either hit the mark or miss it. Until he hits it, however, he would be without religious faith, and even when he has hit upon the teaching of religion and has it firmly in hand, he is not secure against being deprived of it again by some uncertainty that might arise in his mind and corrupt his belief. We are agreed, then, on charging one who behaves in this fashion with sin, even though he be a professional thinker. As for ourselves, the congregation of the children of Israel, we engage in research and speculation in a way other than this. It is this method of ours that I wish to describe and clarify with the help of the Merciful One.

Know, then, and may God direct thee aright, Oh thou that studiest this book, that we inquire into and speculate about the matters of our religion with two objectives in mind. One of these is to have verified in fact what we have learned from the prophets of God theoretically. The second is to refute him who argues against us in regard to anything pertaining to our religion.

Our Master, blessed and exalted be He, has namely given his complete instructions in regard to our religious requirements through the medium of His prophets. [He did this] after [first] confirming for us their possession of the gifts of prophecy by means of [sundry] miracles and marvels. Thus He has enjoined us to accept these matters as binding and observe them. He has furthermore informed us, however, that, if we would engage in speculation and diligent research, inquiry would produce for us in each instance the complete truth, tallying with His announcement to us by the speech of His prophets. Besides that He has given us the assurance that the godless will never be in a position to offer a proof against our religion, nor the skeptics[13] [to produce] an argument against our creed.

These facts are borne out by the statement in which God informs us that all things had a beginning, that He was the Creator who originated them, and that furthermore He was one, having no associate with Him. Thus saith the Lord, the King of Israel, and his Redeemer, the Lord of hosts: "I am the first, and I am the last, and beside Me there is no God" (Isa. 44:6).

He tells us also immediately thereafter that, whatever He has commanded or forbidden us to do or informed us about, has been and will be: "And who, as I, can proclaim—let him declare it and set it in order for Me—since I appointed the ancient people? And the things that are coming, and that shall come to pass, let them declare" (Isa. 44:7).

Next He allays our fear of those who disagree with us, stating that they will not be able to prevail against us in argument, nor be successful in producing convincing proof against us. That is the import of His subsequent remark: "Be not afraid, neither fear ye; have I not announced unto thee of old and declared it? And ye are my witnesses. Is there a God beside Me? Yea, there is no Rock; I know not any" (Isa. 44:8).

When He says: Be not afraid, He means: [Be not afraid] of the character of your opponents, of their numerical strength, their [physical] power and other traits, as He says elsewhere: "And thou fearest continually all the day because of the fury of the oppressor" (Isa. 51:13). The expression *we'al tirhu*, again, is equivalent to *we'al tire'u* (neither fear ye), for by the process of substitution the *he* may stand in place of the *'aleph*. He means thereby that [we must not stand in fear] of the allegation [of our opponents] or their arguments in themselves. This is borne out by what He says elsewhere: "And thou, son of man, be not afraid of them, neither be afraid of their words" (Ezek. 2:6). In a similar vein it is said: "He that feared the word of the Lord" (Exod. 9:20).

God's statement, moreover, "Have I not announced unto thee of old" (Isa. 44:8) refers to the prophetic revelations concerning the future. His remark again, "And I declared" (ibid.) has reference to the prophetic revelations concerning the past. Thus, too, does He say elsewhere: "The former things, what are they? Declare ye, that we may consider, and know the end of them; or announce to us the things to come" (Isa. 41:22).

When, furthermore, He says: "And ye are My witnesses" (Isa. 44:8), He alludes to the marvelous signs and the manifest proofs witnessed by the [Jewish] people. These [were revealed] in many forms,[14] such as the visitation of the ten plagues and the cleaving of the [Red] Sea and the assemblage at Sinai. Personally, however, I consider the case of the miracle of the manna as the most amazing of all miracles, because a phenomenon of an enduring nature excites greater wonderment than one of a passing[15] character. Aye it is hard for the mind to conceive of a scheme whereby a people numbering something like two million souls could be nourished for forty years with nothing else than food produced for them in the air by the Creator. For had there been any possibility of thinking up a scheme for achieving something of this nature, the philosophers of old would have been the first to resort to it. They would have maintained their disciples therewith, taught them wisdom, and enabled them to dispense with working for a livelihood or asking for help.

Now it is not likely[16] that the forbears of the children of Israel should have been in agreement upon this matter if they had considered it a lie. Such [proof] suffices, then, as the requisite of every authentic tradition. Besides, if they had told their children: "We lived in the wilderness for forty years eating naught except manna," and there had been no basis for that in fact, their children would have answered them: "Now you are telling us a lie. Thou, so and so, is not this thy field, and thou, so and so, is not this thy garden from which you have always derived your sustenance?" This is, then, something that the children would not have accepted by any manner of means.

His statement, again, "Is there a God beside Me?" (ibid.) means: "If, now, perchance you be afraid that some of the things, about which I have told you that they had come to pass or some of those concerning which I have told you that they would come to pass, are not true, [that fear on your part might be justified] if a creation had been effected by someone else than Me. In that event I might perhaps not have been posted on what he was making. But inasmuch as I am One, My knowledge embraces everything that I have made and that I will make."

Finally under His statement, "And there is no rock (ṣur) that I do not know"[17] (ibid.) are subsumed the distinguished men of the human race and its sages. For the expression ṣur may be applied to great men. Scripture says, namely: "Look unto the rock (ṣur) whence ye were hewn and to the hole of the pit whence ye were digged. Look unto Abraham your father, and unto Sarah that bore you" (Isa. 51:1, 2). It says also: "Yea, thou makest the rock (ṣur) turn back his sword, and hast not made him to stand in the battle"[18] (Ps. 89:44). What is meant by the verse under discussion is therefore: "There is no wise or distinguished man that I do not know. Hence it is impossible that he should be able to produce an argument against you in the matter of your religion or do injury to your creed, because My knowledge is all-embracing and I have imparted it to you."

In this way, then—may God be merciful unto thee—do we conduct our speculation and inquiry, to the end that we may expound concretely by means of rational intuition and logical inference what our Master has imparted unto us. With this thesis, however, there is intimately bound up a point that we cannot avoid [bringing up]. It consists of the question: "Inasmuch as all matters of religious belief, as imparted to us by our Master, can be attained by means of research and correct speculation, what was the reason that prompted [divine] wisdom to transmit them to us by way of prophecy and support them by means of visible proofs and[19] miracles rather than intellectual demonstrations?"

To this question we should like to give, with the help of God, exalted be He, an adequate answer. We say, then, [that] the All-Wise knew that the conclusions reached by means of the art of speculation could be attained only in the course of a certain measure of time. If, therefore, He had referred us for our acquaintance with His religion to that art alone, we would have remained without religious guidance whatever for a while, until the process of reasoning was completed by us so that we could make use of its conclusions. But many a one of us might never complete the process because of some flaw in his reasoning. Again he might not succeed in making use of its conclusions because he is overcome by worry or overwhelmed by uncertainties that confuse and befuddle him. That is why God, exalted and magnified be He, afforded us a quick relief from all these burdens by sending us His messengers through whom He transmitted messages to us, and by letting us see with our own eyes the signs and the proofs supporting them about which no doubt could prevail and which we could not possibly reject. Thus He said: "Ye yourselves have seen that I have talked with you from heaven" (Exod. 20:19). Furthermore He addressed His messenger in our presence, and made it an obligation to believe him forever, as He said: "That the people may hear when I speak with thee, and may also believe thee forever" (Exod. 19:9).

Thus it became incumbent upon us immediately to accept the religion, together with all that was embraced in it, because its authenticity had been proven by the testimony of the senses. Its acceptance is also incumbent upon anybody to whom it has been transmitted because of the attestation of authentic tradition, as we shall explain. Now God commanded us to take our time with our speculation until we would arrive thereby at these selfsame conclusions. We must, therefore, persevere in this standpoint[20] until the arguments in favor of it have become convincing for us, and we feel compelled to acknowledge God's Torah [that has already been authenticated] by what our eyes have seen and our ears have heard.

So, then, even if it should take a long time for one of us who indulges in speculation to complete his speculation, he is without worry. He who is held back from engaging in such an activity by some impediment will, then, not remain without religious guidance. Furthermore women and young people and those who have no aptitude for speculation can thus also have a perfect and accessible faith, for the knowledge of the senses is common to all men. Praised, then, be the All-Wise, who ordered things thus. Therefore, too, dost thou often see Him include in the Torah the children and the women together with the fathers whenever miracles and marvels are mentioned.

Next I say, in further elucidation of this matter, that one might compare the situation to that of a person who out of a total of 1,000 drachmas weighs out 20[21] to each of five men, and 16 and 2/3 to each of six, and 14 and 2/7 to each of seven, and 12 and 1/2 to each of eight, and 11 and 1/9 to each of nine, and who wishes to check with them quickly on how much money is left. So he tells them that the remainder amounts to 500 drachmas, supporting his statement by the weight of the money. Once, then, it has been weighed by them[22] quickly and found to be 500 drachmas, they are compelled to credit his statement. Then they can take their time until they find out [that] it [is really so] by way of calculation, each one according to his understanding, and the effort he can put into it and the obstacles he might encounter.

One might further compare this case to that of a person who, upon being informed about an illness accompanied by certain pathological conditions, designates it by a natural symptom [whereby it may be] immediately [recognized], until the diagnostician is able by means of [his] investigations to check the matter.[23]

It behooves us also to believe that even before the era of the children of Israel God never left His creatures without a religion fortified by prophecy and miraculous signs and manifest proofs. Whoever witnessed the latter in person was convinced of their authenticity by what he had perceived with his sense of vision. He, again, to whom it was transmitted, was convinced by what he had grasped by means of his sense of hearing. Thus the Torah says about one of these [who lived before the rise of a Jewish nation]:

> "For I have known him, to the end that he may command his children" (Gen. 18:19).

*

To this statement I should like to append what occur to me to be the principal causes responsible for keeping infidels and heretics from believing [in the authenticity of] miracles and marvels, and from engaging in speculation about religious doctrines. Of these I consider eight as being particularly prevalent. The first of these is that human beings find the effort to be naturally burdensome. When, namely, they perceive instinctively a certain matter that ought to be confirmed and corroborated by means of logical proof and be applied practically in religious life, they take flight and run away from it. That is the reason why thou seest many people say: "The truth is burdensome. The truth is bitter." For they desire freedom [from such burdens] and so they flee from them.[24] Of such persons does Scripture say: "Get you far from the Lord! Unto us is this land given for an inheritance" (Ezek. 11:15). They do not realize, these thoughtless individuals, that if they were [consistently] to obey their natural instinct in its tendency to avoid exertion and effort, they would starve to death by virtue of failing to cultivate [the soil] or to build [homes].

The second is ignorance which predominates among many men. [There are, namely, people] who express themselves foolishly, are lazy in their thinking, and say unreflectingly: "There is nothing at all." And this is what they meditate inwardly also. Of such does Scripture say: "Surely now shall they say: 'We have no king; for we feared not the Lord; and the king; what can he do for us?'" (Hos. 10:3). Nor do they consider the fact that if they were to make such inane statements and wild utterances about human rulers, they would court death and destruction.

The third [cause of heresy] is the inclination of the average man toward the gratification of his appetites, such as greediness for every [type of] food and sexual intercourse and acquisition. [On account of this tendency] he hurls himself into such activities hastily [and] without deliberation. It is of individuals of this character that Scripture says: "The fool hath said in his heart: 'There is no God'" (Ps. 53:2). A person of this type does not bear in mind the fact that if he were to act in such a manner in the event of illness—nay even when he is well—eating whatever he lusted for and cohabiting with whomever he found, he would perish therefrom and die.

The fourth [cause of heresy] is an aversion to speculation and an incapacity for listening attentively and engaging in sustained thinking. [All this causes the individual] to be easily contented and say: "I have already looked into the matter and this is all I got out of it." Of such a one does Scripture say: "The slothful man (*remiyyah*) shall not hunt his prey; but the precious substance of men is to be diligent" (Prov. 12:27). The meaning of [this word] *remiyyah* is "one who is without ambition." Such a one does not attain what he needs. Those belonging to this class do not realize that, if they were to employ such tactics in their worldly affairs, they would never be successful in them.

The fifth [cause] is arrogance and conceit, by which a person is so dominated as not to concede the existence of any wisdom that might be hidden from him or of any science that still has to be mastered by him. Of such a one does Scripture say: "The wicked in the pride of his countenance saith: 'He will not require.' All his thoughts are: There is no God" (Ps. 10:4). This type of individual does not perceive that such an argument would do him but little good in the fashioning of a signet ring or in the writing of a letter of the alphabet.

The sixth [cause of heresy] may be a word that a person hears from the mouth of the godless that touches his heart and unnerves it, so that he remains for the rest of his life in this state of nervous prostration, occasioned by this word. It is of such persons that Scripture says: "The words of a whisperer are as dainty morsels and they go down into the innermost parts of the belly" (Prov. 18:8). But why doesn't this [sort of individual] likewise consider the fact that, if he were not to shield himself against heat and cold so that they do not react against him, they [too] would destroy and kill him?

The seventh [cause of heresy] may be some weak, ridiculous argument [in favor of the true belief] that one has heard propounded by a certain monotheist, and that one believes to be typical of all [arguments of this order]. Of persons thus [misled] does Scripture say: "But they laughed them to scorn, and mocked them" (2 Chron. 30:10). Now it does not enter the mind of this sort of individual that the fact that a dealer in fine linens does not know how to describe the costly[25] cloths he offers for sale does not diminish their worth.

The eighth, finally, is the animosity existing between a man and certain monotheists. The unfortunate situation causes him to hate, together with his enemies, also their Master whom the latter worship. It is of persons [who permit themselves to be] thus [carried away by their feelings] that Scripture declares: "My zeal hath undone me, because mine adversaries have forgotten Thy words" (Ps. 119:139). Such a fool does not realize that his enemy is incapable of bringing upon him [so great] an evil as he has brought upon himself, since it is not within his enemy's power to subject him in perpetuity to painful torment.

There may, however, exist a person the error of whose way is due to the fact that in the course of his interpretation of the verses of the Bible he noted something that he regarded as objectionable, or that he had prayed to his Master and received no answer from Him or that he had made a request of Him which was not granted. Or [there may be one] who sees evildoers who are not punished, or who takes exception to the continued existence of the rule of the infidels, or who notes how death indiscriminately gathers in all creatures, or who is unable to grasp with his mind the meaning of God's unity or that of the soul or of reward and punishment. [For the benefit of such let me state that] all these and related subjects will be taken up individually by me in the respective treatises to which they belong and in the appropriate chapter. I shall discourse about them according to my ability, and I hope, if God, exalted be He, is willing, to contribute thereby to the welfare of those that venture into this discussion.

*

And now that our discussion has reached this point, I deem it proper to make mention of the aim of this book and the number of its treatises. This is to be followed by an elaboration upon each subject, it being noted first what the books of prophecy have to say in each case, after which will be presented the rational proofs, as I have stated previously.

I say, then, that the total number of treatises of which this book consists is ten.

The first treatise [aims to prove] that the world, together with all that is in it, was created in time.

The second treatise [aims to prove] that the Creator, may His greatness be magnified, is one.

The third treatise [is concerned with proving] that He, exalted be He, has issued to mankind commandments as well as prohibitions.

The fourth treatise [deals] with [the subjects of] obedience and disobedience [to God].

The fifth treatise [deals] with good and evil deeds.

The sixth treatise [deals] with the soul and the state of death and the hereafter.

The seventh treatise [deals] with the resurrection of the dead.

The eighth treatise [deals] with the redemption of the children of Israel.

The ninth treatise [deals] with reward and punishment.

The tenth treatise [discusses] the question of the best possible behavior for man in [this] nether abode.

In each treatise I shall begin with [an exposition of] what has been imparted to us by our Lord and of whatever corroboration is furnished by reason. This is to be followed by [a citation of] such diverging views as have been reported to me. In each instance there will be given a statement of the thesis as well as of the arguments against it. I shall conclude with the proofs furnished by prophecy bearing on the subject of the treatise in question. On behalf of myself, as well as of anyone who studies this book, I beseech God to make even our path and to enable me to realize my aspirations on behalf of His people and His saints, for He is attentive and near at hand.

Notes

1. "is patterned after"—literally "follows."
2. "All ... says"—literally "and as it says."
3. "mental deterioration"—literally "perdition."
4. "misfortune"—Ibn Tibbon. [i.e., according to Ibn Tibbon's Hebrew translation of Saadya's Arabic – ed.]
5. "thought fit"—Ibn Tibbon and codex M quoted by S. Landauer._[in his 1880 critical edition – ed.]
6. "aim"—so M.
7. "instances"—so M.
8. "recognize"—literally "hold on to," so Ibn Tibbon. Cf. also Abraham Heshel, "The Quest for Certainty in Saadia's Philosophy," *The Jewish Quarterly Review* 33.3 (1943): 290 and n. 139.
9. "sense"—M and Ibn Tibbon.
10. So, acording to the exposition by Abraham ben Hiyya, quoted by Moise Ventura, *La Philosophie de Saadia Gaon* (Paris: J. Vrin, 1934), 85, n. 26.
11. Cf. ibid.
12. "until . . . figure"—added by Ibn Tibbon and M.
13. "skeptics"—Ibn Tibbon.
14. "forms"—Ibn Tibbon and M.
15. "passing"— Ibn Tibbon and M.
16. "not likely"—Ibn Tibbon and M.
17. The usual translation is: "Yea, there is no Rock; I know not any."
18. These quotations are given as in Ibn Tibbon.
19. "and"—Ibn Tibbon.
20. "standpoint," i.e., that of the acceptance of the teachings of the Jewish religion.
21. "20"—according to Landauer's emendation.

22. "them"—M. Cf. Landauer, 26, n. 6.
23. "matter"—literally "his quest."
24. "from them"—Ibn Tibbon.
25. "costly"—Ibn Tibbon. The Arabic text uses the adjective *dabikiyyah*, i.e., a fabric manufactured in Dabik, a town in Egypt (cf. *Jacuts Geographisches Woerterbuch*, ed. F. Wuestenfeld [Leipzig, 1868], II, 548), which was world-renowned during the Abbasid period. (See Philip Hitti, *History of the Arabs* [London, 1937], 346.)

Thirteen Articles of Faith[*]

Maimonides

What I have to mention now (and this is the most correct place for alluding to it) is that the roots of our Law and its fundamental principles are thirteen.

The First Principle of Faith

The existence of the Creator (praised be he!), i.e. that there is an existent Being invested with the highest perfection of existence. He is the cause of the existence of all existent things. In him they exist and from him emanates their continued existence. If we could suppose the removal of his existence then the existence of all things would entirely cease and there would not be left any independent existence whatsoever. But if on the other hand we could suppose the removal of all existent things but he, his existence (blessed be he!) would not cease to be, neither would it suffer any diminution. For he (exalted be he!) is self-sufficient, and his existence needs the aid of no existence outside his. Whatsoever is outside him, the intelligences (i.e. the angels) and the bodies of the spheres, and things below these, all of them need him for their existence. This is the first cardinal doctrine of faith, which is indicated by the commandment, "I am the Lord thy God" (Exod. 20:2).

The Second Principle of Faith

The Unity of God. This implies that this cause of all is one; not one of a genus nor of a species, and not as one human being who is a compound divisible into many unities; not a unity like the ordinary material body which is one in number but takes on endless divisions and parts. But he, the exalted one, is a unity in the sense that there is no unity like his in any way. This is the second cardinal doctrine of faith which is indicated by the assertion, "Hear, O Israel, the Lord our God the Lord is one" (Deut. 6:4).

The Third Principle of Faith

The removal of materiality from God. This signifies that this unity is not a body nor the power of a body, nor can the accidents of bodies overtake him, as e.g. motion and rest, whether in the essential or accidental sense. It was for this reason that the Sages (peace to them!) denied to him both cohesion and separation of parts, when they remarked "no sitting and no standing, no division, and no cohesion" (*Hagiga* 15a). The prophet again said, "And unto whom will ye liken God" (Isa. 40:18), etc., "and unto whom will ye liken me that I may be like, saith the Holy One" (Isa. 40:25). If God were a body he would be like a body. Wherever in the scriptures God is spoken of with the attributes of material bodies, like motion, standing, sitting, speaking, and such like, all these are figures of speech, as the Sages said, "The Torah speaks in the language of men" (*Berachoth* 31b). People have said a great deal on this point. This third fundamental article of faith is indicated by the scriptural expression, "for ye have seen no likeness" (Deut. 4:15), i.e. you have not comprehended him as one who possesses a likeness, for, as we have remarked, he is not a body nor a bodily power.

The Fourth Principle of Faith

The priority of God. This means that the unity whom we have described is first in the absolute sense. No existent thing outside him is primary in relation to him. The proofs of this in the Scriptures are numerous. This fourth principle is indicated by the phrase "The eternal God is a refuge" (Deut. 33:27).

The Fifth Principle of Faith

That it is he (be he exalted!) who must be worshipped, aggrandized, and made known by his greatness and the obedience shown to him. This must not be done to any existing beings lower than he—not to the angels nor the spheres nor the elements, or the things which are compounded from them. For these are all fashioned in accordance with the works they are intended to perform. They have no judgement or freewill, but only a love for him (be he exalted!). Let us adopt no mediators to enable ourselves to draw near unto God, but let the thoughts be directed to him, and turned away from whatsoever is below him. This fifth principle is a prohibition of idolatry. The greater part of the Torah is taken up with the prohibition of idol-worship.

The Sixth Principle of Faith

Prophecy. This implies that it should be known that among this human species there exist persons of very intellectual natures and possessing much perfection. Their souls are predisposed for receiving the form of the intellect. Then this human intellect joins itself with the active intellect, and an exalted emanation is shed upon them. These are the prophets. This is prophecy, and this is its meaning. The complete elucidation of this principle of faith would be very long, and it is not our purpose to bring proofs for every principle or to elucidate the means of comprehending them, for this affair includes the totality of the sciences. We shall give them a passing mention only. The verses of the Torah which testify concerning the prophecy of prophets are many.

The Seventh Principle of Faith

The prophecy of Moses our Teacher. This implies that we must believe that he was the father of all the prophets before him and that those who came after him were all beneath him in rank. He (Moses) was chosen by God from the whole human kind. He comprehended more of God than any man in the past or future ever comprehended or will comprehend. And we must believe that he reached a state of exaltedness beyond the sphere of humanity, so that he attained to the angelic rank and became included in the order of the angels. There was no veil which he did not pierce. No material hindrance stood in his way, and no defect whether small or great mingled itself with him. The imaginative and sensual powers of his perceptive faculty were stripped from him. His desiderative power was stilled and he remained pure intellect only. It is in this significance that it is remarked of him that he discoursed with God without my angelic intermediary.

We had it in our mind to explain this strange subject here and to unlock the secrets firmly enclosed in scriptural verses to expound the meaning of "mouth to mouth"; and the whole of this verse and other things belonging to the same theme. But I see that this theme is very subtle; it would need abundant development and introductions and illustrations. The existence of angels would first have to be made clear and the distinction between their ranks and that of the Creator. The soul would have to be explained and all its powers. The circle would then grow wider until we should have to say a word about the forms which the prophets attribute to the Creator and the angels. The *Shi`ur Qoma* and its meaning would consequently have to enter into our survey. And even if this one subject were shortened into the narrowest compass it could not receive sufficient justice, even in a hundred pages. For this reason I shall leave it to its place, either in the book of the interpretation of the "discourses," which I have promised, or in the book on prophecy which I have begun, or in the book which I shall compose for explaining these fundamental articles of faith.

I shall now come back to the purpose of this seventh principle and say that the prophecy of Moses differs from that of all other prophets in four respects:

(1) Whosoever the prophet, God spake not with him but by an intermediary. But Moses had no intermediary, as it is said, "mouth to mouth did I speak with him" (Num. 12:8).

(2) Every other prophet received his inspiration only when in a state of sleep, as it is asserted in various parts of scripture, "in a dream of the night" (Gen. 20:3), "In a dream of a vision of a night" (Job 33:15), and many other phrases with similar significance; or in the day when deep sleep has fallen upon the prophet and his condition is that in which there is a removal of his sense-perceptions, and his mind is a blank like a sleep. This state is styled "dreams" or "visions," and is alluded to in the expression "in visions of God." But to Moses the word came in the day-time when "he was standing between the two cherubim," as God had promised him in the words "And there I will meet with thee and I will commune with thee!" (Exod. 25:22). And God further said, "Let there be a prophet among you, I the Lord will make myself known unto him in a vision and will speak unto him in a dream. My servant Moses is not so, who is faithful in all mine house. With him I will speak mouth to mouth . . ." (Num. 12:6–8).

(3) When the inspiration comes to the prophet, although it is in a vision and by means of an angel, his strength becomes enfeebled, his physique becomes deranged. And very great terror falls upon him so that he is almost broken through it, as is illustrated in the case of Daniel. When Gabriel speaks to him in a vision, Daniel says: "And there remained no strength in me; for my comeliness was turned in me into corruption and I retained no strength!" (Dan. 10: 8) And he further says: "Then was I in a deep sleep on my face, and my face towards the ground!" (Dan. 10:9) And further: "By the vision my sorrows are turned upon me" (Dan. 10:16). But not so with Moses. The word came unto him and no confusion in any way overtook him, as we are told in the verse "And the Lord spake unto Moses face unto face as a man speaketh unto his neighbour" (Exod. 33:11).

This means that just as no man feels disquieted when his neighbour talks with him, so he (peace to him!) had no fright at the discourse of God, although it was face to face; this being the case by reason of the strong bond uniting him with the intellect, as we have described.

(4) To all the prophets the inspiration came not at their own choice but by the will of God. The prophet at times waits a number of years without an inspiration reaching him. And it is sometimes asked of the prophet that he should communicate a message [he has received], but the prophet waits some days or months before doing so or does

not make it known at all. We have seen cases where the prophet prepares himself by enlivening his soul and purifying his spirit, as did Elisha in the incident when he declared "But now bring me a minstrel!" and then the inspiration came to him. He does not necessarily receive the inspiration at the time that he is ready for it. But Moses our teacher was able to say at whatsoever time he wished, "Stand, and I shall hear what God shall command concerning you" (Num. 9:8). It is again said, "Speak unto Aaron thy brother that he come not at all times into the sanctuary" (Lev. 16:2); with reference to which verse the Talmud remarks "that only Aaron ['not come at all times'], but not Moses." The prohibition applies only to Aaron. But Moses may enter the sanctuary at all times.

The Eighth Principle of Faith

That the Torah has been revealed from heaven. This implies our belief that the whole of this Torah found in our hands this day is the Torah that was handed down by Moses and that it is all of divine origin. By this I mean that the whole of the Torah came unto him from before God in a manner which is metaphorically called "speaking"; but the real nature of that communication is unknown to everybody except to Moses (peace to him!) to whom it came. In handing down the Torah, Moses was like a scribe writing from dictation the whole of it, its chronicles, its narratives, and its precepts. It is in this sense that he is termed "lawgiver." And there is no difference between verses like "And the sons of Ham were Gush and Mizraim, Phut and Canaan" (Gen. 10:6), or "And his wife's name was Mehatabel, the daughter of Matred" (Gen. 36:39) or "And Timna was concubine" (Gen. 36:12) and verses like "I am the Lord thy God" (Exod. 20:2) and "Hear, O Israel" (Deut. 6:4). They are all equally of divine origin and all belong to the "The Law of God which is perfect, pure, holy, and true." In the opinion of the Rabbis, Manasseh was the most renegade and the greatest of all infidels because he thought that in the Torah there were a kernel and a husk, and that these histories and anecdotes have no value and emanate from Moses. This is the significance of the expression "The Torah does not come from heaven," which, say the Rabbis (*Sanhedrin* 99a), is the remark of one who believes that all the Torah is of divine origin save a certain verse which (says he) was not spoken by God but by Moses himself. And of such a one the verse says, "For he hath despised the word of the Lord" (Num. 15:31). May God be exalted far above and beyond the speech of the infidels! For truly in every letter of the Torah there reside wise maxims and admirable truths for him to whom God has given understanding. You cannot grasp the uttermost bounds of His wisdom. "It is larger in measure than the earth, and wider than the sea" (Job 11:9). Man has but to follow in the footsteps of the anointed one of the God of Jacob, who prayed "Open my eyes and I shall behold wonderful things from thy Law!" (Ps. 119:18). The interpretation of traditional law is in like manner of divine origin. And that which we know today of the nature of Succah, Lalab, Shofar, Fringes, and Phylacteries is essentially the same as that which God commanded Moses, and which the latter told us. In the success of his mission Moses realized the mission of "a faithful servant of God." The text in which the eighth principle of faith is indicated is: "Hereby ye shall know that the Lord hath sent me to do all these works; for I have not done them of mine own mind" (Num. 16:28).

The Ninth Principle of Faith

The abrogation of the Torah. This implies that this Law of Moses will not be abrogated and that no other law will come from before God. Nothing is to be added to it nor taken away from it, neither in the written nor oral law, as it is said "Thou shalt not add to it nor diminish from it!" (Deut. 13:1). In the beginning of this treatise we have already explained that which requires explanation in this principle of faith.

The Tenth Principle of Faith

That he, the exalted one, knows the works of men and is not unmindful of them. Not as they thought who said, "The Lord hath forsaken the earth" (Ezek. 8:12; 9:9), but as he declared who exclaimed, "Great in counsel, and mighty in work; for thine eyes are open upon all the ways of the sons of men" (Jer. 32:19). It is further said, "And the Lord saw that the wickedness of man was great in the earth" (Gen. 6:5). And "the cry of Sodom and Gomorrah is great" (Gen. 18:20). This indicates our tenth principle of faith.

The Eleventh Principle of Faith

That he, the exalted one, rewards him who obeys the commands of the Torah, and punishes him who transgresses its prohibitions. That God's greatest reward to man is "the future world," and that his strongest punishment is in "cutting off." We have already said sufficient upon this theme. The scriptural verses in which the principle is pointed out are: "Yet now if thou wilt forgive their sin; but if not, blot me out of thy book" (Exod. 32:32). And God replied to him, "Whosoever hath sinned against me, him will I blot out of my book" (Exod. 32:33). This is a proof of what the obedient and the rebellious each obtain. God rewards the one and punishes the other.

The Twelfth Principle of Faith

The days of the Messiah. This involves the belief and firm faith in his coming, and that we should not find him slow in coming. "Though he tarry, wait for him" (Hab. 2:3). No date must be fixed for his appearance, neither may the scriptures be interpreted with the view of deducing the time of his coming. The sages said, "A plague on those who calculate periods" (for Messiah's appearance) (*Sanhedrin* 97b). We must have faith in him, honouring and loving him, and praying for him according to the degree of importance with which he is spoken by every prophet, from Moses unto Malachi. He that has any doubt about him or holds his authority in light esteem imputes falsehood to the Torah, which clearly promises his coming in "the chapter of Balaam" (Num. 23–24), and in "Ye stand this day all of you before the Lord your God" (Deut. 30:1–10). From the general nature of this principle of faith we gather that there will be no king of Israel but from David and the descendents of Solomon exclusively. Everyone who disputes the authority of this family denies God and the words of his prophets.

The Thirteenth Principle of Faith

The resurrection of the dead. We have already explained this.

When all these principles of faith are in the safe keeping of man, and his conviction of them is well established, he then enters "into the general body of Israel," and it is incumbent upon us to love him, to care for him, and to do for him all that God commanded us to do for one another in the way of affection and brotherly sympathy. And this, even though he were to be guilty of every transgression possible, by reason of the power of desire or the mastery of the base natural passions. He will receive punishment according to the measure of his perversity, but he will have a portion in the world to come, even though he be of the "transgressors in Israel." When, however, a man breaks away from any one of these fundamental principles of belief, then of him is it said that "he has gone out of the general body of Israel," and "he denies the root-truths of Judaism." And he is then termed a "*min*," "*apikorsim*," and a "hewer of the small plants," and it is obligatory upon us to hate him and cause him to perish, and it is concerning him that the scriptural verse says: "Shall I not hate those who hate thee, O Lord?" (Ps. 119:21).

I find that I have prolonged my remarks very much and have departed from the main thread of my thesis. But I have been obliged to do so because I consider it advantageous to religious belief. For I have brought together for you many useful things scattered about in many collections of books. Therefore find happiness in them, and repeat this my discourse many times over, and ponder it well. And if your power of desire make you wish that you grasped its purport after going through it once, or even after reading it ten times, verily God knows that you have been made to desire an absurd thing. And so do not go through it hurriedly, for, of a truth, I have not composed it in random fashion but after reflection and conviction and the attentive examination of correct and incorrect views; and after getting to know what things out of all of them it is incumbent upon us to believe, and bringing to my assistance arguments and proofs for every individual section of the subject. I shall now ask God's assistance to what is right and true, and return to the main theme of the chapter (X of *Sanhedrin*).

Note

* The original version of this essay possesses numerous technical footnotes on the philology of the text, and thus has many Arabic and Hebrew texts. For the reader's and the typesetter's convenience I have omitted these notes. Interested readers should, of course, consult the original. Also, in the original, J. Abelson provides the Hebrew of the biblical quotations. I, however, have rendered them in English and, once again, omitted the Hebrew.

SELECTION FROM ANSWERS TO NAPOLEAN

The Paris Sanhedrin

Declaration adapted by the Assembly, and the answers to the three first questions

Declaration

Resolved, by the French deputies professing the religion of Moses, that the following Declaration shall precede the answers returned to the questions proposed by the Commissioners of His Imperial and Royal Majesty:

> *The assembly, impressed with a deep sense of gratitude, love, respect, and admiration, for the sacred person of his Imperial and Royal Majesty, declares, in the name of all Frenchmen professing the religion of Moses, that they are fully determined to prove worthy of the favours His Majesty intends for them, by scrupulously conforming to his paternal intentions; that their religion makes it their duty to consider the law of the prince as the supreme law in civil and political matters; that, consequently, should their religious code, or its various interpretations, contain civil or political demands at variance with those of the French code, those commands would, of course, cease to influence and govern them, since they must, above all, acknowledge and obey the laws of the prince.*
>
> *That, in consequence of this principle, the Jews have, at all times, considered it their duty to obey the laws of the state, and that, since the revolution, they, like all Frenchmen, have acknowledged no others.*

First Question

Is it lawful for Jews to marry more than one wife?

Answer

It is not lawful for Jews to marry more than one wife: in all European countries they conform to the general practice of marrying only one. Moses does not command expressly to take several; but he does not forbid it. He seems even to adopt that custom as generally prevailing, since he settles the rights of inheritance between children of different wives. Although this practice still prevails in the East, yet their ancient doctors have enjoined them to restrain from taking more than one wife, except when the man is enabled by his fortune to maintain several.

The case has been different in the West; the wish of adopting the customs of the inhabitants of this part of the world has induced the Jews to renounce Polygamy. But as several individuals still indulged in that practice, a synod was convened at Worms in the eleventh century, composed of one hundred Rabbies, with Guerson at their head. This assembly pronounced an anathema against every Israelite who should, in future, take more than one wife.

Although this prohibition was not to last for ever, the influence of European manners has universally prevailed.

Second Question

Is divorce allowed by the Jewish Religion? Is divorce valid when not pronounced by Courts of Justice by Virtue of Laws in Contradiction with those of the French Code?

Answer

Repudiation is allowed by the law of Moses; but it is not valid if not previously pronounced by the French code.

In the eyes of every Israelite, without exception, submission to the prince is the first of duties. It is a principle generally acknowledged among them, that, in every thing relating to civil or political interests, the law of the state is the supreme law. Before they were admitted in France to share the rights of all citizens, and when they lived under a particular legislation which set them at liberty to follow their religious customs, they had the facility of repudiating their wives; but it was extremely rare to see it put into practice.

Since the revolution, they have acknowledged no other laws on this head but those of the empire. At the epocha when they were admitted to the rank of citizens, the Rabbies and the principal Jews appeared before the municipalities of their respective places of abode, and took an oath to conform, in every thing to the laws, and to acknowledge no other rules in all civil matters.

Consequently they can no longer consider as valid the repudiation pronounced by their Rabbies, since, to make it valid, it must have been previously pronounced by competent tribunals; for, in like manner as by an *arrete* of the Consular Government, the Rabbies could not impart the matrimonial benediction till it appeared to them that the civil contract had been performed before the civil officer; in like manner they cannot pronounce repudiation, until it appears to them that it has already been pronounced by a sentence which gives it validity. Supposing even that the aforesaid *arrete* had been silent on this head, still the rabbinical repudiation could not be valid; for, according to Rabbies who have written on the civil code of the Jews, such as Joseph Carro in the *Abeneser*, repudiation is valid only, in case there should be no opposition of any kind. And as the law of the state would form an opposition, in point of civil interests—since one of the parties could avail himself or herself of it against the other—it necessarily follows that, under the influence of the civil code, rabbinical repudiation cannot be valid. Consequently, since the time the Jews have begun to enter into engagements before the civil officer, no one, attached to religious practices, can repudiate his wife but by a double divorce—that pronounced by the law of the state, and that prescribed by the law of Moses; so that under this point of view, it may be justly affirmed, that the Jewish religion agrees on this subject with the civil code.

Third Question

Can a Jewess marry a Christian, and a Jew a Christian woman? Or does the law allow the Jews to intermarry only among themselves?

Answer

The law does not say that a Jewess cannot marry a Christian, nor a Jew a Christian woman; nor does it state that the Jews can only intermarry among themselves.

The only marriages expressly forbidden by the law are those with the seven Canaanean nations, with Amon and Moab, and with the Egyptians. The prohibition is absolute concerning the seven Canaanean nations: with regard to Amon and Moab, it is limited, according to many Talmudists, to the men of those nations, and does not extend to the women; it is even thought that these last would have embraced the Jewish religion. As to the Egyptians, the prohibition is limited to the third generation. The prohibition in general applies only to nations in idolatry. The Talmud declares formally that modern nations are not to be considered as such, since they worship, like us, the God of heaven and earth. And, accordingly, there has been, at several periods, intermarriages between Jews and Christians in France, in Spain, and in Germany: these marriages were sometimes tolerated, and sometimes forbidden by the laws of those sovereigns, who had received Jews into their dominions.

Unions of this kind are still found in France; but we cannot dissemble that the opinion of the Rabbies is against these marriages. According to their doctrine, although the religion of Moses has not forbidden the Jews from intermarrying with nations not of their religion, yet, as marriage, according to the Talmud, requires religious ceremonies called *Kiduschim*, with the benediction used in such cases, no marriage can be *religiously* valid unless these ceremonies have been performed. This could not be done towards persons who would not both of them consider these ceremonies as sacred; and in that case the married couple could separate without the *religious* divorce; they would then be considered as married *civilly* but not *religiously*.

Such is the opinion of the Rabbies, members of this assembly. In general they would be no more inclined to bless the union of a Jewess with a Christian, or of a Jew with a Christian woman, than Catholic priests themselves would be disposed to sanction unions of this kind. The Rabbies acknowledge, however, that a Jew, who marries a Christian woman, does not cease on that account to be considered as a Jew by his brethren, any more than if he had married a Jewess *civilly* and not *religiously*.

Fourth Question

In the eyes of Jews are Frenchmen considered as their brethren? Or are they considered as strangers?

Answer

In the eyes of Jews Frenchmen are their brethren, and are not strangers. The true spirit of the law of Moses is consonant to this mode of considering Frenchmen.

When the Israelites formed a settled and independent nation, their law made it a rule for them to consider strangers as their brethren. With the most tender care for their welfare, their lawgiver commands them to love them: "Love ye therefore the strangers," says he to the Israelites, "for ye were strangers in the land of Egypt" (Deut. 10:19; Lev. 19:34; Exod. 22:21, 23:9).

Respect and benevolence towards strangers are enforced by Moses, not as an exhortation to the practice of social morality only, but as an obligation imposed by God himself. "When ye reap the harvest of your land," says he to them, "thou shalt not make clean riddance of the corners of the field when thou reapest, neither shalt thou gather any gleaning of thy harvest; thou shalt leave them unto the poor and to the stranger; I am the Lord thy God" (Lev. 23:22). "When thou cuttest down thy harvest in the field, and hast forgot a sheaf in the field, thou shalt not go back again to fetch it:

it shall be for the *stranger*, for the fatherless, and the widow: that the Lord thy God may bless the work of thy hands" (Deut. 24:19). "Thou shalt neither vex a stranger, nor oppress him" (Exod. 22:21). "The Lord your God doth execute the judgment of the fatherless and widow, and loveth the stranger, in giving him food and raiment. Love ye therefore the stranger; for ye were strangers in the land of Egypt" (Deut. 10:18, 19).

To these sentiments of benevolence towards the *Stranger*, Moses has added the precept of general love for mankind: "Love thy fellow creature as thyself."

David also expresses himself in these terms: "The Lord is good to all; and his tender mercies are over all his works" (Ps. 145:9). This doctrine is also professed by the Talmud.

"We are bound," says a Talmudist, "to love as our brethren all those who observe the *Noachides* (the precepts given by the Patriarch Noah), whatever their religious opinions may otherwise be. We are bound to visit their sick, to bury their dead, to assist their poor, like those of Israel. In short, there is no act of humanity which a true Israelite is not bound to perform towards those who observe the *Noachides*." What are these precepts? To abstain from idolatry, from blasphemy, from adultery, not to kill or hurt our neighbours, neither to rob or to deceive, to eat only the flesh of animals killed; in short, to observe that rules of justice; and therefore all the principles of our religion make it our duty to love Frenchmen as our brethren.

A Pagan having consulted the Rabbi Hillel on the Jewish religion, and in wishing to know in a few words in what it consisted, Hillel thus answered him: "Do not to others what thou shouldst not like to have done to thy self. This," said he, "is all our religion; the rest are only consequences of this principle."

A religion whose fundamental maxims are such—a religion which makes a duty of loving the stranger—which enforces the practice of social virtues, must surely require that its followers should consider their fellow citizens as brethren.

And how could they consider them otherwise when they inhabit the same land, when they are ruled and protected by the same government, and by the same laws? When they enjoy the same rights, and have the same duties to fulfil? There exists, even between the Jew and Christian, a tie which abundantly compensates for religion— it is the tie of gratitude. This sentiment was at first excited in us by the mere grant of toleration. It has been increased, these eighteen years, by new favours from government, to such a degree of energy, that now our fate is irrevocably linked with the common fate of all Frenchmen. Yes France is our country; all Frenchmen are our brethren, and this glorious title, by raising us in our own esteem, becomes a sure pledge that we shall never cease to be worthy of it.

Fifth Question

In either case, what line of conduct does their law prescribe towards Frenchmen not of their religion?

Answer

The line of conduct prescribed towards Frenchmen not of our religion is the same as that prescribed between Jews themselves; we admit of no difference but that of worshipping the Supreme Being, every one in his own way.

The answer to the preceding question has explained the line of conduct which the law of Moses and the Talmud prescribe towards Frenchmen not of our religion. At the present time, when the Jews no longer form a separate people, but enjoy the advantage of being incorporated with the Great Nation (which privilege they consider as a kind of political redemption), it is impossible that a Jew should treat a Frenchman, not of his nation, in any other manner than he would treat one of his Israelitish brethren.

Sixth Question

Do Jews born in France, and treated by the laws as French citizens, consider France as their county? Are they bound to defend it? Are they bound to obey the laws and to conform to the dispositions of the civil code?

Answer

Men who have adopted a country, who have resided in it these many generations—who, even under the restraint of particular laws which abridged their civil rights, were so attached to it that they preferred being debarred from the advantages common to all other citizens, rather than leave it, cannot but consider themselves as Frenchmen in France; and they consider as equally sacred and honourable the bounden duty of defending their country.

Jeremiah (chapter 29) exhorts the Jews to consider Babylon as their country, although they were to remain in it only for seventy years. He exhorts them to till the ground, to build houses, to sow, and to plant. His recommendation was so much attended to, that Ezra (chapter 2) says that when Cyrus allowed them to return to Jerusalem to rebuild the Temple, forty-two thousand three hundred and sixty only left Babylon; and that this number was mostly composed of the poorer people, the wealthy having remained in that city.

The love of the country is in the heart of Jews a sentiment so natural, so powerful, and so consonant to their religious opinions, that a French Jew considers himself, in England, as among strangers, although he may be among Jews; and the case is the same with English Jews in France.

To such a pitch is this sentiment carried among them, that, during the last war, French Jews have been seen fighting desperately against other Jews, the subjects of countries then at war with France.

Many of them are covered with honourable wounds, and others have obtained, in the field of honour, the noble rewards of bravery.

Seventh Question

Who names the Rabbies?

Answer

Since the revolution, the majority of the chiefs of families names the Rabbi, wherever there is a sufficient number of Jews to maintain one, after previous inquiries as to the morality and learning of the candidate. This mode of election is not, however, uniform; it varies according to place, and, to this day, whatever concerns the elections of Rabbies is still in a state of uncertainty.

Eighth Question

What police jurisdiction do Rabbies exercise among the Jews? What judicial power do they enjoy among them?

Answer

The Rabbies exercise no manner of Police Jurisdiction among the Jews.

The qualification of *Rabbi* is nowhere to be found in the law of Moses, neither did it exist in the days of the first Temple; it is only mentioned towards the end of those of the second.

At these epochas the Jews were governed by the *Sanhedrin* or tribunals. A supreme tribunal, called *the Great Sanhedrin*, sat in Jerusalem, and was composed of seventy-one Judges.

There were inferior courts, composed of three judges for civil causes and for police; and another composed of twenty-two judges, which sat in the capital to decide matters of less importance, and which was called *the Lesser Sanhedrin*.

It is only in the Misna and in the Talmud that the word *Rabbi* is found for the first time applied to a doctor in the law; and he was commonly indebted for this qualification to his reputation, and to the opinion generally entertained of his learning.

When the Israelites were totally dispersed, they formed small communities in those places where they were allowed to settle in certain numbers. Sometimes, in these circumstances, a Rabbi and two other doctors formed a kind of tribunal, named *Bethin*, that is, House of Justice; the Rabbi fulfilled the functions of judge, and the other two those of his assessors.

The attributes, and even the existence of these tribunals, have, to this day, always depended on the will of government under which the Jews have lived and on the degree of tolerance they have enjoyed. Since the revolution those rabbinical tribunals are totally suppressed in France, and in Italy. The Jews, raised to the rank of citizens, have conformed in every thing to the laws of the state; and, accordingly, the functions of Rabbies, wherever any are established, are limited to preaching morality in the temples, blessing marriages, and pronouncing divorces.

In places where there are no Rabbies, the Jew who is best instructed in his religion, may, according to the law, impart the marriage benediction without the assistance of a Rabbi; this is attended with an inconveniency, the consequences of which it certainly would be proper to prevent, by extending to all persons, called upon to bless a marriage, the restrictions which the consular *arrete* places on the functions of Rabbies in this particular.

As to judicial powers, they possess absolutely none; for there is among them neither a settled ecclesiastical hierarchy, nor any subordination in the exercise of their religious functions.

Ninth Question

Are these forms of Election, and that police-judicial-jurisdiction, regulated by the law, or are they only sanctioned by custom?

Answer

The answer to the preceding questions makes it useless to say much on this, only it may be remarked, that, even supposing that Rabbies should have, to this day, preserved some kind of police-judicial-jurisdiction among us, which is not the case, neither such jurisdiction, nor the forms of the elections, could be said to be sanctioned by the law; they should be attributed solely to custom.

Tenth Question

Are there professions which the laws of the Jews forbids them from exercising?

Answer

There are none: on the contrary, the Talmud (*vide* Kiduschim, *chap. 1st.*) expressly declares that "the father who does not teach a profession to his child, rears him up to be a villain."

Eleventh Question

Does the law forbid the Jews from taking usury from their brethren?

Answer

Deuteronomy 23:19 says, "thou shalt not lend upon *interest* to thy brother, *interest* of money, *interest* of victuals, *interest* of any thing that is lent upon *interest.*"

The Hebrew word *nechech* has been improperly translated by the word *usury*: in the Hebrew language it means *interest* of any kind, and not *usurious interest*. It cannot then be taken in the acceptation now given in the word *usury*.

It is even impossible that it could ever have had that acceptation; for usury is an expression relative to, and compared with, another and a lawful interest; and the text contains nothing which alludes to the other term of comparison. What do we understand by usury? Is it not an interest above the legal interest, above the rate fixed by the law? If the law of Moses has not fixed this rate, can it be said that the Hebrew word means an unlawful interest? The word *nechech* in the Hebrew language answers to the Latin word *faenus*: to conclude that it means *usury*, another word should be found which would mean *interest* and, as such a word does not exist, it follows that all interest is usury, and that all usury is interest.

What was the aim of the lawgiver in forbidding one Hebrew to lend upon interest to another? It was to draw closer between them the bonds of fraternity, to give them a lesson of reciprocal benevolence, and to engage them to help and assist each other with disinterestedness.

The first thought had been to establish among them the equality of property, and the mediocrity of private fortune; hence the institution of the sabbatical year, and of the year of jubilee; the first of which came every seventh year, and the other every fifty years. By the sabbatical year all debtors were released from their obligations: the year of jubilee brought with it the restitution of all estates sold or mortgaged.

It was easy to foresee that the different qualities of the ground, the greater or lesser industry, the untowardness of the seasons, which might affect both, would necessarily make a difference in the produce of land, and that the more unfortunate Israelite would claim the assistance of him whom fortune should have better favoured. Moses did not intend that this last should avail himself of this situation, and that he should require from the other price of the service he was soliciting; that he should thus aggravate the misery of his brother, and enrich himself by his spoils. It is with a view to this that he says, *Thou shalt not lend upon interest to thy brother*. But what want could there exist among the Jews, at a time when they had no trade of any kind? When so little money was in circulation, when the greatest equality prevailed in property? It was, at most, a few bushels of corn, some cattle, some agricultural implements; and Moses required that such services should be gratuitous; his intention was to make of his people a nation of husbandmen. For a long time after him, and though Idumea was at no great distance from the sea-shores, inhabited by the Tyrians, the Sidonians, and other nations possessing shipping and commerce, we do not see the Hebrews much addicted to trade: all the regulations of their lawgiver seemed designed to divert their attention from commerce.

The prohibition of Moses must therefore be considered only as a principle of charity, and not as a commercial regulation. According to the Talmud, the loan alluded to is to be considered almost as a family loan, as a loan made to a man in want; for in case of a loan made to a merchant, even a Jew, profit adequate to the risk should be considered as lawful.

Formerly the word *usury* carried no invidious meaning; it simply implied any interest whatever. The word usury can no longer express the meaning of the Hebrew text: and accordingly the Bible of Osterwald and that of the Portuguese Jews, call *interest* that which Sacy, from the Vulgate, has called *usury*.

The law of Moses, therefore, forbids all manner of interest on loan, not only between Jews, but between a Jew and his countryman, without distinction of religion. The loan must be gratuitous whenever it is to oblige those who claim our assistance, and when it is not intended for commercial speculation.

We must not forget that these laws, so humane and so admirable at these early periods, were made for a people which then formed a state and held a rank among nations.

If the remnants of this people, now scattered among all nations, are attentively considered, it will be seen, that, since the Jews have been driven from Palestine, they no longer have had a common country, they no longer have had to maintain among them the primeval quality of property. Although filled with the spirit of their legislation, they have been sensible that the letter of the law could no longer be obeyed when its principle was done away; and they have, therefore, without any scruple, lent money on interest to trading Jews, as well as to men of different persuasions.

Twelfth Question

Does it forbid or does it allow to take usury from strangers?

Answer

We have seen, in the answer to the foregoing question, that the prohibition of usury, considered as the smallest interest, was a maxim of charity and of benevolence, rather than a commercial regulation. In this point of view it is equally condemned by the law of Moses and by the Talmud; we are generally forbidden, always on the score of charity, to lend upon interest to our fellow-citizens of different persuasions, as well as to our fellow-Jews.

The disposition of the law, which allows us to take interest from the stranger, evidently refers only to nations in commercial intercourse with us; otherwise there would be an evident contradiction between this passage and twenty others of the sacred writings.

"The Lord your God loveth the stranger, in giving him food and raiment; love ye therefore the stranger, for ye were strangers in the land of Egypt" (Deut. 10:18, 19); "One law shall be to him that is home-born, and to the stranger" (Exod. 7:49). "Hear the causes between your brethren, and judge righteously between every man and his brother and the stranger that is with him" (Deut. 1:16). "If a stranger sojourn with thee in your land you shall not vex him" (Lev. 19:33). "Thou shall neither vex a stranger nor oppress him, for ye were strangers in the land of Egypt" (Exod. 22:21). "If thy brother be waxen poor, or fallen in decay with thee, thou shalt then relieve him; yea, though he be a stranger or a sojourner" (Lev. 25:15).

This the prohibition extended to the stranger who dwelt in Israel; the Holy Writ places them under the safeguard of God; he is a sacred guest, and God orders us to treat him like the widow and like the orphan.

It is evident that the text of the Vulgate, *Extranei faenaberis et fratri tuo non faenaberis*, can be understood only as meaning foreign nations in commercial intercourse with us; and, even in this case, the Holy Writ, in allowing to take interest from the stranger, does not mean an extraordinary profit, oppressive and odious to the borrower. *Non licuisse Isrealitis*, say the doctors, *usuras immoderatas exigere ab exrtraneis, etiam divitibus, res est per se nota.*

Can Moses be considered as the lawgiver of the universe, because he was the lawgiver of the Jews? Were the laws he gave to the people, which God had entrusted to his care, likely to become the general laws of mankind? *Thou shalt not lend upon interest to thy brother.* What security had he, that, in the intercourse which would be naturally established between the Jews and foreign nations, these last would renounce customs generally prevailing in trade, and lend to the Jews without requiring any interest? Was he then bound to sacrifice the interest of his people, and to impoverish the Jews to enrich foreign nations? Is it not absolutely absurd to reproach him with having put a restriction to the precept contained in Deuteronomy? What lawgiver would have considered such a restriction as a natural principle of reciprocity?

How far superior in simplicity, generosity, justice, and humanity, is the law of Moses, on this head, to those of the Greeks and of the Romans! Can we find, in the history of the ancient Israelites, those scandalous scenes of rebellion excited by the harshness of creditors towards their debtors; those frequent abolitions of debts to prevent the multitude, impoverished by the extortions of lenders, from being driven to despair?

The law of Moses and its interpreters have distinguished, with a praiseworthy humanity, the different uses of borrowed money. Is it to maintain a family? Interest is forbidden. Is it to undertake a commercial speculation, by which the principal is adventured? Interest is allowed, even between Jews. *Lend to the Poor*, says Moses.

Here the tribute of gratitude is the only kind of interest allowed; the satisfaction of obliging is the sole recompense of the conferred benefit. That case is different in regard to capitals employed in extensive commerce: there, Moses allows the lender to come in for a share of the profits of the borrower; and as commerce was scarcely known among the Israelites, who were exclusively addicted to agricultural pursuits, and as it was carried on only with strangers, that is with neighbouring nations, it was allowed to share its profits with them.

It is in this view of the subject that M. Clermont-Tonnerre made use of these remarkable words in the first National Assembly: "It is said that usury is permitted to the Jews; this assertion is grounded only on a false interpretation of a principle of benevolence and fraternity which forbade them from lending upon interest to one another."

This opinion is also that of Puffendorf and of other writers on the law of nations.

The antagonists of the Jews have laid a great stress on a passage of Maimonides, who seems to be represented as a precept, the expression *Anochri tassih* (make profit of the stranger). But although Maimonides has presumed to maintain this opinion, it is well known that his sentiments have been most completely refuted by the learned Rabbi Abarbanel. We find, besides, in the Talmud, a treatise of *Macot* (Perfection) that one of the ways to arrive at perfection is to lend without interest to the stranger, even to the idolator. Whatever besides might have been the condescension of God to the Jews, if we may be allowed the expression, it cannot be reasonably supposed that the common father of mankind could, at any time, make usury a precept.

The opinion of Maimonides, which excited all Jewish Doctors against him, was principally condemned by the famous Rabbies Moses de Gironda and Solomon Benadaret, upon the grounds, first, that he had relied on the authority of Siffri, a private doctor, whose doctrine has not been sanctioned by the Talmud; for it is a general rule that every rabbinical opinion which is not sanctioned by that work is considered as null and void. Secondly, because, if Maimonides understood that the word *Nochri* (stranger) was applicable to the Canaanean people doomed by God to destruction, he ought not to have confounded a public right, arising from an extraordinary order of God to the Israelites, considered as a nation, with the private right of an individual towards another individual of that same nation.

It is an incontrovertible point, according to the Talmud, that interest, even among Israelites, is lawful in commercial operations, where the lender, running some of the risk of the borrower, becomes a sharer in his profits. This is the opinion of all Jewish doctors.

It is evident that opinions, teeming with absurdities, and contrary to all rules of social morality, although advanced by a Rabbi, can no more be imputed to the general doctrine of the Jews, than similar notions, if advanced by Catholic theologians, could be attributed to the evangelical doctrine. The same may be said of the general charge made against the Hebrews, that they are naturally inclined to usury: it cannot be denied that some of them are to be found, though not so many as is generally supposed, who follow that nefarious traffic condemned by their religion.

But if there are some not over-nice in this particular, is it just to accuse one hundred thousand individuals of this vice? Would it not be deemed an injustice to lay the same imputation on all Christians because some of them are guilty of usury?

SELECTION FROM *JUDAISM AND ITS HISTORY*

Abraham Geiger

Akiba, Interpretation of the Scriptures, Mishnah, Babylonian Gemara

Let us continue the view of the period. Akiba, as we have observed, one of the foremost carriers of the tendency of that time (first half of the second century), has in brief words pronounced great eternal truths; he has presented God in pure spirituality and man in his capacity and task to develop out of himself the noblest product. Let us try to complete that representation by a few illustrations. Besides God and man separately, the question arises as to man within mankind, as to the relation of the individual within society. This question also, Akiba, in conjunction with his contemporaries, answers for us. Already the quoted saying of the excellent shape of man gives us in the form of its expression, sufficient guidance. It is, so the words run, a great preference for man to have been created in excellent shape. By that it is announced that man in general, not a separate class of men, not man under certain conditions, of a certain faith, the individual of an exclusive people, alone possesses that excellency, but man in general, all men. To leave no doubt about that meaning, he continues: For Israel, it is an excellency that they have recognized the fatherhood of God and are designated as God's children; what he said earlier of men and his high excellence, he holds to under all forms and conditions. And it corresponds to it, if he repeats the words of Hillel and pronounces: The comprehensive great principle of the law is, Love thy neighbor as thyself. In the most perfect agreement with that is the doctrine of a little earlier contemporary of Akiba, Joshua Ben Chanania, who in general is most like Akiba. In contradiction to some other teachers, he quotes the verse of Psalms: The wicked shall be turned into hell, and all the nations that forget God; and interprets, Only those that forget God are turned into hell, but not any that think of God; all—those outside of Israel as well—who harbor a divine idea, who strive toward higher, nobler development, even if in error now and then, who want to lift themselves toward God by honest endeavor, to all of them is due a share in eternal life, as he expresses it. That is a great thought which occurs here in briefest form, according to the method peculiar to the time, based upon a verse of the bible and without larger development of its contents, but which is of great depth and was for that period and for the long centuries thereafter, the fountain of richest and truly religious stimulation. At a time in which Judaism was forced, in order to defend itself against exterior influences, into exclusiveness, and austerely carried it through, at the selfsame time, it decidedly rejected by that doctrine, all one-sided narrowness which prevailed so mightily on the outside. It preserves to itself the recognition of all that is human, never lets go of the guiding line by which it joins the tie of peace with all humanity. We must apprehend this doctrine so much the more according to its full importance and recognize the indestructibility of the live Jewish religiousness, the more it seems to be in contradiction with the entire attitude and the efforts of the time. And this doctrine did not remain unnoticed; it became valid doctrine for all time in Judaism, even if the rigor from without, did not let it attain to its complete consequences, yet through all periods minded the undisputed doctrine: The pious of all nations and all religions have a share in eternal life.

As to the position of the individual in society, sayings have come down to us from that time, which bear witness of deep insight into the nature of man and his task. Everyone has value who carries within himself endeavor toward reflection, who accepts God's law and develops accordingly; is measured by that, not according to position and rank. There are three crowns: the crown of government, the crown of priesthood, and the crown of the knowledge of the law; yet they are excelled by the crown of a good name. In every condition of life, only the faithful doing of duty which merits good repute is the true crown. Government and priesthood are gifts of birth; knowledge of God's law can be acquired by everybody, and with it he grasps the finest crown, puts it on his head, and thereby attains true nobility. Already, at its first formation, Phariseeism had opposed priestly nobility, and all externals resting on office and birth; the value of learning and of science, as it was then understood, the value of what a man develops under all conditions, was put to the front. Akiba, like Hillel, was a man of the people, not of a higher rank, not endowed with inherited, unearned dignity; but the plain scholar, risen to the greatest importance in Israel, he stands as the hero of his time, and the builder for all times. In this, too, lies an energy of Judaism, which kept it fresh through the long period. It contained many a germ which, if it had belonged to its spiritual essence, must have necessarily developed and led to hierarchy. That this was not the case, proves that the spirit of liberty within it was too powerful for such attempts to succeed, even when they had their historic connecting links and points of departure. Induction into office by laying on of hands as sign of transference of spiritual dignity which in another religion became out-and-out endowment with the holy ghost, dates back into Judaism. Moses inducts Joshua into office in that manner. Yet, such induction never became in Israel a priestly one and was never considered to raise man to higher power. It remained an expression of acknowledgment of attained ability. It bestows the ornament of science, not the scepter of dominion; it was a testimony of the acquisition of scholarship, not a magical consecration and elevation. Therefore, at that time, as in all times, the most modest scholar without position or office, was esteemed in his circle just as much as another who had attained high position and office. This recognition of the love of the spirit and of the power of knowledge gave to Judaism strength and freshness.

Such principles, as we have learned to know them from that time, from a time in which Judaism was driven into externalism and exclusiveness, remained the living force that again gave even to the hulls some spirituality, and this endowed them with endurance; while on the other side, those hulls were necessary to guard the innermost kernel of Judaism from injuries which threatened it in such a terrible manner from that time on. Indeed, the conditions of the time demanded a tighter closing of ranks, a tangible external band, because old ties had been broken. To obtain a correct understanding of how this band was woven, which stretched around the whole life, to be able to correctly estimate the remarkable structure which then arose, we must present yet a few complementary facts which introduce us into the mental tendency that remained ruling within Judaism for a long time.

Already when the exiles had returned from Babylon to restore the state and attempted to rehabilitate the Temple, there had a certain antiquarian endeavor come back alongside of the quick and fresh spirit which they had preserved from the time of the old prophets, and which had become their real energy for overcoming all paganism. That antiquarian sentiment had prevailed in all arrangements. While yet Jeremiah, living about the time of the destruction of the first Temple, announced: "I will put my law in their inward parts and write it in their hearts;" while he, like all genuine prophets, put the emphasis upon the point that the spirit should rule, and not the letter, that not the written word but the live inner meaning should become the measure for thought and action, at the founding of the second Temple, we constantly meet the phrase, "and they found *written*." On all occasions, the books, accepted as written in godly spirit during Israel's early ages, were consulted about their opinions, and even opinions which were but temporary effusions arisen out of the conditions of a definite period, prevailed as general ordinances, valid for all eternity. It was not easy to make up the mind to admit the necessity for development and real, accomplished transformation. The spirit of tradition, which is nothing else than the creative instinct for further development, was at hand and the stream of life ran unconsciously through the whole and did the transforming—but to pronounce with full decision that a new time had arrived which must grow new products out of the old, energetic spirit, for such a decided declaration of their majority they were not ready. Even when Phariseeism arose against the priestly usurpations of the Sadducees, when it battled for the right of practical life and the vigorous body of the people, its importance against the arrogance of those who made regulations for the people as officers of the sacrificial service and the written law, it did not at first know how to give to its sound conviction and energy any other expression, and to apply for their presentation any other remedy than to transfer the letter of the law to themselves as well as to the priests, that it wrapped the whole people in priestly vestment and adjudged every possible priestly thing to them, so that they were more cramped, notwithstanding the liberal, free thought, out of which the resistance had come. In the later time, too, when mainly through Hillel, a free sentiment penetrated still farther, the endeavor was always present to compound with the letter as much as possible. That something else was ordained in the Scripture than that which prevailed in the present—to admit that, courage was lacking. They sought rather to expound one thing out and interpret another into it, to develop something different; in short, they wanted to carry the entire present into the past in order to attain the ease of mind of being really in accord with the past.

Such action was yet easier in the time of the second Temple. With the great political and religious congruence existing in those older conditions, transformations flowed in more unnoticed; the text of the old Scriptures was not as yet fixed and it was in parts treated very much at the pleasure of the copyist, never shrinking from making many changes, in the belief that it must always have read that way, since it could not be imagined to have been differently written according to then present views. The peculiarities of the Hebrew language, like those of the Semitic sister-languages, greatly favored such a change in the interpretation. As is well known, the Hebrew has in its writing, in the cold presentation by letters, only consonants—the mere skeleton of the idea, as it were—which receives its actual life only from the various pronunciations. According to the change in the unwritten vowels, sense, meaning, and importance vary greatly. Thus it was very easy at that time, when the vowels had not been written (for only much later they came to be directly indicated by little marks and points), at that time, when all punctuation was lacking, it was very easy to give new meaning to the text by other vocalization and different punctuation, joining or separating words and phrases. Such continued even when the efforts were made to fix the meaning more exact by vocalization and punctuation, and thus they have gained lasting shape in our present text of the bible. In that way, there was in that time a peculiar identification of one's own conception with the written word, a mutual accommodation, a looking up of one's own in the book which was adjudged to have exclusive validity in all its particulars, and then again a half-conscious carrying into it and soft bending of its general rules. With all veneration for the standard book, they proceeded with a certain degree of freedom; a people's life existed, which formed its wants and peculiarities independently, in which the conditions of living enforced their claims. Separate books were spoken of with boldness, they were rejected, they were accepted, according to the view held of them, according to the propriety of conviction found in them. This determination of the inner consciousness would surely have matured its fruits with a continued free nationality.

But now the time of ruin came. The tie was dissolved; if the members of this faith were to be kept together while they were scattered into the different countries, surrendering the hope of being soon again gathered; if they were not to totally fall apart, a new solid band had to be thrown around them and the spirit had to receive a lasting form by which it could be recognized. Yet the form into which it had already moulded itself was held to be the one authorized and binding for all time; it was the expression of the people to be preserved, and had to be kept with it. They believed that they must cling to the past in all its peculiarities. To ask for reasons, for occasions that might have produced this or that regulation, to measure them by the spirit within them—that seemed a wicked beginning, a presumptuous undertaking. Independence of one's own conviction could now no longer be permitted to prevail over the letter of the Scripture. Proceeding freely with the text, as had been the habit, could no longer be permitted, if everything was not to be made uncertain with the dismemberment of the national life. Accordingly, we then hear for the first time the acceptance as a firm principle (which on the one side became scientifically justified and preventing arbitrary action, had its favorable influence, but on the other side became a great hindrance): The traditional pronunciation—that is, the vocalization of the text, which was then not written but was customary in definite form—is a fence to the law; it must remain as it is now fixed and traditionally delivered to us; it can no longer be permitted that anybody should change it according to his own views.

Nothing should now be different from what the present letter of the Scripture presented, and nothing outside of it. But there were so many transformations and additions in use? That those were actually transformations and additions, could not be admitted. Clinging to the letter, they tried to interpret it as containing everything, all was to have existed as valid from the beginning, even if it was not found in the Scriptures; all should not be simply tradition as born out of the original spirit of the people and fitted to the conditions, but was to have existed in part by having been orally given in all its particulars, with the written law, to Moses, and in part by being indicated and contained in the Scriptures according to an interpretation which was regarded as perfectly justified with a divine book that chooses no superfluous word, no curious form, no irregularity, for nothing. From such seeming indications it was believed the regulations that varied from the natural meaning, and the ordinances that were outside of it, could be sufficiently proved. And thus an exceedingly dangerous method of interpretation was formed, which at first simply tried to bring the actual existing into harmony with the received text, but which, very soon in luxurious growth, created many a new regulation. Akiba and his contemporaries are patterns in this proceeding. Because Akiba demonstrated such an indication for ordinances which, without being given in the Scriptures, had become firmly established, but the validity of which was doubted by earlier teachers because they could not find any warrant for them in the written word—because Akiba demonstrated such an indication for them, he was glorified as a skillful scholar, as a man who had laid new and irremovable foundations for Judaism in its then existing form.

We have noticed a few attempts in which Akiba expounded verses in accordance with his conviction, going far away from the natural meaning. Another sample may suffice to mark the whole proceeding. It is a peculiarity of the Hebrew language that it sometimes indicates the objective case simply by the position of the noun in the sentence and sometimes by the addition of the little word "eth." That was sufficient occasion for those times to look for a particular reason why that little word or particle was used in some passages, although it might just as well have been absent, and to ask for indications in its apparently superfluous presence. That word, but derived from a different root, has the meaning "with." And that was enough for that school to expound it accordingly in that sense and call it "with" in every passage where it occurs. The proceeding grew to such an extent that the interpretation was not limited to discussion of the laws in the schools, but was carried into the bible translations. The want was felt for a new translation for the Jews who spoke the Greek language only. The ancient Greek septuagint version which represented the old position and had been made with great freedom, had lost its former authority, and thus several new Greek translations arose. Among them, the one of Aquila, a contemporary of Akiba, especially wanted to render the new position in full, and he is for that treated with great acknowledgment. It clings to the letter and in that way translates everywhere where that little word occurs as sign of the objective case as if "with" were in the text; it is rendered by the Greek "syn" although it does not fit into the connection and is repugnant to grammatical rules of the Greek language. That proceeding governed the time, and as it faces us in that translation, in the same way it was followed up by the teachers of the Mishnah—the name of the teachers of the law at that time—they expounded every sentence in which the little word was, as if something else was included. In the beginning, God created "the" heavens and "the" earth; here too, the objective case is indicated by "the." Thence their interpretation: "the" heavens, "with the" heavens, all its hosts were created; "the" earth, "with the" earth everything produced that moves and grows upon it. Thus it is said of a contemporary of Akiba, Simon, or Nehemiah the Amsonite, that he had successfully found interpretations for all passages with that sign of the objective case, that he in fact found the mission of his life in that work. But he came across one passage at which he shied: "Thou shalt fear the Lord thy God"; here also the objective case is indicated by that particle. That besides the Lord, others should be given like fear, that another being should be named as on a certain equality with God, that he did not dare to pronounce, and he gave up any attempt at interpretation. Asked for the reason why, after so many interpretations, he abstained from finding one here, he said, "As I hope to receive reward for the interpretations which I made, so I hope to receive reward for abstaining from it in this passage." A fine sense for truth! It did not suffice to Akiba, he had more courage and was more consistent; he found an interpretation: "Besides God, you shall honor the teachers of His law."

This example may be sufficient to show with what anxiety the letter was observed on the one side, and how arbitrarily it was squeezed and pressed into service on the other side in order to interpret the most various things out of it. That anxious clamping and cramping at a given word was a sad necessity, if all was not to fall apart. The spirit could not reveal itself in its freedom. It could not in a fluid and esoteric manner have resisted a world that met it with rudeness and violence; it needed a hard, protecting hull, a sheltering roof, under which the scattered members got closer together. We learn about Akiba that he traveled far about, but we do not exactly know for what purpose. Yet it can hardly be doubted that in those journeys he did not omit to cement together the scattered members in the various countries, so that they remained parts of a whole. That endeavor was a leading principle with more or less clear consciousness. In Palestine, the old ties were dissolved, a new one was to get around them. Indeed, it gradually became a very coarse rope, but it answered the purpose; it held fast together until the time comes when the shell may be burst, and the mind and spirit can unfold freely.

The new movement with seeming convulsive clinging to the old things, effected a complete inner transformation and was decisively pressing to a close. And thus we meet, a short time thereafter, a new book worked out of that movement. It is the Mishnah. The word means "repetition," but is intended for "doctrine." Everything in it was then styled repetition; nothing appeared new, everything had to appear as simply repeated and renewed injunction of what the ancient time had given long ago. What the old law, so they persuaded themselves, had laid down in short words, in dim indications, that was here repeated, but expanded more definitely and more extensively. That Mishnah was closed by Rabbi Juda the Prince about sixty years after Akiba. Akiba himself appears to have started one, but it came to a close only then. It can not be our task here to enter into the particulars of it, but the spirit that rules in it is known by the matter accepted and the manner in which the material is arranged. It is in six divisions. It begins with the divine service and almost leads to the belief that this amounts to a demonstration, the presentation of the great treasure that had been gained, because divine service is the real and lasting conquest of Pharisaic Judaism against the priesthood. Priesthood is on the whole neglected and rather ignored in the Mishnah. And yet one-half of it is filled with instruction about things that had already been removed out of the present. Besides the still-valid ordinances about festivals, marriage relations, civil law matters, and the like, it treats of regulations about the soil, the dues or taxes to be paid from the crops, about sacrifices, cleanness and uncleanness. Those matters fill the greater part of the book, matters which had disappeared out of practical life and had no longer validity in the present, but were a tradition of the past. But they lived in the past and presented it.

That was the last incisive action which affected Judaism from Palestine. That country did not wholly rest during the coming centuries, forced a few sprouts, but they were without particular creative force and did not attain to governing influence upon the remaining Jewish world. The soil of Palestine had become unstable and slippery for Israel and his faith. The entire Roman empire no longer offered a safe spot for him. But a new country opened to him, or rather, a territory came again into the foreground that had once before been a refuge for Israel and in which Jewish seed had once before come up abundantly. Immediately after Rabbi Juda the Prince—that is, after the close of the Mishnah at the beginning of the third century—we find a large number of schools in Babylonia, in the country whither the scattered remnants of the first Temple had been conducted, where they were still germinating and growing, in the country whence Ezra had arisen, who undertook the restoration of the second commonwealth, and from which also Hillel, another rejuvenator of Judaism, had emigrated into Palestine to apply his fresh force to its revival. There we meet fast flourishing schools at Nehardea, Sora, Pumbeditha, and in many other places, schools that did not teach what they had received only, in the manner as it was wretchedly carried on yet for awhile in Palestine, but which took hold of their task with a fresh and live spirit. Heretofore we have mentioned the important words pronounced by a teacher there: He that emigrates from Babylonia to Palestine, commits a sin and transgresses God's command. Palestine, which was regarded as the holy land, whose soil was venerated as a holy one, which was looked upon as endowed with a certain sanctity—to migrate into that land from Babylonia should be prohibited? They felt the new spirit within themselves, felt themselves at home in a vigorous country in which endeavor could develop untrammeled. Here was the only empire into which the power of the Romans did not reach; the rough hand of the Parthians had opened a refuge for the Jews the like of which they hardly found in the remaining civilized world of that time. There were some romantics who looked toward Palestine with fond longing. It is told of such a one—that he secretly withdrew from his teacher and fasted forty days, in order to forget the fresh manner and doctrine of Babylon and get used to the more sober and stunted ways of Palestine; fast days were scarcely necessary for him, because his desire indicates that the right spirit had departed from him. But those were exceptions, few and far between. The fresh spirit which moved about there, penetrated the scholars and invigorated them.

At any rate, life was not outside of the present. Many a thing was felt missing, many earnest hopes had to be deferred to a distant future, yet they did not so completely efface the present as it had become the custom on leaving Palestine. While in that country they dreamed themselves into the past and could picture the future only in order to restore the past in ideal form, a future which could not grow out of the natural course of development, they had in Babylonia a healthier realism. Between this world and the days of the Messiah, said a teacher there, there is no further difference than the pressure of the nations; the world will go on, the pressure only will cease; it is the same development, the same order of the state, only freedom enters with her reviving breath. While they in Palestine regarded the entire government of the time, as it ruled outside of Israel and pressed upon it, as illegitimate; while they recognized no verdict coming from that government machinery as legal because emanating from an illegitimate power and even put up as doctrine that it was only permissible to ask a Jewish court for a verdict and that any other should be rejected, even if the court decided according to the same principles: they taught in Babylonia that the law of the state, because founded on legitimate principles, was effective and legitimate and had religious validity. Such thoughts flow from a view which adjudges to the present its right and knows how to esteem it. Sayings along such lines are reported chiefly of a teacher Samuel, and he is also described as a patron of science. He is said to have been a physician, and learned in mathematics and astronomy. To him is attributed the saying: "The paths of the heavens are as familiar to me as the streets of Nehardea." We do not want to take that too literally and examine into the exact truth of the statement, but it shows to us at any rate, that science was studied there, and if that is especially true of astronomy, the reason is in its close connection with the fixing of the festivals.

For here again we meet a point which reveals the independence of Babylonia in a noteworthy manner. To keep the festivals according to their traditionally-fixed time is something upon which every religious association places great importance. Many controversies were carried on in the early Christian times about the day on which Easter should be celebrated, one side insisting on the fifteenth day of Nissan, and the other side on the following Sunday. Great schisms followed out of it, and at the most various periods the dispute about the celebration of holidays has separated more than inner differences. In Israel, it was formerly the custom to send messengers out upon the high mountains to look for the new moon, and then when its appearance had been proven by their testimony, the beginning of the month, and accordingly the festivals occurring therein, were fixed by the courts, and runners of the court announced the decision to the inhabitants all around. The influence of Palestine became weaker, the ties looser, the want was felt to get out of dependence on Palestine and to order the festivals in a definite manner. That requires great resolution, to arrange a new order of fixing the religious festivals and to depart from the old proceeding of consulting the visible, natural phenomenon as it had been believed to be ordained in the letter of the Scripture and to bear the seal of divinity. Such an undertaking can arise only out of a fresh living time, and it was accomplished then. Its beginnings are hidden from us; it suddenly stands before us, a definite calendar is ordained so that the festivals are ordered according to fixed calculation, without having to observe the appearance of the new moon. With the acceptance of that ordinance, many consequences of the old proceeding fell into disuse. In the olden times, new year often had to be celebrated two days, because they did not know whether the new moon had actually appeared, and often the second day was the correct one. Those who resided far away and learned of the announcement of the appearance of the new moon only towards the middle of the month, could not know the day decided on in Jerusalem, and had to keep other holidays for two days. With a fixed calendar, all doubts disappeared, and the reason for a two days' celebration existed no longer. The two days for the new year were retained. For, said they, when the Temple is rebuilt, the former regulations about observing the appearance of the new moon will be restored, and then the cases when two days have to be kept will occur again, and therefore it is better to leave it in this way. But for the other holidays, they felt a two days' celebration to be unnecessary. Yet from Palestine a message came: "Hold fast to the custom of your fathers." Palestine felt itself injured by a transformation of the former regulation.

Thus in Babylonia a pew order had arisen; and not enough, that calculation had taken the place of seeing the new moon. They shifted in some cases the day of the festival out and out. It was considered burdensome to have Sabbath and a day of atonement follow each other, that the day of atonement should be on a Friday or a Sunday, as had often happened before, and is expressly shown in the Mishnah. To keep two such important rest days and holidays in succession interfered with all conditions of life; and to prevent that, it was ordained that new year should not be celebrated on Wednesday or Friday; the day was shifted if it should happen to fall on one of those days according to the calculation of the moon's course. It was a bold interference, the ordinance cut deep into the arrangements which had till then been valid, but it carried, and became the rule for all time.

In other ways they showed their independence of Palestine. In Palestine, winter is the rainy season, and for this rainy season there is in the prayer-book a fixed formula: "Give dew and rain for a blessing." In Palestine this rainy season begins in the first half of Marcheshvan, in November. But Babylonia has a different climate. The rainy season begins a month later, sixty days after the sun crosses the line in Tishri. "We pray for ourselves," said the Babylonians, "not for Palestine, for the right kind of winter and the growth of vegetation in our own country." And without hesitation, they ordered that the prayer should be made later. Consider the difference between that vigorous time and the periods of weakness following later. Then in Babylonia shortly after their removal from the soil of Palestine when the wound of its loss was still bleeding, near the land which still exerted great influence, they yet dared with decision to break away in prayer from its forms, if they did not correspond to the needs of their own country. The later time stuck to the Babylonian order. We have no rainy season, our seasons are quite different; but still we follow the Babylonian ordinance and use the formula of prayer at the time which was set for that country, with a show of fitness. Nor do we follow the rule of Palestine, which would have some justification in the mind of those who have their view upon the holy land of the future.

In every way, Babylonia had become a spiritual world-power. It had not completely emancipated itself from Palestine, had continued in its spirit, but with independent energy, with boldness and clear mind, so that its influence upon the later time remained a lasting one. A healthy, here and there, a rough realism ruled there, and the religious expressions are sometimes rough and harsh, but never sickly and weak. That rugged nature shows itself also in their tales and legends which often are very sensual, yet at the same time plastic, and proceed from a certain energy of life. Sound nature reveals itself in the vigorous moral sense that breaks through everywhere. Not only is every injustice reproved, but every action, too, which might mislead anybody into erroneous conception, even if that is not their intention. For such, the pictorial expression is used: to commit theft of the supposition of the other man. Desecration of the divine name, it is called, when a man who enjoys high regard as a teacher of religion, does not at once pay for his requirement and causes the appearance as if he would avoid doing so. It was a life of solid core, even if the stuff appears rude here and there.

Thus the schools flourished there for some time. Many a new thing was developed, even if free science could not succeed under the government of the Parthians. With all externalism, a sharp, penetrating sense is revealed so that by the collection of the local discussions Judaism was kept from stagnation. That collection was joined to the

Mishnah. Yet, about the beginning of the sixth century, the schools continued in their debates, a formal closing never took place, but gloomy circumstances came in time and brought it about and all at once completion and inactivity arrived. The Gemara— i.e., learning, completion, as that work which joined the Mishnah was called—the Babylonian Talmud, as the two works were named, was not closed; they closed of themselves. The work was never formally voted on or accepted, it gained validity and kept it until a new spiritual, equally vigorous power arises. A complete, free development could not form itself in those times, but furrows were drawn for later seeding, the soil was kept fresh, that it may be filled with new germ.

In the meantime, the Roman empire had been moving nearer its disintegration. Roman paganism, grown weak, became at last persecution-mad in the consciousness of its impotency; it decayed gradually and could not resist new powers. Christianity in its mediation between paganism and Judaism increased in importance and respect, overcame crumbled paganism and mounted the throne. Even that new force, ecclesiastical life, was not able to rejuvenate the ageing Roman empire, so that it might have resisted the approaching storms; it did not breathe into it a full, new spirit which could have raised a dam against the floods. When the floods of the migration of nations rolled over it, all at once, the Roman empire broke down, barbarism flowed over it, perhaps necessary barbarism to bring fresh, rugged forces into the world. The Church was now the carrier of the only wretched remains of culture as far as it permitted it to be harbored. For Judaism, a hard, gloomy time had come. In comparison with that, its members had formerly only sipped at the cup of sorrows; now they were to empty it to the lees. Even the rude nations did not put up as violent resistance to Judaism, as now the councils of the Church organized it. They prohibited every intercourse with Jews; not only was marriage between them and the members of the Christian Church forbidden under severe penalties, but every tie of friendship, every intimate intercourse is represented as leading to damnation and is warned against. Thus the rudeness of the nations was paired with the refined animosity of a religion which could not pardon another for still existing and remaining among the living while it asserted to have consumed it long ago. Thus it seemed as if mankind would fall completely into barbarism. Yet the spirit of humanity never sleeps altogether; even if a part flags, if it laboriously pants along here under difficulties piled up to giant height, it rises elsewhere with unsuspected energy. All at once, day breaks within a people which had never been looked at and which until then had never been noticed. A new factor entered humanity, and it carried the light in the lead for several centuries— the Arabians.

Setting the Problem, Laying the Ground

Judith Plaskow

The need for a feminist Judaism begins with hearing silence: It begins with noting the absence of women's history and experiences as shaping forces in the Jewish tradition. Half of Jews have been women, but men have been defined as normative Jews, while women's voices and experiences are largely invisible in the record of Jewish belief and experience that has come down to us. Women have lived Jewish history and carried its burdens, but women's perceptions and questions have not given form to scripture, shaped the direction of Jewish law, or found expression in liturgy. Confronting this silence raises disturbing questions and stirs the impulse toward far-reaching change. What in the tradition is ours? What can we claim that has not also wounded us? What would have been different had the great silence been filled?

Hearing silence is not easy. A silence so vast tends to fade into the natural order; it is easy to identify with reality. To ourselves, women are not Other. We take the Jewish tradition as it has been passed down to us, as ours to appropriate or ignore. Over time, we learn to insert ourselves into silences.[1] Speaking about Abraham, telling of the great events at Sinai, we do not look for ourselves in the narratives but assume our presence, peopling the gaps in the text with women's shadowy forms. It is far easier to read ourselves into male stories than to ask how the foundational stories within which we live have been distorted by our absence. Yet it is not possible to speak into silence, to recover our history or reclaim our power to name without first confronting the extent of exclusion of women's experience. Silence can become an invitation to experiment and explore—but only after we have examined its terrain and begun to face its implications.

68

This chapter has two purposes: to chart the domain of silence that lies at the root of Jewish feminism and to take up the methodological presuppositions that inform my thinking. While it is not my primary intention in this book to set out an indictment of Judaism as a patriarchal tradition, criticism is an ongoing and essential part of the Jewish feminist project. Not only is criticism a precondition for imagining a transformed Judaism; without a clear critique of Judaism that precedes and accompanies reconstruction, the process of reconstruction easily can be misconstrued as a form of apologetics. In exploring the territory of silence and describing my methodology, I mean to prevent this misunderstanding by clarifying the stance and intent that underlie my constructive thinking.

Exploring the Terrain of Silence

In her classic work *The Second Sex*, Simone de Beauvoir argues that men have established an absolute human type—the male—against which women are measured as Other. Otherness, she says, is a pervasive and generally fluid category of human thought; I perceive and am perceived as Other depending on a particular situation. In the case of males and females, however, Otherness is not reciprocal: men are always the definers, women the defined.[2] While women's self-experience is an experience of selfhood, it is not women's experience that is enshrined in language or that has shaped our cultural forms. As women appear in male texts, they are not the subjects and molders of their own experiences but the objects of male purposes, designs, and desires. Women do not name reality, but rather are names as part of a reality that is male-constructed. Where women are Other, they can be present and silent simultaneously; for the language and thought-forms of culture do not express their meanings.

De Beauvoir's analysis provides a key to women's silence within Judaism, for, like women in many cultures, Jewish women have been projected as Other. Named by a male community that perceives itself as normative, women are part of the Jewish tradition without its sources and structures reflecting our experience. Women are Jews, but we do not define Jewishness. We live, work, and struggle, but our experiences are not recorded, and what is recorded formulates our experiences in male terms. The central Jewish categories of Torah, Israel, and God all are constructed from male perspectives. Torah is revelation as men perceived it, the story of Israel from their standpoint, the law unfolded according to their needs. Israel is the male collectivity, the children of a Jacob who had a daughter, but whose sons became the twelve tribes.[3] God is named in the male image, a father and warrior much like his male offspring, who confirms and sanctifies the silence of his daughters. Exploring these categories, we explore the parameters of women's silence.[4]

In Torah, Jewish teaching, women are not absent, but they are cast in stories told by men. As characters in narrative, women may be vividly characterized, as objects of legislation, singled out for attention. But women's presence in Torah does not negate their silence, for women do not decide the questions with which Jewish sources deal.

When the law treats of women, it is often because their "abnormality" demands it. If women are central to plot, the plots are not about them. Women's interests and intentions must be unearthed from texts with other purposes, for both law and narrative serve to obscure them.

The most striking examples of women's silence come from texts in which women are most central, for there the normative character of maleness is especially jarring. In the family narratives of Genesis, for example, women figure prominently. The matriarchs of Genesis are all strong women. As independent personalities, fiercely concerned for their children, they often seem to have an intuitive knowledge of God's plans for their sons. Indeed, it appears from the stories of Sarah and Rebekah that they understand God better than their husbands. God defends Sarah when she casts out Hagar, telling Abraham to obey his wife (Gen. 21:12).[5] Rebekah, knowing it is God's intent, helps deceive Isaac into accepting Jacob as his heir (Gen. 25:23; 27:5–17). Yet despite their intuitions, and despite their wiliness and resourcefulness, it is not the women who receive the covenant or who pass on its lineage. The establishment of patrilineal descent and the patriarchal family takes precedence over the matriarch's stories.[6] Their relationship to God, in some way presupposed by the text, remains an undigested element in the narrative. What was the full theophany to Rebekah, and how is it related to the covenant with Isaac? The writer does not tell us; it is not sufficiently important. And so the covenant remains the covenant with Isaac, while Rebekah's experience floats at the margin of the story.

The establishment of patrilineal descent and patriarchal control, a subtext in Genesis, is an important theme in the legislation associated with Sinai. Here again, women figure prominently, but only as objects of male concerns. The laws pertaining to women place them firmly under the control of first fathers, then husbands, so that men can have male heirs they know are theirs. Legislation concerning adultery (Deut. 22:22, also Num. 5:11–31) and virginity (Deut. 22:13–21) speaks of women, but only to control female sexuality to male advantage. The *crime* of adultery is sleeping with another man's wife, and a man can bring his wife to trial even on suspicion of adultery, a right that is not reciprocal. Sleeping with a betrothed virgin constitutes adultery. A man who sleeps with a virgin who is not betrothed must simply marry her. A girl whose lack of virginity shames her father on her wedding night can be stoned to death for harlotry. A virgin who is raped must marry her assailant. The subject of these laws is women, but the interest behind them is the purity of the male line.

The process of projecting and defining women as objects of male concerns is expressed most fully not in the Bible, however, but in the Mishnah, an important second-century legal code. Part of the Mishnah's Order of Women (one of its six divisions) develops laws discussed in the Torah concerning certain problematic aspects of female sexuality. The subject of the division is the transfer of women—the regulation of women who are in states of transition, whose uncertain status threatens the stasis of the community. The woman who is about to enter into a marriage or who has just left one requires close attention. The law must regularize her irregularity, facilitate her transition to the normal state of wife and motherhood, at which point she no longer poses a problem.[7] But it is not even the contents of the order, male-defined as they are, that trumpet most loudly women's silence. In a system in which a division of Men would be unthinkable nonsense, the fact of a division of Women is sufficient evidence of who names the world, who defines whom, in "normative" Jewish sources.

Thus Torah—"Jewish" sources, "Jewish" teaching—puts itself forward as *Jewish* teaching but speaks in the voice of only half the Jewish people. This scandal is compounded by another: The omission is neither mourned nor regretted; it is not even noticed. True, the rabbis were aware of the harshness of certain laws pertaining to women and sought to mitigate their effects. They tried to find ways to force a recalcitrant husband to divorce his wife, for example. But the framework that necessitated such mitigations went unquestioned. Women's Otherness was left intact. The Jewish passion for justice did not extend to Jewish women. As Cynthia Ozick puts it, one great "Thou shalt not"—"Thou shalt not lessen the humanity of women"— is missing from the Torah.[8]

For this great omission, there is no historical redress. Indeed, where one might expect redress, the problem is compounded. The prophets, those great champions of justice, couch their pleas for justice in the language of patriarchal marriage. Israel in her youth is a devoted bride, subordinate and obedient to her husband/God (for example, Jer. 2:2). Idolatrous Israel is a harlot and adulteress, a faithless woman whoring after false gods (for example, Hos. 2, 3). Transferring the hierarchy of male and female to God and his people, the prophets enshrine in metaphor the legal subordination of women.[9] Those who might have named and challenged women's marginalization thus ignore and extend it.

The prophetic metaphors mark an end and a beginning. They confront us with the injustice of Torah; they link that injustice to other central Jewish ideas. If exploring Torah means exploring a terrain of women's silence, this is no less true of the categories of Israel or God. Israel, the bride, the harlot, the people that is female (that is, subordinate) in relation to God is nonetheless male in communal self-perception. The covenant community is the community of the circumcised (Gen. 17:10), the community defined as male heads of household. Women are named through a filter of male experience: that is the essence of their silence. But women's experiences are not recorded or taken seriously because women are not perceived as normative Jews. They are part of but do not define the community of Israel.

The same evidence that speaks to women's silence in the tradition, to the partiality of Torah, also reflects an understanding of Israel as a community of males. In the narratives of Genesis, for example, the covenant moves from father to son, from Abraham to Isaac to Jacob to Joseph. The matriarchs' relation to their husbands' God is sometimes assumed, sometimes passed over, but the women do not constitute the covenant people. Women's relation to the community is also ambiguous and unclear in biblical legislation. The law is couched in male grammatical forms, and its content too presupposes a male nation. "You shall not covet your neighbor's wife" (Exod. 20:17). Probably we cannot deduce from this verse that women are free to covet! Yet the injunction assumes that women's obedience is owed to fathers and husbands, who are the primary group addressed.

The silence of women goes deeper, however, than who defines Torah or Israel. It also finds its way into language about God. Our language about divinity is first of all male language; it is selective and partial. The God who supposedly transcends sexuality, who is presumably one and whole, comes to us through language that is incomplete and narrow. The images we use to describe God, the qualities we attribute to God, draw on male pronouns and experience and convey a sense of power and authority that is clearly male. The God at the surface of Jewish consciousness is a God with a voice of thunder, a God who as lord and king rules his people and leads them into battle, a God who forgives like a father when we turn to him. The female images that exist in the Bible and (particularly the mystical) tradition form an underground stream that occasionally reminds us of the inadequacy of our imagery without transforming its overwhelmingly male nature.

This male imagery is comforting and familiar—comforting because familiar—but it is an integral part of a system that consigns women to the margins. Since the experience of God cannot be directly conveyed in language, imagery for God is a vehicle that suggests what is actually impossible to describe. Religious experiences are expressed in a vocabulary drawn from the significant and valuable in a particular culture. To speak of God is to speak of what we most value. In attributing certain qualities to God, we both attempt to point to God and offer God's qualities to be emulated and admired. To say that God is just, for example, is to say both that God acts justly and that God demands justice. Justice belongs to God but is also ours to pursue. Similarly with maleness, to image God as male is to value the quality and those who have it. It is to define God in the image of the normative community and to bless men—but not women—with a central attribute of God.

But our images of God are not simply male images; they are images of a certain kind. The prophetic metaphors for the relation between God and Israel are metaphors borrowed from the patriarchal family—images of dominance softened by affection.

God as husband and father of Israel demands obedience and monogamous love. He repays faithfulness with mercy and loving-kindness, but punishes waywardness, just as the wayward daughter can be stoned at her father's door (Deut. 22:21). When these family images are combined with political images of king and warrior, they reinforce a particular model of power and dominance. God is the power over us, the One out there over against us, the sovereign warrior with righteousness on his side. Family and political models of dominance and submission are recapitulated and rendered plausible by the dominance and submission of God and Israel. The silence and submission of women becomes part of a greater pattern that makes it appear fitting and right.

What emerges then is a "fit," a tragic coherence between the role of women in Jewish life, and law, teaching, and symbols. Women's experiences have not been recorded or shaped the contours of Jewish teaching because women do not define the normative community; but of course, women remain Other when we are always seen through the filter of male interpretation without ever speaking for ourselves. The maleness of God calls for the silence of women as shapers of the holy, but our silence in turn enforces our Otherness and a communal sense of the "rightness" of the male image of God. Moreover, if God is male, and we are in God's image, how can maleness not be the norm of Jewish humanity? If maleness is normative, how can women not be Other? And if women are Other, how can we not speak of God in a language of Otherness and dominance, a language drawn from male experience?

Confronting these interconnections is not easy. But it is only as we hear women's silence as part of the texture of Jewish existence that we can place our specific disabilities in the context in which they belong. Women's exclusion from public religious life, women's powerlessness in marriage and divorce are not accidental; nor are they individual problems. They are pieces of a system in which men have defined the interests and the rules, including the rules concerning women. Manipulating the system to change certain rules—even excision of many of them—will not of itself restore women's voices or women's power of naming. On the contrary, without awareness of the broader context of women's silence, attempts to redress concrete grievances may perpetuate the system of which they are part. Thus, as feminists demand that women be allowed to lead public prayer, the issue of language is often set aside. Traditional modes of liturgical expression are assumed to be adequate; the only issue is who has access to them. But women's leadership in synagogue ritual then leaves untouched the deeper contradictions between formal equality and the fundamental symbols of the service, contradictions that can be addressed only through the transformation of religious language. Similarly, attempts to solve particular legal (*halakhic*) problems often assume the continued centrality and religious meaningfulness of *halakhah* (law). But halakhah is part of the system that women did not have a hand in creating. How can we presume that if women add our voices to tradition, law will be our medium of expression and repair? To settle on halakhah as the source of justice for women is to foreclose the question of women's experience when it has scarcely begun to be raised.

Clearly, the implications of Jewish feminism reach beyond the goal of equality to transform the bases of Jewish life. Feminism demands a new understanding of Torah, Israel, and God. It demands an understanding of Torah that begins by acknowledging the injustice of Torah and then goes on to create a Torah that is whole. The silence of women reverberates through the tradition, distorting the shape of narrative and skewing the content of the law. Only the deliberate recovery of women's hidden voices, the unearthing and invention of women's Torah, can give us Jewish teachings that are the product of the whole Jewish people and that reflect more fully its experiences of God.

Feminism demands an understanding of Israel that includes the whole of Israel and thus allows women to speak and name our experience for ourselves. It demands we replace a normative male voice with a chorus of divergent voices, describing Jewish reality in different accents and tones. Feminism impels us to rethink issues of community and diversity, to explore the ways in which one people can acknowledge and celebrate the varied experiences of its members. What would it mean for women *as women* to be equal participants in the Jewish community? How can we talk about difference without creating Others?

Feminism demands new ways of talking about God that reflect and grow out of the redefinition of Jewish humanity. The exclusively male naming of God supported and was rendered meaningful by a cultural and religious situation that is passing away. The emergence of women allows and necessitates that the long-suppressed femaleness of God be recovered and explored and reintegrated into the Godhead. But feminism presses us beyond the issue of gender to examine the nature of the God with male names. How can we move beyond images of domination to a God present in community rather than over it? How can we forge a God-language that expresses women's experience?

Methodological Underpinnings

Although I intend to devote the rest of this book to exploring the implications of feminism for the transformation of Jewish life, I must touch first on another foundational aspect of my feminist reconstruction of Judaism. My basic critique of Judaism as a male-defined religion rests on a number of assumptions concerning texts, sources, experience, and authority, assumptions that inform my efforts at construction as much as they do my critique. My perspective as a Jewish feminist is shaped not simply by the personal experiences I delineated in the introduction, but also by a series of theological and methodological presuppositions that are influenced by my experiences but cannot be reduced to them. These presuppositions are as essential to my argument as my understanding of Judaism as a patriarchal tradition.

Women's Experience

"Women's experience" is an important and problematic phrase I mention repeatedly in the preceding pages. At several points in discussing women's silence, I turn to this term to name an element missing in Jewish sources and Jewish communal life. The phrase is sufficiently obvious to be overlooked, and at the same time fraught with significant difficulty. It conceals a number of problems and comprehends a major methodological decision.

On one level, the term "women's experience" is quite straightforward. I mean it to refer to the daily, lived substance of women's lives, the conscious events, thoughts, and feelings that constitute women's reality. To say that women's experience is not part of the Jewish tradition is to say that we do not know the world as women have perceived it. We do not have women's account of Jewish history in its large and small moments, filtered through women's perceptions and set in a framework of their making.

On this definition, "women's experience" is not an essence or abstraction. It does not refer to some innate capacity of women, some eternally female mode of being that is different from male being. If women's experience is distinct from men's—and I believe it is—the reasons are primarily historical and social. The different socialization of men and women, present in different ways in every culture, nurtures divergent capacities and divergent experiences of the world. But also, insofar as women are projected as Other, women's experience is doubled in a peculiar way. Knowing she is just herself, a woman must nonetheless measure herself against a standard that comes from outside. If she would act against prevailing stereotypes, she must do so being aware of their existence, and this adds an extra burden to whatever she undertakes.[10] Like the Jew, who is always a Jew in the eyes of the world, a woman is assessed in terms of her particularity. The social and historical situation of the Other is not the same as the situation of one who takes identity for granted.

If "women's experience" is primarily a product of culture rather than of some innate female nature, however, then it is also not unitary or clearly definable. The problem with the phrase "women's experience" is that it implies uniformity where—even if we restrict ourselves to Jewish women—there is great diversity. One can delineate certain common elements to women's situation: shared biological experiences, common imposition of Otherness, exclusion from the encoding of cultural meanings. But women have appropriated, interpreted, and responded to these elements very differently, both as individuals and as members of different (Jewish) cultures. It is too easy for one dominant group—in this case, the North American Ashkenazi Jew—to define women's experience for all women, forgetting that even Jewish women's experience is a great tapestry of many designs and colors. Since no woman's work can ever include the whole tapestry, each must remember she speaks from one corner, the phrase "women's experience" qualified by a string of modifiers that specify voice.

Yet, despite the real danger of defining it monolithically, the phrase "women's experience" can hardly be avoided. It is indispensable both for signifying a terrain of silence—no group of Jewish women has had the privilege of defining Jewish reality—and for signaling an important methodological choice. In a system in which women have been projected as Other, there is no way within the rules of the system to restore women to full personhood. The conviction that women are fully human is a critical and disruptive principle that comes from outside. Commitment to "women's experience" marks precisely an a priori commitment to women's humanity. It is the fundamental feminist methodological move. Without the presupposition of women's full humanity, there is no bridge from the male Jewish tradition to a feminist Judaism. All one can do is manipulate the rules of the system to alleviate women's disabilities, without altering the assumptions from which those disabilities arise. To commit oneself to recovering women's experiences within Judaism, on the other hand, is to say that women as well as men define Jewish humanity and that there is *no Judaism*— there is only male Judaism—without the insights of both. This is the starting point for a feminist Judaism, and it represents a basic realignment of the feminist's relationship to tradition.

Suspicion and Remembrance

If insistence on the full humanity of women represents a deliberate and important break with Jewish tradition, it clearly has important implications for the feminist's relationship to Jewish sources. Insofar as Jewish sources assume women's Otherness, are they simply evidence for women's oppression? Do they have anything of value to teach Jewish women? How does one sort out the oppressive from the nonoppressive elements in Jewish sources? How does one decide that a certain fundamental presupposition—like the presupposition of woman's Otherness—must be disavowed? These questions are part of the critical issue of authority that commitment to women's experience raises. Since this is an issue with many ramifications, it needs to be approached deliberately and from several sides.

Attitude toward sources is one dimension of the issue of authority. In discussing the deep-rooted sexism of the Jewish tradition, I use the *Tanakh* (Hebrew Scriptures) to demonstrate women's silence in Jewish writings. In doing so, I presuppose a dual and paradoxical relationship to the biblical text. I take for granted my critical freedom in relation to the Bible; but I also take for granted my connection to it, the value of examining its viewpoint and concerns. I pronounce the Bible patriarchal; but in taking the time to explore it, I claim it as a text that matters to me. This double relation is not unthinking. It stems from my belief that the Jewish feminist must embrace with equal passion (at least) two different attitudes to Jewish sources. These are described by Elisabeth Schüssler Fiorenza, who in developing feminist principles of interpretation for the study of the New Testament, distinguishes between a "hermeneutics of suspicion" and a "hermeneutics of remembrance," both of which must inform a feminist appropriation of religious texts.[11]

A hermeneutics of suspicion "takes as its starting point the assumption that biblical texts and their interpretations are androcentric and serve patriarchal functions."[12] Since both the Tanakh and rabbinic literature come from male-dominated societies and are attributed to male authors, they need to be examined for androcentric assumptions and content, and for their attention, or lack of it, to women's experiences and concerns. While mainstream sources may have much to say to women, they cannot be accepted uncritically.[13] All too often, they serve to consolidate or reinforce patriarchal values or to inculcate models of power that are destructive or oppressive.

Moreover, it is not just a few obviously patriarchal texts that must be subjected to critical examination and judgment. Feminists cannot assume that any traditional source is entirely free from sexism. Some years ago, referring to Phyllis Trible's project of "depatriarchalizing" the Bible, Mary Daly quipped that a depatriarchalized Bible would make a nice pamphlet.[14] While the comment is clever, it could have gone further: a depatriarchalized text would not exist. Biblical insights are formulated in a patriarchal culture and expressed in patriarchal terms. The husk and kernel interpenetrate; each can be named, but they cannot be divided. Thus the fact that the prophets expressed their concern for justice in the language of patriarchal marriage does not make that concern trivial or unreal. But it does mean that, in different contexts, the very same texts can be liberating or oppressive. To ignore this fact—to talk about justice without reference to the patriarchal metaphors in which justice is described—is to leave the oppressive aspects of texts to do their work in the world.

At the same time Jewish sources must be viewed with mistrust, they are, however, the sources we have. If suspicion is one side of the feminist's relationship to tradition, the other side is remembrance. Jewish sources have formed us for good and for ill, and they remain our strongest links with the Jewish historical experience. Since, in Schüssler Fiorenza's words, "the enslavement of a people becomes total when their history is destroyed and solidarity with the dead is made impossible," feminists must appropriate Jewish sources not simply as witnesses to women's oppression but as testimonies of "liberation and religious agency." A "hermeneutics of remembrance" insists that the same sources that are regarded with suspicion can also be used to reconstruct Jewish women's history. Just as no source, however neutral or liberating it may seem, is exempt from feminist scrutiny, so even the most androcentric text can provide valuable information about Jewish women's past.[15] Biblical legislation concerning menstruation, for example, can serve as the basis for reconstructing women's understanding of menstruation taboos. Prophetic injunctions against idolatry can furnish clues concerning women's participations in polytheistic traditions.[16] Read with new questions and critical freedom, traditional sources can yield "subversive memories" of past struggles for liberation within and against patriarchy, memories that link contemporary women to transformative history.[17]

Critical Method and Religious Unity

The distinction "suspicion/remembrance" suggests a dual attitude toward Jewish texts that is central to feminist critical appropriation of Jewish sources. Other aspects of the problem of authority and textual interpretation plague modern readers more generally and thus enter into feminist concerns. Modern scientific criticism, for example, has left many people with a divided relationship to religious texts different from the division "suspicion/remembrance." The same religious sources that claim to give overarching significance to life, and that may indeed provide frameworks of meaning, are simultaneously seen as human creations, culture-bound expressions of past religious values. The distinction "critical method/religious unity" points to a second tension in attitudes toward religious texts, a tension not unique to feminism but with which feminists must grapple.

On the one side, modern scientific thought and historical scholarship have eroded the sacred authority of traditional sources. Religious texts, they tell us, are not a transcript of divine revelation but the work of human beings living in particular social and historical contexts and responding to historical and cultural needs. The same critical tools, literary and historical, that one would bring to reading any text are appropriate to religious sources. We cannot understand either "biblical attitudes" toward women or women's roles in "the biblical period," for example, without taking into account that biblical texts span a thousand years of history and come from very different cultures. We should not expect that the roles of women in the period of early Israelite settlement would be the same as women's roles under the monarchy or in the postexilic period. Similarly, a rabbinic midrash on a biblical text reflects the questions and concerns of the rabbinic period. It does not give us the meaning of the Tanakh for biblical times. Thus, in my earlier discussion of the narratives of Genesis as an instance of women's silence, I did not consider the ways later midrash takes up and elaborates the themes of the stories, sometimes shifting their emphasis or meaning. That is not relevant to the changing biblical silence concerning women, which can be examined in its own right.

But while religious texts can be broken down literarily and historically, as received tradition, they come to us whole. One may divide and analyze for purposes of criticism or historical reconstruction. The religious meaning of a work, however, may lie in its historical impossibilities, the tensions of the final editing, or the rhythm of the narrative heard as a totality.[18] Scholars may debate, for instance, whether there was an Exodus from Egypt, what proportion of the future Israelite community dwelt in Egypt, and how the Exodus narrative became part of Jewish experience. Whatever they decide, however, the Exodus story, as a *story*, is constitutive for Jewish self-understanding. As such, it has a claim on contemporary Jews, who must wrestle with its meaning. An analogous point can be made for rabbinic midrash. Midrash may not tell us what the Bible meant in its own time, but it often tells us how particular narratives are comprehended by the Jewish community, and therefore how certain texts have shaped communal values. It may therefore be appropriate sometimes to consider the midrashic meaning of a text as if it were its true meaning, for it may be through the midrash that a text is read and known.

Suspicion/remembrance and critical method/religious unity are aspects of textual appropriation that, on first consideration, may appear to correspond. Critical methods are appropriate to suspicion, for they allow us to see sources in their patriarchal contexts; while to remember our history, we seem to need texts whole. In fact, however, the categories are interwoven. Critical methods are necessary both in analyzing androcentric texts and in historical reconstruction. They can help us recover both the patriarchal setting of our sources and the religious possibilities the sources conceal. Similarly, a text may be considered as a unity or in the light of later interpretation both in order to scrutinize its sexism and in order to get at its religious meaning. Traditional stories may be mediated to us through androcentric midrash, but midrash can also unveil in a text religious import that would otherwise go unseen.

A complex view of texts, then, can be part of any reading. Indeed a multi-layered consciousness can be difficult to avoid. The modern reader may find it hard to look for religious meaning without a critical view of sources intruding in the background.[19] This divided awareness is both burdensome and liberating. A critical reading can yield results that are disturbing to religious faith, but it can also free texts for deeper appropriation. To approach texts critically is not to dismiss them. On the contrary, it can be part of what it means to take sources seriously as a modern person. When we understand the meaning of a religious text in and for its time, we are freer to take the text and apply it to our own time. Seeing how particular sources answered the religious needs of some people in the period in which they were written allows us to look at contemporary needs and to interpret for today. Thus awareness of how midrash dealt with rabbinic questions might lead us to write midrash that deals with women's questions. Awareness of women's silence in the narratives of Genesis might lead us to restore women's voices, connecting to the text in fresh ways.

Authority

To use Jewish texts as a basis for historical reconstruction and to take them seriously as literary units is nonetheless different from investing them with final authority. Particularly since neither the intent nor direction of feminist reconstruction is derived from Jewish sources, the issue of the authority of these sources for feminist thought needs to be pressed further. How do a "hermeneutics of suspicion" and the use of critical methods accord with the authority of traditional texts? In the process of interpretation, where does authority finally reside? While this question intersects with a number of issues to be considered in other chapters, it is too central to any project of religious transformation to be treated only piecemeal. It will be necessary to anticipate some later discussion, therefore, to take it up in this context.

Modernity has brought increasing awareness of both the global diversity of religious beliefs and practices and the cultural location and historical development of individual religious traditions. This awareness has undermined the authority of traditional religions and weakened their claims to universality or to eternal truth. Feminists have participated in confronting the breakdown of old authority structures, and have responded to the problem of authority in several different ways. While some religious feminists have used the weakening authority of the western traditions to criticize and move outside them entirely, others have sought within their traditions authority structures consonant with their beliefs. A number of Christian feminists, for example, have sought to find a "real (that is, nonsexist) Paul" or a feminist Jesus who can function as models for Christians today.[20] This nonsexist strand of the tradition is identified with "true" Christianity, while sexist Christianity is false and must change. Other feminist thinkers have acknowledged the basic androcentrism of biblical thinking, but have found within Scripture minority themes that submit the Bible to self-criticism. Some have focused on the prophetic tradition—not necessarily as a set of texts, but as an ongoing process of criticizing the status quo. Others have pointed to the equality of the original creation or to the presence of female God-language throughout the Bible.[21] While such themes are not statistically the norm, they may function as *normative* in that they provide a scriptural basis for feminist faith.

The problem with attempting to ground feminist (or any contemporary) conviction in Scripture, however, is that it denies or disguises the authority of the reader. When one element of a text is declared true or normative, where does authority actually lie?

Do biblical texts themselves provide a sure basis for judging between their conflicting perspectives? The contrary uses to which the Bible has been put suggest that the needs and values of a community of readers are as much a source of norms as the texts themselves. Different communities have different stakes in maintaining and defending the authority of the Bible, but the selection of particular texts or passages as central or normative can seldom be justified on purely textual grounds.

It is not the Bible itself that tells us which parts are authoritative, authority must rest in some outside source. In our individualistic American culture, this source is often identified as the individual, who picks and chooses among texts according to "personal preference." If we do not have the divine word, ostensibly we are left with only our own words, words that are changeable and subject to sway.[22] From a feminist perspective, however, human choices are not reducible to God/text or whim. Human beings are fundamentally communal; our individuality is a product of community, and our choices are shaped by our being with others.[23] Scripture itself is a product of community. It may be revelatory or communicate lasting values, but revelation is communally received and molded. Revelation is the experience of a reality that transcends language, that cannot be captured or possessed in words. The communal experiences of God's presence and power that lie at the origins of Jewish existence were crystallized by certain sensitive individuals, and recreated in language to be stored in memory. Language bears witness to revelation. It allows the possibility that, centuries after the original event, one may find reverberating in a text the extraordinary experience in which it was formed.[24]

But language bears witness to the enduring in words that are limited. Not only must it suggest rather than chronicle the revelatory experience, it does so within the cultural framework that language itself inscribes. Revelation may surprise us and destroy our preconceptions, but it must compete with language already in place. The Bible emerged in a context in which patriarchal modes of social organization were being consolidated and justified. The record of revelation is for the most part assimilated to this task and never decisively breaks with it.[25] As we have seen, women's revelatory experiences are largely omitted from the sources; narratives are framed from an androcentric perspective; the law enforces women's subordination in the patriarchal family. Insofar as biblical texts silence women and serve to oppress them, they must be criticized as "revealing" patriarchy.

The authority that grounds this criticism, however, is not individual experience or some private intuition. It is rather the experience of particular communities struggling for religious transformation.[26] For example, the community that is my central authority is the Jewish feminist community, for it is in this community my identity finds fullest expression. But beyond it lie the *havurah* and broader feminist communities, the wider Jewish community, and the communities of all those working for religious and political change. Just as Jews of the past experienced God and interpreted their experiences in communal contexts that shaped what they saw and heard, so we also read their words and experience God in communities—communities in continuity with, but different from, theirs. It is the contemporary feminist community that has taught me to value and attend to women's experience. It is this community that has taught me that Jewish sources have been partial and oppressive, occasionally ugly and simply wrong.

It is true that through and behind the androcentrism of Jewish teaching may lie profound and important insights and frameworks of meaning. Jewish sources have a claim on me to be read and heard and taken seriously. But the claim is not final. I am responsible first to the Jewish feminist community and its struggle to create a Judaism that includes all Jews. To say that this community is my central source of authority is not to deny the range of ideas or disagreements within it, or the other communities of which I am part. It is simply to say that I have been formed in important ways by Jewish feminism; without it I could not see the things that I see. It is to say that my most important experiences of God have come through this community, and that it has given me the language with which to express them. To name this community my authority is to call it the primary community to which I am accountable. It is to claim that its vision enhances life beyond itself—that it can enhance Jewish life and life on this planet.

To locate authority in particular communities of interpreters is admittedly to make a circular appeal. Yet it is also to acknowledge what has always been the case: that in deciding what is authoritative in sacred texts, deciding communities take authority to themselves. When the rabbis said that rabbinic modes of interpretation were given at Sinai, they were claiming authority for their own community—just as other groups had before them, just as feminists do today.

A Word about Theology

In the last several pages, I have addressed certain of my theological presuppositions, but not my reasons for writing a theology. Yet it may seem that if my goal is a feminist Judaism, feminist theology is a peculiar place to begin. Theology, after all, has had only a limited role in Jewish religious life.[27] Reflection on God, the mission of Israel, the nature of human life has more often been confined to the interstices of rabbinic discussions or dealt with midrashically than considered independently in works on such subjects. While there is a history of Jewish philosophy from Philo to the present, philosophy is generally left to a few with the interest in and inclination to such things. The main energy of Jewish intellectual life has gone into the elaboration of the law, and it is observance of the law, rather than adherence to theological principles, that marks one a religious Jew. Law takes precedence over beliefs and feelings, which are expected to flow from action rather than to ground it.

But if the law maintains its primacy in Jewish self-understanding, theology affects Jewish practice in important, unseen ways. Indeed, there is a mutually reinforcing relationship between Jewish theology and Jewish religious practice and institutions.

Patriarchal theology, while it cannot of itself give rise to patriarchal structures, supports patriarchy as a religious and legal system. When Torah is thought of as divinely revealed in its present form, the subordination of women is granted the seal of divine approval. When God is conceived of as male, as a king over his universe, male rule in society seems appropriate and right. The correlate of this relationship between patriarchal theology and religious structures is that feminist theology may help to undermine patriarchal institutions, and at least will no longer support them. When Torah embraces the experience of women and men as full members of the Jewish people, it will no longer be possible to base women's subordination on appeals to the divine will. When we think of God as male/female friend and lover, or as the ground and source of being, new images of human relating will be fostered in our imaginations, and we will not be able consciously or unconsciously to appeal to metaphors for God to justify male social domination.

So long as theology is dismissed as unimportant, the sexism built into certain basic Jewish ideas is aided and abetted by the neglect of theology. It is difficult to confront the structural implications of God's maleness, for example, if the community is not really interested in thinking about God anyway. The issue of the gender of God can always be jettisoned on the grounds that theology is trivial, at the same time old images continue to work their effects. Only when the basic categories of Jewish thought are reconstructed in the light of women's silence will unexamined theological assumptions cease to operate at woman's expense.

The fact that theology surreptitiously affects many aspects of Jewish practice may make theology relevant even to secular Jewish feminists. Jewish literature and communal life, radicalism and ethnic identity are governed by a host of presuppositions concerning which Jews are normative, what constitutes Jewish values, the proper ways to order community, and the proper tasks of life. Many of these presuppositions have infiltrated from the theological sphere but remain doubly hidden when religion as well as theology is rejected. Theological analysis, because it lays bare some of the assumptions that operate unnamed in secular Jewish movements, can provide secular feminists with more power to transform these assumptions.

But there is another reason why theology is important. When a religious system has become established and its structures self-perpetuating, it often loses contact with the experiences at its root. Rabbis need not stand at Sinai with the first generation to make legal decisions. They must read the works of their predecessors and follow the appropriate rules. Moreover, insofar as Jewish identity is based on orthopraxis, there is no necessary relation between practice and religious experience; practice is self-justifying, it makes one a Jew. But for those who would transform the tradition, the situation is different: Reform always begins in conviction and vision. Jewish feminism, like all reform movements, is rooted in deeply felt experience and a powerful image of religious change. Wherever the individual feminist locates her active interests—in liturgy, theology, midrash, law—she acts out of commitment to an animating vision that has important repercussions for community life and practice. My central reason for writing a Jewish feminist theology, then, is to articulate one version of this vision and to foster its growth. If feminist theologies help to reanimate the connection between practice and belief in the Jewish world more generally, they will have made another important contribution to Jewish religious life.

Notes

1. Carol P. Christ, "Spiritual Quest and Women's Experience," in *Womanspirit Rising: A Feminist Reader in Religion*, ed. Carol P. Christ and Judith Plaskow (San Francisco: Harper & Row, 1979), 229.
2. Simone de Beauvoir, *The Second Sex*, trans. H. M. Parshley (New York: Bantam Books, 1961), xv–xvii.
3. Dina's birth is mentioned in Gen. 30:21; her story is found in Gen. 34. In naming their anthology of Jewish feminist writing *The Tribe of Dina: A Jewish Woman's Anthology* (1986; reprint ed., Boston: Beacon Press, 1989), Melanie Kaye/Kantrowitz and Irena Klepfisz restore Dina to her rightful place.
4. The following discussion is based on my article, "The Right Question is Theological," in *On Being a Jewish Feminist: A Reader*, ed. Susannah Heschel (New York: Schocken Books, 1983), 223–33.
5. The fact that God takes Sarah's side does not alter the problematic nature of the relationship between Sarah and Hagar, which has been explored especially powerfully by black women. See, for example, Delores Williams, "Womanist Theological Perspectives on the Hagar-Sarah Story" (paper delivered at Princeton University, May 17, 1988).
6. See Savina Teubal, *Sarah the Priestess: The First Matriarch of Genesis* (Athens, OH: Swallow Press, 1984) and "Sarah and Hagar: Power in Ritual" (paper delivered at the 1985 Annual Meeting of the American Academy of Religion).
7. Jacob Neusner, *A History of the Mishnaic Law of Women*, 5 vols. (Leiden: E.J. Brill, 1980), 5:13f, 271f.
8. Cynthia Ozick, "Notes Toward Finding the Right Question," *Lilith* 6 (1979): 19–29; reprinted in Heschel, *On Being a Jewish Feminist*, 120–51; quotation, 149.
9. See T. Drorah Setel, "Prophets and Pornography: Female Sexual Imagery in Hosea," in *Feminist Interpretation of the Bible*, ed. Letty M. Russell (Philadelphia: Westminster Press, 1985), 86–95.
10. De Beauvoir, *The Second Sex*, 641–42. See Judith Plaskow, *Sex, Sin, and Grace: Women's Experience and the Theologies of Reinhold Niebuhr and Paul Tillich* (Washington, DC: University Press of America, 1980), ch. l, for an extended discussion of "women's experience" and its relation to prevailing cultural role definitions.
11. Elisabeth Schüssler Fiorenza, *Bread Not Stone: The Challenge of Feminist Biblical Interpretation* (Boston: Beacon Press, 1984), 15ff.
12. Ibid., 15. "Androcentric" and "androcentrism" refer to the assumption that maleness is constitutive of humanity. See Rita Gross, "Androcentrism and Androgyny in the Methodology of the History of Religions," in *Beyond Androcentrism: New Essays on Women and Religion*, ed. Rita Gross (Missoula, MT: Scholars Press, 1977), 7–21.
13. See my "The Jewish Feminist: Conflict in Identities," in *The Jewish Woman: New Perspectives*, ed. Elizabeth Koltun (New York: Schocken Books, 1976), 4.

14. Mary Daly, "Post-Christian Theology: Some Connections between Idolatry and Methodolatry, between Deicide and Methodicide" (address given at the 1973 Annual Meeting of the American Academy of Religion); for a more general reference see the paper of the same name in Joan Arnold Romero, *Women and Religion: 1973 Proceedings* (Tallahassee, FL: American Academy of Religion, 1973), 33. For Phyllis Trible's discussion of depatriarchalizing, see her *God and the Rhetoric of Sexuality* (Philadelphia: Fortress Press, 1978).

15. Schüssler Fiorenza, *Bread Not Stone*, 19–20.

16. See T. Drorah Setel, "Power and Pollution: The Ritual Purity/Impurity System in the Hebrew Bible" (paper delivered at the 1982 Annual Meeting of the American Academy of Religion); Merlin Stone, *When God Was a Woman* (New York: Dial Press, 1976), ch. 8.

17. Schüssler Fiorenza, *Bread Not Stone*, 19–20. The phrase in quotation marks is Johann Baptist Metz's.

18. See, for example, Richard Elliot Friedman, *Who Wrote the Bible?* (New York: Summit Books, 1987), ch. 14.

19. Emil Fackenheim calls this divided consciousness that characterizes modern faith "immediacy after reflection" (*God's Presence in History: Jewish Affirmations and Philosophical Reflections* [New York: New York University Press, 1970], 47–49), while Paul Tillich talks about "broken myths" (*Dynamics of Faith* [New York: Harper & Row, 1957], 50–51).

20. In editing *The Woman's Bible* (1898; reprint ed., Seattle: Coalition Taskforce on Women and Religion, 1974), Elizabeth Cady Stanton took advantage of the advent of biblical criticism to radically question biblical authority from a feminist perspective. Today the whole women's spiritualism movement takes place outside the authority structures of Judaism or Christianity. See Charlene Spretnak, ed., *The Politics of Women's Spirituality: Essays on the Rise of Spiritual Power within the Feminist Movement* (Garden City, NY: AnchorBooks/Doubleday, 1982) for a range of examples. For a Christian response to the problem of authority, see Robin Scroggs, "Paul and the Eschatological Woman," *Journal of the American Academy of Religion* 40 (September 1972): 283–303, and Scroggs, "Paul and the Eschatological Woman: Revisited" and Elaine Pagels, "Paul and Women: A Response to Recent Discussion," *JAAR* 42 (September 1974): 532–49 for a small sample of the debate on Paul. Leonard Swidler was the first to propose the "Jesus was a feminist" argument which has been reiterated innumerable times; see "Jesus Was a Feminist," *Catholic World* 212 (January 1971): 177–83.

21. On the prophetic tradition, see Rosemary Ruether, *Sexism and God-Talk: Toward a Feminist Theology* (Boston: Beacon Press, 1983), 22–27 and "Feminist Interpretation: A Method of Correlation," in Russell, *Feminist Interpretation*, 118–22. On the themes of equality in creation and female God-language, see Trible, *God and the Rhetoric of Sexuality*. Russell's book provides a general overview of feminist hermeneutics, as does Adela Yarbro Collins, ed., *Feminist Perspectives on Biblical Scholarship* (Chico, CA: Scholars Press, 1985). Jewish feminist hermeneutics is in the earliest stages of development.

22. For example, at a major symposium on "Cultural and Religious Relativism" held at 92nd Street YM-YWHA, January–February 1986, the issue of authority was presented as a conflict between communal imperatives rooted in divine sanction and individual choice. Martha Ackelsberg helped me to see and criticize this dichotomy.

23. See chapter 3, 76–81, for a fuller discussion of this point.
24. Martin Buber ("The Man of Today and the Jewish Bible," in *On the Bible* [New York: Schocken Books, 1968], 1–13 and *Moses: The Revelation and the Covenant* [New York: Harper & Row, 1958]) and H. Richard Niebuhr (*The Meaning of Revelation* [New York: Macmillan, 1941]) are the theologians who have most influenced my view of revelation.
25. See Norman K. Gottwald, *The Tribes of Yahweh* (Maryknoll, NY: Orbis Books, 1979), 685. "Yahweh's asexuality was apparently not invoked to challenge or shatter male dominance in the Israelite society as a whole—in the decisive way, for example, that class dominance was challenged and shattered by Yahweh's liberating action."
26. In this, I agree with Elisabeth Schüssler Fiorenza, *In Memory of Her: A Feminist Theological Reconstruction of Christian Origins* (New York: Crossroad, 1983), 29, 32 and *Bread Not Stone*, 3.
27. Both Louis Jacobs (*A Jewish Theology* [West Orange, NJ: Behrman House, 1973], 10–12) and Michael Wyschogrod (*The Body of Faith: Judaism as Corporeal Election* [San Francisco: Harper & Row, 1983], xiii) begin their Jewish theologies by addressing this point.

Part II

The Contours of Judaism

Apartheid Comparative Religion in the Second Century: Some Theory and a Case Study

Daniel Boyarin

Jacques Derrida has written of the frontier between "speech" and "writing" as "the limit separating two opposed places. Like Czechoslovakia and Poland, [they] resemble each other, regard each other; separated nonetheless by a frontier all the more mysterious ... because it is abstract, legal, ideal."[1] This metaphor can be extended into a virtual allegory to sketch a picture of the historical situation of Judaism and Christianity in the second, third, and fourth centuries, as the borderlines between them came to be instituted. Like Czechoslovakia and Poland, they too resembled each other and regarded each other, eventually coming to be separated by a frontier that is abstract, legal, and ideal.

Heresiology—the "science" of heresies—inscribes the borderlines, and heresiologists are the inspectors of religious customs. Authorities on both sides tried to establish a border, a line that, when crossed, meant that someone had definitively left one group for another. But, extending Derrida's metaphor, Paul de Man wrote, there is "no way of defining, of policing, the boundaries that separate the name of one entity from the name of another; tropes are not just travelers, they tend to be smugglers and probably smugglers of stolen goods at that."[2] The heresiologists tried to police the boundaries so as to identify and interdict those who respected no borders, those smugglers of religious ideas and practices newly declared to be contraband, nomads of religion who would not recognize the efforts to institute limits, to posit a separation between "two opposed places," and thus to establish clearly who was and who was not a "Christian," a "Jew."[3]

They named such folk "Judaizers" or "*minim*," respectively, and attempted to declare as out of bounds their beliefs and practices, their very identities.

Heresiologists don't describe and classify heresies so much as produce them as such, or perhaps more subtly put, in studying heresiology, we are investigating a sort of "feedback loop," within which social difference is being rationalized as ideological difference and the ideological difference, in turn, reproducing and intensifying the social difference. This notion of the "feedback loop" is closely related to the concept of "dynamic nominalism" elaborated by Arnold Davidson and Ian Hacking. As Hacking puts it, "categories of people come into existence at the same time as kinds of people come into being to fit those categories, and there is a two-way interaction between these processes."[4] We could say with some justice that "Christianity" and "Judaism" were invented in order to make sense of the fact that there were Jews and Christians. Groups that are differentiated in various ways by class, ethnicity, and other forms of social differentiation become transformed into "religions" in large part, I would suggest, through discourses of orthodoxy/heresy. Heresiology, whatever else it is, is largely the work of those who wished to eradicate the fuzziness of the borders, semantic and social, between Judaism and Christianity and thus produce them as fully separate (and opposed) entities—as religions.[5]

For nearly two decades now, scholars of early Christianity have been advancing a major revision of the history of Christian heresiology. Working within a Foucauldian paradigm, Alain Le Boulluec has been central—even the prime mover—in this shift in research strategy.[6] Aside from his specific historical achievements and insights, Le Boulluec's most important move was to shift the discourse away from the question of orthodoxy and heresy, understood as essences (even constructed ones) as had Walter Bauer before him,[7] and to move the discussion in the direction of a history of the representation of orthodoxy and heresy, the discourse that we know of as heresiology, the history of the idea of heresy itself.

Similarly, where scholars of rabbinic Judaism have looked for evidence of response to Christianity at specific points within rabbinic texts—e.g., denunciation in the form of *minut* or imitation of or polemic against certain Christian practices and ideas—we can follow Le Boulluec's lead in taking up Foucault's notions of discourse and shift our investigation from the specifics of what was thought or said to the *episteme* or universe of possible knowledge within which heresiological concepts and expressions could be thought or said. Continuing Derrida's "border" conceit and invoking a well-known joke might help to make clearer the shift that I'm talking about here. Every day for thirty years a man drove a wheelbarrow full of sand over the Tijuana border-crossing. The customs inspector dug through the sand each morning but could not discover any contraband. He remained, of course, convinced that he was dealing with a smuggler. On the day of his retirement from the service, he asked the smuggler to reveal what it was he was smuggling and how he had been doing the smuggling. The answer, of course, was that he was smuggling wheelbarrows.[8] Where until now, it might be said, scholarship has been looking for what is hidden in the sand (with more success than the customs inspector),[9] I prefer to look at smuggled wheelbarrows as the vehicles of language within which identities are formed and differences are made.[10] If Bauer, we might say, was still looking for some contraband treasures in the sand, it was Le Boulluec who taught us to look for smuggled wheelbarrows. But, of course, it wasn't only the modern scholar who was searching for the contraband but the heresiologists themselves. Little did they suspect, I warrant, that in struggling so hard to define who was in and who was out, who was Jewish and who was Christian, what was Christianity and what was Judaism, it was they themselves who were smuggling the wheelbarrows, the discourses of heresiology and of religion as identity.

Hybrids and Heretics

Generally, scholars have seen the orthodox topos that Christian heretics are "Jews" or "Judaizers" as a sort of side-show to the real heresiological concern, the search for the Christian doctrine of God, to put it in Hanson's terms.[11] According to this view, heresiology is primarily an artifact of the contact between biblical Christian language and Greek philosophical categories, which forced ever more detailed and refined definitions of godhead, especially, in the early centuries, in the face of the overly abstract or philosophical approaches of the "Gnostics." The naming of heretics as Jews or Judaizers is treated, in such an account, as a nearly vacant form of reprobation for reprobation's sake. Without denying that interpretation's validity for the history of Christian theology,[12] I nonetheless hypothesize that it is not epiphenomenal that so often heresy is designated as "Judaism" and "Judaizing" in Christian discourse of this time,[13] nor that a certain veritable obsession with varieties of "Jewish-Christianity" (Nazoreans, Ebionites) became so prominent in some quarters precisely at the moment when Nicene orthodoxy was consolidating.[14] Furthermore, it is not a necessary outcome that even a very refined theological discourse and controversy (on such issues as the relations of the persons of the trinity) produced a structure of orthodoxy and heresy without some other cause or function intervening.[15] At least one major impetus for the formation of the discourse of heresiology, on my reading, is the construction of a Christianity that would not be Judaism. The "Jews" (i.e., for this context, heretics so named), the Judaizers, and the Jewish-Christians—whether they existed and to what extent is irrelevant in this context—thus mark a space of threatening hybridity, which it is the task of the religion-police to eliminate.[16]

Note that these religion-police, the border guards, were operating on both sides; hybridity was as threatening to a "pure" rabbinic Judaism as it was to an orthodox Christianity.[17] An elegant example is the fair of Elone Mamre, which, according to the church historian Sozomen, attracted Jews, Christians, and pagans, who each commemorated the angelic theophany to Abraham in their own way: the Jews celebrating Abraham; the Christians the appearance of the Logos; and the pagans, Hermes.[18] Here is, perhaps, the very parade instantiation of Bhabhan "interstitial" spaces that bear the meaning of culture. The rabbis prohibited Jews from attending at all,[19] thus reinscribing the hybridity as something like what would later be called "syncretism," and banishing it from their orthodoxy. This is an oft-repeated phenomenon at this particular time.[20]

A recent writer on the history of comparative religion, David Chidester, has developed the notion of an "apartheid comparative religion." By this (working out of the southern African situation as a model for theorization), Chidester means a system that is "committed to identifying and reifying the many languages, cultures, peoples, and religions of the world as if they were separate and distinct regions." The point of such a knowledge/power regime is that "each religion has to be understood as a separate, hermetically sealed compartment into which human beings can be classified and divided."[21] I locate the beginnings of such ideologies of religious difference in late antiquity. Following Chidester's descriptions, I want to suggest that the heresiologists of antiquity were performing a very similar function to that of the students of comparative religion of modernity, conceptually organizing "human diversity into rigid, static categories [as] one strategy for simplifying, and thereby achieving some cognitive control over, the bewildering complexity of a frontier zone."[22] Heresiology is, I might say, a form of apartheid comparative religion, and apartheid comparative religion, in turn, a product of late antiquity.

One of the most important themes of postcolonial theorizing is its emphasis on the hybridity of cultural identifications and the instability of dominating cultural paradigms, paradigms that must be constantly reproduced, that must constantly assert their own naturalness while asserting hybridity as unnatural, monstrous.[23] Homi Bhabha has written that cultures interact, not on the basis of "the exoticism of multiculturalism or the *diversity* of cultures, but on the inscription and articulation of culture's *hybridity*." Bhabha concludes, "it is the 'inter'—the cutting edge of translation and negotiation, the *in-between* space—that carries the burden of the meaning of culture."[24] The instability of colonial discourse makes possible the subaltern's voice, which colonizes, in turn, the discourse of the colonizer. As Bhabha puts it, "in the very practice of domination the language of the master becomes hybrid—neither the one thing nor the other."[25] Robert Young glosses this insight: "Bhabha shows that [the decentering of colonial discourse from its position of authority] occurs when authority becomes hybridized when placed in a colonial context and finds itself layered against other cultures, very often through the exploitation by the colonized themselves of its evident equivocations and contradictions."[26] Bhabha focuses on the faultlines, on the border situations and thresholds, as sites where identities are performed and contested.[27] Borders, I might add, are also places where people are strip-searched, detained, imprisoned, and sometimes shot. Borders themselves are not given but constructed by power to mask hybridity, to occlude and disown it. The localization of hybridity in those others who are called hybrids and heretics serves that purpose.

I thus argue that hybridity is double-edged. On the one hand, the hybrids "represent … a difference 'within,' a subject that inhabits the rim of an 'in-between' reality,"[28] but on the other hand, the literal ascription of hybridity on the part of hegemonic discourses to one group of people, one set of practices, disavows the very difference within by externalizing it. Hybridity itself is the disowned other. It is this very disowned hybridity that supports the notion of purity. Following this mode of analysis, the commonplace that orthodoxy needs heresy for its self-definition can be nuanced and further specified. "Heresy" is marked not only as the space of the not-true in religion but also as the space of the syncretistic, the difference that enables unity itself. A similar point has been made in another historical context by Young who writes, "The idea of race here shows itself to be profoundly dialectical: it only works when defined against potential intermixture, which also threatens to undo its calculations altogether."[29] Young helps us see that it is not only that "white" is defined as that which is "not-black" but that the very system of race itself, the very division into white and black as races, is dependent on the production of an idea of hybridity, over against which the notion of the "natural" pure races comes into discourse. This way of thinking about hybridity in the classification of humans into races can be mobilized in thinking about heresy and the classification of people and doctrines into religions as well. This provides a certain corrective, then, to those versions of a postcolonial theory that would seem to presuppose pure essences, afterwards "hybridized," thus buying into the very activity of an apartheid they would seek to subvert.[30]

Historian Seth Schwartz, providing us with a nonessentialist model for approaching the question of hybridity, has urged us to think about the constructedness of religious identities:

> We should not be debating whether some pre-existing Jewish polity declined or prospered, or think only about relatively superficial cultural borrowing conducted by two well-defined groups. In my view, we should be looking for *systemic change*: the Jewish culture which emerged in late antiquity was radically distinctive, and distinctively late antique—a product of the same political, social and economic forces which produced the no less distinctive Christian culture of late antiquity.[31]

By systemic change, Schwartz means changes in entire systems of social, cultural, and, in this case, religious organization that affect Jews, Christians, and others equally, if not identically. This seems just right to me, but calls for a bit more emphasis on the differentiating factors in that very same productive process, in addition to highlighting the forces tending toward similarity.

In looking at that differentiating process within the context of a shared systemic change, I will propose a tentative hypothesis for understanding one of the factors that set this systemic change in motion; in other words, I will suggest an answer to the question "Why was that border written?" In my historical construction, a serious problem of identity arose for Christians who were not prepared (for whatever reason) to think of themselves as Jews, as early as the second century, if not at the end of the first. These Christians, whom I will call by virtue of their own *self*-presentation, Gentile Christians ("The Church from the Gentiles, *ek tōn ethnōn*"), were confronted with a dilemma: thinking of themselves as no longer "Greeks" and not "Jews," to what kind of a group did these converts belong? We are told it was in Antioch that the disciples were first named "Christians" (Acts 11:26).[32] I think it no accident that this act of naming occurs in a context where the entry of "Greeks" into the Christian community is thematized. Nor is it an accident that Justin is our earliest source for both heresiology and the notion that the Gentile church has replaced the Jews as God's "Israel."

These Christians had to ask themselves: What is this *Christianismos* in which we find ourselves? Is it a philosophical party, a new *gens*, a new *ethnos*, a third race that is neither Jew nor Greek, or is it an entirely new something in the world, some new kind of identity completely?[33] One important strand of early Christianity, beginning with Ignatius and Justin Martyr, decided to see *Christianismos* as an entirely novel form of identity. Christianity was a new thing, a community defined by adherence to a certain canon of doctrine and practice. For these Christian thinkers, the question of who's in and who's out became the primary way of thinking about Christianicity. And the vehicle for answering that question was the determination of orthodoxy and heresy. "In" was to be defined by correct belief, "out" by willful adherence to false belief.

In adopting the language "had to ask themselves," I don't mean to ascribe actual inevitability to the question. There are particular classlike interests that are served by the ideological posing of the question itself and the production of particular answers. The interests that are served by the ideological discourse (by ideological nonstate apparatuses, to adapt Althusser) can be investments in other sorts of power and satisfaction for elites of various types within a given social formation.[34] The discourses of orthodoxy/heresy, and thus, I will argue, of religious difference, of religion as an independent category of human identification, do not necessarily serve the interests of an economic class—it would be hard to describe the rabbis of late Roman Palestine or Sassanid Babylonia or the bishops of Nicaea as an economic class[35]—but they do serve in the production of ideology, of hegemony, the consent of a dominated group to be ruled by an elite (hence "consensual orthodoxy," that marvelous mystification). This makes an enormous difference, for it leads to the Althusserian notion of ideology as having a material existence, as having its own material existence in that it "always exists in an apparatus, and its practice, or practices."[36] Ania Loomba's statement of the current theoretical position that "no human utterance could be seen as innocent," that, indeed, "any set of words could be analysed to reveal not just an individual but a historical consciousness at work," is crucial for me, for it is this postulate that enables my work as a historian.[37] This set of notions, to which I can more or less only allude in this context, does not quite dissolve completely (as sometimes charged) but surely renders much more permeable any boundary between linguistic (or textual) practice and "the real conditions" of life within a given historical moment and society, thus empowering the study of texts not as reflective of social realities but as social apparatuses that are understood to be complexly tied to other apparatuses via the notion of a discourse or a *dispositive*. In the case study that follows, I hope to make a contribution to the genealogical study of the discourse of orthodoxy, or, more generally, of "religion."[38]

Ignatius and the Invention of Judaism

One of the earliest of the religious customs inspectors was the first-century "bishop" of Antioch, Ignatius.[39] Ignatius was one of the first thinkers to attempt to name and define what is (and what is not) Christianity, and, as such, one of the first (perhaps the first) to define a "Judaism," as well. C. K. Barrett has observed, "Ignatius was one of the most notable representatives of the first age to understand Christianity, and especially Christian controversy, in terms of orthodoxy and heresy, catholicism and schism, and the relation of Ignatius to Jewish Christians is a significant part of this development."[40] Barrett goes too far in ascribing to Ignatius the concept of orthodoxy and heresy, for, as Walter Schoedel has written, "disunity, not false teaching is uppermost in Ignatius' mind."[41] The letters of Ignatius, nevertheless, provide us with some rich bread to chew on, as these are arguably the earliest documents that would prefigure Christian heresiology. In Ignatius we find, too, one of the first attempts to make a difference between *Christianismos* and *Ioudaismos*, which is not surprising since he is the earliest known writer to use the term *Christianismos* as the name for his "religion."[42] From its very conception, then, the word *Christianismos* has been defined over against *Ioudaismos*, a term which, like *Hellenismos* or *Medismos*, had earlier signified political, ethnic, and cultural entities.[43]

In terms of the most elementary structuralist notions of language (and even without these), it will be seen that the invention of *Christianismos* as the binary opposite of *Ioudaismos* completely re-signifies the latter term as well. The point (worth repeating) is not, of course, that there was no religion in *Ioudaismos* but rather that *Ioudaismos* included much that we would not call religion, or rather, as Elizabeth Castelli has well phrased it,

> From the vantage point of a post-Enlightenment society that understands the separation of the political and the religious as an ideal to be protected, the Roman imperial situation requires careful attention to the myriad ways in which "Roman religion" might, it could be defensibly argued, not quite exist. That is, insofar as practices that could conventionally be called "religious" intersected so thoroughly with political institutions, social structures, familial commitments, and recognition of the self-in-society, there is very little in ancient Roman society that would not as a consequence qualify as "religious."[44]

In the process of entering into a new paradigm, *Ioudaismos* itself (and later *Hellenismos* too) was re-signified from the name of a political/cultural/religious entity to the name of a religion. Frances Young has made the point quite plain: "*Hellēnismos*, *Ioudaismos* and *Romanitas* were originally terms referring to culture; only in response to Christianity did paganism or Judaism, or for that matter at a later date Hinduism, become a belief-system as distinct from a whole culture."[45] The Christian heresiologist was among the major agents of that re-signification, and Ignatius, that precursor of heresiology, anticipated this function as well.[46] The bishop and future martyred saint inveighed mightily against those who blurred the boundaries between Jew and

Christian. His very inveighings, however, are indicative of the ideological work that he is performing—work that in the fullness of time led to the making of both Christianity and Judaism. In Ignatius's time (and, I will hypothesize, for many generations after), *Ioudaismos* and *Christianismos* constituted a very fuzzy set of categories.[47] The "fuzzy category" is referred to by Ignatius as the "monster": "It is monstrous to talk of Jesus Christ and to practice Judaism" (Magnesians 10:3; *Ignatius*, 126), he proclaims, thus making both points at once: the drive of the nascent orthodoxy—understood as a particular social location and as a particular form of self-fashioning and identity-making—toward separation and the lack of clear separations "on the ground."[48] In a related context, Schoedel remarks that "Ignatius tends to shape the world about him in his own image."[49]

The question of names and naming is central to the Ignatian enterprise. Near the very beginning of his letter to the Ephesians, in a passage whose significance has been only partly realized in my view, Ignatius writes, "Having received in God your much loved name, which you possess by a just nature according to faith and love in Christ Jesus, our Savior—being imitators of God, enkindled by the blood of God, you accomplished perfectly the task suited to you" (Eph. 1:1; *Ignatius*, 40). Although this interpretation has been spurned by most commentators and scholars of Ignatius, I would make a cornerstone of my construction a reading of this comment as a reference to the name *Christians*.[50] It was, after all, in Ignatius's Antioch that Christian believers were first called by that name (Acts 11:26). Ignatius is complimenting the church in Ephesus as being worthy, indeed, to be called by the name of Christ owing to their merits.[51] Indeed, as Schoedel does not fail to point out, in Magnesians 10:1, Ignatius writes, "Therefore let us become his disciples and learn to live according to Christianity [*Christianismos*]. For one who is called by any name other than this, is not of God" (*Ignatius*, 126).

Even more to the point, however, is Magnesians 4:1: "It is right, then, not only to be called Christians but to be Christians" (see also Romans 3:2; *Ignatius*, 170). Ignatius tells the Ephesians, then, that they are not just called Christians but are Christians by nature (φύσει) as it were.[52] Ignatius goes on in verse 2 to write, "For hearing that I was put in bonds from Syria for the common name and hope, hoping by your prayer to attain to fighting with beasts in Rome, that by attaining I may be able to be a disciple, you hastened to see me" (*Ignatius*, 40). Once again, the interpretative tradition seems to have missed an attractively specific interpretation of name here that links it to the name in the previous verse. It is not so much the name of Christ that is referred to here as the name Christian, which equals disciple (cf. again Acts 11:26: "And the disciples were called Christians first in Antioch").[53] The "common hope" is Jesus Christ (cf. Eph. 21:1 and Trallians 2:2; *Ignatius*, 95, 140), but the common *name* is *Christian*.

I would suggest that Ignatius represents here the theme of the centrality of martyrdom in establishing the name Christian as the legitimate and true name of the disciple; this, in accord with the practice whereby *Christianus sum* (or its Greek equivalent) were the last words of the martyr, the name for which the martyr died.[54] Similarly in the next passage, Ignatius explicitly connects martyrdom with "the name":

"I do not command you as being someone; for even though I have been bound in the name, I have not yet been perfected in Jesus Christ" (Eph. 3:1; *Ignatius*, 48). The name in which Ignatius has been bound (i.e., imprisoned and sent to Rome for martyrdom) is the name *Christianos*.[55] The nexus between having the right to that name and martyrdom or between martyrdom and identity, and the nexus between them and heresiology, separating Christianity from Judaism, is also clear.[56] In opening his letters with this declaration, I think, Ignatius is stating one of his major themes for the entire corpus of his writings: the establishment of a new Christian identity, distinguished and distinguishable from Judaism. If this is seen as a highly marked moment in his texts, then one can follow this as a dominant theme throughout his letters, and the protoheresiology of Ignatius is profoundly related to this theme, as well.[57]

This issue is most directly thematized, however, in Ignatius's letter to the Magnesians. He exhorts, "Be not deceived by erroneous opinions nor by old fables, which are useless. For if we continue to live until now according to Judaism, we confess that we have not received grace" (Mag. 8:1; *Ignatius*, 28).[58] *Ioudaismos* consists, for Ignatius, of erroneous opinions and old fables, but what precisely does he mean? Let us go back to the beginning of the letter. Once more, Ignatius makes a reference to the *name*: "For having been deemed worthy of a most godly name, in the bonds which I bear I sing the churches" (Mag. 1:1; *Ignatius*, 104). Here, as Schoedel recognizes, it is almost certain that only the name *Christian* will fit the context. This thought about the name is continued explicitly in Ignatius's famous, "It is right, then, not only to be called Christians but to be Christians" (Mag. 4:1; *Ignatius*, 108). On my reading, it is the establishment of that name, giving it definition, "defining, ... policing, the boundaries that separate the name of one entity [Christianity] from the name of another [Judaism]" that provides one of the two thematic foci for the letter (and the letters) as a whole, the other related one being, of course, the establishment of the bishop as sole authority in a given church.[59]

Near the end of the letter to the Magnesians, Ignatius writes, "(I write) these things, my beloved, not because I know that some of you are so disposed, but as one less than you I wish to forewarn you" (Mag. 11; *Ignatius*, 128).[60] Although Schoedel and others treat this compliment, "not because," as mere rhetoric—i.e., that some of them *were* so disposed and Ignatius is either being ingratiating or purposefully idealizing, I suggest rather that we take his statement literally, as an indication that Ignatius knows that they are *not* so disposed, that what he is doing is constructing borders, delimiting what will be understood as legitimate Christianity, the proper name, and what will be excluded as Judaism.

As a sort of thought experiment, at any rate, I would like to take seriously the possibility that the "heterodox" ideas anathematized by Ignatius were, indeed, in some important sense *Ioudaismos*, that is, that the believers who held them might well have thought of themselves as, in some important sense, *Ioudaioi*, at the same time, of course, that they were "Christians" (perhaps, for them, *avant la lettre*). The issue joined by Ignatius then is the making of the Christian name as something distinct and different, an opposed place to Judaism, "defining and policing the boundaries that separate the name of one entity from the name of another," preventing the smuggling of contraband.

Ioudaismos so far for Ignatius does not seem to mean what it does in other writers of and before his time, namely, that it signifies "false views and misguided practice" or refers especially to "the ritual requirements of that system."[61] Ignatius troubles to let us know that this is not the case, as we learn from a famous and powerful rhetorical paradox in his letter to the Philadelphians:

> But if anyone *expounds* Judaism to you, do not listen to him; for it is better to hear Christianity from a man who is circumcised than Judaism from a man uncircumcised; both of them, if they do not speak of Jesus Christ, are to me tombstones and graves of the dead on which nothing but the names of men is written. (Phil. 6:1; *Ignatius*, 200, my emphasis)

After considering various options that have been offered for the interpretation of this surprising passage, Schoedel arrives at what seems to me the most compelling interpretation: "perhaps it was the 'expounding' (exegetical expertise) that was the problem and not the 'Judaism' (observance)."[62] I would go further than Schoedel by making one more seemingly logical exegetical step, to assume that for Ignatius *Ioudaismos* is a matter of expounding, just as *Christianismos* is. In Ignatius, I suggest, Ioudaismos no longer means observance per se (except insofar as expounding itself is an observance). In other words, for him Judaism and Christianity are two *doxas*, two theological positions, a wrong one (ἑτεροδοχία [Mag. 8:1; *Ignatius*, 118]) and a right one, a wrong interpretation of the legacy of the prophets and a right one.[63] The right one is that which is taught by the prophets "inspired by his grace," and which is called "Christianity" since it is "revealed through Jesus Christ his Son, who is his Word" (8:1). Ignatius's point may in fact be even more radical, that *Ioudaismos* is comprised by the study of the prophets, or by any scripture at all. The words quoted certainly seem to mean that *Christianismos* consists of "speaking of Jesus Christ"—the Gospels still oral of course—while *Ioudaismos* is concerned with devoting oneself to the study of scripture.[64] Although, to be sure, in chapter 9 of Magnesians Ignatius mentions one aspect of practice—the abandonment of the Sabbath for "the Lord's Day," assuming that the plausible translation "Lord's Day" for κυρίακη is correct[65]—nevertheless Schoedel seems correct in asserting that it was too much attention to the meaning of biblical texts and not practicing of "the Law" that was at issue, that is, a scripturally based Christianity versus an exclusively apostolic faith based only on the disciples' teaching.[66] Ignatius explicitly links those who have not abandoned the Sabbath for the Lord's Day as those who deny Christ's death as well (Mag. 9:1; *Ignatius*, 123), a point that will take on greater significance below.

For Ignatius, seemingly, *Ioudaismos* and *Christianismos* are both versions of what we would call Christianity, since his opponents are those who say, "If I do not find it in the archives, I do not believe (it to be) in the gospel" (Phil. 8:2; *Ignatius*, 207). Ignatius's antagonists, real or imagined, are not actually what we today would call Jews, since Gospel seems to be a relevant concept for them, but were Christians, even uncircumcised ones, who preached some heterodox attachment to Christ, or even merely an insistence that everything in Christianity be anchored in scriptural exegesis, the Old Testament being the scripture they had.[67] They do not put Christ first, and therefore they are preaching *Ioudaismos*, and they are "tombstones."

What is this *Ioudaismos*, and how does it define *Christianismos*? A closer reading of the passage will help answer this question:

> I exhort you to do nothing from partisanship but in accordance with Christ's teaching. For I heard some say, "If I do not find (it) in the archives, I do not believe (it to be) in the gospel." And when I said, "It is written," they answered me, "That is just the question." But for me the archives are Jesus Christ, the inviolable archives are his cross and death and his resurrection and faith through him—in which, through your prayers, I want to be justified. (Phil. 8:2; *Ignatius*, 207)

The Greek of this passage allows for two translations at a crux. "ἐν τῷ εὐαγγελίῳ ου πιστεύω" can either be taken, following Schoedel, as "I do not believe (it to be) in the gospel," or, as Bauer would have it, "[When I do not find it (also) in the Archives], I do not believe it, [when I find] it in the gospel."[68] Schoedel gives his reasons for adopting his translation:

> Ignatius could not have accomplished anything by twisting his opponents' words that badly (I take it for granted that they regarded themselves as believers in the gospel)... Conceivably a group of Christians could have declared rhetorically their unwillingness to believe the gospel unless it was backed up by Scripture simply to make clear the importance of Scripture to them. But then why would Ignatius have replied by saying, "It is written"? And why would they have challenged him on that as if to suggest that the truth of the gospel itself was in doubt? The answer may be that the group was actually made up of Jews closely associated with Christianity but doubtful of its central tenets. But surely Ignatius has in mind Christians in danger of being attracted to Judaism (cf. Phd. 6.1)—people close enough to other members of the congregation that they almost "deceived" Ignatius (Phd. 11.1). When Ignatius indicates that "repentance" and a turning to the unity of the church is in order or this group (Phd. 8.1), it is likely that they were recognizably Christian.[69]

The possibility that Schoedel refuses to consider is that Jews who insist that the true Gospel must contain only ideas, histories that can be backed up from scripture, might have been precisely "people close to other members of the congregation," and even, *quel horreur*, "recognizably Christian." The group in Philadelphia to which the future martyr is objecting so strongly would be, on this reading, Christian Jews who insisted that the Gospel contained only scriptural truth, a position that was acceptable to the Philadelphian congregation with whom they were in communion.

Schoedel's incredulity is generated by his assumption that Jew and Christian are separate identities by the time of Ignatius, an assumption that I would seriously put into question. If we do not make this assumption and recognize that the very content of the probably oral Gospel is under question at this time, then where do those "central tenets of Christianity" come from that these Jews close to Christianity might be said to doubt? That is exactly the question that they put to Ignatius: "they answered me, 'That is just the question,'" to wit: Who are you, Ignatius, to determine what is or is not Gospel? Ignatius, however, for whom some nonscriptural kerygma is central, sees, as he insists over and over, such reliance on scripture as itself *Ioudaismos*, the following of Jewish scriptures, and not as *Christianismos*, the following of Christ's teaching alone. This opposition between Ignatius and these other Christian Jews has been symbolized by him already as an opposition between those who keep the Sabbath and those who observe only the Lord's Day. Here Ignatius draws it out further through an epistemological contrast between that which is known from scripture (i.e., *Ioudaismos*) and that which is known from the very facts of the Lord's death and resurrection (i.e., χρίστομαθία). As we have seen above, for Ignatius, those who observe the Sabbath are implicated as those who also deny the Lord's death (Mag. 9:1). Schoedel believes that "the link between Judaizing and docetism was invented by Ignatius" and, moreover, "that the form of the polemic compelled Ignatius to look for a serious theological disagreement where none existed."[70] I have argued elsewhere, however, that Jews who held a version of Logos theology, and perhaps might even have seen in Christ the manifestation of the Logos, might yet have balked at an incarnational Christology, that is, rather than the "low" Christology of which so-called Jewish Christians were usually accused, their Christology might have been, indeed, too "high" for Ignatius's taste.[71] What is not found in the "archives," then, is precisely the notion that the Logos could die! That is exactly what Ignatius himself claims distinguishes the Gospel over against the Old Testament: "the coming of the Savior, our Lord Jesus Christ, his passion and resurrection" (Phil. 9:2; *Ignatius*, 207). This suggests strongly that, if not precisely the same people, it is the same complex of Christian-Jewish ideas—accepting Jesus, accepting the Logos, denying actual physical death and resurrection—which Ignatius names as *Ioudaismos*, the product of overvaluing scripture against the claims of the Gospel, which alone must be first and foremost for those would have the name Christian, that name for which Ignatius would die.[72] This suggestion is also borne out strongly in Magnesians where we find a strong association between those who keep the (Jewish) Sabbath and those who deny Christ's actual death (Mag. 9:1; *Ignatius*, 123).

In any case, Schoedel has surely advanced our understanding by showing that "it was Ignatius and not they [the heretics] who polarized the situation."[73] Ignatius produced his *Ioudaismos* (and perhaps his docetic heresy as well) in order to define more fully and articulate the new identity for the disciples as true bearers of the new name, *Christianoi*. Ignatius is, in some important sense, the inventor of Judaism as a religion as part and parcel of his invention of Christianity. Justin, whose cause will be taken up in the next section, adopts and refines Ignatius's strategy of defining Christian identity over against Jews and heretics, already somewhat more clearly defined in the Christian mind by Justin's time.

Justin Makes a Difference

Le Boulluec found that it was Justin Martyr who was a crucial figure (if not *the* crucial figure) in the Christian shift from understanding *hairesis* as a "party or sect marked by common ideas and aims" to "a party or sect that stands outside established or recognized tradition, a heretical group that propounds false doctrine in the form of a heresy."[74] As Le Boulluec put it so pithily, the result of his research is that, "Il revient à Justin d'avoir inventé l'hérésie."[75] As we see at several points in Justin's *Dialogue*, Justin is very concerned to portray Trypho as not believing in the second divine person, this in spite of what I think to be the case, namely, that most (or at any rate numerous) non-Christian Jews did see the Logos (or his sister, Sophia) as a central part of their doctrines about God.[76] I would suggest that an important motivation for this expenditure of discursive energy is precisely to *deny* the second person to the Jews, to take it away from them, in order that it be the major theological center of Christianity, in order to establish a religious identity for the believers in Christ that would, precisely, mark them off as religiously different from Jews. Since this claim has recently been misunderstood, let me explain it a bit more. I believe that it can be shown (and indeed that I have shown) that well into the Christian era there were many non-Christian Jews (if not most) who found the notion of a *deuteros theos*, of one name or another, quite theologically compatible with their monotheism and indeed would have interpreted many of Justin's prooftexts for this concept quite similarly to the way that he did. Through his portrayal, therefore, of Trypho as an implacable opponent of any such notion, Justin is, without of course saying so explicitly, doing two kinds of work. He is, on the one hand, constructing/producing a point of uniqueness of "Christianity" over against "Judaism," but at the same time delegitimizing certain Christian opponents, rejectors of the notion of second gods, as Judaizers or Jews.

The question that I ask, assuming that Le Boulluec is right, is what precipitated this cataclysmic shift in the notion of identity specifically in Justin's time and place.[77] Justin's identity crisis is articulated by him through the medium of Trypho's challenging: "You do not distinguish yourselves in any way from the Gentiles" (*Dialogue* 10.3), providing, as it were, the justification, the articulation of the need for the *Dialogue* as an attempt for the Gentile Christian to so distinguish himself. There is more, however. Justin tells us that he is being accused of ditheism from within the "Christian" world, owing precisely to his Logos theology. The *Dialogue*, by establishing a binary opposition between the Christian and the Jew over the question of the Logos accomplishes, then, two purposes at once. It articulates Christian identity as *theological*. Christians are those people who believe in the Logos; Jews cannot, then, believe in the Logos. Secondly, Christians are those people who believe in the Logos; those who do not, are not Christians but heretics. This is the double motion of Christian heresiology that I am seeking to articulate in this study. The double construction of Jews and heretics, or rather, of Judaism and heresy effected through Justin's *Dialogue*, thus serves to produce a secure religious identity, a self-definition for Christians. It will be seen why for Justin the discourse about Judaism and the discourse about heresy would have been so inextricably intertwined. If Christian identity is theological, then orthodoxy must be at the very center of its articulation. According to Rowan Williams, "orthodoxy" is a way that a "religion," separated from the locativity of ethnic or geocultural self-definition as Christianity was, asks itself: "[H]ow, if at all, is one to identify the 'centre' of [our] religious tradition? At what point and why do we start speaking about 'a' religion?"[78] For Justin, belief in the Logos is the very touchstone of that center, the very center of his religion. I should not be understood, then, as claiming either that Justin invented "heresy" in order to make a difference between Christianity and Judaism, or that he pursued Jewish difference (via the *Dialogue*) in order to condemn heretics, but rather that these two projects (in both senses of the word) were imbricated, like tiles of a Mediterranean roof, in such a way as to finally be, if not indistinguishable, impossible without each other.

Justin, of course, was not just reflecting an actually existing situation; he was actively participating on one side of a discursive process, the setting of limits, that brought such situations into existence. There is an interesting moment of inconsistency in Justin's discourse, a moment of paradox, or at any rate of incongruity within Justin's text, that may afford us insight into the gap between the reality being constructed by the *Dialogue* and the social reality that Justin knows:[79]

> For even if you yourselves have ever met with some so-called Christians, who yet do not acknowledge ... [the] resurrection of the dead ... do not suppose that they are Christians, any more than if one examined the matter rightly he would acknowledge as Jews those who are Sadducees, or similar sects of Genistae, and Meristae, and Galileans, and Hellelians, and Pharisees and Baptists (pray, do not be vexed with me as I say all I think), but (would say) that though called Jews and children of Abraham, and acknowledging God with their lips, as God Himself has cried aloud, yet their heart is far from Him. (*Dialogue* 80.3–4)[80]

The implication of his last sentence, especially without the editorial insertion "would say," which is not in the Greek, is that Jews who do not deny the resurrection or participate in other "heresies" do, indeed, have their hearts "close to God." Just as in the Pseudo-Clementine texts, in which there are clearly Jews, identified there as Pharisees, who are deemed close to "orthodox" Christianity, closer indeed than some Christians in their insistence on the resurrection, in this moment in Justin's text, the lines are *not* clearly drawn between "Judaism" and "Christianity."[81] Instead, in at least one isogloss, belief in resurrection, which marked the difference between orthodox and heretic for the Rabbis and Justin and the Pseudo-Clementines alike, the line is drawn between Jew and Jew and between Christian and Christian, thus marking a site of overlap and ambiguity between the two "religions" that the text is at pains to construct as different.[82]

The gap which this textual moment uncovers allows us to begin to excavate further, beyond textual relations as such, and begin to assemble fragments of the social realities of which they were a part. It gives us access to the ambiguities of a situation in which the ideal, abstract, and legal borders being constructed by the heresiologists were constantly being transgressed by those who simply did not recognize them or abide by them, those who did not regard them as in any way normative, definitive, and in that sense "real."

There is at least one more site within the *Dialogue* in which the new notion of heresy and the issue of Judaism are intimately intertwined. It is certainly suggestive that it is in Justin Martyr that we find for the first time *hairesis* in the sense of "heresy" attributed to Jewish usage as well:

> I will again relate words spoken by Moses, from which we can recognize without any question that He conversed with one different in number from Himself and possessed of reason. Now these are the words: And God said: Behold, Adam has become as one of Us, to know good and evil. Therefore by saying as one of Us He has indicated also number in those that were present together, two at least. For I cannot consider that assertion true which is affirmed by what you call an heretical party among you, and cannot be proved by the teachers of that heresy, that He was speaking to angels, or that the human body was the work of angels. (*Dialogue* 62.2, my emphasis)

Justin quotes Gen. 3:22 to prevent the Jewish teachers' "distortion" of Gen. 1:26, "let us make," since in the latter verse it is impossible to interpret that God is speaking to the elements or to himself. In order, however, to demonstrate that his interpretation that God is speaking to the Second Person (the Logos) is the only possible one, Justin has to discard another possible reading that some Jewish teachers, those whom Trypho himself would refer to as a *hairesis*, have offered but cannot prove, namely, that God was speaking to angels.[83] On this text Marcel Simon comments:

> However, when this passage, written in the middle of the second century, is compared with the passage in Acts, it seems that the term *hairesis* has undergone in Judaism an evolution identical to, and parallel with, the one it underwent in Christianity. This is no doubt due to the triumph of Pharisaism which, after the catastrophe of 70 C.E., established precise norms of orthodoxy unknown in Israel before that time. Pharisaism had been one heresy among many; now it is identified with authentic Judaism and the term *hairesis*, now given a pejorative sense, designates anything that deviates from the Pharisaic way.[84]

The text is extremely difficult, and the Williams translation does not seem exact, but it nevertheless periphrastically captures the sense of the passage in my opinion. A more precise translation (although still difficult) would be: "For I cannot consider that assertion true which is affirmed by what you call an *hairesis* among you, or that the teachers of it are able to demonstrate."[85] "It" in the second clause can only refer to *hairesis*, so Williams's translation is essentially correct although somewhat smoothed out. Justin cannot consider the assertion true, nor can he consider that the teachers of the *hairesis* can prove it. There are two reasons for reading *hairesis* here as "heresy." First, this is consistent with the usage otherwise well attested in Justin with respect to Christian dissident groups and, therefore, seems to be what Justin means by the term in general; and second, the phrase "what you call" implies strongly a pejorative usage. It seems to me, therefore, that Simon's interpretation is well founded.

The literary dialogue between Justin and Trypho, a fictional, non-rabbinic Jew, provides us with a way to examine what Justin knew of Judaism and how he knew it, allowing us to interrogate the social formations underlying nascent Gentile Christianity and nascent rabbinic Judaism in a way that gets beyond the efforts to produce differences between them. As Demetrios Trakatellis has concluded, "Justin knew and presented rather accurately some basic aspects of the Judaism of his day" and "[i]t is plausible then to suggest that, when Justin described Trypho within the framework of his *Dialogue* the way he did, he was reporting a reality related to the theological contacts between Jews and Christians in his time."[86] The Judaism described by Justin as that which "your teachers" promulgate bears many significant parallels to actually attested rabbinic opinions.[87] In a recent monograph, David Rokeah argues, however, that there was little, if any, contact between Justin and "actual Jewish"—by which he means Pharisaic or rabbinic teachers.[88] Rokeah adopts Oskar Skarsaune's suggestion that much (if not all) of Justin's knowledge of Jewish practice and lore is dependent on an early Jewish-Christian text, very likely the same one that is embedded in the Pseudo-Clementines.[89]

The evidence for Rokeah's position seems strong to me, but leads me to a different revision of our understanding of the history of Jewish/Christian interactions in the early centuries. There is no contradiction between Justin knowing a fair amount about early rabbinic Judaism and his major source being the Jewish-Christians in the background of the Pseudo-Clementines. Indeed, this lack of contradiction is precisely the point. Since, as has recently been well argued, the Jewish-Christians who are the source of the Pseudo-Clementine text were indeed very proximate to the early Rabbis and probably in close (and irenic) contact with them, groups such as theirs can be adduced as the medium of contact and the means by which knowledge was transferred between Gentile Christians and rabbinic Jews.[90] For that reason, they were a source of restlessness on the newly invented borders, indeed, perhaps, one important catalyst for the invention of heresy on both sides of that border under construction. They numbered among them the "others" that both sides sought to exclude by naming heretics as heretics. As Albert Baumgarten has argued:

> The Pseudo-Clementine texts exhibit detailed and specific knowledge of rabbinic Judaism. Their awareness is not of commonplaces or of vague generalities which might be based on a shared biblical heritage, but of information uniquely characteristic of the rabbinic world. There can be no doubt that we are dealing with two groups in close proximity that maintained intellectual contact with each other. The authors of the Pseudo-Clementines quite obviously admired rabbinic Jews and their leaders.[91]

The "authors" of the Pseudo-Clementines, then, considered themselves at least fellow travelers of the Rabbis. Justin's representation of Trypho as a Jew who "took the trouble to read them [the Gospels]" (*Dialogue* 10.2) and of the Jewish "teachers" as opposing such association (38.1) is very important as providing evidence that there were such Jews and that they may very well have been seen as troubling by other Jews and Jewish leaders.[92] A Pharisaic-law-abiding group that was very knowledgeable in the ways of the Rabbis, but believed in Jesus as Messiah, or was strongly attracted to the Jesus movement, one like the group that produced the Pseudo-Clementines, certainly would have transgressed the very limits that the heresiologists on both sides were so intent on instituting.[93] Justin's acceptance of such "Jewish Christians" into communion with "orthodox" Christians (*Dialogue* 47.1–2) would, if anything, have made them more "dangerous" to the Rabbis, for then the border between that which is "Jewish" and that which is "Christian" becomes impossible to locate.[94] The existence of law-abiding Jewish-Christian groups (so-called "Nazoreans"), such as the circle behind the Pseudo-Clementine literature as possible mediators between rabbinic Jews who were non-Christians and even Gentile Christians such as Justin, provides suggestive evidence that Judaism and Christianity should be conceived as connected dialects of one language and not as separate languages, as it were, to borrow the great linguist Jespersen's definition of a "language as a dialect with an army," perhaps, indeed, up until the time of Theodosius.[95] They were the "smugglers" who crossed the lines between Czechoslovakia and Poland that the heresiologist border-guards sought to draw carrying with them the contraband of religious knowledge and ideas.

Making History of Theory

"Judaeo-Christianity," not Jewish Christianity, but the entire multiform cultural system, should be seen as the original cauldron of contentious, dissonant, sometimes friendly, more frequently hostile, fecund religious productivity out of which ultimately precipitated two institutions at the end of late antiquity, orthodox Christianity and rabbinic Judaism. Ignatius's letters and Justin's *Dialogue* can be read as representations and symptoms of broader discursive forces within Judaeo-Christianity, as a synecdoche of the processes of the formation of nascent orthodoxy and nascent heresiology, as well as of the vectors that would finally separate the Christian church from rabbinic Judaism. Seen in this way, the factors that induced the production of the notion of heresy in the second century are strikingly like those that produced "apartheid comparative religion" in the nineteenth. The historical situation of the second century, I would submit, is arguably best revealed when we reread the ancient texts with an eye for notions of hybridity bred in the hothouse of postcolonial theory.

Notes

1. Jacques Derrida, *Glas*, trans. John P. Leavey, Jr., and Richard Rand (Lincoln: University of Nebraska Press, 1970), 189b. And it is perhaps worth mentioning that that very

border has taken on entirely different meanings since Derrida's writing, not least because Czechoslovakia no longer exists.

2. Paul de Man, "The Epistemology of Metaphor," in *On Metaphor*, ed. Sheldon Sacks (Chicago: University of Chicago Press, 1779), 17.

3. See, e.g., Daniel Boyarin, "Martyrdom and the Making of Christianity and Judaism," *Journal of Early Christian Studies* 6.4 (1778): 577–627; and Boyarin, *Dying for God: Martyrdom and the Making of Christianity and Judaism* (Stanford, CA: Stanford University Press, 1779), 93–130, where I argue that people attending both synagogue and church in third-century Caesarea were the "smugglers" who transported discourses of martyrology in both directions across the "abstract, legal, and ideal" frontier between Judaism and Christianity. I would add here "Jewish Christian" communities, such as those behind the Pseudo-Clementine texts.

4. Ian Hacking, "Five Parables," in *Philosophy in History: Essays on the Historiography of Philosophy*, ed. Richard Rorty, J. B. Schneewind, and Quentin Skinner (Cambridge: Cambridge University Press, 1984), 22. For Davidson's role in the elaboration of this concept, see Arnold I. Davidson, *The Emergence of Sexuality: Historical Epistemology and the Formation of Concepts* (Cambridge, MA: Harvard University Press, 2002), 227 n. 32.

5. Karen King has made the point that for early Christian writers, "heresy" was always defined with respect to Judaism; too much Judaism, and you were a Judaizer, too little, a "gnostic." Karen L. King, *Making Heresy: Gnosticism in Twentieth-Century Historiography* (Cambridge, MA: Harvard University Press, 2003). See, too, Daniel Boyarin, "The Christian Invention of Judaism: The Theodosian Empire and the Rabbinic Refusal of Religion," *Representations* 85 (2004): 21–57.

6. Alain Le Boulluec, *La notion d'hérésie dans la littérature grecque IIe-IIIe siècles* (Paris: Études Augustiniennes, 1985). See especially, partially in the wake of Le Boulluec, Virginia Burrus, *The Making of a Heretic: Gender, Authority, and the Priscillianist Controversy* (Berkeley, CA: University of California Press, 1995); and J. Rebecca Lyman, "The Making of a Heretic: The Life of Origen in Epiphanius *Panarion* 64," *Studia Patristica* 31 (1997): 445–51.

7. Walter Bauer, Gerhard Krodel, and Robert A. Kraft, *Orthodoxy and Heresy in Earliest Christianity*, ed. Gerhard Krodel (Philadelphia: Fortress Press, 1971).

8. This tale was suggested to me for this context by Ishay Rosen-Zvi.

9. A very diligent and instructive recent effort in the former direction is Israel Jacob Yuval, *Two Nations in Your Womb: Perceptions of Jews and Christians*, in Hebrew (Tel Aviv: Alma/Am Oved, 2000). See, however, Galit Hasan-Rokem, "Narratives in Dialogue: A Folk Literary Perspective on Interreligious Contacts in the Holy Land in Rabbinic Literature of Late Antiquity," in *Sharing the Sacred: Religious Contacts and Conflicts in the Holy Land First-Fifteenth Centuries C.E.*, ed. Guy Stroumsa and Arieh Kofsky (Jerusalem: Yad Izhak Ben Zvi, 1998), 109–29, for a very different approach, one that focuses less on processes of differentiation as "polemic" and more on shared traditions. Also see Elchanan Reiner, "From Joshua to Jesus: The Transformation of a Biblical Story to a Local Myth; A Chapter in the Religious Life of the Galilean Jew," in *Sharing the Sacred*, 223–71.

10. See also, partially anticipating Le Boulluec, H.-D. Altendorf, "Zum Stichwort: Rechtglaubigkeit und Ketzerei in ältesten Christentum," *Zeitschrift für Kirchengeschichte* 80 (1969): 61–74.

11. R. P. C. Hanson, *The Search for the Christian Doctrine of God: The Arian Controversy, 318–381 A.D.* (Edinburgh: T & T Clark, 1988).

12. For critique of this view, see Elaine Pagels, "Irenaeus, the 'Canon of Truth,' and the Gospel of John: 'Making a Difference' through Hermeneutics and Ritual," *Vigiliae Christianae* 56 (2002): 339–71.

13. Rudolf Lorenz, *Arius judaizans? Untersuchungen zur dogmengeschichtlichen Einordnung des Arius* (Göttingen: Vandenhoek and Ruprecht, 1979). For a notable example of this discursive phenomenon, see Gregory of Nyssa's *Life of Moses*, trans. Abraham J. Malherbe and Everett Ferguson, preface by John Meyendorff (New York: Paulist Press, 1978), 184 and n. 294.

14. This point is important for understanding the virulence of the Quartodeciman controversy at this time as well, which, I think, also was largely about establishing a Christianity that is completely separate from Judaism.

15. In the Middle Ages, there was as rich and technical a theological controversy on the nature of godhead among Jews as there had been in late antiquity among Christians, yet it did not issue in a structure of orthodoxy and heresy.

16. An elegant exemplification of the hybridity of hybridity itself can be found in the fact that Rebecca Lyman reads Justin himself under the sign of postcolonial hybridity. J. Rebecca Lyman, "The Politics of Passing: Justin Martyr's Conversion as a Problem of 'Hellenization,'" in *Conversion in Late Antiquity and the Early Middle Ages: Seeing and Believing*, ed. Anthony Grafton and Kenneth Mills (Rochester, NY: University of Rochester Press, 2003), 36–60. Note especially her remark: "Ironically, due to Justin's and later Irenaeus' successful polemics about 'deviant' teachers, we hesitate to give him as a 'teacher' a central place in the construction of orthodox Christian identity."

17. Daniel Boyarin, "Two Powers in Heaven; or, the Making of a Heresy," in *The Idea of Biblical Interpretation: Essays in Honor of James L. Kugel*, ed. Hindy Najman and Judith H. Newman (Leiden: E. J. Brill, 2004), 331–70.

18. Arieh Kofsky, "Mamre: A Case of a Regional Cult?" in *Sharing the Sacred*, ed. Stroumsa and Kofsky, 19–30.

19. Palestinian Talmud, *'Avodah Zarah* 1.5.39d.

20. Daniel Boyarin, *Border Lines: The Partition of Judaeo-Christianity* (Philadelphia: University of Pennsylvania Press, 2004), 209–10.

21. David Chidester, *Savage Systems: Colonialism and Comparative Religion in Southern Africa* (Charlottesville: University Press of Virginia, 1996), 4.

22. Ibid., 22–23.

23. For the persistence of the "monster" as a modern trope for human hybrids, see Rudyard Kipling and Thomas Carlyle as quoted in Robert Young, *Colonial Desire: Hybridity in Theory, Culture, and Race* (London: Routledge, 1995), 3, 5 respectively.

24. Homi K. Bhabha, *The Location of Culture* (London: Routledge, 1994), 38–39, original emphasis; and see Chidester, *Savage Systems*, xv.

25. Bhabha, *Location of Culture*, 33.

26. Young, *Colonial Desire*, 161.

27. This language has been adopted from the otherwise nearly scurrilous essay, Marjorie Perloff, "Cultural Liminality/Aesthetic Closure? The 'Interstitial Perspective' of Homi Bhabha," at http://wings.buffalo.edu/epc/authors/perloff/bhabha/html.

28. Bhabha, *Location of Culture*, 13.

29. Young, *Colonial Desire*, 19.

30. For another critique that problematizes the notion of "pure precolonial" selves as projected by certain versions of postcolonial analyses, see Ania Loomba, *Colonialism/ Postcolonialism* (London: Routledge, 1998), 181–82. Richard King argues that "Bhabha's notion of 'hybridity' implies that the colonial space involves the interaction of two originally 'pure' cultures (the British/European and the native) that are only rendered ambivalent once they are brought into direct contact with each other" (*Orientalism and Religion: Postcolonial Theory, India, and the Mystic East* [London: Routledge, 1999], 204). While I am somewhat doubtful as to whether this critique is properly applied to Bhabha, it does seem relevant to me in considering the postcolonial model for reading Judaism and Christianity in antiquity, which, we might say, are always/already hybridized with respect to each other.

31. Seth Schwartz, *Imperialism and Jewish Society from 200 B.C.E to 640 C.E.* (Princeton, NJ: Princeton University Press, 2001), 184, original emphasis.

32. This is a point that will be further developed below. I do not enter here into the question as to whether *Christiani* was a derogatory epithet taken by the Christians themselves as an instance of reverse discourse (the view of Harold Mattingly, "The Origin of the Name *Christiani*," *Journal of Theological Studies* n.s. 9 [1958]: 26–37, to which view I am inclined) or a name that they named themselves originally (the view of Elias Bickerman, "The Name of the Christians," *Harvard Theological Review* 42 [1949]: 109–24). Most recently, supporting Mattingley's position, see Judith Lieu, "'I Am a Christian': Martyrdom and the Beginning of 'Christian' Identity," in *Neither Jew Nor Greek? Constructing Christian Identity* (Edinburgh: T & T Clark, 2003). See also Lieu, *Image and Reality: The Jews in the World of the Christians in the Second Century* (Edinburgh: T & T Clark, 1996), 23–24.

33. On *hairesis* (philosophical party) in the pre-Christian sense, see Marcel Simon, "From Greek *Hairesis* to Christian Heresy," in *Early Christian Literature and the Classical Intellectual Tradition: In Honorem Robert M. Grant*, ed. William R. Schoedel and Robert L. Wilken (Paris: Beauchesne, 1979), 101–16. On *Christianismos* as a new race, see Denise Kimber Buell, "Race and Universalism in Early Christianity," *Journal of Early Christian Studies* 10.4 (2002): 429–68.

34. For Althusser's terminology, see Louis Althusser, "Ideology and Ideological State Apparatuses (Notes Toward an Investigation)," in *Mapping Ideology*, ed. Slavoj Zizek (London: Verso, 1994), 100–140.

35. See, however, Lee I. Levine, *The Rabbinic Class of Roman Palestine in Late Antiquity* (New York: Jewish Theological Seminary of America, 1989), not, to be sure, a *Marxisant* work.

36. Althusser, "Ideology and Ideological State Apparatuses," 126.

37. Loomba, *Colonialism/Postcolonialism*, 37.

38. For a more detailed study of "religion" per se as a *dispositive*, see Boyarin, "The Christian Invention."

39. The scare quotes are an indication that it was, in fact, a large part of Ignatius's very project to invent the bishop, and he, himself as one, but that is beyond my scope here.

40. C. K. Barrett, "Jews and Judaizers in the Epistles of Ignatius," in *Jews, Greeks, and Christians: Religious Cultures in Late Antiquity; Essays in Honor of William David Davies*, ed. Robert Hamerton-Kelly and Robin Scroggs (Leiden: E. J. Brill, 1976), 243.

41. William R. Schoedel, *Ignatius of Antioch: A Commentary on the Letters of Ignatius of Antioch*, ed. Helmut Koester, trans. and ed. William R. Schoedel (Philadelphia: Fortress

Press, 1985), 203. Further citations of Ignatius's writings are cited in the text (*Ignatius*) by chapter and verse of the works followed by page numbers.

42. Paul's two uses of the term *Ioudaismos* (unique in the New Testament) in Galatians 1:13–14 mean the mores/way of life (ἀναστροφήν) traditional among Jews. It is surely clear that Paul had no sense of a not-yet-coined *Christianismos* as the name for a new religion, opposed to Judaism as the religion of Israel. For Paul, the relevant opposition is Greek and Jew, of course. As Conzelmann has put it, "The classifying of mankind from the standpoint of salvation history as Jews and Greeks is a Jewish equivalent for the Greek classification 'Greeks and barbarians.'" Hans Conzelmann, *I Corinthians: A Commentary on the First Epistle to the Corinthians*, ed. George W. MacRae, trans. James W. Leitch, with James W. Dunkly (Philadelphia: Fortress Press, 1976), 46. We surely do not have here, then, a differentiation of religions.

43. Jonathan A. Goldstein, trans. and ed., *II Maccabees: A New Translation with Introduction and Commentary*, Anchor Bible 41a (New York: Doubleday, 1983), 192. And see now discussion in Daniel Boyarin, "Semantic Differences; or, 'Judaism'/ 'Christianity,'" in *The Ways That Never Parted: Jews and Christians in Late Antiquity and the Early Middle Ages*, ed. Adam H. Becker and Annette Yoshiko Reed (Tübingen: Mohr Siebeck, 2003), 65–86.

44. Elizabeth A. Castelli, *Martyrdom and Memory: Early Christian Culture-Making* (New York: Columbia University Press, 2004), 50.

45. Frances Young, *Biblical Exegesis and the Formation of Christian Culture* (Cambridge: Cambridge University Press, 1997), 49–50.

46. Rowan Williams, "Does It Make Sense to Speak of Pre-Nicene Orthodoxy?" in *The Making of Orthodoxy: Essays in Honor of Henry Chadwick*, ed. Rowan Williams (Cambridge: Cambridge University Press, 1989), 1–23.

47. See Boyarin, "Semantic Differences."

48. See Lieu, *Image and Reality*, 28, for an exploration of the anxieties brought on by this fuzzy border. This position is partially *pace* Keith Hopkins, "Christian Number and Its Implications," *Journal of Early Christian Studies* 6.2 (1998): 187, who regards such fuzziness (or "porosity" in his language) as particularly characteristic of Christianity. Hopkins's article is very important and will have to be reckoned with seriously in any future accounts of Judaeo-Christian origins and genealogies. See also Lyman, "Politics of Passing."

49. Schoedel, *Ignatius*, 49. Schoedel also explicitly connects Ignatius's heresiological work with his assertion of the authority of the monarchial bishop as instances of Ignatius's constructive world-making (12).

50. See Schoedel, *Ignatius*, 41; and Henning Paulsen and Walter Bauer, *Die Briefe des Ignatius von Antiochia und der Brief des Polykarp von Smyrna* (Tübingen: Mohr Siebeck, 1985), 25.

51. Other interpretations seeing Ignatius's comment as a reference to the name *Ephesus* seem to me quite far-fetched.

52. For this sense of being "by nature" Christians, see Trallians 1:1 and Schoedel's discussion, *Ignatius*, 138.

53. See Schoedel, *Ignatius*, 43, for a contrary opinion.

54. Lieu, "I Am a Christian," in *Neither Jew Nor Greek?*; Carlin A. Barton, "The 'Moment of Truth' in Ancient Rome: Honor and Embodiment in a Contest Culture," *Stanford Humanities Review* 6 (1998): 16–30.

55. Similarly, it seems to me that in Eph. 7:1 where Ignatius writes, "For some are accustomed with evil deceit to carry about the name, at the same time doing things unworthy of God" (*Ignatius*, 59), it is *not* the name *Christ* that these folks are carrying about (*pace* Schoedel: "that is, they move from place to place looking for converts to their version of Christianity"), but the name *Christian*. See Justin's remark that, "For I made it clear to you that those who are Christians in name, but in reality are godless and impious heretics, teach in all respects what is blasphemous and godless and foolish." *Dialogue* 80.3–4, ed. and trans. A. Lukyn Williams, *Justin Martyr: The Dialogue with Trypho* (London: SPCK, 1930); Justin, *Dialogus Cum Tryphone*, ed. Miroslav Marcovich (Berlin: Walter de Gruyter, 1997). Further citations of the *Dialogue* are given in the text by chapter and line numbers.

56. As Lieu remarks, "I Am a Christian," in *Neither Jew Nor Greek?*, 215, "The claiming of this identity involves the denial of other alternatives," hence the importance of the name, martyrdom, and *Ioudaismos* in Ignatius. If one can be a Jew and a Christian, then Ignatius's martyrdom would, indeed, be in vain.

57. Schoedel, *Ignatius*, 12, sees *heresy* and *heterodox* as quasitechnical terms in Ignatius. But cf. *Ignatius*, 147: "But we should note first that in referring to the 'strange plant' as 'heresy' Ignatius is mainly concerned about the false teachers themselves rather than their teaching. 'Heresy', then, is still basically a matter of people who disrupt unity and create 'faction.'"

58. See also Barrett, "Jews and Judaizers," 220–44.

59. The quoted material is from de Man, "Epistemology of Metaphor," in *On Metaphor*, ed. Sacks, 17.

60. *Ignatius*, 128.

61. See Schoedel, *Ignatius*, 118, who considers Ignatius's usage of *Ioudaismos* to be the same as in 2 Maccabees, Paul, and the pastoral epistles.

62. Ibid., 202–3.

63. Contra Schoedel, *Ignatius*, 118, I do not see here a near-technical term for heresy, preferring the view of Martin Elze, "Irrtum und Haresie," *Kairos* 71 (1974): 393–94.

64. Schoedel, *Ignatius*, 201.

65. Ibid., 123 n. 3.

66. Ibid., 123–24: "But Ignatius makes a characteristic move when he links the resurrection with the mystery of Christ's death and emphasizes the latter as that through which faith comes. For it is Christ's death that stands out as a 'mystery' in Ignatius's mind (Eph. 19:1). One purpose of Ignatius here is to present the passion and resurrection (not Scripture as misinterpreted by the Jews and Judaizers) as that which determines the shape of Christian existence (and makes sense of Scripture)."

67. For further discussion of this difficult passage, see Schoedel, *Ignatius*, 207–9; and especially William R. Schoedel, "Ignatius and the Archives," *Harvard Theological Review* 71 (1978): 97–106. Oddly enough, these Jewish Christians sound like Sadducees: "the Sadducean group reject [the oral traditions], saying that one should consider as rules [only] those which have been written down, and that it is not necessary to keep the regulations handed down from the ancestors" (Josephus, *Antiquities* 13.297). See also Birger Pearson, "The Emergence of the Christian Religion," in *The Emergence of the Christian Religion: Essays on Early Christianity* (Harrisburg, PA: Trinity Press International, 1997), 11–14; Einar Molland, "The Heretics Combatted by Ignatius of Antioch," *Journal of Ecclesiastical History* 5 (1954): 1–6; Paulsen and Bauer,

Die Briefe, 85–86; and the important argument of C. K. Barrett in "Jews and Judaizers," in *Jews, Greeks, and Christians*, ed. Hamerton-Kelly and Scroggs, 233, who argues that "Ignatius has heard this preaching, must mean that the persons in question were Christian, even if (in Ignatius' eyes) unsatisfactory Christians. Ignatius is unlikely to have made his way into the synagogue."

68. Paulsen and Bauer, *Die Briefe*, 85.

69. Schoedel, *Ignatius*, 207.

70. Ibid., 118–19. I disagree with Schoedel's remark that "Ignatius speaks of Judaism where Paul would more naturally have spoken of the law," that this contrast is "between grace and Judaism and not, as in Paul, between grace and law." I think that Ignatius simply does not operate with an opposition between grace and law at all, as we can see from Mag. 2: "because he is subject to the bishop as to the grace of God and to the presbytery as to the law of Jesus Christ."

71. Daniel Boyarin, "The Gospel of the Memra: Jewish Binitarianism and the Crucifixion of the Logos," *Harvard Theological Review* 94.3 (2001): 243–84.

72. This interpretation was generated in conversation with my colleague Rebecca Lyman for whose koinonia I am especially grateful. While it must be conceded that Ignatius does not mention *Ioudaismos* in the letters (Trallians and Smymeans) where he is most explicit in his attacks on "docetics," I still find it quite plausible to see the same tendencies at work in these instances, with perhaps a somewhat varying emphasis. In all instances, it does seem to be denial of Christ's passion that is at work. Similarly in Ephesians, where it is generally conceded that Ignatius combats "docetic" teachers (Schoedel, *Ignatius*, 59, 231), Ignatius does not name the "heresy" either but merely refers to those "who are accustomed with evil deceit to carry about the name" (7:1), but there, too, he emphasizes positively the reality of the Incarnation, death, and resurrection, "first passible and then impassible [of] Jesus Christ our Lord," who is, moreover, "God in death." According to this interpretation we must understand those mentioned in Smyrneans 5:1, "whom the prophecies did not persuade nor the law of Moses, nor indeed until now the gospel" (*Ignatius*, 230), as meaning that they were not persuaded to interpret those documents and traditions (for the Gospel is almost surely oral for Ignatius) as proof of the Gospel of incarnational Christology. As Schoedel, himself an adherent of the view that two groups of "heretics" are comprehended in Ignatius, writes:

> As we have seen, Ignatius thinks of the appeal to the Scriptures as making sense only if it is recognized that they point forward to Christ and find their fulfillment there. The prophets and Moses gain their significance from the events of the Lord's ministry (cf. *Phd.* 5.2; 8.2; 9.2) and the commitment of the martyr (cf. *Phd.* 5.1; 8.2). Thus arguments that Ignatius had used against Judaizers to subordinate the Scriptures to Christ are used here (in a modified form) against docetists to confirm the reality of the humanity of Christ. (*Ignatius*, 234)

Given, however, that it seems most plausible (in my view) to see the issue between Ignatius and those who "expound *Ioudaismos*" in Magnesians and Philadelphians as also about the death of the Logos, it seems most elegant to assume as well that the same arguments are used with the same goals in mind in both groups of texts, thus supporting the view of Theodor Zahn, *Ignatius von Antiochien* (Gotha, 1873), 356–99, esp. 370; and J. B. Lightfoot and J. R. Harmer, trans., *The Apostolic Fathers*,

2nd. ed., rev. Michael W. Holmes (Grand Rapids, MI: Baker Book House, 1989), 359–75. This interpretation is supported by the fact that Ignatius uses precisely the same terms, *heterodoxy* and *grace*, as the terms of opposition in Mag. 8:1 and Smyr. 6:2. Cf. the awkwardness to which Schoedel is forced: "In any event, his arguments rely most heavily … on the nature of the gospel, and he finds it possible to adapt his views on the subject either to those who overemphasize the Scriptures (as in Philadelphia) or to those who teach docetism (as in Smyrna)" (*Ignatius*, 242). A further possible objection to this interpretation is the fact that Ignatius accuses his opponents at Smyrna of having no concern for "the widow, none for the orphan, none for one distressed, none for one imprisoned etc." (6:2; *Ignatius*, 238), a set of objections that would seem hardly to have been directed at Judaizing. However, against this objection we can put Schoedel's own obviously correct assertion that "[i]t would be naive, however, to think that the bishop was describing the behavior of his opponents accurately. What is true, perhaps, is that they valued their theology highly enough to be unwilling to sacrifice it simply to avoid the threat of disruption to the community" (*Ignatius*, 240). This would be just as true of alleged Judaizers who deny the physical death and resurrection as of so-called Gnostics. In my view, the interpretation that Ignatius deals with two groups of "heretics," Jewish Christians who keep the Law and have too low a Christology and "Gnostics" who have too high a Christology, owing to their over-allegiance to pagan philosophies, is a product of the (later) heresiological schema itself, argued for compellingly by Karen King, in *Making Heresy*, wherein all heresy is either a matter of being too Jewish or not Jewish enough, as it were. The very assertion of the existence of a real entity called "Gnosticism" is, following Michael Allen Williams, *Rethinking "Gnosticism": An Argument for Dismantling a Dubious Category* (Princeton, NJ: Princeton University Press, 1996), and the even more far reaching King, is to buy into the (Justinian, Irenaean) heresiological ideology itself.

73. Schoedel, *Ignatius*, 234. To be sure, Schoedel would see this view as being applicable only in the case of the "Gnostic docetics," while I would extend the point, either by seeing all of Ignatius's opponents as essentially one and the same, particularly so if they are being polarized by Ignatius himself, or as seeing it as applicable to both of the cases if the "two heresy" view holds.

74. This lucid summary of Le Boulluec's thesis is given by David T. Runia, "Philo of Alexandria and the Greek *Hairesis-Model*," *Vigiliae Christianae* 53.2 (1999): 118.

75. Le Boulluec, *La notion d'hérisie*, 110.

76. Boyarin, "The Gospel of the Memra." For the prominence of Logos theology within the *Dialogue*, see M. J. Edwards, "Justin's Logos and the Word of *God*," *Journal of Early Christian Studies* 3.3 (1995): 261–80.

77. In recent discussions, my friend and colleague Marc Hirshman disagreed sharply with this assessment, arguing, in effect, that it is too dependent on Le Boulluec's acceptance of Nautin's argument that much of Irenaeus's work includes a copy of a lost work of Justin's against heresies. Even without the grandiosity of the larger argument, however, I believe that the texts cited and discussed from the *Dialogue* below here are sufficient to establish Justin's great concern for heresy as a negative—and not neutral—category. If he is, as he seems to be, the first author to use *hairesis* in this pejorative sense, then Le Boulluec's argument stands whether or not we accept Nautin's reconstruction. I would like to thank Hirshman for providing the critical stimulus to come back to this question.

78. Rowan Williams, "Does It Make Sense to Speak of Pre-Nicene Orthodoxy?" in *The Making of Orthodoxy*, 3.
79. This inconsistency in Justin's text was pointed out to me by Shamma Boyarin.
80. For the crucial (Platonic) distinction between being called a Jew and being one, see Shaye J. D. Cohen, *The Beginnings of Jewishness: Boundaries, Varieties, Uncertainties* (Berkeley, CA: University of California Press, 1998), 60–61. See on this passage Le Boulluec, *La notion d'hérésie*, 71, who considers that "La représentation hérésiologique a cependant besoin de déformer la conception juive des divers courants religieux pour attendre son efficacité entière." In my view, this is less of a deformation than Le Boulluec would have it.
81. On the Pseudo-Clementine texts, see Albert I. Baumgarten, "Literary Evidence for Jewish Christianity in the Galilee," in *The Galilee in Late Antiquity*, ed. Lee I. Levine (New York: Jewish Theological Seminary of America, 1992), 39–50.
82. On the distinction between orthodox and heretic by the Rabbis, see Christine E. Hayes, "Displaced Self-Perceptions: The Deployment of *Minim* and Romans in *B. Sanhedrin* 90b-91a," in *Religious and Ethnic Communities in Later Roman Palestine*, ed. Hayim Lapin (Potomac: University Press of Maryland, 1998), 249–89.
83. Edwards, "Justin's Logos," has made a compelling argument that in the *Dialogue* as much as in the *Apologies*, Justin's Logos theology is being elaborated, indeed that his Logos theology is a product of the biblical interpretation promulgated in the *Dialogue*. However, since this claim is perhaps controversial (and indeed proved controversial to a recent audience of my work), I will stick here with the more general formula of the Second Person, whether deemed the Logos or not. There can be no doubting then that Justin argues several times with Trypho over the latter's alleged denial of a Second Person. Since, as I am arguing, Second Person theology was nearly ubiquitous in pre-Christian Judaism and was not uncontested in early Christianity, my reading strategy is to purport that Justin had a stake in making this be a (if not the) difference that marks off himself (Christian) from his opponent (Jew) and thus the marker of that self-definition, such that any Second-Person-deniers immediately confess, as it were, that they are really Jews and not Christians.
84. Simon, *"Hairesis,"* 106.
85. I am grateful for Erich Gruen's and Chava Boyarin's help with construing this passage in the *Dialogue*, although neither are responsible for my interpretation of it. Cf. the old translation in *The Apostolic Fathers, Justin Martyr, Irenaeus*, Ante-Nicene Fathers, vol. 1, ed. Alexander Roberts and James Donaldson (Grand Rapids, MI: Eerdmans, 1989), 228: "For I would not say that the dogma of that heresy which is said to be among you is true, or that the teachers of it can prove that [God] spoke to angels, or that the human frame was the workmanship of angels." David T. Runia for his part translates in "'Where, Tell Me, is the Jew. . . ?': Basil, Philo, and Isidore of Pelusium," *Vigiliae Christianae* 46.2 (1992): 178: "For personally I do not think the explanation is true which the so-called sect among you declares, nor are the teachers of that sect able to prove that he spoke to angels or that the human body is the creation of angels."
86. Demetrios Trakatellis, "Justin Martyr's Trypho," *Harvard Theological Review* 79.1-3 (1986): 287, 297. A recent scholar from the side of rabbinics, Marc Hirshman, however, argues that Justin's knowledge of rabbinic exegesis is "on the whole unimpressive." Marc Hirshman, *A Rivalry of Genius: Jewish and Christian Biblical Interpretation in Late Antiquity*, trans. Batya Stein (Albany: State University of New York Press, 1996),

65. My preliminary assessment is that Hirshman's somewhat skeptical remarks derive in part from an attempt to find in Justin the echoes of what are really later, detailed developments in rabbinic exegesis per se, while Trakatellis is essentially right that the general *kind* of Judaism that "Trypho" represents (and the voice of Justin himself telling Trypho what "your teachers say" even more so) is not far from what we can imagine as the religious ethos of nascent forms of Judaism close to the Rabbis in the second century.

87. For excellent examples, see Darrell D. Hannah, *Michael and Christ: Michael Traditions and Angel Christology in Early Christianity* (Tübingen: Mohr Siebeck, 1999), 111–12. Note that for our purposes it doesn't make any difference whether Trypho is a "real" person or one made up; the only significant point is whether the Judaism that he expresses and that, therefore, Justin knows can be shown to be a realistic possibility. See also A. H. Goldfahn, "Justinus Martyr und die Agada," *Monatschrift für Geschichte und Wissenschaft des Judentums* 22 (1873): 49–60, 104–15, 145–53, 193–202, 257–69; and see Hirshman, *Rivalry of Genius*, 31–42, 55–66. In spite of the recent work on this subject, this is a matter that will repay further research.

88. David Rokeah, *Justin Martyr and the Jews* (Leiden: Brill, 2002).

89. Oskar Skarsaune, *The Proof from Prophecy—A Study in Justin Martyr; Proof-Text Tradition: Text-Type, Provenance, Theological Profile* (Leiden: Brill, 1987), 316–20; Rokeah, *Justin Martyr and the Jews*, 30. What remains, however, is to consider the question of the dating of that source, its possible connections with rabbinic or associated traditions, and the dating of those traditions. Both Skarsaune who accepts such connections and Rokeah who rejects them rely on the assumption that material attributed to second-century Rabbis in fifth-century (and even eighth-century!) texts can be dated to the second century (Skarsaune, *Proof from Prophecy*, 319; Rokeah, *Justin Martyr and the Jews*).

90. Baumgarten, "Literary Evidence," in *The Galilee in Late Antiquity*, ed. Levine.

91. Ibid., 46–47.

92. As Williams, ed. and trans., *Dialogue with Trypho*, 74–75, points out, the Gospel is only represented in rabbinic literature with cacophemisms: e.g., '*Awen Gilayon* (The Scroll of Falsehood) or '*Awon Gilayon* (The Scroll of Sin). The contrast with Trypho's "admirable and great" is striking, although vitiated somewhat by the fact that Williams is much too credulous in accepting the ascription and therefore the dating of this talmudic notice, which may be much later. One's confidence in this ascription to early Palestinian sources is certainly not raised by the fact that it seems only to occur in this Babylonian talmudic citation and in a context which shows much Babylonian diction. See also Frédéric Manns, *Essais sur le Judéo-Christianisme* (Jerusalem: Franciscan Press, 1977), 131. The prohibition on conversation with Christians is not attested in rabbinic texts redacted before the mid-third century (albeit in the name of the early-second-century Rabbi Tarfon, who has even been—temptingly but implausibly—identified with Trypho), and even then, clearly was honored as much in the breach (within Palestinian and even rabbinic circles) as in the observance, *pace* Leslie W. Barnard, *Justin Martyr: His Life and Thought* (London: Cambridge University Press, 1967), 40, 45, who at least understands that the *Dialogue* is indicative of "closer intercourse between Christians and Jews in the first half of the second century than has usually been supposed," but still imagines that the "rabbis of Jamnia" had sought to "enforce a pattern of Pharisaic orthodoxy which forbad contacts with the *Minim*, i.e.

Christians." See also Barnard's crucial point that "[Trypho] warns us against identifying the linguistic frontier between the Greek and Semitic worlds with the cultural frontier between Hellenism and Judaism" (Justin Martyr, 42). All Judaism is, by definition, Hellenistic, precisely under the definition of Hellenism itself as the creative adaptation of Greek to Asiatic (and therefore also, ipso facto, Semitic) cultural forms and societies; see Lee I. Levine, *Judaism and Hellenism in Antiquity: Conflict or Confluence* (Seattle: University of Washington Press, 1998). By the time we can speak of anything recognizable as "Judaism" at all, it is, by definition, Hellenistic. As Seth Schwartz has remarked, *Imperialism and Jewish Society*, 25, "When Alexander the Great conquered the east coast of the Mediterranean in 332 B.C.E., he found there a world which was not completely foreign to him, in which certain aspects, at least, of Greek culture already enjoyed widespread acceptance." For a compelling general argument that binary oppositions between Judaism and Hellenism are a (problematic) scholarly construct, see also Erich S. Gruen, *Heritage and Hellenism: The Reinvention of Jewish Tradition* (Berkeley: University of California Press, 1998), 292. Also Schwartz's remark, "Hellenization was so pervasive and fundamental that it has little utility as an analytic category" (*Imperialism and Jewish Society*, 12). I am working here with the same assumption that motivates Schwartz's work, namely, "that the Israelite religion, as practiced before the destruction of the Kingdom of Judah by the Babylonians in 586 B.C.E., was distinct from the religion practiced by the Israelites' putative descendants, the Jews, in the Second Temple period" (19). "Judaism" is, then, entirely a product of the Second Temple period and, therefore, almost from the beginning an integral part of the Hellenistic world.

93. Gedaliah Alon, "Jewish Christians: The Parting of the Ways," in *The Jews in Their Land in the Talmudic Age (70–640 C.E.)*, ed. and trans. Gershon Levi (Jerusalem: Magnes Press, 1984), 288–307; Baumgarten, "Literary Evidence," in *The Galilee in Late Antiquity*, ed. Levine; F. Stanley Jones, *An Ancient Jewish Christian Source on the History of Christianity: Pseudo-Clementine "Recognitions" I.27-71* (Atlanta: Scholars Press, 1995). See also James D. G. Dunn, *The Partings of the Ways between Christianity and Judaism and their Significance for the Character of Christianity* (London: SCM Press; Philadelphia: Trinity Press International, 1991), 233.

94. I am in full agreement with Joan E. Taylor that the term *Jewish Christian* is very problematic and would insist that we conceive of those people who were both Jewish and Christian, even as late as the fourth century, not as "combining two religions," but as representing one form on a continuum of Judaeo-Christian religious identity and praxis. Joan E. Taylor, "The Phenomenon of Early Jewish-Christianity: Reality or Scholarly Invention," *Vigiliae Christianae* 44 (1990): 314–15. All Christian heresiologists other than Justin himself seem to have immediately realized this "danger." Justin himself realizes that he is unusual in this respect.

95. Dunn, *Partings of the Ways*, 5, has also spoken of "first-century reality … as a more or less unbroken spectrum across a wide front from conservative Judaizers at one end to radical Gentile Christians at the other." I would emend this statement by substituting for "conservative Judaizers" non-Christian Jews, thus also answering to Dunn's own call for a recognition of "the importance of the continuing Jewish character of Christianity," within the very same model; and also I would consider this situation as obtaining quite a bit after the first century. For the literalness of my Jespersenian conceit, see *Codex Theod.* 16.1.2, ed. Theodor Mommsen, Paul Martin Meyer, and

Jacques Sirmond, *Theodosiani Libri* XVI *Cum Constitutionibus Sirmondianis et Leges Novellae Ad Theodosianum Pertinentes* (Dublin: Apud Weidmannos, 1970), vol. 1, pt. 2, 833. Cf. Richard Lim, *Public Disputation, Power, and Social Order in Late Antiquity* (Berkeley: University of California Press, 1994), 177.

Who Were the Jews? Problems In Profiling the Jewish Community Under Early Islam

Steven M. Wasserstrom

The end of late antiquity is a period of Jewish history best known for being unknown. Salo Baron emphasizes the darkness of this terra incognita: "In the first three and one half dark and inarticulate centuries after the conclusion of the Talmud (500–850), Jewish intellectual leadership laid the foundations upon which the vocal and creative generations of the following three and one half centuries (850–1200) erected the magnificent structure of medieval Jewish biblical learning."[1] S. D. Goitein likewise states unequivocally that "the centuries both preceding and following the rise of Islam are the most obscure in Jewish history."[2] Not long ago, a leading specialist in this period presumed this problem once again: "We all know that the two hundred years that preceded the Arab conquest and the two hundred years that followed are among the most obscure in the history of the Jewish community in Palestine; very few historical documents of that period have reached us."[3] And Leon Nemoy, the leading student of Islamicate Karaism, recently reiterated a point he has emphasized throughout his career: "This whole period of Jewish history [remains] dark and puzzling."[4]

The darkest of all periods of postbiblical Jewish history occurred, however, at a turning point in the history of the Middle East. Henri Pirenne says: "The Middle Ages were ... beginning. The transitional phase was protracted. One may say that it lasted a whole century—from 650 to 750. It was during this period ... that the tradition of antiquity disappeared, while the new elements came to the surface." And Peter Brown adds, "The late seventh and early eighth century ... are the true turning points in the history of Europe and the Middle East."[5]

At this extraordinarily important moment, blackout overcomes the history of the Jews. This fact is all the more remarkable when one recalls Jane Gerber's estimate that "between 85 and 90% of world Jewry lived in the Muslim world in the period from the eighth through the tenth century."[6] To the extent, then, that so few datable Jewish sources survive from this period, the status of the Jews at this point remains perhaps the best-kept secret of Jewish history. What can we really know concerning the Jewish community at the end of antiquity?

I shall start with Jewish professions in the first two centuries of Islamic rule, working toward a profile of the Jewish community at the end of antiquity by first surveying the kinds of work undertaken by Jews of that time. After this rough assessment of the class structure of eighth-century Judaism, I shall then describe what may be called the crisis of mobility on the part of the Jewish leadership. My conclusions will concern the ways in which the end of Jewish antiquity was brought about by a "third power," beyond the Jewish laity and Jewish leadership. This power from outside was a Muslim caliph, whose manipulation of power struggles among the Jews ironically turned out to be something of a boon to the Jews.

The Jewish Professions

"Upper" Professions

Perhaps the most salient of the "upper" Jewish professions was long-distance trade. In part because the Jews were neither Muslims, Christians, Indians, Chinese, nor Slavs, they were particularly well suited to moving goods among these various peoples.[7] Accordingly, Jewish merchants by the eighth century specialized in plying the trade routes between China, India, Russia, Persia, Western Europe, and their home bases in the Muslim world.[8] The goods they traded included slaves, spices, and other luxury items. The skilled, capital intensive, and lucrative nature of this vastly dispersed enterprise placed long-distance traders among the highest levels of the Jewish economic elite. Indeed, the travelling merchant eventually helped pave the way for the subsequent creation of an international banking system, for such a trader was uniquely situated to convey letters of credit (*suftaja*) from country to country.[9]

But long-distance trade was not the only route to Jewish wealth. The Jews of the Banu Nadhir tribe, for example, controlled a palm-growing oasis in central Arabia, which was conquered by the Prophet Muhammad in the year 625. When Muhammad drove them from their home oasis, the Banu Nadhir Jews proudly paraded "their women decked out in litters wearing silk, brocade, velvet, and fine red and green silk. People lined up to gape at them. They passed by in a train one after the other, borne by 600 camels... They went off beating tambourines and playing on pipes."[10] The Jews of the Arabian oases also earned their livelihoods by selling wine and importing silk. One pre-Islamic Arabic poet evoked his desert landscape as multicolored, "just as if the Jews had extended their cloth of silk, their shimmering sashes."[11] These and other Jews of central Arabia were economically powerful enough that Muhammad's earliest political maneuvers were at least in part designed to come to terms with these entrenched Jewish merchants and agriculturalists.[12]

Jews in the seventh and eighth centuries also were active in the precious and not-so-precious metal businesses. When one of the Seven Wonders of the Ancient World, the Great Colossus of Rhodes, was scrapped in the eighth century, the remains were sold to a Jewish scrap-metal dealer.[13] The Jews in the oases around Muhammad's Mecca not only raised date palms but were celebrated goldsmiths.[14] And at the turn of the eighth century a Jew was named the head of Umayyad general's mint. This Jew, one Sumayr, was successful enough in his position of head minter that his coins were named *sumariyya* after him.[15]

In the earliest years of new Islam, upper Jewish professionals gravitated to the caliphal centers of power, which provided pivotal points from which to further pursue their scattered economic interests. Jewish physicians, astrologers, poets, and, eventually, viziers attended the affairs at court, if not to the caliph himself.[16] Perspicacious caliphs naturally took advantage of these readily available Jewish skills. For example, when the 'Abbasid dynasty overtook the Umayyads in 750, the new 'Abbasid regime decided to establish its capital city at Baghdad. The man appointed to plot out the city plan for this ideal city was a Jew, the celebrated physician and astrologer Mashallah.[17] This Jewish scientist calculated that the day of the historic groundbreaking should be July 30, 762. Thus, from its vary inception, the 'Abbasid dynasty, who ruled from this capital of Baghdad for the succeeding five centuries, utilized Jews in positions of technical and cultural authority.

For the ambitious young Jew already in the eighth century, then, a position of influence at the center of the Muslim world-empire was not entirely an unrealistic aspiration. And, indeed, Jewish skills continuously were co-opted in the interests of the Islamic state. By the tenth century the role of the Jews in international banking and commerce, often at the behest of the caliph, expanded considerably. The tenth century, in the phrase of Goitein, constituted "the golden age of the high bourgeoisie" for Jews as well as for Muslims.[18]

The Jewish community eventually prospered, along with its neighbors, in what Goitein termed the "bourgeois revolution," engendered by the economic boom following in the wake of the Arab conquests.[19] Certainly by the tenth century Jewish middle classes of Egypt and Mesopotamia enjoyed the pivotal advantage of powerful friends at court. But beneath these well-documented and overemphasized few success stories were squeezed a silent and apparently degraded Jewish majority.

Reviled Occupations

By the tenth century the Jewish community had become a "religious democracy," with wealthy classes caring for the poor through efficient social services, as Goitein has shown from Geniza documents.[20] My concern at this point, however, lies with the earlier, less organized situation. I therefore now turn to the neglected "lower" levels of Jewish life, with special reference to what (little) we know of the eighth and ninth centuries. Jewish court poets, town planners, caliphal astrologers, ambassadors, and monied courtiers of that day, I suggest, did not represent their people. Indeed, for however much evidence there may be concerning court Jews and their apparent influence, there is that much more proof that the Jewish masses were in a generally miserable condition.[21]

This grim situation can best be illustrated by a look at the most frequently mentioned of all Jewish professions in the first centuries of Islamic rule. I refer to cloth-making—mere manual labor, which almost universally was considered to comprise the lowest level of society.[22] It was assumed that mercantile activity possessed social status, while manual labor did not. Moreover, the social status of those engaged in laboring on cloth and fur—tanners, fullers, carders, weavers—was that of a despised underclass.[23] And of workers engaged in the manufacture of cloth, the weavers were derogated as the lowest of them all.[24]

This was an ancient prejudice. As early as the first century, Flavius Josephus describes the general Roman loathing for weavers.[25] Rabbinic Jewish views were much the same: a passage from *Tosefta* designates weaving as "the lowest trade in the world."[26] No wonder weaving has been deemed by one scholar as "the most despised profession in the East."[27] And the prejudice against weavers common in other traditional societies seems particularly acute in the medieval Muslim social world.

It is striking, then, that garment work, with its derogatory implications, was associated widely with Jews in the first centuries of Islam. An Arabic essayist tells us that the Jews of the ninth century were dyers, tanners, cuppers, butchers, and tinkers. About the same time, a geographer notes that many of the Jews of Egypt and Syria were dyers and tanners. The most striking castigation derives from a source dated between the eighth and tenth centuries: In this source, an Arabic-speaking Christian reviles a Jew in his way: "As for you, God has replaced the status of his Son and his delight with malediction, wrath and exile; instead of Royalty, the job of weaver; instead of Prophet, the profession of tanner; instead of Priest, that of barber, potter, glassblower and other vile professions." And we find this image corroborated by another Eastern Christian, who asserted that "no Jew has been raised to a position of exalted honour … [and] the humbler among them are engaged as tanners or dyers or tailors."[28]

This depressing background should be kept in mind in order to comprehend the full pathos of the Jewish rebellions of the eighth century, for rebellious Jews are repeatedly associated with various kinds of cloth work. It is interesting to note that garment workers in particular have been perennially associated with something more than their low class standing. They were also—not inaccurately—held responsible for social agitations. The conjunction of cloth workers and rebellion is known outside the Muslim world. Jewish women working in the imperial Roman weaving establishment converted Christian women to Judaism. The Jewish women weavers accomplished this in such numbers that the disturbance required a special proviso in the Theodosian Code (398 CE) in order to allow converted women back into Christianity.[29] Even in the Europe of the High Middle Ages, several millenarian peasant uprisings were instigated by semiskilled weavers and fullers.[30]

Furthermore, more than one of the widely vilified eighth-century proto-Shiʻi prophets was said to be a weaver. The medieval Muslim historian who reports this fact dryly comments "that his claim [to prophecy] should have been raised by them in favor of a weaver is strange indeed!"[31] And, certainly, these eighth-century Shiʻi rebels propagandized on the effectively populist appeal of their own lower-class origins.[32]

We should therefore not be surprised to find that contemporaneous Jewish rebels, closely associated with these originators of Shiʻi Islam, seem to have appealed similarly to their underclass status in their uprisings. One of these Jewish rebels arose in Mesopotamia around the year 720. Around him gathered Jews who were "weavers, carpetmakers and launderers."[33] Though his rebellion was quickly put down, others were soon to follow.

The greatest of all these Jewish cloth-worker revolutionaries—indeed, the most significant Jewish Messianic figure from Bar Cochba in the second century to Shabbetai Zevi in the seventeenth century—was Abu ʻIsa al-Isfahani.[34] A reliable source says that Abu ʻIsa was "an ignorant tailor who could neither read nor write"—another lowly, illiterate cloth worker.[35] Despite—or because of—his humble origins, his movement apparently was a mass movement. Indeed, Goitein argued that Abu ʻIsa's movement, the ʻIsawiyya, was at least symbolically responsible for the decline of Jewish village life starting in the second century of Muslim rule.[36]

The way Maimonides tells this tragic story is instructive. He refers to "an exodus of a multitude of Jews, from the East beyond Isphahan, led by an individual who pretended to be the Messiah. They were accoutered with military equipment and drawn swords, and slew all those that encountered them." The caliph stops them by proving their leader to be a phoney and then bribing his followers to return home. When pacified, the "Caliph ordered them to make a special mark on their garments, the writing of the word 'cursed' and to attach one iron bar in the back and one in the front. Ever since then the communities of Khorasan and Ispahan have experienced the tribulations of the Diaspora."[37] Goitein may have been correct to extrapolate that "it may well be that the disappearance of Jewish village population in the Arab East was partly caused by the negative outcome of such Messianic upheavals."[38]

Goitein's suggestion may be corroborated by two further indications of the serious extent of these movements. First, classical Muslim traditions have it that the Dajjal, the monstrous Antimessiah who will oppose the Messiah, "will emerge from Isfahan followed by 70,000 Jews wearing Persian shawls."[39] Note the motif of Jewish cloth—but more importantly, note that this mythical terrible uprising of Jewish peasants is permanently embodied in Muslim tradition as a sign of the end of time.

Christian tradition provides a second indication of the impact of the weaver rebels. Their widespread appeal made their way into a later Eastern Christian report: "A weaver wanted to be a prophet. The people told him, Never has there been a prophet who was a weaver. He, however, replied to them: Shepherds with all their simplicity have been employed as prophets, why should not weavers be fit for it?"[40]

It is no surprise, of course, to find that underclasses revolt—all the more so, to be sure, in a society in which reviled occupations were so isolated and stigmatized. Nevertheless, it still seems extraordinary to realize that, in the first centuries of Islam, Jews filled so many of the occupations conveniently named by a Muslim author listing "professions that damn": blacksmith, butcher, conjurer, policeman, highwayman, police informer, night watchman, tanner, maker of wooden and leather pails, maker of women's shoes, burier of excrement, well digger, stoker of baths, felt maker, masseur, horse trader, weaver, ironsmith, pigeon racer, and chess player.[41]

Extraordinarily, there were Jewish occupations even more reviled and undesirable than any of these. It was common enough, in fact, from ancient times through the decline of Muslim power, to use Jews for dirty work—not only the smelly and offensive work of tanning or fulling, but even more repulsive occupations. One of the worst of these was the universally loathed jailer. We already hear of Jewish jailers in sixth- and seventh-century Persia.[42] Moreover, in the Babylonian Talmud (Taanit 22a) the prophet Elijah appears in a contemporary marketplace and declares that a man there has a share in the world to come. That man was a Jewish jailer.

Jews were used not only as jailers, but even as executioners. Middle Eastern rulers, in other words, utilized Jews for the very worst jobs for well over a millennium. In illustration, I have translated a description of such activities deriving from events in fifteenth-century Lebanon. On Wednesday night, the twenty-ninth day of the month of Shawwal, in the year 1462,

> a slave and a black bondswoman conspired against their mistress at Tripoli. Her husband was away at the time and they murdered her… A Jew was put in charge of their execution, as was their custom in that land, for whenever such a thing occurred they would call upon a Jew at random, whoever it might be. The Jew was then ordered to execute by whatever manner of punishment the criminal deserved, out of the apprehension that one of [the Muslim community] should have to do [that undesirable deed].[43]

There was, then, a full spectrum of Jewish professions. Beyond legal occupations, Jews operated outside the law as outlaws.[44] Indeed, we possess a precious account of a Jewish highwayman at the turn of the ninth century. Because of its rarity and intrinsic interest, I translate it here (from *The History of the Rulers of Damascus and the Biography of Ibrahim ibn al-Mahdi*) in its entirety:

> 'Ali ibn al-Mughira al-Athram said: "Ibrahim ibn al-Mahdi [a professional singer, uncle of the caliphs al-Amin and al-Ma'mun] told me that he ruled the emirate of Damascus for two years, after which for a period of four years no one was waylaid in his province. I was told that disaster eventually did occur in the form

of highway robbery, by Diama and Nu'man, two *mawali* [client-tribesmen] of the Umayyads, and by Yahya ibn Yirmia of the Balqa' Jews. They refused to submit to the authority of a governor, so when I came to office I wrote letters to them. Nu'man wrote to him with a solemn oath that he would not despoil his district so long as he was governor. Diama came to me 'hearing and obeying.' He told me that Nu'man had been true and had kept his promise. He told me that the Jew had written to him, 'I am going out to dispute you. So write me a note of assurance swearing to me in it that you won't do anything to me until I return to my place of safety.' I acceded to this request.

A youth with scant hair, wearing an ornamented outer garment, a girdle, and a Mahalla sword, approached me. He entered the House of Mu'awiyya while I was in its courtyard. He greeted me off the carpet. So I said to him, 'Get on the carpet.' He said, 'O Amir! The carpet carries with it an obligation which frightens me from staying seated on it. For I don't know what on earth you will impose on me.' So I replied, 'Convert! Hear and Obey!' He said, 'As for obedience, I hope to do so. But as for Islam, there's no way. Let me know what is in it for me if I don't convert to Islam.' I said, 'There is no way for you to avoid rendering the *jizya* [head tax] to me.' To which the Jew replied, 'No way to do that.' [The Jew] then answered back, 'I am leaving in accordance with my pledge of safe conduct,' and I permitted that. And I ordered them to water his horse as he went out to it. When he saw that, he called for a hired horse, mounted it, and abandoned his own steed. He said, 'I'm not in a position to take anything with me which I received from you for mere convenience, for I will wage war on you upon it.' I appreciated that coming from him, and I requested that he come back inside.

And when he entered, I said, 'Praise God, who made me victorious over you without a contract or a pact.' He asked, 'How is that?' I answered, 'Because you turned away from me and then returned to me.' He said, 'You imposed as condition that you should send me away to my sanctuary. If your abode is my sanctuary, then I shouldn't be scared. But if my sanctuary is my own abode, then return me to Balqa.' I tried hard to have him comply with my request to pay the jizya, [even] on condition that I grant him two hundred dinars a year, but he wouldn't do it. He returned and stirred up mischief in his area.

Sometime thereafter, monies were transported to 'Ubaidallah ibn al-Mahdi in Egypt. The Jew went out to intercept this [shipment]. I wrote back to him, commanding him to war against the Jew if he interfered with the money. When ['Ubaidallah ibn al-Mahdi] encountered the Jew, both knights were escorted militarily. Al-Nu'man asked the Jew to leave the field, but he refused. He said, 'You wish me to come out to you all alone while you come out in your escort. If you so desire, we should meet in single combat. If I vanquish you, your companions will revert to me, and they will share booty with me. And if you beat me, my companions will revert to you.' Al-Nu'man said to him, 'O Yahya! Woe unto you, you youth! You have been inflated with conceit—even if you were one of the Quraysh, your hostility to the government wouldn't be possible. This amir is the caliph's brother, and I, even though we are of different religions, would prefer not to have the murder of a knight on my hands. If you wish what I wish of security, then he will not be afflicted by you and by me.'

They both went out together at the time of the Asr [late afternoon] prayer, remaining in duel till dusk. Each stayed on his horse, supporting his weight on his lance. Al-Nu'man had his eyes poked out. The Jew thrust at him, and the spearhead of his lance got caught in al-Nu'man's girdle. The girdle revolved and the spearhead started to turn in the girdle toward the rear. At this point al-Nu'man grabbed him and said to him, 'Double-cross, O son of a Jewish woman!' Yahya replied, 'O the fighter sleeps, O son of a handmaid!' Al-Nu'man then leaned his full weight on him in his embrace and fell on top of him. Al-Nu'man was a huge man, and so, immobilizing the Jew, he cut his throat. He thereupon dispatched his head to the caliph. None after him opposed me.[45]

By the tenth century, then, Jews worked in virtually every known profession. From the documentary evidence of the Cairo Genizah, Goitein counted over 250 manual occupations and 170 types of activities in commerce, the professions, education, and administration.[46] I want to emphasize that there was a smaller but still quite considerable range of professions already occupied by Jews by the eighth century, from the highest merchant ranks to the most reviled, including those operating outside the law.

Finally, I must add that there were un-Jewish Jewish successes: ironically, the professional Jewish convert. These converts were learned Jewish men who converted to Islam and then proceeded to spend a lifetime Islamicizing Jewish traditions. These "professional Jewish converts" partly were responsible for the Islamic assimilation of reams of Halakha and Aggada.[47]

The best known of these professional converts, Wahb b. Munnabih, was flogged to death in the early 720s.[48] It is strange to hear that he was executed, for he spent a long life as a Muslim loyally transposing Jewish traditions into Islamic guise, in which garb they were rapidly recognized as being Muslim traditions. Wahb and other Jewish converts thereby played an invaluable role of enormous consequence in the self-definition of new Islam. But they seem to have been rather unwelcome in either of their religious communities: otherwise respectable works of Jewish history of this period do not even mention these converts. But Wahb cannot be shrugged out of Jewish history. That the professional Jewish convert posed a certain threat to the Jewish community is obvious on the face of it. Jacob Katz argues persuasively, however, that such apostates do still belong to Jewish history. In discussing two nineteenth-century French Jewish brothers who converted to Catholicism and subsequently became celebrated Catholic thinkers, Katz argues that "their lives were given much attention by Catholics but entirely ignored by Jews—wrongly so, in my opinion, for failures, no less than successes of Jewish society, belong to Jewish history."[49]

Clearly, we possess insufficient data upon which to draw defensible specifications concerning class conflict among the Jews of the eighth century. That being said, it seems clear enough, in general, that classes of Jews were in conflict. We know, at the broadest level, that Jews were heavily represented in the lower classes and that they participated in conflicts, even military rebellions, in which class difference played a part. To the extent that the majority of Jews at this time apparently suffered from the ugly reputation associated with those classes, it is reasonable to conclude that they also suffered the consequence of such a reputation.[50]

Leadership and the Crisis of Mobility

Although I began by bemoaning the absence of sources, we do possess sufficient sources to assemble a roughly accurate picture—a moving picture, for whatever sources survive are marked by an inescapably vivid sense of motion. There were Jewish conversions and Jewish revolutions, inspiring Jewish rises and catastrophic falls. Things were in flux and reflux. The end of antiquity conveys such a sense of motion, in fact, that I would argue that this period of Jewish history constituted an epochal crisis of mobility for the Jewish community.

Thus far I have tried to show that some few Jews at the mid-eighth-century end of antiquity wielded power and influence, while the majority were variously alienated enough to convert, rebel, and even form new sects. These were the two obvious poles of Jewish experience, though neither of these were obviously *the* Jewish experience. There were, after all, non-Jewish courtiers and non-Jewish peasants, so neither the Jewish courtiers nor the Jewish peasants represents the essentially Jewish Zeitgeist, the characteristic Jewish spirit of the age. Who, then, did? Who led the Jewish community? The answer to that question is that Jewish authority—then, as now—was made up of an interlocking and sometimes internally contested network of leadership. I have to this point described the socioeconomic pluralism of the Jewish community because that complexity provides the bases for these rival parties struggling for the center of Judaism.

Under early Islam, the very definition of Jewish authority and legitimacy were being reconstituted. What, in fact, comprised Jewish constitutional authority in the eighth century? Who was the properly constituted leader of the community? Who could legitimately lead? These questions, which we ask today of our own community, were being aggressively pursued then. Then, as now, Jewish authority was being anxiously reassessed.[51]

This critical reassessment was brought to a head at a brief but pivotal moment of Jewish history. I refer now to the twenty-one years of the reign of the second 'Abbasid caliph, Abu Ja'far al-Mansur (754–75).[52] It is precisely then that I would locate the climactic confrontation of powerless Jews with newly empowered Muslims, as they converged around the center of real political power. During the two decades of the reign of al-Mansur, major challenges for supreme Jewish leadership emanated from three distinct Jewish parties: the Gaons, the exilarchs, and the laity. I shall discuss each in turn and try to show how al-Mansur apparently manipulated each of these Jewish challenges.

The shattering peoples' uprising of Abu 'Isa in Isfahan, as described by Maimonides, may be the best example of the politics of the Jewish underclass.[53] Maimonides refers to a unnamed caliph who cleverly halts the dangerously spreading movement. Other sources specify that this caliph was none other than al-Mansur.[54] Here is Maimonides' account of how al-Mansur dealt with this Jewish revolution:

> [Al-Mansur] said to all the Jews of his kingdom: "Let your Rabbis go out to meet this multitude and ascertain whether their pretension is true and he is unmistakably your Expected One. If so, we shall conclude peace with you under any conditions you may prefer. But if it is dissimulation, then I shall wage war against them." When the Rabbis met these Jews … they asked them: "Who instigated you to make this uprising?" Whereupon they replied: "This man here … whom we know to be a leper at night, arose the following morning healthy and sound." They believed that leprosy was one of the characteristics of the Messiah…
>
> Whereupon the Rabbis explained to them that their interpretation was incorrect, and that he lacked even one of the characteristics of the Messiah, let alone all of them. Furthermore the Rabbis advised them: "O fellow Jews, you are still near your native country, and have the possibility of returning there. If you remain in this land, you will not only perish but also undermine the teachings of Moses by misleading people to believe that the Messiah has appeared and has been vanquished…" [The rebels] were persuaded by the Rabbi's arguments. [Al-Mansur] then turned over to them so many thousands of *denars* by way of hospitality in order that they should leave his country.[55]

Then, once the rebels had been bribed to depart, al-Mansur turned around and punished the Jews of his own realm![56] Al-Mansur indeed operated as a textbook Machavellian. In fact, a full analysis of his relations with religions, ethnic groups, and minorities would reveal, it would seem, the genius that leads Dunlop to consider al-Mansur "the virtual founder of the 'Abbasid dynasty."[57] In short, fundamental religiopolitical reorganizations were affected by al-Mansur, including such major parties as the Manicheans and the Imamiyya (Twelver Shi'ites).[58]

He certainly knew how to get Jews to work for him. As noted above, he employed a Jewish tax collector and a Jewish town planner, who plotted his capital city of Baghdad in 762. In addition to his adroit manipulation of both the Jewish peasantry and Jewish administrators, al-Mansur was equally effective in handling the Jewish scholarly elite. He certainly used rabbis for his own ends, according to the above report of Maimonides. But the most telling of al-Mansur's meddling in the affairs of the rabbis took place in his brilliant manipulation of Gaons and exilarchs.

Gaons (Geonim), as the heads of the Babylonian Jewish academies, along with their Palestinian counterparts, constituted the supreme court of the Jewish world.[59] Indeed, their academies constituted, at once, the high court, university, and parliament of all Jewries under their jurisdiction.[60] Vying for power with the Gaons were the exilarchs. The exilarch, Leader of the Exile (Hebrew, *rosh golah*; Aramaic, *resh galuta*; Arabic, *ra's jalut*) were Jewish civil leaders who derived their authority from a claim of direct descent from King David.[61] The exilarchs under the caliphs served as "ministers of Jewish affairs": the Jewish community paid taxes to them, who in turn passed them on to the caliph (after taking a cut). The exilarchs, in short, were wealthy courtiers who literally dwelled at the court in Baghdad. They were also, it seems, cozy with the caliphs: a ninth-century Gaon inveighs against an exilarch "who cannot control Bible or Talmud nor make practical decisions but is powerful through money and closeness to the throne."[62]

It may be instructive that we possess numerous Muslim tales of the Jewish exilarchs but no Muslim tale of the Gaons.[63] This disparity may be due to the fact that exilarchs were creatures of the courts, where they were openly and regularly observed by Muslims, who unavoidably noted their presence. This fact also implies that exilarchs were not "of the people." That the Geonim, on the other hand, must have been socially rather closer to the people than to the caliphal court we know from a variety of evidence. For example, in the late ninth century, a certain Yom Tov Kohen became a Gaon, as a later Gaon put it, *"even though he was a weaver."*[64]

Between them, the Gaons and the exilarchs purported to represent the totality of Jewry—Catholic Israel, as Solomon Schechter translated "Kelal Yisrael"—in other words, all classes of Jews. However, during the mid-eighth-century regime of al-Mansur, the high-class exilarchs and the relatively declassé Gaons were together bitterly engaged in the "age-old drive of the scholarly class for supreme control of the Jewish community."[65] Their rivalry became, at this moment, a pointed struggle of contending legitimacies. The specific situation was the following: Already for several decades of the early eighth century, Gaons and exilarchs had been vigorously deposing each other, attempting to impose their choices on the others and generally jockeying for that "supreme control of the Jewish community." Then the Muslim dynasties changed hands at the century's midpoint, in the year 750. By the time al-Mansur ascended to the throne in 754, the Jewish community would appear to be in almost unparalleled disarray. The last caliph they needed was what they got with al-Mansur: a single-mindedly calculating political genius all too inclined to widen the already gaping visions in the Jewish leadership.

Al-Mansur insinuated himself into these shaky Jewish affairs, and his ploys were to have a sustained impact on Jewish life for centuries to follow. The story has two parts. These were the two times that we know of in which al-Mansur directly intervened in the Gaon-exilarch struggle. Both incidents involved ancient conflicts and resulted in substantial and permanent changes in the Jewish structure of authority. The first of these interventions came with al-Mansur's decision to personally resolve the dispute between two lineages over the exilarchate.[66] Al-Mansur chose "the Persian lineage," which already owed a century of obligations to the Muslim caliphs. It must surely have been due to this debt that the grateful exilarch, probably at al-Mansur's behest, moved the seat of the exilarchs to al-Mansur's new capital of Baghdad.

Meanwhile, as Baron puts its, "even more portentous was the conflict between 'Anan, the founder of the Karaite schism, and his brother Hananiah, which resulted in the permanent schism of the Karaite sect from the main Rabbanites."[67] 'Anan ben David was the son of the exilarch and a disciple of the greatest scholar of the generation. Perhaps because 'Anan seemed too arrogant, the Gaons, who elected the exilarchs, chose 'Anan's younger brother over him. 'Anan refused to recognize the decision and was consequently thrown into the dungeon by al-Mansur. According to his (apocryphal) account, 'Anan then successfully freed himself by convincing al-Mansur that he would not contest the decision but rather would start his own religion. Al-Mansur gladly freed 'Anan, perhaps because the Muslim ruler was content to let the new sectarian leader of the "disgruntled intellectuals of Baghdad" further divide the Jewish community.[68]

Thus a crisis of mobility paradoxically paralyzed the Jewish leadership of the mid-eighth century. This gridlock of multiple leaders, I assert, was consciously encouraged by the deftly manipulative al-Mansur, a conniving master of the technique of divide and conquer. Al-Mansur used Jewish leaders against Jewish leaders to his own exquisite advantage. The canny al-Mansur knew what he was doing; just as he had pitted the Gaons against the rebels of Abu 'Isa, so he pitted the exilarchs against the Gaons. As a result there sprang from the time of his rule the two most significant Jewish sects—the *only* important Jewish sects after the destruction of the Second Temple—the 'Isawiyya and the Karaites. In dealing with al-Mansur, the Jewish community would seem to have played a politics of catastrophe. Or did it? To be sure, the world history of the Jews at this moment made it appear ripe for a rebirth of a Jewish commonwealth: about 740 a Jewish kingdom was established by the Turkish Khazars of Central Asia; in 768 a Jewish princedom was (said to have been) established in southern France; and the Persian Jewish rebel Abu 'Isa tried to do the same in Persia at roughly the same historical moment.[69] Did the Babylonian Gaons and exilarchs, so strategically situated at the center of the Muslim empire, fail to seize that moment?

They did not seize the day, because al-Mansur did that for them. However, while the Khazar and the French and Persian Jewish attempts at political power ultimately did fail, we are not entitled to speak of the Jewish political catastrophe under al-Mansur—for the devious caliph in fact left the Jewish community with a legacy he himself desired: stability. And with the coming of his stability, after the end of a rather chaotic late antiquity, the darkness of our sources finally lifts. With this added information we know that the crisis of mobility of the Jewish leadership in the eighth century, culminating in the reign of al-Mansur, eventually resulted in a dialectically positive effect on the Jewish community. When the dust settled, the rabbinical and Karaite communities had reconciled themselves to being complementary if contending Jewish parties; the smaller Jewish sects were scattered and ineffectual, their power neutralized; the Jewish court bankers, like the Jewish weavers and tanners, went about their business. And the great caliphs residing in Baghdad rested properly comfortably with this quiescent state of affairs. Jewish antiquity was at its end, and its long medieval creativity, stimulated by new stability and new plurality, was underway.

Thus through disorientation new forms of authority were instituted. Through this novel complexity, the Jewish community grew plural without actually breaking apart entirely.[70] Did the caliph al-Mansur in fact do Judaism a favor? Is that how the Jews of his day understood him? Remarkably, we can read contemporaneous Jewish responses to al-Mansur. Of the surviving handful of Jewish texts from this time, we luckily have two or three sources arguably dating from the reign of al-Mansur. These Jewish texts include apocalypses, books of revelation revealed by an angel. The most significant of these apocalypses, *The Secrets of Shimon bar Yochai*, describes the landmark reign of al-Mansur in euphorically Messianic terms. *The Secrets of Shimon bar Yochai* seems to consider its own days as the last days of history; it even describes Muslim rule as a sign of the final redemption of the Jews.[71] The eighth-century end of Jewish antiquity was, then, immediately perceived by some Jews as being momentous: the Jewish community perceived itself to be verging on a new age.

Of course, in the absence of accurately prognosticating prophets, they could not actually know just how much was about to change. The transformative events of the mid-eighth century did reconstitute Jewish leadership. After al-Mansur's meddling, new structures of Jewish authority grew secure enough that the now more broadly based Jewish community could rest relatively more securely on them in that challenging new era. In this new age, however, the old social structures remained, however realigned. Thus a Muslim poet sang,

> Fear of God alone gives standing and nobility—to love the world makes you poor and destitute. As long as he keeps his fear of God unimpaired, it is no shortcoming for the servant of God even to be a weaver or a cupper.[72]

Moses Maimonides (1135–1204), in so many ways, marks the end of the creative symbiosis between Jews and Muslims. To what extent this shift in relations reflects internal breakdowns in Jewish leadership remains to be seen. But Maimonides rejected the preceding Jewish establishment, and with telling phrases: "It is better for you to earn a drachma as wages for the work of a weaver, tailor or carpenter, rather than to be dependent on the license of the Exilarch."[73]

Though few solid conclusions can be established concerning the precise profile of the Jewish community in the eighth century, its occupational and class-differentiated pluralism seems beyond dispute. I leave aside (as beyond my purview) the consolidation of rabbinic leadership in this period. But the evidence points to an "ascendency of Babylonian ritual," as Urbach puts it.[74] In any event, my concern to this point is not to write a fully rounded history of the Jews nor to study rabbinic developments. Rather, I have been concerned to show that the Jewish community, divided against itself geographically, "sectually," and between classes, could hardly have been expected to present a unified front to the Muslims around them. Thus the symbiosis did not take place on the part of some spuriously reified "Jewry," but rather on the part of many different Jews.

The Question of Sectarianism

A certain consensus of scholars prevails concerning Jewish sectarianism in the pre-Gaonic period. On this hypothesis, there had been extant several identifiable Jewish groups in Mishnaic times, but none of these survived the Roman destruction of Jerusalem or of the Temple and its cult. This watershed disaster is therefore considered a certain terminus ad quem for Jewish sectarianism: no Jewish sects have been proven to exist during the long talmudic period, roughly 200–600. The title of a recent article expresses this consensus succinctly: "The Significance of Yavneh: Pharisees, Rabbis, and the End of Jewish Sectarianism."[75]

And yet, to be sure, with the coming of Islam, Jewish sectarianism dramatically reemerged from its long night of (purported) seclusion.[76] The problem is simple yet intractable: What, if any, are the continuities between the Jewish groupings under the early Muslim Church and the Jewish groupings under the early *umma* (Muslim community)? How do we account for similarities such as those between the Qumran Jews and the Karaites?[77]

Primordial Karaism, while still obscure in detail, remains a pointedly salient—if still relatively little explored—promontory on the contours of Jewish historiography. Indeed, even though a "pan-Karaite" theory held sway for some years, we still do not understand even such rudiments as, for example, the social setting of the origins of Karaism.[78] Our map of Jews and Judaism after Muhammad, to be sure, will remain a pastiche of speculations and extrapolations until such questions have been thoroughly reinvestigated. Only after such studies will the light generated by Jewish internal proliferations illumine our dim understanding of Muslim-Jewish relations under the Geonim.

This imperative seems more pressing in the case of extra-Karaite Jewish sectarianism. How, after all, does one sensibly go about streaming these obscure Jewish groups under early Islam? One largely obsolete method has been to follow uncritically the rubrics concocted by heresiographers. These doxographies are Muslim, Christian, and Karaite; rabbis themselves never listed their dissident groups under the umbrella rubric of "Judaism." Still, despite rabbinic silence, no one suggests that organized subgroupings of Jews did not exist; no one, that is, believes that rabbinic abstinence from naming sectarian names betokens anything more than "the silent treatment." In short, given the amplitude of the evidence, there is simply no reason to believe that Jews were monolithically "unified" at the end of antiquity. But, of course, this supposition merely leads to the more serious question: How, then, was this Jewish diversity organized?

Obviously, a historical rethinking of Jewish group organization is required. In order to transcend its confounding of folklore and philology and miscellaneously precious data, I analyzed (elsewhere) the literary-critical questions involved in interpreting Muslim heresiography of the Jews. Such source analysis is propaedeutic to a systematic reassessment of the historicity of such groups.

I should reiterate that the present work is not that study of Jewish history as such—though I did find it necessary to sketch a social description of Jews under early Islam in the preceding section of this chapter. The present work, however, is an effort to comprehend the diversity of interreligious systems of meanings as they were exchanged and transformed in the first centuries of Islamic culture. Since there exists no serious objection to the proposition that extrarabbinic, extra-Karaite groups did exist, and since I present a history of the largest of them, the 'Isawiyya, in the following chapter, my concern at this point lies more generally with the dynamics of Jewish pluralism.

After all, the history of Jews and Judaism in the first centuries after Muhammad will remain dark until the pluralism of the Gaonic period has been thoroughly reinvestigated. In short, a rethinking of Jewish group organization at the end of antiquity is required. It was with this desideratum in mind that I therefore undertook a systematic analysis of Muslim heresiography (that literature devoted to the classification and description of religious groups) of the Jews. In that work, I analyzed the surprisingly rich range of classical Arabic sources concerning Jewish sectarianisrn.[79] Here I present some of the results of that research, supplemented by subsequent discovery and analysis of texts.

The first problem one encounters in this field of research is the paucity of datable Jewish sources. We possess almost no Rabbanite sources that specify the identities of non-Rabbanite Jewish groups. The Geonim were famously disciplined in giving the silent treatment to their opposition and rivals; they did not "name namcs." Thus, aside from a few responsa and indirect statements as well as some allusions in *piyyutim* and other poems, no Jewish sectarians are specified by name by the Geonim. Some rabbis do refer to contemporaneous *minim*; Saadya cryptically criticized a group of "people who are called Jews" (*anashim she-nikraim Yehudim*); and, occasionally, a polemicist referred to *apikorsim* or, in Arabic, Khawarij.[80] These derogations often simply referred to Karaites or to dissident Rabbanites.[81] Rarely can any other firm sectarian identity be teased from these oblique clues.

A second point with regard to Jewish sources is in order. The Cairo Geniza, which one might expect to be as rich a source on this subject as it is on so many other realms of Judaica, seems almost as silent as do the Geonim with reference to sectarians. Exceptions from the Geniza include the few texts (such as the Damascus Document) associated with the Qumran Jews;[82] a fascinating tenth-century polemical text of unknown origin studied only, and incompletely, by Jacob Mann;[83] some miscellaneous hints gleaned from documents;[84] and some works claimed by Shlomo Pines and his students to be Jewish Christians.[85] This apparent paucity of Geniza evidence, however, may be misleading. We have reason to believe that important texts relevant to the study of Jewish sects under Islam exist in the Firkovitch collection in Leningrad.

The following, then, represents an attempt based largely on Muslim sources—as well as on Karaite, Christian, and Rabbanite sources, though only secondarily—to survey the state of the question concerning the smaller Jewish sects under early Islam. I have searched for groups who are called or call themselves Jews; were considered to be or considered themselves to be somehow Jewish; and/or were neither Rabbanite,

Karaite, or Samaritan. Thus, this search particularly concerns Jewish groups possessing a distinctive body of doctrine and practice, whose organization and whose self-definition set them apart from being Rabbanites, Karaites, and Samaritans but not necessarily apart from being "Jews."

Given these general criteria, one could argue repeatedly for the existence of a handful of non-Karaite Jewish sects. On my reading of the sources, however, sufficient evidence exists to assert seriously the historicity of only three of these: the 'Isawiyya, the Jewish Gnostics, and the Jewish Christians.[86] Inasmuch as I will study the 'Isawiyya and the Jewish Gnostics in chapters to follow, I shall now look at one sectarian trajectory, that of the so-called Jewish Christians, and one geographic region, the Persianate orbit. I have chosen these two areas because, in both areas, burgeoning research reveals substantial internal differentiation in these locations. Rather than review acceptably consensual reconstructions, however, I have therefore chosen to be suggestive and to try to evoke the possibilities apparent in these two identifiable areas of Jewish extrarabbinic, extra-Karaite activity.

The So-Called Jewish-Christians

Not all scholars have yet transcended the old dictum of Harnack: "Islam is a transformation on Arab soil of a Jewish religion which itself had been transformed by Gnostic Judeo-Christianity."[87] For example, not so long ago, Danielou was still saying much the same, though without the emphasis on Gnosticism: "[Jewish Christian] survival in the East can be traced from the third and fourth centuries... Some were absorbed by Islam, which is itself in some ways an heir of Judaeo-Christianity." Schoeps, in the final lines of his major study of Jewish Christianity, Hegelianizes the old argument: "And thus we have a paradox of world-historical proportions, the fact that Jewish-Christianity indeed disappeared in the Christian Church, but was preserved in Islam and thereby extended some of its basic ideas even to our own day." Finally, and not accidentally, such theosophically oriented writers as Henry Corbin and N. O. Brown have returned to Harnack's original Gnostic emphasis: "Islam picks up and extends the notion, already present in Jewish (Ebionite) Christianity, of the unity of the prophetic spirit."[88]

These sweeping historiosophic assertions concerning so-called Jewish Christians and their purportedly profound impact on original Islam are to be contrasted with a remarkable series of closely argued, erudite researches. That is, the question of the survival of Jewish Christians after the Muslim conquests has been extensively surveyed and substantially extended in recent years in the brilliant, if ultimately problematic, studies undertaken by the late Israeli historian of philosophy, Shlomo Pines. In the late 1960s, Pines captured headlines in the popular press when he published his initial study of what he interpreted to be an anti-Pauline Jewish Christian tract, preserved verbatim, so he argued, in the theological encyclopedia of the tenth-century Mu'tazilite 'Abd al-Jabbar.[89] While several early Church historians eagerly embraced his reading, Pines's former coworker on this subject, S. M. Stern, forcefully responded that this sensationalist discovery merely represented another surviving apocryphal gospel, a species of text quite well known in Muslim letters.[90]

While the book remains open on the identification of 'Abd al-Jabbar's source, Pines's corollary research has turned up numerous data suggesting the presence of Jewish Christians—of one kind or another—in the first centuries of Islam. From my point of view, it is therefore all the more remarkable to see that Pines, after two decades of strenuous effort devoted to his Jewish Christians, came to rest on the 'Isawiyya as the sole identifiable group of such sectarians.[91] This is yet another reason to write the history of this unusual group; I attempt to do so in the following chapter.

For the moment, I restrict my concern to the sheer presence of Christianizing and Christianized Jews. I conclude, along with some of the aforementioned scholars, that sufficiently manifold evidence demonstrates, within a reasonable margin of doubt, the existence of some such phenomenon. And, with Pines, I have found only one distinguishable and identifiable Jewish Christian group in this period—the 'Isawiyya.

The varieties of evidence for so-called Jewish Christian groups has been all-too-often muddled. These currents of evidence include: preachments of an interconfessional revelation; theological sympathies for various aspects of Christian doctrine; ostensible "remnants" of groups descending from the primordial Christian Church; and miscellaneous syncretists with an uncertain relationship to these broad currents. Similar confusions plague the issue of Judaizing Christians—as opposed to Christianizing Jews, under consideration here—confusions that contaminate much of the scholarship on this benighted subject. For example, the laws and councils of the seventh-century Visigoths Recceswinth and Erwig do reveal that these authorities were exercised by what Parkes calls "Hebrew Christians."[92] A parallel problem apparently existed in Syria. A seventh-century Syriac disputation between a stylite and a Jew, in the opinion of its editor, Hayman, was authored to combat real Judaizing.[93] Marcel Simon even argues that such Judaizing among the Christians of Syria continued from the first through the thirteenth centuries.[94]

Clearly, then, the distinction between Christianizing Jews and Judaizing Christians must be maintained wherever possible. With this caveat in mind, I shall review some of the (considerably varied) literature evincing the presence of Christianizing Jews in the centuries just before and after the rise of Islam.

There would appear to have been some diffuse attraction to Christianity in these years. During the lifetime of Muhammad in the seventh century a "rabbi" was heard to say, "I fear lest the Christ, who came first, whom the Christians worship, was himself he that sent by God."[95] Many Jews were attracted to Christianity in the Byzantine period.[96] Early in the eighth century, under divergent circumstances, a Syrian monk and a Mesopotamian monk independently pronounced themselves to be Jewish prophets. Both garnered Jewish followers.[97]

Even as the institutionalization of Islam progressed, some Christianizing of Jews seems to have continued. In the year 796, the Nestorian patriarch of Elam, Timotheos, wrote his now-famous letter. The patriarch stated that, ten years earlier, he had learned from trustworthy Jews, who had just recently been instructed as converts to Christianity, "that some old Hebrew manuscripts had been discovered in a cave in Jericho." He has Jewish scholars confirm that these documents included "texts of our New Testament which are not even mentioned in the Old Testament, neither in our Christian texts or in their Jewish text."[98]

This discovery, so closely parallel in circumstance to the Dead Sea Scrolls find, seems to have uncovered texts belonging to that very same ancient sect dwelling at Qumran.[99] A Jewish sect with curious, quasi-Jewish demiurgic beliefs, the Maghariyya, seem to have received this apellation, "cave people," by virtue of their utilization of these speleologically retrieved texts.[100] Moreover, it is now widely recognized that five apocryphal psalms, three of which were rediscovered in 1948 at Qumran as well, were translated into Syriac subsequent to the eighth-century discovery of them.[101] In other words: Christians, Jews, Jewish converts to Christianity, and perhaps a Christianized Jewish sect all apparently read and translated these eight-hundred-year-old sectarian documents subsequent to their rediscovery in the eighth century.

Other Christianized Jews seem to have been in the environs. Ibn al-Nadim, a reporter celebrated for his reliability, describes several such Mesopotamian groups, including the so-called Ashuriyyin: "In some things they agree with the Jews and about other things they disagree with them. They seem to be a sect of Jesus.'" In all, Ibn al-Nadim cites five groups that bear both explicitly Jewish and explicitly Christian features.[102]

Perhaps the best known of these Christianizing Jews, aside from the 'Isawiyya, are the eighth-century Athiganoi, Byzantine Samaritan Gnostics. This group, on the argument of Crone and Jeffrey, certainly appears to be "fully" Jewish Christian: "The Athinganoi ... accepted Christ as a mere man, replaced circumcision by baptism or had neither one nor the other, observed the Sabbath, at least when with Jews, and also Levitical purity and Mosaic law in general: [they also had] Jewish preceptors."[103]

A rivulet of Christianizing Jews also trickled through early Karaism. Qirqisani cites several Karaites with varying degrees of sympathy for Jesus as prophet.[104] Perhaps the most striking of these is one Meswi al-'Ukbari. Baron even suggests that Meswi "not only professed Christianity—[a Karaite opponent] chides him by comparing him with Matthew, John, Paul and Luke—but also 'served three deities simultaneously in his old age,' that is, he simultaneously professed belief in the God of Israel, Jesus, and Muhammad."[105]

It has not been my intention to review comprehensively the question of so-called Jewish Christians. Rather, I have sketched out the variety of some fairly clear evidence, leaving aside the highly complex literary analyses underway in the Pines circle. In this "darkest of all periods in post-Biblical Jewish history," it is instructive, even striking, to see such vividly vague patterns emerging. Just what were the implications of such attractively live options? And how were they activated—put into play—within the limits of Jewish life? The following chapters comprise exploratory investigations of these concerns.

The Question of the East: Persia and Beyond

It may not be accidental that the 'Isawiyya developed as a nonrabbinic force east of Babylonia. The Persian and eastern geographic sphere, even more than the Arabian Peninsula of the seventh century, constituted a veritable crucible of Jewish heterodoxy in the early years of Islam. This vast area sheltered, in addition to Abu 'Isa of Isfahan, such prominent figures of nonrabbinic Judaism such as Hiwi of Balkh and Benjamin of Nehawend. Evidence for Jewish life in this area is sparse, but it is worth reviewing, for this was a notorious arena of Jewish pluralism.

The portrait of the miscellaneously nonrabbinical character of the Jewry of the eastern provinces of early Islamicate Persia is only just now being drawn.[106] Certainly, a high percentage of the mixed reports that survive suggest this extrarabbinic profile. Already in the eighth century, for example, a Jew of Khurasan, Marwan ibn Abi Hafsa, can be found serving the 'Abbasid court as a poet.[107] In distant Bukhara, this extrarabbinism resulted in a certain marranism.[108] According to the tenth-century Karaite Salmon b. Yeruhim, "[when the Jews of Samraqand] say 'God is One' (*allah Wahid*) [people who hear this] testify that by [saying] this they have become Muslims."[109]

The town of Hamadan serves as an instructive locus for such phenomena. The great disturbances initiated by Abu 'Isa of Isfahan in the eighth century were to extend, in the following two centuries, to Rayy, Qumm, Arrajan, and Hamadan.[110] In 1163, R. Benjamin of Tudela reports that there were four Jewish communities living between Susa and Hamadan and that they joined the side of the Isma'ilis in battle.[111] Heterodox teachings also emanated from Hamadan. The obscure Joseph of Hamadan was a purveyor of early proto-Kabbalistic teachings; his works were to influence the earliest European Kabbalists.[112]

Some relation between the Jews of Persia and various Gnostic communities is suggested by the sources. Interreligious relationships are not uncharacteristic of eastern Islamicate provinces in general. As Daniel puts it, the "profusion of religions in one area necessitated a measure of religious tolerance and contributed to much syncretism among the different groups. Thus Central Asia had a traditional role as a refuge for religious non-conformists of all persuasions."[113]

We know of at least one specific instance of this common Gnosticizing milieu, that of the Mazdakiyya. It remains unclear whether Mazdak's initial revolt garnered Jewish support, as some of the (contradictory) evidence suggests.[114] It does seem, at least, rather clearer that Mazdak's teachings on the cosmogonic potency of the alphabet are somehow related to similar Isma'ili and Jewish teachings. The *raza rabba*, "great mystery," which was apparently Mazdak's central mystery, was also a key term in what Scholem posits as being the urtext of *Sefer ha-Bahir*. [115]

Moreover, Khurasan, in Central Asia, was the home of extensive Gnosticizing revolutions in the eighth and ninth centuries, including that of Ishaq Turk, who Daniel suggests may have been a Jew.[116] Khurasan still housed Marcionists and Manicheans in the tenth and eleventh centuries.[117] Some of the earliest documentary—

as opposed to literary—evidence suggests that the Jews of early Islamicate Persia inhabited communities contiguous with those of the Manicheans. The earliest surviving inscriptions in the Persian language are in a dialect of Judeo-Persian. These were discovered in the great Central Asian silk-route entrepôts of Tang-i-Azao and Dandan Uiliq, crossroads communities that also have yielded substantial evidence of Manichean habitation from the same period.[118] And some fascinating, if spotty, literary evidence linking Jews and "Manicheans" remains as well. Theodore bar-Khonai, eighth-century Nestorian bishop of Central Asian Kashgar, reports on a number of quasi-Jewish, quasi-Manichean groups, whose teachings he apparently knew firsthand.[119] This evidence points to the existence of organized Jewish Gnostic sects.[120]

Other indications also point toward the far eastern provinces as liminally Jewish. Natan ha-Bavli reports that R. Judah b. Mar Samuel (906–18) persuaded the Khurasani Jews to conform to Babylonian Halakha, which would imply their nonconformity through the ninth century.[121] This implication is corroborated by other sources. The best known of these concerns the infamous ninth-century "heretic" Hiwi al-Balkhi.[122] Hiwi elicits numerous unmistakable parallels with the contemporaneous Gnosticizing critiques of the Bible. Abu Hatim al-Razi, in refuting the Bible critique of Muhammad Zakariyya al-Razi—who may have been Hiwi's teacher and whose Bible critique asks many of the same questions—explicitly reports that his opponent sought the aid of Manichean anti-Jewish teachings.[123] Ninth-century Central Asian Jews could thus be close enough to some kind of "Manichean"-style thought virtually to the point of apostasy.

Central Asian Jews, then, possessed some access, from their vantage point at the center of Eurasia, to heterodoxies. This very geographic centrality, indeed, may itself have played a role in such syncretizings. The convergence of long-distance trade and religious liminality evident, for example, in the Persian Karaite Tustari family, was not accidental but rather seems to have been in fact characteristic of Central Asian socioreligious patterns.

What were these patterns? Karaism may provide a useful example. Karaism itself, the most profoundly far-reaching heterodoxy of the Jews under early Islam, founded several of its strongest early communities in Persia.[124] While Friedlaender opposed the idea, Baron, Nemoy, and, most recently, Shaked, have listed reasonable parallels between the origins of Shi'ism and the origins of Karaism.[125] But Persia, it appears, was the home of the development of these two preeminent groups, rather than of their origins. The Persian communities, situated at the easternmost edges of Islamicate civilization, far from cultural and political centers, were ill suited to the creativity required to initiate sects of sustained conception, especially those possessing seriously threatening power. These communities however, were well suited to serve as refuges far from the Mesopotamian centers of authority. Indeed, recent researches tend to converge on Mesopotamia as the source of earliest Karaism and of earliest Shi'ism, whence these Jewish and Muslim groups shifted some of their subsequent bases of power to the east.[126]

The free development of ideas operated in the open markets of Central Asia. The pre-eleventh-century Persian Karaites not only experienced considerable religious variation but some noticeable economic success as well. Persian Karaite merchants are well documented in the Cairo Geniza.[127] Indeed, the earliest known documents in the Judeo-Persian dialect are Karaite. These two characteristics could merge in a family of Persian Karaites such as the Tustaris. Both a business empire and (to a certain extent) a religious subgroup, the Tustaris are both well known from literary sources and from Geniza sources.[128] That some of them apparently acknowledged Muhammad as prophet may be only another indication of the extent to which a weakening of "Jewish" self-consciousness could dovetail with economic expedience.

In the hypothesis of Pritsak, Central Asian Jews were noted for a distinctive social organization typified by "the harmonious co-existence of religious, commercial and scholarly interests... The long-distance traders, residing in the oases and towns, who knew several languages and had a keen interest in philosophical matters ... should be credited with the alleged religious tolerance of the nomads."[129] The Jews of Persia and Central Asia, in this hypothesis, may have been among the most amenable of all the early Islamicate Jewish communities to a certain syncretism because they represented a larger Central Asia religioeconomic complex. Pritsak extends this hypothesis to make the Radhaniyya responsible for the Judaization of the Khazar kingdom.[130] This amalgamating was not infrequently associated with a certain degree of intermediate Gnosticization. This milieu, in particular, was the same cultural sphere out of which the Central Asian school of Isma'ilism also emerged, under analogous circumstances.

The Jewish communities from Fars to the Central Persian provinces of Khuzistan and Mazanderan, then, were apparently not firmly under the control of the Babylonian Geonim. They lived in a milieu of "traditional syncretism," whose comminglings were not only Jewish. Fischel notes that at least three instances under early Islam of Muslim Hebraism where quotations "presuppose direct contact and cooperation with Jewish scholars in Khorasan."[131] Major heterodoxies of both Judaism and Islam emerge from these peripheries. The free movement of goods and ideas along the frontier may not have been conducive to brilliant conception but provided fructifying soil for basic social and intellectual cross-fertilization.

From Periphery to Center

The question of Jewish pluralism at the end of antiquity requires a multiple approach if it is to be fully comprehended. In the foregoing, I have only sampled the possibilities. I have looked at Jewish leaderships, professions, sects, and cultural geography. What conclusions can be drawn from such data? Where is the center of Jewish life in the first centuries of Islam? What is normative, and what is peripheral?

No responsible answer can be given to this question until much more work is done. I have not, for example, included Jewish literature as such within my purview. The very dating of Jewish texts in this period remains to be systematically reassessed.[132]

Social history from Gaonic halakhic sources, likewise, has barely begun.[133] And more serious analyses of midrashim and piyyutim would no doubt provide added insights.[134] I have not even attempted such work here. Instead, and by way of counterpoint, I have tried to show that other, equally underexplored approaches—those of the historian of religions—also wait to be exploited.

That being said, the common problem that remains is the problem of symbiosis. If Judaism under early Islam is still an underdefined entity, how is it then possible to isolate precisely what was symbiotic with Muslim civilization? Would it perhaps be helpful to posit *Judaisms* in this regard? Or would this be a merely semantic, and not substantive, innovation in our understanding of "the darkest period in all of post-Biblical Jewish history"?

Conventional historiography depicts this darkness as lifting with the "ascension" of Saadya Gaon (892–942) from Egypt to Babylonia. Saadya Gaon, "the first in all fields," in the (still-accepted) characterization of Ibn Ezra, spurs a rabbinic counterattack that successfully consolidates rabbinic leadership under the Babylonian Geonim. And yet it remains to be demonstrated—and not merely asserted—that the Geonim before Saadya represented either a majority Judaism or an essential Judaism. I do not know that they did not. But they themselves simply do not provide us with the evidence we need to answer this question, for their surviving works are, naturally, normative, being intended to provide primarily halakhic norms for their community. And the historian of religions takes it as self-evident that normative texts in themselves do not provide sufficient foundation for any fully rounded history.

In short, rabbinic literature—leaving aside its radical paucities and discontinuities in this period—is incapable of resolving single-handedly the problem of symbiosis. Rabbinic literature constitutes part but obviously not all of the multiplex picture necessary for reimagining the fullness of this interreligious civilization, for the historical study of religions should follow Gregory Bateson's Two Laws of Discovery— keep data moving through the system, and the always-the-multiple approach. Only by the utilization of all available sources, from whatever religion, will the historical study of religions eventually achieve adequate "thick description." Such description, given the paucity of sources for the present study, obviously is out of the question. But the consistent utilization of Muslim sources at least brings us closer to this ideal.

The literature of the rabbis is rich indeed, but it represents only itself. The rabbis are simply not explicit about extrarabbinic Jewish diversity: we have no rabbinic heresiography of the Muslims. But Muslim scholars are thus explicit, and we do possess a ramified Muslim heresiography of the Jews. Nor is this all. Indeed, the utilization of the panorama of Muslim sources for the writing of Jewish history remains to be maximized. Here, as in many other aspects of Judeo-Arabica, the example of other areas of Jewish studies should be emulated. The obvious model for the student of the Jews under the formative *umma* is that of the Jews under the early Church. After all, it is universally recognized that any full history of the Jews in late antiquity must take account of Greek and Latin, Syriac and Persian, sources.

My work here is therefore entirely propaedeutic. We cannot yet write a satisfactory history of the Jews under early Islam. I am not attempting to do so here. Rather, the following chapters tentatively reinterpret certain aspects of civilizational symbiosis from the point of view of the history of religions. The Judaist would write one history of this period; the Islamicist would write another. As a historian of religions, I have written a third kind of study. My study is not incidentally but rather essentially concerned with symbiosis, for the history of religions is perhaps best situated to comprehend the self-understandings of religions as they operate in synergy with one another.

Notes

1. Salo W. Baron, *Social and Religious History*, 18 vols. (New York and Philadelphia, 1958–), 6:312. For the beginnings of a social and economic history of the Jews in this period and later, see Eliyahu Ashtor, "Prolegomena to the Medieval History of Oriental Jewry," *Jewish Quarterly Review* 50 (1959), 55–68, 145–66. With regard to Palestine, we also now possess an overview in English: Moshe Gil's *History of Palestine*, translated by Ethel Broido (Cambridge: Cambridge University Press, 1992).

2. Shlomo Dov Goitein, *Jews and Arabs: Their Contacts Through the Ages*, 3rd ed. (New York: Schocken Books, 1974), 95.

3. Avraham Grossman, "Aliyah in the Seventh and Eighth Centuries," *Jerusalem Cathedra* 3 (1983): 176–87.

4. Personal correspondence, October 22, 1981. Very recently, Nemoy has reiterated that most of Karaite history "(including, alas, the initial—medieval and most productive—period of it) is wrapped in an almost total darkness" (L. Nemoy, "Stroumsa's Edition of al-Muqammis's '*Ishrun Maqalah*," *Jewish Quarterly Review* 82 [1991], 233).

5. Henri Pirenne, *Mohammed and Charlemagne* (New York: Barnes and Noble, 1931.), 285; Peter Brown, *World of Late Antiquity* (London: Norton, 1981), 200. I have explored some of the implications of this turning point in my article "The Moving Finger Writes: Mughira ibn Sa'id's Islamic Gnosis and the Myths of its Rejection," *History of Religions* 25 (1985), 1–29.

6. Jane S. Gerber, "Judaism in the Middle East and North Africa Since 1992," *Encyclopedia of Religion*, vol. 8: 158.

7. For a still useful overview of Jewish occupations in the Middle Ages, see Israel Abrahams, *Jewish Life in the Middle Ages* (New York: Macmillan, 1973 [1896]), 211–51.

8. See Charles Verlinden, "Les Radaniya et Verdun: A Propos de la traité des esclaves vers l'espagne musulmane au IVe et Xe siecles," in *Estudios en Homenaje a Don Claudio Sánchez Albornoz en Sus 90 Anos* (Buenos Aires: Instituto de Historia de España, 1983), 2:105–32, with reference to the previous literature.

9. Shlomo Dov Goitein, *Mediterranean Society: The Jewish Communities of the Arab World as Portrayed in the Cairo Genizah*, 5 vols. (Berkeley and Los Angeles: University of California Press, 1967–1988), 1:242–45. This practice developed fully only in subsequent centuries, however.

10. Al-Waqidi, *Kitab al-Maghazi* 1:136, cited in Ignaz Goldziher, "Mélanges Judeo-Arabes," *Revue des études juives* 43 (1901), 273.

11. Goldziher, "Mélanges Judeo-Arabes," 273.

12. Norman Stillman, *Jews of Arab Lands* (Philadelphia: Jewish Publication Society of America, 1979), 3–22.

13. In the year 627, according to the *Chronographia* of Theophanes. See Baron, *Social and Religious History* 3:235 n. 16.

14. Gordon D. Newby, *A History of the Jews of Arabia* (Columbia, SC: University of South Carolina Press, 1988), 49–78.

15. Dietrich, "al-Hadjdjaj b. Yusuf," *Encyclopedia of Islam*, 2nd ed., 3:41, citing Ibn al-Athir; Walter J. Fischel, *The Jews in the Economic and Political Life of Medieval Islam* (London: The Royal Asiatic Society, 1937), xvii n. 9; Gil, *History of Palestine*, 110 n. 34.

16. I provide a number of additional examples of Jewish scientists and astrologers in "*Sefer Yesira* and Early Islam: A Reappraisal," *Journal of Jewish Thought and Philosophy* 3 (1993), 1–30.

17. David Pingree, "Masha'alah: Some Sassanian and Syriac Sources," in *Essays on Islamic Philosophy and Science*, ed. G. F. Hourani (Albany, NY: State University of New York Press, 1975), 5–13; Pingree and E. S. Kennedy, trans., *The Astrological History of Masha'allah* (Cambridge: Harvard University Press, 1971); Majid Fakhry, *A History of Islamic Philosophy*, 2nd ed. (New York: Columbia University Press, 1983), 8–9.

18. S. D. Goitein, "The Rise of the Near Eastern Bourgeoisie in Early Islamic Times," *Journal of World History* 32 (1956–57), 583–604.

19. Ibid., 603; Michel Abitol, "Juifs Maghrébins et commerce Transsaharien du VIIe au XVe siècle," *Revue française d'histoire d'outre-mer* 66 (1979), 561–77.

20. Goitein, *Mediterranean Society*, vol. 2.

21. See the subtle and useful observations on this question made by J. Sadan, "Some Literary Problems Concerning Judaism and Jewry in Medieval Arabic Sources," in *Studies in Honour of David Ayalon* (Jerusalem and Leiden: Brill, 1986), 356. See more generally Raphael Mahler, *Karaimer* (New York, n.p., 1947).

22. Robert Brunschvig, "Métiers vils en Islam," *Studia Islamica* 16 (1962), 41–60.

23. As Adam Mez put it, "the lowest class of tax-payers were the Jewish money-changers, tanners, shoe-makers and particularly dyers" (*Renaissance of Islam* [Patna: Jubilee, 1937], 39, with reference to various sources).

24. Israel Friedlaender, "The Heterodoxies of the Shi'ites in the Presentation of Ibn Hazm," *Journal of the American Oriental Society* 29 (1908), 96.

25. Israel Friedlaender, "Jewish-Arabic Studies," *Jewish Quarterly Review*, n.s., 3 (1912–1913), 282 n. 346.

26. Friedlaender, "Heterodoxies," 96, citing Tosefta Eduyot 1:2.

27. Friedlaender, "Jewish-Arabic Studies," 282 n. 346, provides numerous Jewish, Muslim, and Christian sources. In his section "Social Position" (281–85), he surveys the literature on this question.

28. Jahiz, in an often-cited essay translated by Stillman, in *Jews of Arab Lands*, 170; Fischel, *Jews in the Economic and Political Life*, 7, citing Muqaddasi; Georges Vajda, "Un traité de polemique christiano-Arabe contre les Juifs attribué a Abraham de Tibériade," *Bulletin de l'Institut de recherches et d'histoire des texts* 15 (1969), 147; my translation from the French of Vajda; Fischel, *Jews in the Economic and Political Age*, 106, citing Bar Hebraeus.

29. Bernadette Brooten, *Women Leaders in the Ancient Synagogue* (Chico, CA: Scholars Press, 1982), 146.

30. Norman Cohn, *The Pursuit of the Millennium*, 2nd ed, revised and expanded (New York: Harper, 1970), 58–60, 101–2. On the twelfth-century edicts against certain heretics known as "Piphili ... those vilest of people, the weavers," see Jeffrey B. Russell, *Dissent and Reform in the Early Middle Ages* (Berkeley and Los Angeles: University of California Press, 1965), 218–21. One might note that the cultural abhorrence of weavers can be found even in India. The great Sakhi poet Kabir is despised for his origins in the Julaha weaving class. See Charlotte Vaudeville, *Kabir* (Oxford: Clarendon, 1971), 1:83.

31. Friedlaender, "Heterodoxies," 64.

32. They are denigrated variously as *safala* ("lowlife": see Abu 'Amr al-Kashshi, *Rijal al-Kashshi* [Karbala: n.p., 1962], 250); *'amma* ("common folk": Kashshi, *Rijal*, 249); *ghauga'* ("riffraff": see Heinz Halm, "Das 'Buch des Schatten': Die Mufaddal-Tradition der Gulat und die Ursprünge des Nusairiestums," *Der Islam* 58 [1981], 17). For a list of the professions of the *ghulat*, see Halm, "Schatten," 85. See especially Friedlaender, "Jewish-Arabic Studies," 3: 281–85.

33. Baron, *Social and Religious History* 5:1–84.

34. See chapter 2 below.

35. Qirqisani, *Jewish Sects and Christianity*, trans. Wilfrid Lockwood (Frankfurt am Main: n.p., 1984), 103.

36. Goitein, *Jews and Arabs*, 169.

37. Maimonides, *Iggeret Teiman*, trans. Boaz Cohen, in *A Maimondes Reader*, ed. Isadore Twersky (New York: Schocken Books, 1972), 458–59.

38. Goitein, *Jews and Arabs*, 169.

39. A. H. Siddiqi, ed., *Sahih Muslim* (Lahore, n.p., 1975), 4:15–25. The bad reputation of Isfahani Jews was reflected in their association with "low" occupations. See for example Abu Nu'aim, who says that the Jews of Isfahan were workers in cupping, tanning, fulling, and butchering (Mez, *Renaissance of Islam*, 39 n. 8).

40. Bar Hebraeus, cited in Friedlaender, "Jewish-Arabic Studies," 3:282 n. 398.

41. Louis Massignon, *The Passion of Al-Hallaj*, trans. Herbert Mason (Princeton: Princeton University Press, 1982), 1:267.

42. J. B. Segal, "Jews of North Mesopotamia before the Rise of Islam," *Eres Israel* 17 (1964), 55.

43. Habib Zayyat, "The Jews in the 'Abbasid Caliphate" (in Arabic), *Al-Machriq* 35 (1937): 37–40, 172–73, reproducing the text of 'Abd al-Basit al-Hanafi's *Al-Rauda al-Basam*, 55.

44. Perhaps "lowest" of all were the Jewish criminals. Jewish travelers (Eldad ha-Dani and Benjamin of Tudela) in the Middle Ages noted the presence of Jewish robbers. See, for example, Louis Ginzberg, *An Unknown Jewish Sect* (New York: Jewish Theological Seminary of America, 1976), 387 n. 140. For a portrayal of later Jewish weavers, see S. D. Goitein, "Portrait of a Yemenite Weaver's Village," *Journal of Jewish Studies* 16 (1955), 3–26.

45. Zayyat, "Jews in the 'Abbasid Caliphate," 155–57. This report comes from *The History of the Rulers of Damascus and the Biography of Ibrahim ibn al-Mahdi* and dates to the reign of al-Rashid (786–809). See also Joel L. Kraemer, "Apostates, Rebels and Brigands," *Israel Oriental Society* 99 (1979), 34–74.

46. Goitein, "Jewish Society and Institutions under Islam," in *Jewish Society Through the Ages*, ed. H. Ben-Sasoon and S. Ettinger (New York: Schocken Books, 1975), 175.

47. I discuss some of these figures, as well as the general phenomenon of Isra'iliyyat, more fully in chapter 6 below, with special reference to 'Abdallah ibn Salam.

48. Nizar Faruqi, *Early Muslim Historiography* (New Delhi: Idarah-i Adabiyat-i Dell i, 1979), 92–110; Josef Horowitz, "The Earliest Biographies of the Prophet and their Authors," *Islamic Culture* 1 (1927), 530–55; Nadia Abbott, "Wahb b. Munabbih: A Review Article," *Journal of Near Eastern Studies* 36 (1977), 103–12.

49. Jacob Katz, "Religion as a Uniting and Dividing Force in Modern Jewish History," in *The Role of Religion in Modern Jewish History*, ed. Jacob Katz (Cambridge, MA: Association for Jewish Studies, 1975), 6. In this regard, it is striking that Reuben Ahroni does not discuss Wahb or 'Abdallah ibn Saba' in his *Yemenite Jewry* (Bloomington, IN: Indiana University Press, 1987).

50. On accusations against one's enemies as belonging to the *'amma*, see Michael Cook and Patricia Crone, *Hagarism: The Making of the Muslim World* (Cambridge: Cambridge University Press, 1980), 230 n. 24. For the relationship of this label to the rebellions in the early period, see Jan Olav Blichfeldt, "*Khassa* and *'amma*: On Slogans, Concepts and Social Settings in Islamic History," *Oriental Suecana* 38–39 (1989–1990), 14–20.

51. For the best overview of the political history of Jewry in this age, see Baron, *Social and Religious History*, 5:3–82.

52. Theodore Noldeke's essay, "Caliph Mansur," in his *Sketches from Eastern History* (London: A and C Black, 1892), is still a valuable introduction.

53. There was a rebellion against al-Mansur in Isfahan, in the year 755–56. In 767, Mansur thought of making Isfahan his capital, though it was mere rubble at the time (E. G. Browne, "Account of a Rare Manuscript History of Isfahan," *Journal of the Royal Asiatic Society* [1901], 419). See also Walter J. Fischel, "Yahudiyya: On the Beginnings of Jewish Settlement in Persia" (in Hebrew), *Tarbis* 6 (1935), 523–26.

54. That is the dating of Shahrastani, which I follow.

55. Maimonides, *Iggeret Teiman*, 458–59.

56. Ibid. Al-Mansur was hereby reinforcing the "counterrevolution," which he had already initiated against other insurgents. See Elton J. Daniel, *The Political and Social History of Khurasan under Abbasid Rule, 747–820* (Minneapolis: Bibliotheca Islamica, 1979), 157, on the "striking revival of Caliphal power"; and the profile of his power relations in Marshall G. S. Hodgson, *Venture of Islam* (Chicago: University of Chicago Press, 1974), 1:284–89.

57. D. M. Dunlop, *Arab Civilization to 1500* (New York: Praeger, 1971), 257.

58. On an anti-*dhimmi* decree generally, see the older account concerning al-Mansur in T. W. Arnold, *Preaching of Islam: A History of the Propagation of the Muslim Faith* (New York: C. Scribner's Sons, 1913), 75. On the Manicheans, see the account of the Miqlasiyya in Ibn al-Nadim, *Fihrist of Ibn al-Nadim* 2:793–94. And on the Imamis, see al-Mansur's relations with Ja'far al-Sadiq. The Ithna 'Ashariyya believe that Mansur killed Ja'far: see D. M. Donaldson, *The Shi'ite Religion: A History of Islam in Persia and Irak* (London: Luzac, 1933; reprint New York, n.d.), 131–32.

59. Gerson Cohen impressively surveyed the historiography in "Reconstruction of Gaonic History," in *Texts and Studies in Jewish History and Literature*, vol. 1, ed. Jacob Mann (New York: Ktav, 1972 [1931]). See also Israel Friedlaender, "The Jews of Arabia and the Gaonate," *Jewish Quarterly Review*, o.s., 19 (1907), 249–52.

60. S. D. Goitein repeats this characterization in various places, for example, in "Minority Self-Rule and Government Control in Islam," *Studia Islamica* 31 (1970), 114.

61. The sources on the exilarchate in this period have now been conveniently and thoroughly collected by Avraham Grossman, *The Babyloniun Exilarchate in the Gaonic Period* (in Hebrew) (Jerusalem: n.p., 1984).

62. Daniel Jeremy Silver, *Maimonidean Criticism and the Maimonidean Controversy, 1180–1240* (Leiden: Brill, 1965), 61.

63. See chap. 3 below for numerous Shiʿi tales of the rosh golah. The role and function of the Gaon seem to have been almost unknown to Muslim letters.

64. Baron, *Social and Religious History*, 5:74–75, citing Sherira Gaon.

65. Baron, *Social and Religious History*, 5:13. It can hardly be a coincidence that the first attempt to bring Palestinian Jewry under Babylonian sway was under Yehudai Gaon, ca. 760.

66. Ibid.

67. Ibid., 221.

68. This tale is reviewed by Nemoy in "'Anan ben David": A Re-appraisal of the Historical Data," in *Karaite Studies*, ed. Philip Birnbaum (New York: Hermon Press, 1971), 309–18. See also Martin Cohen, "'Anan ben David and Karaite Origins," *Jewish Quarterly Review* 68 (1977), 129–45, 224–34; the most important recent work on ʿAnan has been done by Haggai Ben-Shammai. See his "Between Ananites and Karaites: Observations on Early Medieval Jewish Sectarianism," *Studies in Muslim-Jewish Relations* 1 (1993), 19–31.

69. On the Judaization of the Khazars see D. M. Dunlop, *The History of the Jewish Khazars* (Princeton: Princeton University Press, 1983; reprinted New York: Schocken Books, 1967); P. B. Golden, *Khazar Studies: An Historical-Philological Inquiry in the Origins of the Khazars* (Budapest: Akadémiai Kiadó, 1980); Norman Golb and O. Pritsak, *Khazar Hebrew Documents of the Tenth Century* (Ithaca: Cornell University Press, 1982). On the purported "Jewish princedom" in southern France see Arthur J. Zuckerman, *A Jewish Princedom in Feudal France, 768–900* (New York: Columbia University Press, 1972), to be used with caution; and for the rebellion of Abu ʿIsa see below, chapter 2, on the history of the ʿIsawiyya.

70. Credit certainly must be given to the rabbinic leadership on this score, for example, their generous embrace of the former followers of the pseudo-prophet Serene. See the conciliatory responsum of Gaon Natronai Gaon, in Franz Kobler, trans., *Letters of Jews Through the Ages* (New York: East and West Library, 1952), 1:69–70.

71. As translated and annotated in Bernard Lewis, "Apocalyptic Vision of Islamic History," *Bulletin of the School of Oriental and African Studies* 13 (1950), 305–38. Remarkably, Muslim sources would seem to corroborate this great hope that some placed in al-Mansur. A sect known as the Rawendiyya, in the Persian province of Khorasan (ca. 758) believed that al-Mansur was the Mahdi. See Freidlaender, "Jewish-Arabic Studies," 2:503–7.

72. Abu 'l-Atahiya, citing from the *Kitab al-Aghani*, in Gustave E. Von Grunebaum, *Medieval Islam* (Chicago: University of Chicago Press, 1969), 124.

73. Letter to Joseph ibn ʿAqnin, cited in Kobler, *Letters of Jews through the Ages* 1:207.

74. Ephraim Urbach, "Center and Periphery in Jewish Historic Consciousness: Contemporary Implications," in *World Civilization and the Present State of Jewry*, ed. Moshe Davis (New York, 1977), 233–37. Yehudai Gaon, ca. 760, attempted this

regularization under al-Mansur. See Paul Kahle, *The Cairo Geniza*, 2nd ed. (Oxford: Blackwell, 1959), 40.

75. Shaye Cohen, "The Significance of Yavneh: Pharisees, Rabbis and the End of Jewish Secterianism," *Hebrew Union College Annual* 55 (1984), 27–53.

76. A history of the smaller Jewish sects under Islam remains a desideratum. Aside from the Samaritans and Karaites, who have received continuous scholarly attention over the last two hundred years, the smaller sects have not yet been studied using the full battery of available historical sources.

    The best history of the smaller sects under Islam is in S. Baron, "Messianism and Sectarian Trends," in *Social and Religion History of the Jews* 5:138–209. Somewhat out of date, but still extremely useful, is Friedlaender's "Jewish-Arabic Studies." Perhaps the fullest collections of texts and general discussions continue to be written in Hebrew, as they have been since Simhah Pinsker's *Likkute Kadmoniot* of 1860. Of more recent Hebrew-language collections, two are essential: A. Aeshcoly, *Messianic Movements in Israel* (Jerusalem, 1956), 117–32; B. Z. Dinur, *Judaism in the Israel* (Tel Aviv and Jerusalem, 1958–72), 207–34, and the notes thereon, 268–75.

    Two other points concerning the history of the Jewish sects under Islam should be made at this point. First, it is instructive to note that next to no direct information concerning medieval non-Karaite Jewish sectarianism came out of the otherwise rich Cairo Geniza. One may hope that the Firkovitch collection of Leningrad may well contain much information on this subject, since it contains numerous Karaite works. The second point, which helps us understand the first, is that medieval Jews, like medieval Muslims, were largely unconcerned with postbiblical Jewish history. The Jewish disregard for its own historiography is well reported by Yosef Hayyim Yerushalmi in *Zakhor* (Seattle: University of Washington Press, 1982). Likewise, there exists a vast Muslim literature pertaining to figures and events of the Banu Isra'il, but very little historical (or legendary) discussion of postbiblical Jews and Judaism.

77. Solomon Zeitlin led the charge of an Anglo-American revisionist argument, which asserted that the scrolls found at Qumran were to be assigned to the Karaites (*Zadokite Fragments*).

    Golb explored this argument for a time ("Literary and Doctrinal Aspects of the Damascus Covenant in the Light of Karaite Literature," *Jewish Quarterly Review* 48 [1956], 354–74; "The Dietary Laws of the Damascus Covenant in Relation to Those of the Karaites," *Journal of Jewish Studies* 7 [1957], 51–69; "The Qumran Covenanters and the Later Jewish Sects," *Journal of Religion* 41 [1961], 38–50). Sidney Hoenig also worked this vein in "Qumran Rules of Interpretation," *Revue de Qumrans* 6 (1969), 559–67 and "Pre-Karaism and the Sectarian (Qumran) Scrolls," in *Jubilee Volume in Honor of Dr. Joshua Finkel* (New York, 1974), 71–93.

    The fullest statement of this position is articulated impressively by Naphtali Wieder, *The Judean Scrolls and Karaism* (London: East and West Library, 1960). The consensual position of scholarship rejected this hypothesis: "The Karaite hypothesis … is simply untenable in the light of the combined evidence of archeology, paleography, and literary contents" (Geza Vermes, "Essenes and History," *Journal of Jewish Studies* 32 [1981], 23). But the numerous indisputably striking parallels between the Qumran and Karaite systems have yet to be explained in historical terms. Some scholars still hold for a genetic relationship. This position is summarized by Bernard Dupuy, "Les karaites sont-ils les descendents des esseniens?" *Istina* 29 (1984), 139–51.

78. The best attempts thus far have been Mahler's Marxian reading, *Karaimer*, and H. H. Ben-Sasson's Zionist "The First of the Karaites: The Trend of their Social Conceptions" (in Hebrew), *Zion* 15 (1950), 42–55.

79. Steven M. Wasserstrom, "Species of Misbelief: A History of Muslim Heresiography of the Jews" (PhD dissertation, University of Toronto, 1985).

80. Jacob Mann, "An Early Theologico-Polemical Work," in *The Collected Articles of Jacob Mann* (Gedara: M. Shalom, 1971), 411–59.

81. Bruno Chiesa, "Il Guidaismo Caraita," in *Correnti Culturali e Movimenti Religiosi de Guidaismo*, ed. B. Chiesa (Rome, 1987), 163–69.

82. Ginzberg, *Unknown Jewish Sect.*

83. Mann, "Early Theologico-Polemical Work."

84. Mordechai Friedman, "Menstrual Impurity and Sectarianism in the Writings of the Geonim and of Moses and Abraham Maimonides" (in Hebrew), *Maimonidean Studies* 1 (1980), 1–23.

85. See the works of Pines on Jewish Christians listed in the Bibliography below, as well as P. Crone, "Islam, Judeo-Christianity, and Byzantine Iconoclasm," *Jerusalem Studies in Arabic and Islam* 2 (1980), 59–95; Yehudah Liebes, "Who Makes the Horn of Jesus to Flourish?" *Jerusalem Studies in Jewish Thought* 3 (1984), 313–48; and Menahem Kister, "Plucking the Grain on the Sabbath and the Jewish-Christian Debate" (in Hebrew), *Jerusalem Studies in Jewish Thought* 3 (1984), 349–66.

86. I deal with the 'Isawiyya in chapter 2 below.

87. Adolf von Harnack, "Der Islam," in *Lehrbuch der Dogmengeschichte* (Darmstadt: Wissenschaftliche Buchgesellschaft, 1964), 2:537.

88. Jean Danielou, "Christianity as a Jewish Sect," in *The Crucible of Christianity*, ed. Arnold Toynbee (London: World Publishing Co., 1969), 282; Hans Joachim Schoeps, *Jewish Christianity* (Philadelphia: Fortress Press, 1969); Norman O. Brown, "Prophetic Tradition," *Studies in Romanticism* 21 (1982), 371.

89. Pines's voluminous work in this area includes: "'Israel, My Firstborn,' and the Sonship of Jesus," in *Studies in Mysticism and Religion* (Jerusalem: Magnes Press, 1967), 177–90; "Judaeo-Christian Materials in an Arabic Jewish Treatise," *Proceedings of the American Academy for Jewish Research* 55 (1967), 187–217; "The Jewish Christians of the Early Centuries of Christianity According to a New Source," *Proceedings of the Israel Academy of Sciences and Humanities* 2 (1968).

90. Samuel M. Stern, "New Light on Judaeo-Christianity?" *Encounter* (May 1987), 53–57.

91. Pines, "A Preliminary Note on the Relation Posited by Ibn Hazm between the Author of the *Book Yosippon* and the 'Isawiyya Sect and on the Arabic Version of This Book," *Jerusalem Studies in Arabic and Islam* 6 (1985), 145–53.

92. James Parkes, *The Conflict of the Church and the Synagogue: A Study in the Origins of Anti-Semitism* (New York: Atheneum, 1974), 358–66.

93. A. Hayman, ed. and trans., *The Disputation of Sergius the Stylite Against a Jew* (Louvain: Secretariat du CorpusSCO, 1973), 75. For example, "I am amazed how there are among you some Christians who associate with us in the synagogue and who bring offerings and at the time of the Passover send unleavened bread" (75). More generally, see A. Hayman, "The Image of the Jew in the Syriac Anti-Jewish Polemical Literature," in *To See Ourselves as Others See Us*, ed. J. Neusner and E. S. Frerichs (Chico, CA: Scholars Press, 1985), 423–43.

94. On the case of Syria, as well as Africa, Spain, Anatolia, and others, see Marcel Simon, *Verus Israel*, trans. H. McKeating (Oxford: Littman Library, 1986), 306–38. See more generally Gilbert Dagron, "Judäiser," *Travaux et Mémoires* 11 (1991), 359–80.

95. Jacob Neusner, *A History of the Jews in Babylonia* (Leiden: Brill, 1970), 5:130, citing *Domina Jacobi Nuper Baptizati*. On this text see Sidney H. Griffith, "Jews and Muslims in Christian and Arabic Texts of the Ninth Century," *Jewish History* 3 (1988), 86–87. I thank Professor Griffith for sharing this article with me prior to its publication. See now the definitive work of Gilbert Dagron and Vincent Déroche, "Juifs et Chrétiens dans l'orient du VIIe Siècle," *Travaux et Mémoires* 11 (1991), 17–46; and the edition of Déroche, ed., "*Doctrina Jacobi Nuper Baptizati*," *Travaux et Mémoires* 11 (1991), 47–275.

96. Robert D. Wilken, "The Restoration of Israel in Biblical Prophecy: Christian and Jewish Responses in the Early Byzantine Period," in *To See Ourselves as Others See Us*, ed. J. Neusner and E. S. Frerichs (Chico, CA: Scholars Press, 1985), 443–73.

97. These cases are discussed more fully below in chapter 2, in the section titled "The Jewish Messiahs of Early Islam."

98. O. Braun, "Ein Brief des katholikos Timotheos I über biblische Studien des 9 Jahrhunderts," *Oriens Christianus* 1 (1901), 299–313, first edited and translated this letter.

99. Norman Golb, "Who were the Magariya?" *Journal of the American Oriental Society* 80 (1960), 347–59; Ernst Bammel, "Hohlenmenschen," *Zeitschrift für die neutestamentliche Wissenschaft* 49 (1958), 77–88; Harry Austryn Wolfson, "The Pre-Existent Angel of the Magharians and Al-Nahawandi," *Jewish Quarterly Review* 51 (1960), 89–106.

    Much of the subsequent literature on this sect has come from scholars of Gnosticism, who believe that this sect has much to tell them—negatively or positively—on this subject. R. M. Grant, "Les êtres intermediares dans le judaïsme Tardif," in *Le Origini dello Gnosticismo* (Leiden: Brill, 1967), 159, for example: "Among the Maghariya we find then realized the possibility for Jewish heterodoxy, that an angel created the world, but we also find confirmed there the impossibility—for Jewish thought—that he was evil" (my translation from the French of Grant).

    Gilles Quispel found, contrarily, a "Jewish Gnostic" origin of the Maghariya demiurge: "The Origins of the Gnostic Demiurge," in *Kyriakon: Festschrift Johannes Quasten*, ed. P. Granfield and J. A. Jungmann (Munster: Aschendorff, 1970), 1:271–76; "Jewish Gnosis and Mandaean Gnosticism," in *Les Textes des Nag Hammadi: Colloque sur la bibliotheque copte de Nag Hammadi*, ed. J. É. Menard (Leiden: Brill, 1975), 82–122, at 121. The argument for a Gnostic Maghariya has been rebutted by G. Stroumsa, "Le Couple de l'ange de l'esprit: Traditions juive et chretiennes," *Revue biblique* 88 (1981), 42–61, esp. 49–52, where he argues that this sect was in fact anti-anthropomorphic. Fossum has now achieved the fullest treatment on this question in his "Magharians." Two recent contributions are of interest: R. T. Beckwith, "The Essene Calendar and the Moon: A Reconsideration," *Revue de Qumran* 59 (1992), 462–66; and Simon Szyzsman, "Compte rendu," *Bulletin des études karaites* 2 (1989), 105–6, where he reports a tantalizing (if far-fetched) possibility of modern remnants of the Maghariyya.

100. That is, they found texts in caves—not that they were cave dwellers.

101. Other texts found in Qumran also were channeled into the Islamicate (Jewish, Christian, and Muslim) world, perhaps through the Timotheos find. Among those texts were several which found their way into the Cairo Geniza. These include the Damascus Document, Hebrew Sirach, and Aramaic Testament of Levi.

   A particularly interesting discussion has arisen around the apocryphal psalms found at Qumran, which find their close parallels in the later Syriac and Arabic psalms. See Marc Philonenko, "L'origine essenienne des 5 Ps. Syriaquues de David," *Semitica* 9 (1959), 35–48; Andre Dupont-Summer, "Le psaume CLI dans 11QPs^a et le probleme de son origin essenienne," *Semitica* 14 (1964), 25–62; John Strugnell, "Notes on the Text and Transmission of the Apocryphal Ps. 151, 154 (=Syr 2) and 155 (=Syr 3)," *Harvard Theological Review* 59 (1966), 258; M. M. Goshen-Gottstein, "Psalms Scroll 11 QPs^a," *Textus* 5 (1966), 32 n. 45; J. Magne, "Recherche sur les psaumes 151, 154, et 155," *Revue de Qumran* (1975), 503–8.

102. Ibn al-Nadim, *Fihrist*, 2:813, 810–13.

103. Crone, "Islam, Judeo-Christianity and Byzantine Iconoclasm," 75. The definitive study of the Athinganoi remains Joshua Starr, "An Eastern Christian Sect: The Athinganoi," *Harvard Theological Review* 29 (1936), 93–106. Sidney H. Griffith vigorously rejects the interpretation of Crone concerning the Athinganoi ("Bashir/Beser: Boon Companion of the Byzantine Emperor Leo II. The Islamic Recension of His Story in *Leiden Oriental MS 951 (2)*," *Le Muséon* 104 [1990], 311).

104. Nemoy, "The Atttitudes of the Early Karaites towards Christianity," in *Salo Wittmayer Baron Jubilee Volume*, ed. Saul Lieberman and Arthur Hyman (Jerusalem and New York, 1974–75), 1:697–715.

105. Baron, *Social and Religious History*, 5:196–97. Zvi Ankori announced the publication of a study of this sectarian, but it has never appeared.

106. There is no adequate study devoted to this subject. But see Walter J. Fischel, "The Jews of Central Asia (Khorasan) in Medieval Hebrew and Islamic Literature," *Historia Judaica* 7 (1945), 29–49; and Michael Zand, "Jewish Settlements in Central Asia in Ancient Times and in the Early Middle Ages" (Hebrew), *Pe`amim* 35 (1988), 4–23.

107. Fischel, "Jews of Central Asia," 34 n. 22, citing Ibn 'Abd Rabbihi, *Kitab al-Aghani* 9:36–78, and secondary literature. His family is listed in Ibn al-Nadim, *Fihrist* 1:352–53.

108. For the survival of this phenomenon, see Zand, "Bukhara," in *Encyclopaedia Judaica Yearbook 1976*, 183–92.

109. Cited by Haggai Ben-Shammai, "The Attitudes of Some Early Karaites: Observations on Early Medieval Jewish Sectarianism," in *Studies in Medieval Jewish History and Literature*, ed. Isadore Twersky (Cambridge, MA: Harvard University Press, 1984), 10.

110. See my full discussion of the sources in chapter 2 below.

111. See chapter 3 below.

112. Moshe Idel, *Kabbalah: New Perspectives* (New Haven: Yale University Press, 1988), s.v. "Joseph of Hamadan."

113. Daniel, *Political and Social History*, 139.

114. O. Klima, "Mazdak und die Juden," *Archív Orientálni* 24 (1956), 420–31; I. A. Solodukho, "The Mazdak Movement and the Rebellion of the Hebrew Population of Iraq in the First Half of the Sixth Century," in *Soviet Views of Talmudic Judaism*, ed. Jacob Neusner (Leiden: Brill, 1973), 67–86; Baron, *Social and Religious History*, 2:399

n. 15; Werner Sundermann, "Neue Erkenntnisse über die mazdakitische Soziallehre," *Das Altertum* 34 (1988), 183–88.

115. Erik Peterson, "Urrchristentum und Mandaismus," *Zeitschrift für neutestamentliche Wissenschaft und die Kunde der älteren Kirche* 27 (1928), 81; Werner Müller, "Mazdak and the Alphabet Mysticism of the East," *History of Religions* 3 (1963–64), 72–82; Heinz Halm, "Die Sieben und de Zwolf, die isma'ilitische Kosmogonie und das Mazdak-Fragment des Shahrastani," in *18 Deutscher Orientalistententag* (Vortrage, 1972), 172–77; and the citation in the fully annotated French translation of Shahrastani, *Livre des religions*, 663–65. The "great mystery" of Mazdak, the "*raza rabba*" of the Mandeans, and the "*raza rabba*" of Jewish mysticism appear to have been technical terms in a common late-antique Mesopotamian cosmic semiotics.

116. Daniel, *Political and Social History*, 132.

117. Wilfred Madelung, "Abu 'Isa al-Warraq über die Bardesaniten, Marcioniten und Kantaer," in *Studie zur Geschichte und Kultur des Vonderen Orients*, ed. H. R. Roemer and A. Noth (Leiden: Brill, 1981), 220.

118. W. B. Henning, "The Inscriptions of Tang-i-Azao," *Bulletin of the School of Oriental and African Studies* 20 (1957), 335–42; Bo Utas, "The Jewish-Persian Fragment from Dandan-Uiliq," *Orientalia Sueccana* 17 (1968), 123–37; Jes Asmussen, *Studies in Judeo-Persian Literature* (Leiden: Brill, 1973), 4; G. Lazard, "La Dialectologie de Judeo-Persan," *Studies in Bibliography and Booklore* 7 (1968), 79. For the publication of some remarkable inscriptions, see Karl Jettmar, "Hebrew Inscriptions in the Western Himalayas," *Orientali Iosephi Tucci Memoriae Dicata*, ed. G. Gnoli and L. Lanciotti (Rome, 1987), 667–70.

119. Theodore Bar-Khonai, *Livre des scholies (recension de Seert)*, trans. R. Hespel and R. Draguet (Louvain: Peeters, 1982), 255–61. This eighth-century bishop was in possession of many rare sources; research into the sources of the eleventh book of scholia is surely very desirable.

120. I argue this point more fully in chapter 3 below.

121. Jacob Mann, "The Responsa of the Babylonian Geonim as a Source of Jewish History," *Jewish Quarterly Review* 7 (1916–17), 471; see further W. J. Fischel, "The Beginnings of Judeo-Persian Literature," in *Mélanges d'orientalisme oferts a Henri Massé* (Teheran: n.p., 1963), 141–51; Shaul Shaked, "On the Early Heritage of the Jews of Persia" (in Hebrew), *Pe'amim* 23 (1985), 22–37.

122. Israel Davidson, ed., *Saadia's Polemic Against Hiwi al-Balkhi* (New York: Jewish Theological Seminary of America, 1915); Judah Rosenthal, "On the History of Heresy in the Era of Saadia" (in Hebrew), *Horeb* 9 (1946), 21–37; Judah Rosenthal, *Hiwi al-Balkhi: A Comparative Study* (Philadelphia: Jewish Publication Society of America, 1949); Julius Guttmann, "On the Question of the Sources of Hiwi al-Balkhi," in *Alexander Marx Jubilee Volume* (New York: Jewish Theological Seminary of America, 1950), 95–103; Martin Plessner, "Heresy and Rationalism in First Centuries of Islam" (in Hebrew), in *The Ulama and Problems of Religion in the Muslim World: Studies in Honor of Professor Uriel Heyd*, ed. G. Baer (Jerusalem: n.p., 1979), 3–10; Ezra Fleischer, "A Fragment from Hivi al-Balkhi's Criticism of the Bible" (in Hebrew), *Tarbis* 51 (1981), 49–57. For more on Hiwi, see chapter 4 below.

123. See a discussion of this encounter in chapter 4.

124. Shaul Shaked, "Persia and the Origins of the Karaite Movement," *Association for Jewish Studies Newsletter*, 7–9.

125. Ibid.
126. See chapter 3 below for more on the role of Shi'a-Jewish relations, inside Persia and without.
127. See Gil, *History of Palestine.*
128. Moshe Gil, *The Tustaris, Family and Sect* (in Hebrew) (Tel Aviv: n.p., 1981); and *History of Palestine.*
129. O. Pritsak, "The Role of the Bosporus Kingdom and Late Hellenism as the Basis for the Medieval Cultures of the Territories North of the Black Sea," in *Mutual Effects of the Islamic and Judeo-Christian Worlds*, ed. A. Ascher, T. Halasi-Kun, and Bela Kiraly (Brooklyn: Brooklyn College Press, 1979), 13.
130. O. Pritsak, "The Khazar Kingdom's Conversion to Judaism," *Harvard Ukranian Studies* 2 (1980), 280.
131. Discussed more fully below in chapter 3, in regard to the Isma'ili al-Kirmani.
132. Cohen, "Reconstruction of Gaonic History," xiii–xcvi.
133. Pirkei ben Baboi has been closely scrutinized in this regard: the research is summarized in Grossman, "Aliya," 184 n. 1; and esp. in the study of Shalom Spiegel, "On the Interpretation of the Polemics of Pirkoi ben Baboi" (in Hebrew), in *H. A. Wolfson Jubilee Volume* (Jerusalem, 1965), 243–74. See also Shalom Rosenberg, "Link to the Land of Israel," in *World Jewry and the State of Israel*, ed. E. E. Urbach and Moshe Davis (New York: Arno Press, 1977), 157. Daniel Lasker notes that the *She'iltot* of Ahai Gaon (citing the discussion in Tchernowitz, *Toldot haPoskim*, 62–69) may allude to pre-Ananite sectarians: "Rabbinism and Karaism: The Quest for Supremacy," in *Great Schisms in Jewish History*, ed. Raphael Jospe and Stanley M. Wagner (Denver and New York: Ktav, 1981), 68 n. 13. Examples could be multiplied, but not indefinitely. The sources available for the eighth century are sparse.
134. *Pirke de Rebbe Eliezer* is one midrash that has been so studied, though much work remains to be done. See, for example, Bernhard Heller, "Muhammedanisches und Antimuhammedanisches in den Pirke Rabbi Eliezer," *Monatsschrift für Geschichte und Wissenschaft des Judentums* 69 (1925), 47–54. Another such work would be the so-called apocalypse of Zerubabel: see the studies by Israel Levi, "L'apocalypse de Zorobabel et le roi de Perse Siroes," *Revue des etudes juives* 69 (1919), 108–21; and Brannon M. Wheeler, "Imagining the Sasanian Capture of Jerusalem: The 'Prophecy and Dream Zerubbabel' and Antiochus Strategos' Capture of Jerusalem," *Orientalia Christiana Periodica* 57 (1991), 69–85. For *piyyutim*, Yosef Yahalom, *Poetic Language in the Early Piyyut* (Jerusalem: Magnes Press, 1985) reviews the current state of research. For an example of scholarly redating that provides us with potentially important new light on Jewish responses to the advent of Muhammad, see Ezra Fleischer, "Solving the Qiliri Riddle" (in Hebrew), *Tarbis* 51 (1981), 383–429. For other useful directions, see Jacob Mann on polemical piyyut in the tenth century, *Texts and Studies in Jewish History and Literature* (New York: Ktav, 1972 [1931]), 2:116–20. The history of piyyut no doubt sheds light on intra-Judaic communal conflicts. See Baron, *Social and Religious History*, 7:100: "From the eighth century on, the Babylonian leaders' growingly intensive drive for power and control of world Jewry made such liturgical creativity suspect, because it was both uncontrollable and Palestinian."

The Rejudaization of "the Nation"

Miriam Bodian

Reeducation

Members of virtually all immigrant groups seek to preserve and share among themselves deeply ingrained linguistic and cultural patterns from the "old country." What differentiates the "Portuguese" in Amsterdam was the need to integrate the Iberian experience into their new lives while at the same time taking on quite a different project: that of rejudaization.

Reclaiming rabbinic Judaism was a collective enterprise, but it required individual effort. Some emigres were more willing and eager than others to invest that effort. But all emigres from the Peninsula needed instruction in the basics of Jewish observance if they were to participate in the life of the community. For adults, this could be exhilarating but difficult. There was a language barrier to overcome—and psychocultural ones as well.

Isaac de Pinto's memoirs offer vivid insight into the process. When Pinto and members of his family arrived in Rotterdam from Antwerp, they immediately set about, as Pinto recalled, "instructing ourselves about Judaism and learning to read Hebrew." A month or so later, when his father and uncle arrived safely from Antwerp, the males of the family sent to Amsterdam for a *mohel*, or circumciser, and underwent circumcision. At the ceremony three of Pinto's brothers and his uncle, who had not hitherto done so, adopted Hebrew names. A fortnight later, Pinto and his father, both of them first-born sons, underwent the festive ritual of "redemption of the first-born" (*pidyon ha-ben*), usually performed a month after birth.[1] (This is an interesting detail, given the family's claim to priestly status, since *kohanim* do not redeem their first-born.) These ceremonies, so closely linked to birth, were individual manifestations of the rebirth of the community, and were experienced in that way.

Judging from his memoirs, the early days of Pinto's life in the Netherlands were thrilling and liberating. "We were willing to believe anything," he wrote of being persuaded to settle in Rotterdam rather than Amsterdam, "so happy we were to have become Jews in the service of God."[2] Like many emigres, he seems to have been prepared by the family's converso legacy and the religio-ethnic defiance sparked by inquisitorial persecution to accept the discipline of rabbinic life. Having the means to reattach themselves to Jewish life in grand style, the Pintos rented a house to be used as a synagogue and sent to Amsterdam for a *hakham*. (They were able to hire Yoshiahu Pardo, a grandson of Joseph Pardo.)[3] It is not entirely clear why the family first settled in Rotterdam and only later in Amsterdam, but it is abundantly clear that they at once established themselves as practicing Jews. Though settled for the time being in Rotterdam, Pinto was aware of the excitement surrounding the growth of the community in Amsterdam, and the rapid development of its administrative, welfare, and educational institutions. All of this must have seemed a vindication of his family's decision to leave the Iberian realm.

Entering the rabbinic realm, however, was not without its problems. Neither Pinto nor his father ever achieved facility in studying rabbinic texts. But they were able to compensate for this by supporting talmudic scholars, as wealthy Jews had traditionally done. Pinto's father took his role of patronage quite seriously. Until his death in 1668 he lived "removed and secluded from worldly matters, betaking himself every day to the *Midrash* [house of study] which he had instituted there for twelve scholars to study throughout the morning and afternoon."[4] This is poignant testimony to the often uninformed yet impassioned attachment of emigres to a tradition the access to which they felt they had been denied.

Most emigres could not build private synagogues or support a dozen talmudic scholars. But otherwise the initiation into Jewish life Pinto describes must have been similar to that of others. The act of circumcision was a particularly crucial rite of passage—not merely an act of compliance with Jewish law, but a ritual replete with powerful symbolic meanings. In the converso imagination, circumcision took on a transcendental transitional significance, perhaps akin to that of a Christian sacrament. The ex-converso apologete Isaac Cardoso spoke of it as a "mysterious sacrifice," an act that compensated for the original sin of Adam, and one without which a Jew could not be saved.[5] (Unfortunately, women left no record of what they thought of such an idea.)[6] Notions like this existed in the Peninsula and outside it as an integral part of converso folklore. A rejudaized converso who later returned to Spain related to the Madrid Inquisition in 1635 that after coming to Bordeaux, before departing for Amsterdam, several conversos in Bordeaux "tried to persuade him that he be circumcised before departing, because if he should die at sea without doing so he would not qualify for salvation, and it would be better if he would bear the mark of the

Lord."[7] Perhaps this converso was only concocting a story to try to absolve himself of responsibility for having later been circumcised in Amsterdam.[8] But if so, he was echoing notions that would have been familiar and perhaps persuasive to the inquisitors.

From a rabbinic point of view, the idea of the salvific power of circumcision was both bizarre and misguided. Still, such an idea did serve to impel the male converso being initiated into Jewish life to endure the pain of adult circumcision. Less helpful in the transition, however, was another common converso idea about circumcision— one that apparently *inhibited* emigres' willingness to be circumcised. This was the notion that without circumcision a Jew was not obligated to observe the Law. To the rabbinic leadership, it was important to dispel this misconception, and the Venetian Sephardi rabbi Samuel Aboab condemned it roundly. The emigres must be disabused, he wrote, of

> the vain idea which has spread among almost all the sons of our people who come from the servitude of the soul [i.e., the Peninsula] …, that so long as a man is not circumcised he is not *part of Israel* [my emphasis] [and] his sins are not sins… And some claim that the day of their circumcision is the first day on which their sins begin to count.

All of this, Aboab stressed, was contrary to Jewish law, which holds that "circumcision is [merely] a commandment like all the rest of the Torah" and anyone of the "seed of Israel" is bound by all the precepts, whether circumcised or not.[9] This was an eloquent insistence on rabbinic standards by someone deeply sympathetic to converso needs.

The belief in the religio-ethnic defining power of circumcision, like many "converso" beliefs, was not an arbitrary aberration. It had served an important function in the Peninsula, assuaging the conscience of conversos who were unable to observe Jewish law, allowing them to believe they were not strictly bound to observe it. It made the "Egyptian condition" more bearable. Among the emigres, one of the effects of placing so high a value on circumcision was that the circumcision ceremony evolved into a much-needed rite of passage.

The centrality of circumcision in the ritual of "return" is vividly reflected in the inquisitorial case of Cristóbal Méndez, a converso who settled in Venice in 1643, but was arrested in Madrid in 1661 while on a business or personal mission. Under interrogation he revealed the story, step by step, of how he had been inducted as a "returning" Jew into the Ponentine (largely "Portuguese") community of Venice. His uncle and an ex-converso rabbi urged him to undergo circumcision, which despite his hesitations he agreed to do. For a month before the circumcision ceremony, the rabbi gave him some rudimentary instruction, using a Bible in Spanish translation. Immediately after the circumcision, he was given a prayer shawl and phylacteries. Presumably it was at this time that Méndez adopted the name Abraham Franco de Silveira. When he had recovered from the surgery, he made his debut at the Sephardi synagogue, where he put on the prayer shawl and phylacteries and was called to the ark to recite the blessing of deliverance, which he repeated word for word in Hebrew after the cantor. This cluster of ceremonies became a life-cycle event for the male ex-converso. Even if Méndez was already a Jew, as Aboab argued, these ceremonies served to mark his "return."[10]

In the period after his or her induction into Jewish life, emigres began to learn not only how the Law of Moses was understood by rabbinic authorities in the seventeenth century, but also the rhetoric of the community, the nature of its institutions, and its expectations of him or her. The doting attention of the "old-timers" no doubt eased the transition. But the emigres also faced the difficulties of overcoming their considerable ignorance of traditional Jewish life. Converso cryptojudaizing undoubtedly provided a certain preparation for a rabbinically regulated life, exposing conversos to concepts and focal rituals which would strike them as familiar with their entry into Jewish communities. But by the seventeenth century, the gap between normative Jewish observance and converso judaizing was enormous. By this time "judaizing" had largely been reduced to the relatively safe undertaking of holding a set of attitudes and ideas. It will be helpful to examine some of these, to grasp something of the crypto-Jewish culture the emigres brought with them.

Crypto-Jewish ideas often took the form of attacks on Catholicism rather than direct affirmations of Jewish belief. Indeed, such is the prominence of anti-Catholic motifs in converso belief that Stephen Gilman was led to cryptojudaizing as "a kind of worship in reverse."[11] But in doing so Gilman overlooked the fundamentally Jewish character of "converso" refutations of Catholicism. When conversos scorned images of the saints and the Holy Family—for example, when the Portuguese conversa Isabel Lopes stated in 1583 that "the painted saints were nothing more than pictures that somebody had painted"[12]—they were affirming Jewish belief by attacking an aspect of Catholic worship that Jews regarded as idolatrous.

Denials of Catholic belief were expressed in a variety of colorful ways, often in statements that were pithy and barbed, primed to stick in the memory and, given their rhetorical power, easily disseminated among conversos. Such were the countless witticisms conversos produced about the virgin conception and birth. Characteristic were the remarks of Joao Lopes, "You can't make cheese without curds [i.e., male seed]"[13] and Garcia Mendes d'Abreu, "How can you draw a yolk out of an egg without breaking the shell?"[14] Another converso conveyed the message by referring to Mary as "our stork."[15] Important also in the converso repertoire were denials of the divinity of Jesus. The taboo-like nature of ascribing divinity to a man of flesh and blood reportedly caused the converso family of Isabel Núnez to avoid saying the name *Jesucristo*, referring to him rather as "Christóbal Sánchez."[16] Less cautiously, Simão Vaz of Lisbon reportedly stated that God "had no need of putting himself into the womb of a woman and that the messiah was not God."[17] However these ideas were put, they tended to deflate Catholicism from a generally Jewish point of view and implied a counterview.

Not surprisingly, judaizers also produced formulas to nullify the Catholic rituals they were required to perform. We have already seen this with Isaac de Pinto, who in childhood was taught to say the *Shema* when he entered a church. Similarly, the Portuguese New Christian Gonçalo Vaz was reported in 1543 to have said (under his breath) at the moment the host was elevated by the priest, "Old bread and wine—I believe in the Law of Moses."[18] Yet more trenchant was the formula taught to Marina de Avila by her half-sister in the late sixteenth century. When the priest raised the host, she would say, "I see a piece of bread; I worship you, Lord, instead [*Una torta de pan veo, en ti Senor adoro y creo*]."[19]

But crypto-Jews like these were also likely to hold a few central affirmative Jewish convictions. As we have noted, an important historian of the conversos cited three crypto-Jewish notions that seem ubiquitous in judaizing circles: a) the rejection of Catholicism as a form of idolatry, b) the conviction of belonging to the Jewish people which worships the only true God and which will be redeemed by the Messiah, and c) the belief—a Jewish counterclaim to a central Catholic doctrine—that personal salvation is achieved only through the Law of Moses.[20]

Of these, only the last was truly problematic. Belief in the salvific power of the Law of Moses was indeed widespread among crypto-Jews. In the testimony of conversos accused of judaizing, the "Law of Moses" was invoked in an almost abstract way, like the Zion imagined by the medieval Jew—a notion to cling to rather than an intrinsic aspect of everyday life. A natural result of this situation was the emergence of the idea among judaizers, quite alien to rabbinic Judaism, that the actual observance of precepts was not necessary—that it was sufficient to "believe in one's heart." This conviction appeared surprisingly early. It was suggested, as early as 1503 by a rabbinic scholar—one who, forcibly converted in Portugal, had escaped to Salonica. God would view the forced converts in Portugal, he said, "by their thoughts, not by their deeds." (It is noteworthy that at a later time this same scholar would thoroughly condemn such a view.)[21] In subsequent generations, the belief in the sufficiency of inner allegiance to the Law of Moses became a persistent theme in crypto-Jewish thinking. One converso related that when his father initiated him into crypto-Judaism, he told him "that one must perform many ceremonies and rituals, but that one could not perform them in this realm because of the danger of being discovered." But he assured the boy that "for now it was enough to fix his heart on one single God and be aided in this by the Great Fast which falls on the tenth day of the new moon of September [i.e., Yom Kippur]."[22] Similarly António Homem, a passionate judaizer and professor of canon law at the University of Coimbra, who was burned at the stake in 1624, was said to have preached in a Yom Kippur sermon in 1615 that "while living in persecution it was sufficient to have in mind the intention of performing the precepts of the Law."[23] The idea became so entrenched that it took on a life of its own. The conversa Catarina Fernandes reported that "because she was blind and could not control the use of her hands," she "only lit the sabbath candles in her heart."[24] Such ideas reflected a reverence—not without its own power—for a way of life that had become alien. But believing in the Law of Moses was not, obviously, the same as observing it.

Moreover, conversos often expressed their allegiance to the Law of Moses within a conceptual theological framework that was Catholic. Their religious thinking was permeated with an anxiety about personal salvation which they had absorbed from their environment—a goal which virtually eclipsed the sense of everyday purposefulness inculcated by rabbinic Judaism through the notion of covenantal obligation. Numerous judaizers stated that they were driven to choose Judaism over Christianity because they were convinced that the Law of Moses was the only law through which one could be saved. The concern for salvation was internalized so thoroughly that, astonishingly, a conversa of Trancoso told the Coimbra Inquisition in 1574 that it was "for the salvation of her soul" that she baked unleavened bread for Passover![25] There is here an echo of a more general phenomenon in the history (not mystique) of resistance: a determined rejection of a repressive social order accompanied by an unwitting embrace of some of its deepest impulses.

And even its liturgy. Crypto-Jews naturally longed for time-honored vehicles of religious expression such as those they observed in church. Given the absence of Jewish devotional material, it is not surprising that some conversos improvised, using readily available Catholic texts and developing syncretistic "Jewish" liturgical practices. A converso tried in Évora in 1637 was said to have taught local conversas "to recite two Pater Nosters and two Ave Marias *and offer them to Moses*" (my italics).[26] Another converso told the same Inquisition in 1591 that he said the Pater Noster because he did not know any Jewish prayers.[27] To be sure, such testimony cannot always be relied upon. But judging from the Christian sources cited in works written outside the Peninsula by ex-conversos to *support their own positions*, including the works of contemporary Spanish theologians, it appears that crypto-Jews drew heavily from the only body of spiritual and theological literature at their disposal to give content to their "Jewish" spirituality.[28]

But expressions of Jewish allegiance varied enormously among judaizers. It may be recalled that the prayer composed by Jacob Israel Belmonte, while devoid of specifically Jewish content, was influenced by Catholic formulations. At the other extreme were converso prayers that are extraordinarily rich in material drawn from the rabbinic liturgy. The most easily obtained material was that found in the Bible: psalms in particular and, in at least one case, the story of the sacrifice of Isaac from Genesis.[29] But, remarkably, rabbinic formulations were sometimes preserved and transmitted as late as the second half of the sixteenth century. In 1583 a conversa who appeared before the Coimbra tribunal recited most of the first benediction said before the *Shema* in the evening prayers, in an almost verbatim Portuguese translation.[30] And in 1584 another conversa recited a version of the morning benedictions (*birkhot ha-shahar*).[31] To see these texts in sixteenth-century inquisitorial documents is truly astonishing, and clear testimony to the careful preservation and transmission of rabbinic liturgical formulations in some converso circles.

Thus, while "converso" Judaism was always impoverished relative to Judaism practiced outside the Peninsula, the degree of its remoteness from rabbinic Judaism varied greatly. For those who sought it out, information about postbiblical Judaism was available. Ironically, Iberian society sometimes freely offered conversos information of which they might otherwise have been ignorant. The "Edicts of Faith," for example— proclamations calling for judaizers to come forth and confess their crimes, and for the faithful to denounce judaizers—provided detailed lists of Jewish rituals in order to inform potential denouncers what to look for. Ironically, such lists also furnished valuable information to judaizers to whom the Inquisition had systematically denied access to such knowledge. Autos-da-fé were also a source of information. In Coimbra in 1574 Belchior Fernandes was accused of having said that "if he knew about them [the Laws of Moses], it was from having heard them read in the copies of the sentences that the students from the village of Sea wrote down from the autos-da-fé and read to them."[32]

The more educated the judaizer, the greater access he and members of his family had to knowledge of rabbinic practices. Those who knew Latin were especially equipped to acquire postbiblical Jewish knowledge, piecing together a conception of rabbinic Judaism, however shadowy, from references to rabbinic ideas and practices in writings of the Church Fathers as well as contemporary anti-Jewish sermons and polemical writings. Y. H. Yerushalmi has shown how the converso physician Isaac Cardoso, and presumably others as well, were able to accomplish this.[33] Such figures, needless to say, did not keep their findings to themselves. We have already noted in chapter two how the learned physician Eliahu Montalto became a mentor to members of his immediate and extended family, virtually head of a network of judaizers. We also know that the university-educated physician Juan de Prado, who was disciplined for disseminating heterodox ideas in Amsterdam, had earlier proselytized in the Peninsula among members of his family and others, urging them to adhere to Judaism.[34] At least some judaizers, then, were able to catch a glimpse of the great edifice of postbiblical rabbinic reasoning which the Inquisition sought so systematically to suppress.

Still, what emerged from even the most sophisticated of such efforts was a seriously skewed picture. As new information was acquired, it was inevitably assimilated into a theological framework that was heavily influenced by Catholicism. That is, rejudaization, in the true sense of the word, required more than absorbing new information. It entailed a transformation of religious experience—an understanding of the experiential characteristics of Jewish worship and practice, a conditioning to the rhythms of the synagogue and the Jewish year, a grasp of how *halakhah* (Jewish law), in all its minutiae, was integrated into everyday activity.

No book teaches such things. In these matters, a crucial role was played by the *hakhamim*, as well as by emigres who had spent time in other Jewish communities and by a few "old" Sephardim—descendants of Spanish exiles—who settled in the Netherlands. Especially in the early years of the community, the *hakhamim* had to muster all their skills of tact, firmness, and human understanding to alter ingrained ideas and patterns of behavior. We have caught a glimpse of this in the anecdote (mentioned in chapter two) about the intervention of the *hakham* Joseph Pardo to abolish the custom of mourning the destruction of the Temple in the synagogue on the three sabbaths preceding the Ninth of Ab (a major fast day).[35]

Unfortunately, few anecdotes such as this survive. The considerable literature of rejudaization available to the emigres provides the best material for understanding the approach adopted to aid the neophyte emigres' entry into the world of rabbinics.

As Yerushalmi put it, "The returning Marrano was essentially an autodidact and, like all autodidacts, he needed books to read."[36] In response to the demand, there was a burst of activity in the printing of Jewish books in Portuguese and Spanish: apologetic and ethical works, guides to Jewish practice, and translations of classic Jewish texts. By the mid-seventeenth century, a sizable library of such works had been produced. While in the early years of the seventeenth century Venice turned out most of these books, Amsterdam soon took the leading role.[37]

The works most needed in translation were the Hebrew Bible and the prayer book. As we have noted, Spanish—a language with which native-born Portuguese were acquainted—rather than Portuguese was the language used for all editions of these texts. Spanish was also the language of instruction in the schools. Perhaps because the literary status of Spanish was superior to that of Portuguese, it was felt that Spanish would better convey the sanctity of Scripture and the liturgy, or perhaps Spanish was used because it was the language that united the Sephardi diaspora as a whole.[38] Since the prayer service and Torah reading in the synagogue were in Hebrew—a language the adult newcomers could not easily acquire—some important prayers were transliterated, that is, printed in Hebrew in Latin characters. Italian printers and booksellers did a brisk business supplying the Amsterdam community with Spanish prayer books and Bibles until local presses began producing their own editions.

It was not long before Amsterdam became a center for the printing of such works. As early as 1612, the merchant and devoted communal leader Isaac Franco financed the publication of a three-volume festival prayer book in Spanish translation.[39] Numerous editions of liturgical works in translation (or in Hebrew with accompanying translation) followed.[40] Among them are a prayer book for the High Holidays (1617) and a Passover Haggadah (1622), both in Spanish translation, printed by the merchant David Abenatar Melo, whose religious conversion experience we have discussed. (The books were printed at a press he himself set up in Amsterdam in 1616.)[41] Amsterdam presses also produced many editions of the Hebrew Bible in Spanish translation (all based on the famous Ferrara Bible of 1553), the first appearing in 1611.[42]

Essential as these texts were for a grasp of Judaism, they became the foundation of a living tradition only when the themes that spoke most immediately to the "Portuguese" public were drawn from them and elucidated. The Bible was interpreted to the "Portuguese" in sermons and through an extensive polemical and apologetic literature produced largely in Venice and Amsterdam by figures like Saul Levi Mortera, Menasseh ben Israel, Immanuel Aboab, Isaac Aboab da Fonseca, Isaac Orobio de Castro, Isaac Cardoso, and others. These polemicists and exegetes drew from centuries of Jewish interpretation but, consonant with their own needs and those of their readers, they tended to read the biblical text from an uncommonly anti-Christian point of view. While such polemical interpretations were no doubt intended to win over the unconvinced, they also served to enhance "Portuguese" solidarity by giving expression to shared hostility to Catholicism.[43]

"Portuguese" presses also turned out numerous translations of the classics of medieval Jewish thought. The texts chosen were invariably of Spanish-Jewish origin.

In part, this reflected the special interest of the "Portuguese" in a Sephardi legacy they wished to reclaim. But this was not the only reason for a partiality to Sephardi works. The great philosophical and ethical works of eleventh- and twelfth-century Spanish Jewry were interpretations of rabbinic tradition by Jews living in a highly sophisticated Greco-Arabic culture. For the "Portuguese," with their experience of what might be called a Greco-Christian culture, these texts resonated in a way that Ashkenazi works, with their more alien rabbinic style, did not. Moses Maimonides, however remote in time, was much closer to them than Moses Isserles.

Many of the translations of these works were produced and published in Amsterdam. Among them were the eleventh-century ethical treatise *Duties of the Heart* (*Hovot ha-levavot*), published in Spanish translation in 1610 and in Portuguese in 1670;[44] Judah Halevi's *Kuzari* (1663);[45] Maimonides' "Laws of Repentence" from his *Mishneh Torah* (1613); and the latter's enumeration of the 613 precepts, *Sefer ha-mizvot* (1652).[46] With these and other works available in translation, emigres with little knowledge of Hebrew could discover a Jewish legacy no less sophisticated than the Catholic culture they had known in the Peninsula.

At a more mundane level, the emigres needed help learning the details of Jewish practice. This was important for the overall character the community was to assume, but it was also important for assuring the status of the community in the wider Jewish world. The proud merchants who dominated *K.K. Talmud Torah* were not likely to accept a less than honorable place in that world. With the cooperation of the rank and file of the community, they were able to achieve it. Even so, bringing norms of practice in Amsterdam into relative harmony with practice in older Jewish communities like Salonica or Venice—not to mention Prague or Cracow—was a huge task.

Much of what occurred in effecting this transformation is hidden from the view of the historian. Judging from behavior in similar circumstances—the initiation of newcomers into Jewish circles in Moscow in the 1970s, for example, or the "rabbinization" of Ethiopian Jews in Israel in recent years—nothing would have been more important in encouraging the successful adaptation of the new emigres than the welcoming embrace of those already conditioned to observing some of the finer points of Jewish law in the home, synagogue, and workplace.

The only concrete remains of this effort are the many manuals of Jewish practice published in Spanish and Portuguese, many in Amsterdam. At the time they were published, the accepted basis for practice throughout most of the Jewish diaspora was Joseph Karo's code, the *Shulhan arukh*, which first appeared in 1564. Even in translation, this work was too demanding (and overwhelming) for the "Portuguese" emigres. An abridgment in Ladino (Judeo-Spanish written in Hebrew characters, prevalent among Balkan Sephardim) appeared in 1568, shortly after publication of the original work. But there was some reluctance to produce a translation into Spanish or any other language in Latin characters since this would make the work readily accessible to gentiles. An abridged version of the *Shulhan arukh* appeared in Spanish only in 1609, with the publication in Venice of Moses Altaras's *Libro de Mantenimiento de la Alma*.[47] Other works with a similar purpose appeared subsequently, most notably

Isaac Athias's *Tesoro de Preceptos* (Venice 1627, Amsterdam 1649) and Menasseh ben Israel's *Thesouro dos Dinim* (Amsterdam 1645–47), written in Portuguese "for the use of our Portuguese nation."[48]

Somewhat different from these manuals, because it presented Jewish law within a larger and more theoretical framework, was the work of the Amsterdam physician and merchant Abraham Farar, *Declaração das seiscentas e treze Encomendanças da nossa Sancta Ley* (Amsterdam 1627), a description of the traditionally accepted 613 Jewish precepts, including those no longer of practical significance, presented in the order prescribed by Maimonides in his *Sefer ha-mizvot*, a work which, as mentioned, was published in translation by an Amsterdam press in 1652. Those who wanted more direct contact with talmudic texts could consult a Spanish translation of the Mishnah, with the classic commentaries of Maimonides and Ovadiah Bertinoro (Venice 1606, Amsterdam 1663).

These works reflect an interest in thorough, not minimal, practice, and—in the case of Farar's book and the translation of the Mishnah—even in the complex halakhic structure underlying practice. This does not mean that they offer an accurate reflection of the interests of the emigres. As in all societies, there was a wide spectrum of interest and commitment. But these works would not have appeared if there were no demand for them, nor would they occupy so much space in present-day collections of Sephardica if they had not been bought.

For those emigres and their descendants who took to heart the obligation of the adult male Jew to study Torah at appointed times (and who had achieved sufficient facility with rabbinic texts to do so), it was natural to seek out companions for study, and eventually this led to the organization of societies for the study of Torah. This in itself was hardly novel in a Jewish community. What may have distinguished these associations (aside from the language in which discussions took place) is hidden from our view, since we are largely dependent on De Barrios for information about them, and cannot glean much about their character from his discussion.[49] It is worth noting, however, that according to De Barrios the members of one such society, Torah Or, founded in 1656 and initially headed by Isaac Aboab da Fonseca, met six days a week for half an hour to study "the book by Maimonides" (presumably the *Mishneh Torah*).[50] The choice of a quintessentially Sephardi rabbinic text for study was altogether in keeping with "Portuguese" inclinations, and educated members of the community would no doubt have appreciated Maimonides' systematic distillation of Jewish law from its unruly rabbinic sources.

More basic in the effort of the Amsterdam "Portuguese" elite to perpetuate its ideals were the steps it took in educating its children (to be more precise, its boys). In this area of communal life as in others, the *Mahamad* did not hesitate to deviate from time-honored patterns in Jewish society. Its organizational and pedagogical innovations were keenly noted by two Ashkenazi visitors to Amsterdam. The first, the rabbinic scholar Shabbetai Shefiel Horowitz, son of the renowned Polish talmudist and kabbalist Isaiah ben Abraham Horowitz, spent time in Amsterdam in the early 1640s, and described, like a traveler in a strange country, how the school for the

"Portuguese" children was divided into grades to meet the needs of children of different ages, each grade studying subjects suited to its age group.[51] This was indeed a striking feature of the community's educational policies. In Ashkenazi communities, as Jacob Katz has put it, education was typified by "the lack of systematization and comprehensiveness in educational goals."[52] Children of different ages would attend a school or *heder* under the tutelage of one teacher or *melamed*, and would study the Pentateuch or *halakhah* in a haphazard manner determined not by pedagogical common sense, but by the weekly order of synagogue Torah readings or the need to learn certain aspects of *halakhah* for practice. In contrast, the Amsterdam community's merger agreement of 1639 lays out a well-ordered course of study for seven grades, each with its own teacher or *rubi* and its own curriculum. A child would advance from the study of the alphabet and addition in first grade, to the study of the Pentateuch from beginning to end ("from 'in the beginning' [Gen. 1:1] to 'in the sight of all Israel' [the last verse of Deuteronomy]," as Sheftel Horowitz put it approvingly), to the study of *halakhah* and finally to the study of Talmud under the *hakham* Saul Levi Mortera in the seventh grade.[53] Having described this curriculum, Sheftel Horowitz penned a little cry of distress: "Why don't we do thus in our land? Would that this custom would spread through the entire Jewish diaspora!"

The second visitor, the rabbinic scholar Shabbetai Bass of Prague, who visited Amsterdam in 1680, echoed Horowitz's admiration for the system of graded education but gave a more thorough overview of its organization.[54] The *Mahamad*, he noted, assumed the role of supervising the education of all children, wealthy and poor alike, appointing teachers and paying their salaries. (In fact, the details of administration were handled by the directors of the *Talmud Torah* society who were, however, subordinate to the *Mahamad*.)[55] This stood in stark contrast to the norm elsewhere in Jewish society, where communal government took responsibility only for the education of the poor, leaving the wealthy to hire tutors for their children.[56] Given the marginality of the poor, in such a system communal leaders had a limited interest in the quality of education it provided, while the tutors to the wealthy, unsupervised by the community, were totally dependent on the parents who hired them. In contrast, Shabbetai Bass observed, in Amsterdam the teachers had a measure of dignity and independence.[57]

The *Mahamad*'s insistence on supervising education seems to have been a policy pursued consistently at least from 1639. Well before the unification of the congregations, perhaps as early as 1616, a society known as *Ets Haim* was established to provide financial assistance to needy students who might otherwise be forced to drop their studies. With the unification of 1639, this became an integral part of the communal apparatus, its treasurer being one of the *parnasim* of the *Talmud Torah* society.[58] But the communal leadership also insisted on supervising the education of the affluent. This is vividly illustrated by the steps the *Mahamad* took in 1659 to prevent dissatisfied parents of means, unhappy with a certain teacher hired by the community, from establishing a separate school. After more than twenty students had been withdrawn from the *Talmud Torah* school to study privately with the learned Moses d'Aguilar—leaving the teacher hired by the community with "only those boys who receive stipends (*aspacha*—Heb. *haspakah*) and a few others"—the *Mahamad* decided to act. Jealous of its authority to supervise education, it offered a high salary to Moses d'Aguilar to persuade him (successfully) to replace the teacher who had caused the exodus.[59]

Shabbetai Bass was also impressed by the fact that most of the "Portuguese" schoolchildren in Amsterdam were "expert ... in the science of grammar, in writing verses and poetry in meter, and in speaking correct Hebrew." Even if the "Portuguese" curriculum did not produce the educational miracles he reported, it was, as he recognized, a pedagogically effective curriculum, and unlike the Ashkenazi institution of the *heder* included in its goals the child's aesthetic development.

In general, innovation was a necessity in the rejudaization of the Amsterdam community. An educational system was required that would be consistent both with rabbinic tradition and with "Portuguese" intellectual tastes. And there was a need to introduce adults to the basics of Judaism, including the Hebrew alphabet, without offending their mature sensibilities. Given the demands of adult life, it is remarkable how many men born and raised in the Peninsula (and perhaps women, though they left little evidence) maintained a steady course in their effort to repossess Judaism. It is just as remarkable that this neophyte community was able, by the 1630s, to produce its own rabbis—personalities of the stature of Menasseh ben Israel and Isaac Aboab da Fonseca. More importantly, collectively speaking, is the fact that for every rabbi and theological thinker produced there were many members of the community who were willing and able to participate actively in its life, whose knowledge of Jewish tradition was adequate, if not brilliant.

The Ambivalent and the Heterodox

In such a community there were also bound to be persons who would not adapt to or comply with the enterprise of rejudaization. Not everyone responded to the rhetoric of "restoration" or accepted the authority invested in the *parnasim*. What happened when persuasion failed to bring cooperation? And given the difficulties of the transition the emigres were expected to make, what could reasonably be expected of them and their children? For the early communal leaders, a crucial task was that of establishing their authority, defining the boundaries of acceptable behavior, and dealing with deviance.

Theoretically, the powers of the *parnasim*, like those of the leaders of every Jewish community (*kehilah* or *kahal*), derived from Jewish law and centuries-old patterns.[60] Jewish law did not prescribe a particular system of governance but did recognize the constituted authorities, however chosen, as representing the entire community and granted them full juridical and disciplinary powers. The Amsterdam merger agreement of 1639 and other evidence suggest that the particular model for the governance of the new community was the "Ponentine" ("Portuguese") community in Venice.[61] Indeed, its name, *K.K. Talmud Torah*, was borrowed from that community.

Unfortunately, the degree to which the Amsterdam community borrowed from "Ponentine" patterns of organization cannot be fully established, since the statutes of the Venetian community have not been preserved.

The basic principle behind the community's organization was concentration of authority in the hands of a few. The *Mahamad* dominated every aspect of community life. The matter was put bluntly in the very first article of the 1639 communal statutes (called *haskamot*, a Hebrew term used in Sephardi cornmunities),[62] which stated that "the *Mahamad* shall have authority over everything."[63] The *Mahamad* was a self-perpetuating body in which the outgoing members chose the incoming ones, so that a group of "insiders" shared power among themselves. The oligarchical character of the community's government reflected the trend in Jewish communities everywhere in the early modern period, a result of the emergence of a stratum of extremely wealthy families which paid a large portion of the communal taxes. But the power of the *Mahamad* also represented deeply-ingrained patriarchal patterns in "Portuguese" society. Given the highly corporate structure of Dutch society, it is not surprising that Dutch authorities were willing to recognize the wide powers of the *Mahamad*. They did not, though, regard its authority as absolute, and on occasion the magistrates chose to interfere in internal communal matters.[64]

The members of the *Mahamad* (*parnasim*, or *senhores do Mahamad*, as they were known) were entrusted, along with other tasks, with maintaining rabbinic norms. The major instruments they possessed to impose discipline were censorship, denial of synagogue or burial privileges, and ultimately the *herem*, or ban. But using these measures required a certain delicacy. On the one hand, communal officials did not wish to alienate the ambivalent, especially since one of their goals was to bring into the sphere of Jewish communal life all "Jews of the Portuguese exile." On the other hand, they were committed to establishing a community that would be recognized as legitimate within the wider Jewish world, a goal that required adherence to rabbinic norms.

There were various degrees and types of resistance to the program and authority of the *Mahamad*. There were those who lived at the fringes of communal life and declined to pay the communal *finta* tax assessed by communal leaders, as well as the voluntary taxes or *promesas*.[65] Such marginal persons who otherwise possessed social status did not exist in most Jewish communities, where social status required communal participation. Moreover, the marginal "Portuguese" knew they had the option of living, as they long had, in Christian society, and they sometimes chose that option, joining one or another of the Christian sects in the Netherlands.

For all its formal power, then, the *Mahamad* suffered from inherent weakness. This can be seen in a case from 1646 when a member of the community, Samuel Marques, was faced with excommunication for adultery. He was offered the alternative of leaving Amsterdam, but he spurned it, saying outspokenly that he did not recognize the members of the *Mahamad* as his leaders.[66] He was apparently not threatened by banishment from the community since he had never really lived within it. A similar case was recorded in 1622, when the *Mahamad* gave a certain Francisco Lopez

Capadosse an ultimatum to have himself and his sons circumcised and join the community by a certain time or be put under *herem* (a ban). Unmoved, Capadosse replied that members of the community could "do whatever they please."[67]

The ultimatum given to Capadosse is worth closer consideration. We have discussed the great importance the ex-converso initiates placed on the act of circumcision and the need rabbis felt to dispel misconceptions about it. Nevertheless, rabbis frequently cooperated in making circumcision a precondition for full acceptance in "Portuguese" communities. *Some* criterion was clearly needed to draw a line between those who attached themselves to the community, however superficially, and those who arrived in a place of freedom yet lingered "outside Judaism." Interesting in this respect is the decision of a rabbinic court in Livorno in the seventeenth century as to whether a Portuguese Jew who had not been circumcised—because, it was explained, he had assets in the Peninsula and might want to return there—might hold a Torah scroll. A rabbinic scholar in Pisa (Jacob Seneor) ruled that it was entirely permissible for him to do so. The Livorno court did not disagree with this ruling in principle, but taking into consideration the particular circumstances of the "Portuguese" decided to make a contrary ruling:[68]

> We rule that although the law is thus [i.e., permits this], the times are such as to make this inappropriate. So you must not give them [the uncircumcised] equal status with fully practising Jews [*yisra'elim gemurim*] by allowing them to touch sacred objects… This would result in ruin, for they would put off entering the Covenant of Abraham if they saw that although uncircumcised they are denied nothing and may touch sacred objects just like fully practising Jews. Such an unacceptable situation will not develop if an explicit distinction is made.

Rulings that drew barriers between circumcised and uncircumcised became common in the "Portuguese" diaspora. In 1620, the Bet Israel congregation in Amsterdam ruled that persons who had not undergone circumcision by the upcoming sabbath prior to Rosh Hashanah would not be permitted to enter the synagogue, and that newcomers would be given two months to be circumcised.[69] One of the earliest ordinances of the London community barred any uncircumcised male, as well as members of his family, from burial in the communal cemetery.[70] Among the "Portuguese" of Amsterdam this was apparently not the case, since at least two persons buried at Ouderkerk were circumcised after death.[71] But as the Capadosse case of 1622 shows, this does not mean that circumcision was not viewed in Amsterdam as a key criterion for belonging to the community.

Denial of the right of burial was used by the *Mahamad* in Amsterdam, if not to encourage circumcision, to pressure a few of the emigres to undergo formal conversion to Judaism. These were persons who unquestionably belonged to "the Nation" but, because of known female Old Christian ancestors on their mother's side, were not Jewish according to rabbinic law, which held that Jewishness was transmitted through the mother. These persons were required to undergo ritual immersion (as well as circumcision, in the case of males) in order to be recognized as Jews. To encourage compliance, a ruling of April 1624 denied Jewish burial to any person "who was of the gentile race [*que tenha raca de goy*]" in the "feminine line."[72]

It is interesting that the few cases recorded in which such persons were denied Jewish burial involved marginal members of the community: an illegitimate son of a "Portuguese" man, a mulatto woman, and a daughter of a person identified only as "the English Jew."[73] Partly, this was a result of the very strong endogamous marriage patterns among the "Portuguese" in the Peninsula. Most of the emigres did not have Old Christian maternal figures in their genealogies. But it may also reflect a "don't ask, don't tell" policy on the part of the *Mahamad*. Communal leaders probably hesitated to act on such matters unless, as in the cases mentioned, the problematic female relative was a very recent ancestor and a person whose gentile status was well known. Given "Portuguese" ideas about the purity of Jewish blood, members of the *Mahamad* would not have been eager to uncover gentile blood in respected families.

For figures like Francisco Lopez Capadosse, who scorned the community's threats, the available sanctions had little significance. But these were the exception. Most emigres, whatever their degree of commitment to Judaism, wished to live among their own, belong to the community and participate fully in its social and ritual life. This powerful social need was an important bulwark of the *Mahamad*'s authority.

It was precisely this social need that made the *herem*, or ban, an effective sanction. It was not a measure of last resort, nor was it necessarily a severe measure.

Indeed, for certain violations of communal norms it was used quite routinely—and lifted just as routinely. It is thus often quite misleading to translate the term *herem* as "excommunication."[74] Persons who committed relatively minor infractions, like publicly insulting other members of the community or buying meat from an Ashkenazi butcher, could incur the *herem*.[75] Menasseh ben Israel was banned for a period of one day for verbally attacking the *Mahamad* in the synagogue over a measure he found personally insulting.[76] Sometimes the *herem* meant only that a person would be denied a particular privilege. In 1656, for example, the *Mahamad* declared that Abraham Gabay Mendez would not receive the honor of being called to the Torah or any other synagogue honor for two years because when he was in London he did not worship in a *minyan* with the Jews there (or even identify himself as a Jew), although he had been circumcised.[77] While the offenses that were punished by *herem* differed (in some cases they were not even stated), the most frequent were journeys (usually for business) to "lands of idolatry" where Judaism could not be observed;[78] overt challenges to the *Mahamad*'s authority; and violations of sexual norms.[79]

Members of the *Mahamad* clearly understood that the sanctions they wielded to punish such behavior derived from rabbinic law. But their actions sometimes betray a penchant to follow norms with roots in the Peninsula. A look at violations of sexual norms in the community and their punishment (or nonpunishment) is revealing in this respect. Jewish law, as well as civil law in most Christian states, prohibited sexual relations between Jews and gentiles; and in Ashkenazi communities attitudes strongly reinforced these prohibitions among upstanding members of the community. But as mentioned in chapter three, it was not unusual for "Portuguese" merchants to have sexual relations with Dutch or other gentile women, often maidservants. In the period between 1600 and 1623, thirteen such cases appear in published notarial records—and of course we learn of such cases only when something went wrong, usually a pregnancy.[80] Some of the men involved in these affairs were pillars of the Portuguese-Jewish community. One of them—Duarte Fernandes (Joshua Habilho), accused of fathering a child by a nineteen-year-old Dutch girl in 1600—later went on to become an important figure in the community, a founding member of the *Dotar* and one of the three persons who drafted the 1639 *Haskamot*.[81] Another who admitted a liaison ending in pregnancy was Jeronimo Henriques (Joseph Cohen), a member of the Bet Jacob congregation as well as one of the founders of the *Dotar* (and twice an officer of that institution after the birth of an illegitimate child by his Norwegian maidservant).[82] The children of such unions were often recognized by their fathers, who made some monetary compensation to the mother, sometimes considerable. In the case of Jeronimo Henriques's illegitimate child, the girl actually lived in Henriques's house for seven years. Antonio Lopes Suasso (Isaac Israel Suasso), the enormously wealthy financier who married a Pinto in 1653, and his son Francisco Lopes Suasso (Abraham Israel Suasso), both maintained gentile mistresses (in addition to "Portuguese" wives) who bore them illegitimate children, for whom they took some responsibility.[83] Such behavior was undoubtedly regarded with disapproval by the *hakhamim* and more pious members of the community. But no action was taken to punish it.

However, communal officials did impose the *herem* in cases in which other sexual norms were breached: adultery (or even suspected adultery) within the community, the marriage of youths without the knowledge of parents or communal leaders, and bigamy. Concerning adultery, relations between a "Portuguese" man and a "Portuguese" married woman were regarded with special severity. To be sure, this was consistent with Jewish law. But such relations also brought into play the issue of "Portuguese" honor. This can be seen in a case from 1654, when the *Mahamad* placed Jacob Moreno, Moreno's wife, and Daniel Castiel under the ban because, despite repeated warnings that Daniel Castiel refrain from entering Moreno's home in the husband's absence, Castiel continued to do so.[84] The *herem* was not imposed for adultery per se—nothing had been proved—but rather defiance of the *Mahamad*. What is significant is that this was not the kind of offense the *Mahamad* could overlook.

The allegiance of communal leaders to Iberian sociosexual norms is displayed most unambiguously in the policies of that quintessentially "Portuguese" institution, the *Dotar*. According to its statutes, illegitimate girls of "Portuguese" fathers were allowed to enter the *Dotar* dowry lottery, despite the fact that Jewish law did not recognize them as Jews. (Presumably they converted to Judaism to receive a dowry.) However, illegitimate daughters of "Portuguese" mothers, who were Jewish from birth according to Jewish law, were not permitted to apply for a dowry "under any circumstances."[85] The reinforcement of Iberian sociosexual attitudes, even when these were at odds with rabbinic principles, is particularly conspicuous in this stipulation. Its clear message was that extramarital relations between a "Portuguese" man and a gentile woman (presumably of inferior class) did not constitute a blemish on "Portuguese" honor, while extramarital relations involving a "Portuguese" woman were a scandal and a disgrace.

Whether supporting "Portuguese" or rabbinic norms, the members of the *Mahamad* showed themselves to be deeply conservative in spirit. They worked to create a traditional, ethnically tight-knit society that was both an enclave of Iberian social values and a bastion of traditional Jewish thinking. They cultivated an ideal with roots in Iberian converso society, but adapted it in a way which must have seemed natural to them in the new conditions of the diaspora. The ideal cultural type that emerged was very complex indeed, yet coherent and reproducible. In Amsterdam and Hamburg, there were many who seemed to represent this ideal. They were, of course, men. Each was an important figure in a far-flung family-cum-commercial network, possessed a coat of arms or even an aristocratic title, was a regular synagogue-goer with a prestigiously located seat, and played an active role in communal affairs. Such a person, be his name Belmonte, Texeira, Pinto, Curiel, Azevedo, Senior Coronel, or any number of others, had achieved the pinnacle of social success in the "Portuguese" diaspora.

The conservative character of Amsterdam's Portuguese-Jewish commual elite has sometimes been masked by its cultural cosmopolitanism. In comparison to Ashkenazi communal leaders, the "Portuguese" were better able to absorb new trends in European society because of their command of European languages and their interest in European culture. And, indeed, the libraries of the "Portuguese" reflected intellectual interests that extended beyond the rabbinic world. However, what is significant is not the fact of "European" interests among the Portuguese Jews—this was entirely natural—but the conservative nature of these interests. Their libraries reflect a pursuit of the safe and the comfortable—classics, "histories," travel literature, and the like.[86] Even the erudite physician Orobio de Castro, a spokesman for the communal elite in the 1660s and, unlike his fellows, a man unusually well acquainted with new philosophical trends, adhered to quintessentially conservative ideas about both Judaism and medicine.

Yet even the somewhat antiquated cosmopolitanism of the "Portuguese" posed a threat to the ethos the communal leadership wished to promote. The themes and images of European belles lettres which had taken root in the New Christian imagination naturally continued to thrive in ex-converso minds despite the rites of passage of rejudaization. The *Mahamad*, as we have noted elsewhere, did not attempt to eliminate all expressions of Iberian culture from communal life. It banned theater productions from the sacred sphere of the synagogue, but did not otherwise interfere with the freedom of community members to indulge their appetite for European, and especially Iberian, literary works.

The *Mahamad* did, however, claim the right to censor the literary output of members of the community. This was stated unequivocally in clause 37 of the 1639 statutes, which stipulated that no member of the community might print—either in Amsterdam or outside it—books in Spanish or Portuguese (*livros ladinos*), or in Hebrew without the *Mahamad*'s approval.[87] The *Mahamad*'s authority in this matter was less than it laid claim to, though, since it had no power to enforce its ruling outside Amsterdam, members of the community could (and did) publish offensive or potentially offensive books in Antwerp or Brussels.[88] Some Amsterdam "Portuguese" authors even managed to print books in Amsterdam under the *Mahamad*'s nose by citing a false place of publication.[89] The *Mahamad* did have the power to prevent such books from circulating in the community, however, and could thus limit their sales.

What kind of material did the *Mahamad* seek to repress? The books it censored tended to fall into three categories: 1) works with openly erotic content; 2) works emphasizing pagan mythological motifs; and 3) literary works which presented scriptural narratives in a "profane" manner.

One document that reveals much about the leadership's conception of its role as censor is a memorandum drawn up by a board of rabbis reviewing Daniel Levi de Barrios's *Coro de las Musas*, which the author had had printed in Brussels in 1672. Before detailing the reasons for condemning the book, the rabbis pointed to two general aspects of its contents which disturbed them: matters that jeopardized the "honor of our Jewish faith" and "lascivious [matters]." They did not invoke *halakhah*. Indeed they opened with a list of three features of the book which, "while not totally prohibited, were somewhat scandalous." These were a) the author's way of referring to planets and other creatures by the names of pagan gods; b) the author's use of the title "saint" for "idolatrous and impure Christians"; and c) the author's readiness to grant Christians and idolators a place in heaven. There follows an enumeration of a number of even more obviously insincere (many of them trivial) passages in the book that were deemed offensive.[90] The members of the board were well aware that Barrios was not championing pagan practices or endorsing the Church's dogma on saints. He was courting and flattering Christian readers and patrons, for pecuniary reasons. But in succumbing to the all-too-easy posturing of the converso (and not for the first time)[91]— in playing the admirer of both pagan and Christian Rome—De Barrios was violating important taboos.

In censorship cases in which books, not their authors, were banned—most notably those of De Barrios and Jacob (Manuel) de Pina[92]—the communal leaders were not facing a frontal attack on the community's values, but rather a threat to its image (or, as they would put it, its "honor"). Erotic verses and pagan imagery were deplored, their authors chastised and resocialized, and the little storm passed.

The greatest threat to the community was part of a far broader phenomenon in European culture, namely the criticism of religious tradition. A few generations later, the attack on clerical authority would begin to pose a challenge to all traditional European Jewish societies. But in the seventeenth century, the northern European communities of ex-conversos were unique among European Jewries as crucibles for sweeping, ideologically anchored attacks on rabbinic Judaism. There is a paradoxical aspect to this. Most of the emigres responded to the traumatic Iberian experience by embracing a self-affirming ancient religious tradition and a secure "Portuguese" collective existence. But others were driven by the same experience to reject vehemently this new orthodoxy. To the consternation and concern of the leadership, anticlerical and deistic ideas similar to those being cultivated in small intellectual circles throughout Europe surfaced fairly early. From 1616 to 1657, several searching and provocative souls openly challenged the very premise on which the community was built, namely the obligation of Jews to observe the Law of Moses as interpreted by the rabbis.

It is difficult to characterize the response of the members of the *Mahamad* to these subversive ideas, since they left little record of their thoughts. With the exception of Orobio de Castro they probably did not grasp the import of new philosophical currents. What is perhaps most profoundly reflected in their behavior is not their piety or stringency, but their rejection of the principle of individual freedom of conscience. They led a profoundly collective existence anchored in belief in the divine scheme of things. They had built a community that successfully integrated large numbers of emigres, educating their children, supporting the poor, attracting (and eventually producing) important rabbinic figures. This community had presses that were renowned throughout the Jewish world; it was a nerve center second to none for "the Nation"; it had worked out a uniquely favorable modus vivendi with the Dutch authorities. All of this had been achieved painstakingly, for the sake of "the Nation" and the service of God and, of course, for the ego rewards communal leadership offered. These leaders were not likely to tolerate repeated public statements by persons who challenged the foundations and significance of this enterprise (as well as their own authority).

Sensitivity to potential challenges appeared early, in an episode discussed briefly in chapter two. A person in Amsterdam (probably the physician David Farar) insisted in 1615 that the Torah could be interpreted properly only according to the plain meaning of the text (*peshat*). This represented a rejection of the large and highly revered body of traditional homiletic commentary. Members of the communal elite were troubled, and one of them—presumably one of the *hakhamim*—turned to an eminent rabbinic authority in Venice, Leon de Modena. Modena held that the position the nonconformist had adopted was legitimate and indeed implicitly criticized those who questioned it.[93] Modena, who was not a Sephardi Jew[94] and spoke from the firmly established Venice community, may not have appreciated the fears awakened in a community of neophytes by a person who openly criticized any aspect of tradition.

The following year witnessed a far more threatening challenge to rabbinic tradition by a member of "the Nation" then living in Hamburg. The rebellious spirit was Uriel da Costa, an ex-converso from Porto and a former student of canon law at the University of Coimbra. Da Costa threw down the gauntlet when he sent a written statement to communal leaders in Venice attacking the rabbinic tradition (the so-called Oral Law) as a gross distortion of the Law of Moses. No copy of his written attack has been preserved, but its contents are described at length in a Hebrew refutation, *Magen ve-zinnah*, by Leon de Modena.[95] According to Modena's summary, Da Costa argued that the Oral Law was not an integral part of the Torah but rather a "new Torah" contradicting the old.[96] Modena became involved when the Venetian leaders referred Da Costa's composition to him.[97] He must have seen at once that, unschooled as Da Costa was in rabbinics, his arguments had a powerful and persuasive aspect—especially among ex-conversos, who were more likely to be struck by Da Costa's view than Jews educated from childhood to accept traditional teachings justifying rabbinic innovation. Modena wrote to the Hamburg community demanding that Da Costa be excommunicated if he persisted in his views. When he did persist, the Venetian community, in August 1618, formally imposed a ban on him and his followers, and this ban was promulgated in Hamburg as well.[98]

The *Mahamad* in Amsterdam was not involved in this episode, although it was surely aware of it. It took action only when Da Costa arrived in Amsterdam in May 1623 with the intention of publishing a book there elucidating his heretical views. The *Mahamad* imposed a *herem* on him in February 1623.[99] This did not prevent Da Costa from having his book published in that city in the spring of 1624 by a Christian printer.[100] The first part of the book is simply a revised version of Da Costa's earlier attack on the Oral Law. But in the second part Da Costa attacked another teaching of Jewish tradition, the doctrine of the immortality of the soul: he argued that it was an innovation with no basis in Scripture. With heavy-handed sarcasm, Da Costa argued that "the saintly Pharisees"—the talmudic sages—were "the real renegades and heretics who are accursed."[101] As if intent on offending his readers, he went on to declare converso martyrdom (and Jewish martyrdom in general) a futile act since, according to his reading of Scripture, God did not require (or want) such a sacrifice.[102] He moreover mocked persons he had encountered who deluded themselves that mere lip service to "the Law" ensured their salvation. Likewise, he scorned those who cited a certain rabbinic saying—"All Israel have a share in the world to come"—as proof that salvation was assured for anyone of Jewish blood. Ridiculing this convenient conviction, he wrote:

> Except for a wretch like me—heretic, excommunicated, excluded from your midst—all the rest of you, in one pack [*fornada*] or another, by means of a prayer or some other measure, will find yourselves in the world-to-come because you are the children of Israel and as such you possess that privilege and so can sleep in peace.[103]

Da Costa's attack was not just on rabbinic Judaism, but on the ex-converso establishment in general, with its entrenched belief in salvation through the Law of Moses. At this point he was clearly enraged, and struck at the most sensitive and charged areas of Portuguese-Jewish belief. There is no better guide to the collective ideology of this community than Da Costa's assault on it.

It has been argued that Da Costa was disciplined for publishing this book because he was jeopardizing the community in Christian eyes. In repudiating in print the doctrine of the immortality of the soul, he was repudiating a basic doctrine not only of Judaism but of Christianity as well. The "Portuguese" were already suspected—not without reason—of harboring skeptics among them. Only a few years before the Da Costa episode, Hugo Grotius had addressed the issue of "unbelief" among the Jews in his recommendations concerning the terms of Jewish settlement in Holland. One of the three beliefs he insisted each Jew must hold in order to be tolerated was that "after death there shall be another life in which the just will be rewarded and the evil punished"—precisely what Da Costa denied. Even more pointedly, Grotius noted that "among the Jews as well as among those of other religious convictions, there are often some atheists and impious people who should not be tolerated in any good republic."[104] While Grotius's recommendations never became law, they do indicate what was undoubtedly the opinion of most Dutch magistrates. By publishing his ideas, Da Costa was threatening the well-being of the community.

It would be a mistake, however, to conclude that Da Costa was excommunicated primarily because he endangered relations between the Portuguese-Jewish community and the Dutch authorities. No doubt the *Mahamad* was concerned about the opinion of the authorities in this matter. But this was one aspect of the problem. Da Costa's opponent Samuel da Silva, who published a rebuttal of Da Costa's opinions on the immortality of the soul, articulated the deeper concerns of the "Portuguese" when he spoke of the need of the community to protect itself from "this hypocrite, or any others of his type who, excellent as their stock may be [!], do in some rare instances degenerate into monsters."[105] That is, Da Costa was a kind of mutant who threatened the community's arduously achieved Jewish gestalt. The *Mahamad* banned him—as Modena had earlier insisted he be banned—primarily because he had overstepped the boundaries of tolerable dissent within the Jewish world.

Da Costa formally recanted in 1628 and rejoined the Amsterdam community. But according to his autobiography which, however unreliable (and partly spurious) it may be,[106] has been shown to be based on historical fact,[107] he was banned once more in 1632 or 1633 and ended his life as a deist, denying not only the Oral Law but also the revealed character of Scripture and the providential nature of God. He committed suicide in 1640[108] after undergoing a second and, by his account, exceedingly humiliating ceremony of penance in the synagogue.

Da Costa must have been bitterly amused during his second period of excommunication by a debate that broke out in the community in the mid-1630s. A group of enthusiasts around the young *hakham* Isaac Aboab da Fonseca insisted that regardless of his or her sins no Jew would suffer eternal punishment, justifying this belief with the saying of the Sages, "All Israel have a share in the world to come." Da Costa had already, it may be recalled, ridiculed persons with such complacent views. But these views apparently played a special function in a community of ex-conversos. As the scholar who analyzed the episode suggested,[109] such a community had particular anxieties which were relieved by assurance that all Jews were, so to speak, automatically saved. While the emigres and their children living "in Judaism" believed they had hope for salvation through the Law of Moses, they would have been tormented by the thought that their forefathers and other loved ones who had lived (or were living) "in idolatry" would suffer eternal punishment. An idea of blanket salvation connected with Jewish identity offered a vision of a people who were scattered and divided in this world but united in the world to come.

Comforting as it was, the belief that any Jew, regardless of his or her sins, would enjoy a "portion in the world to come" contradicted traditional Jewish teaching. The "orthodox" rallied around Saul Levi Mortera, who insisted that only righteous Jews would be rewarded and that evil Jews would be punished for all eternity.[110] The strife between the two parties threatened to disrupt the community. Once again a sensitive issue of collective boundaries (this time in the afterlife) was referred to Venice.

In this case, the Venetian rabbinic authorities made explicit their concern about the reactions of the gentile world to this debate. The idea that sinners, as long as they were Jewish, would be saved was not only bad theology, it was offensive and heretical in the eyes of Christians. The rabbis therefore asked that the dispute not be brought formally before a Jewish court:[111]

> We know for certain that if knowledge of the dispute spreads among the gentiles, immense damage will arise for us from having suggested that matters could be in doubt among us, the more so if they hear [that there is a belief among the Jews] that even the soul that has sinned will attain eternal salvation.

But gentile anger was not the only issue. The dispute was a clear case of "converso" innovation confronting rabbinic orthodoxy, and ultimately rabbinic orthodoxy won the day. The Venetian authorities chastised and silenced the young Aboab—who was to emerge in years to come, older and wiser, as a major rabbinic figure in the Amsterdam community.

Thus in the cases of both Da Costa and Aboab—the skeptic and the kabbalistic enthusiast—the Amsterdam leadership cooperated with the more established Venetian leadership to suppress manifestations of converso extremism. Both types of extremists resurfaced, however, in subsequent years.

The kabbalistic enthusiasts were important in fanning the flames of excitement during the messianic movement around the figure of Shabbetai Zvi in 1665–66. This convulsive episode has been discussed in great detail by scholars, most exhaustively by Gershom Scholem in his monumental work on the movement.[112] It is true that the Jews of Amsterdam, both Ashkenazi and "Portuguese," played an important role in the spread of the movement among European Jews after news arrived from Palestine in November 1665 about a curious figure who soon became known as the King Messiah and about his "prophet" Nathan of Gaza. Many of the major figures in the Amsterdam community, merchants and rabbis alike (including Isaac Aboab da Fonseca), were gripped by messianic fervor. But this was not particular to Amsterdam or to "Portuguese" communities. On the contrary, pillars of Jewish communities throughout the Jewish diaspora joined in the excited anticipatory activity. It is difficult to say whether this relatively brief episode and its denouement (Shabbetai Zvi converted to Islam under coercion in September 1666) were handled by the "Portuguese" elite in Amsterdam differently because of the particular characteristics of the community. To determine this would require a detailed comparative study that lies beyond the scope of this book.[113]

In any case, what is known about the episode throws little light on the issues of self-definition and boundary maintenance that concern us. The roots of the movement lay elsewhere in the Jewish world, in the Ottoman Empire. The communal elite of Amsterdam was faced by a complex situation, but not with a challenge to its authority, since it shared in the enthusiasm. Nor did its behavior raise eyebrows in the wider Jewish world, since members of Jewish elites of all backgrounds were behaving similarly, from Tunisia to Palestine, Poland to Yemen. And while aspects of sabbatianism *after* Shabbetai Zvi's conversion do have a "converso" dimension,[114] the rabbinic leadership in Amsterdam did not view it as a major threat. Indeed, the vehemently anti-sabbatian rabbi Jacob Sasportas treated one of the post-conversion "believers" (none other than Daniel Levi de Barrim) with considerable indulgence.[115] Thus, in my view, the sabbatian movement did not play a significant role in the development of "Portuguese" identity in Amsterdam, and we will focus here on more specifically "Portuguese" issues of skepticism and heterodoxy.

The greatest crisis involving militant unbelievers in the community arose in 1656, when three articulate, vocal, and provocative persons with somewhat similar deistic views began teaching their ideas, primarily to the young.[116] Two of them, Juan de Prado and Daniel Ribera, were emigres from the Peninsula. Prado had flirted with deistic ideas even before he left Spain.[117] The third, Baruch Spinoza, was a young man of twenty-four, born and raised in a merchant family in the Amsterdam Portuguese-Jewish community.

Of the three figures, the one whose ideas at this time are least-known is, ironically, Spinoza, about whose later ideas we know so much. He was excommunicated in July 1656. But the *herem* imposed on him, severe as it was, was extremely vague, speaking only of his "abominable heresies [*horrendas heregias*]" and "monstrous deeds [*ynormes obres*]."[118] Unfortunately his *Apologia para justificarse de su abdicación de la Synagoga*, said to have been written after his excommunication, either has not been preserved or was never written. The most revealing description of Spinoza's views in this period is a brief statement given to the Madrid Inquisition by an Augustinian friar who met Spinoza and Prado together in Amsterdam in late 1658 or early 1659. The friar reported that the two said they had come to hold three key beliefs antithetical to rabbinic Judaism—that "the Law was not true, and that the soul dies along with the body, and that God exists only philosophically"—and that they had been expelled "from the synagogue" for these beliefs.[119] If, as seems to be the case, Spinoza and Prado insisted on disseminating such ideas, the *Mahamad* could hardly have ignored them. In early February 1657, after Spinoza's excommunication, the *Mahamad* launched an investigation into the teachings of Prado and Ribera (though the latter had apparently left Amsterdam). The relatively abundant testimony about the two men indicates that they denied the election of Israel and the divine origin of the Law of Moses. Ribera was even said to reject the existence of God. They were far from quiet about their beliefs and, moreover, openly vented their hostility toward the *hakhamim* and the *Mahamad*.[120] It is not surprising that when the investigation was completed Prado was excommunicated.

Scholars have debated to what degree the *Mahamad*, in banning Spinoza and Prado, was acting to placate Amsterdam's civil and ecclesiastical authorities. There is no way to know. Certainly one could be severely disciplined in Dutch society at this time for disseminating such ideas, as Spinoza understood clearly when he later published (or decided not to publish) his works.[121] Moreover, the Portuguese Jews still felt their position was precarious, as a minority in a Christian state. However tolerant the Dutch authorities had become regarding philosophical ideas that did not conform to the basic tenets of the churches, the *Mahamad* did not wish to jeopardize the image of the Portuguese Jews as good citizens who adhered to the principles of an ancient religion.[122]

Nevertheless, the *Mahamad* seems to have been concerned first and foremost with internal issues. This is reflected in the role assumed in the Prado affair by the newly arrived emigre Isaac Orobio de Castro. Technically, Orobio was not permitted to correspond with the banned Prado, then living in Antwerp, even though Orobio had known Prado in Spain and felt an obligation to try to bring him back to Judaism.[123] But the *Mahamad*, while carefully regulating (and even censoring) the correspondence between the two, not only did nothing to punish Orobio but even allowed Orobio's first letter to circulate in manuscript.[124] Orobio thus became a spokesman for the community and its ideals and an important ideologue in the conflict.

He was particularly well suited for this role. He was soon himself a member of the communal elite, playing a significant role in communal affairs in the years after his arrival.[125] But unlike other members of this elite, Orobio had academic training and the theological sophistication to rebut Prado's arguments. What is striking, however, is that in many ways he was not far from the habits of mind of the Pintos and Belmontes. However intellectualized his position vis-à-vis Prado was, it resonated with the ideology and instincts of the merchant elite. The central argument in his correspondence with Prado was that an individual's reasoning can easily lead him astray, whereas an ancient tradition about which learned men agree, as long as it does not directly contradict reason, should be accepted as the basis for faith.[126] It was an argument for perpetuating the ancestral faith that deeply harmonized with crypto-Jewish ways of thinking. Ultimately, truth was validated by collective ethnic consent.

In general, Orobio regarded novel ideas as suspect. In a revised version of the prologue to his first letter, his *Epistola invectiva contra Prado*,[127] he denounced the search for novelty as a moral vice. He depicted those who invented new notions as self-promoting, even malicious, while those who submitted to tradition demonstrated their dignity and reason. To attack Scriptures which had been preserved uncorrupted for centuries was a sign of moral weakness. "The unworthy and frivolous claims that malicious innovation [*la innovadora malicia*] produces against this inalterable truth," he wrote of those who attacked the divinity of Scripture, "are worthy neither to be recorded nor discussed."[128] Speaking primarily of Prado, he asserted that this man, "who loves his [own] opinion so much," should "submit himself to a judgment … which our ancestors have possessed for three thousand five hundred years without interruption and which, rather than declining, is continually being enhanced."[129]

While Orobio's intellectual instincts may have been related to his experience as a converso, he perhaps found support for them in contemporary European society. Orobio's biographer has pointed out the similarity between some of his arguments and those of certain contemporary Christians who were battling skepticism, especially the Jansenists and those whom Richard Popkin has referred to as "fideistic skeptics."[130] These defenders of faith argued—to simplify and generalize their beliefs greatly—that while human reason was important for evaluating beliefs, it could easily lead one astray if used alone, without reliance on authority. Whether or not Orobio was familiar with these ideas, he anchored his defense of rabbinic Judaism in similar arguments, arguments that spoke to wider questions about faith in early modern European society.

But Orobio's emphasis on antiquity and collective ancestral judgment as the foundations of authority seems to draw at least as much from "Portuguese" sources as from Christian polemics against skepticism, of which Orobio, as far as we know, knew nothing.[131] Orobio's line of thinking resonated quite naturally among the "Portuguese," with their drama (as they conceived of it) of repression in the Peninsula and "restoration" on free soil, of heroism at the stake and stubborn adherence to ancestral beliefs. In contrast, the individualistic, universalistic, and mercilessly unsentimental notions of Da Costa, Prado, and Spinoza ran deeply against the grain of their own religio-ethnic intuitions as well as their idealized conception of the community. If the converso experience had contributed to the conviction of a few rugged souls that they could rely on no truths except those arrived at through their own powers of reasoning, it seems to have persuaded other conversos—indeed most of the emigres—that in turning away from the Church they could rely only on an ancient countervailing tradition.

Relations with Other Jews: Tudescos, Polacos, Italianos

That ancient tradition had at its core an ethnic, collective conception of religious responsibility, of which the ex-conversos were well aware. Being a Jew meant being a part of the Jewish people; and the "return" to Judaism implied a "return" to the Jewish people as well—an entity that had hitherto been mainly an abstraction. For a group with so complex and tenuous an identity, this aspect of restoration was fraught with problems.

For early converso settlers in southwest France, Holland, Hamburg, and London, the "Jewish people" remained mainly an abstraction even after emigration, since there were few Jews in these places who did not have Iberian origins. Before long, however, this situation changed dramatically. As conditions for Jews in central and eastern Europe deteriorated, and as the governments of the developing Atlantic states began to readmit Jews, Ashkenazi Jews began to trickle—and then flood—westward, settling among other places in the centers of the northern "Portuguese" diaspora. For the conversos, the encounter with these alien Jews was highly problematic. The first to arrive were German Jews fleeing the Thirty Years War, arriving in Amsterdam from the 1620s onward. They were not only culturally foreign to the "Portuguese," but tended to be poor and uneducated as well. Most were from the lowest social strata—butchers, peddlars, beggars, and the like. Often they became menial employees of Portuguese Jews. They did not conform to the self-image of the Portuguese Jews in any way, and were regarded by the latter with distaste from the start. Initially they were permitted to worship with the "Portuguese" and to bury their dead in Ouderkerk (in a separate plot, for those not of "the Nation"),[132] but they were not accepted as members of the congregations.

The term used to identify the German Ashkenazim was borrowed from Venetian usage, where the Italian *tedesco* (German) was used to refer to Jews of German-Ashkenazi origin. This term was adopted into the Portuguese language of the ex-conversos in Amsterdam, where it became *tudesco* and was given an Iberian plural ending—that is, *tudescos* (or *todescos*) rather than the Italian *tedeschi*.[133] Ashkenazi Jews were referred to as *tudescos* in some of the earliest records of the Amsterdam community, the first mentioned being a "Mahir [Meir] Tudesqo" who was buried in the Ouderkerk cemetery in March 1618.[134] As this instance illustrates, among the "Portuguese," Ashkenazi origins became part of one's name, a key identifier.

The exclusivist tendency of the "Portuguese" became more pronounced as the number of Ashkenazim increased. The *tudescos* formed their own congregation in 1635; and though for several years they remained somewhat dependent on the Portuguese-Jewish community, they soon had their own synagogue and rabbis.[135] In 1642, the "Portuguese" helped the Ashkenazim finance the purchase of their own cemetery in Muiderberg, which made it possible, among other things, to deny them the right to bury their dead in Ouderkerk.[136] The two groups also tended to live in different streets or neighborhoods. In the first decades of the seventeenth century, most of the *tudescos* lived near the Turfsteeg and in Ververstraat. Later, the poorer Ashkenazim lived in the crowded, shabby district of Marken and Uilenberg, while the poor of the Portuguese Jews lived in the Nieuwe Kerkstraat.[137]

The Ashkenazim were generally persons for whom poverty had become a way of life, while in contrast many of the "Portuguese" poor (though not all) were recently impoverished or did not feel themselves to be part of a permanent culture of poverty. These were the "shame-faced poor," the *vergonzantes*, as they were known in Spain. The *Dotar* records offer a glimpse of the pride and humiliation of such persons. A certain Daniel Campos, despite his genuine poverty,[138] refused to allow his daughter to accept the dowry she won in 1631. He insisted that he had not even known of his daughter's application.[139] Likewise, the winner of a dowry living in Venice requested that the dowry be sent to her before the wedding (contrary to the *Dotar*'s principles) because if the groom found out that she was marrying with the help of the dowry society—"which he views as charity"—the wedding would not take place.[140] It appears that for many of the poor among the "Portuguese," poverty was an affliction, not a way of life; and it can be understood why even those who lived off communal charity shunned contact with their Yiddish-speaking Ashkenazi counterparts, who were accustomed to begging door-to-door or at the gates of the synagogue, and were repeatedly berated for their begging, idleness, and "vices" by the *Mahamad*.[141]

As unattractive as these Ashkenazim seemed to the "Portuguese," however, they were unquestionably Jews. From the point of view of Jewish law, it was impossible to refrain from establishing ties of solidarity with them. Like other Jews, the "Portuguese" were obligated to relate to the wider Jewish world both conceptually (as reflected in liturgy and rabbinic literature) and in practice (in the areas of welfare and intercommunal cooperation).

In practice, the policies of the communal leaders toward the wider Jewish world made sense, given the discomfort they felt in actual contact with other Jewish ethnic groups. In matters concerning Jews in danger or distress, the community cooperated with Ashkenazi communities, sending aid to those in distress in Poland and in the German states. The community also granted aid to poor Ashkenazim who arrived in Amsterdam. However, it was not interested in encouraging such refugees to settle in Amsterdam. An episode from 1656 reflects this attitude. That year, when about three hundred Ashkenazi refugees arrived in Amsterdam from Poland and Lithuania, members of the "Portuguese" community received them, providing them with food, clothing, and shelter. But they also took pains to help many of the refugees continue on to destinations outside the Dutch Republic.[142]

The farther away the needy Ashkenazim were, the friendlier the attitude to them. When distant Ashkenazi communities suffered in times of war, the *Mahamad* was willing to offer substantial assistance. It granted a large sum, for example, to the Jews of Kremzier in Moravia in 1643 after that community had been destroyed by the Swedish army.[143] Similarly, in 1677 it contributed to the redemption of Polish Jews taken captive and held in Constantinople.[144] These are but two examples of the routine role the community assumed in offering aid and relief to Ashkenazi communities in distress.

There is no reason to doubt the sincerity of the expressions of solidarity that sometimes accompanied the decisions to grant such aid. In 1642, the community contributed a considerable sum to assist Ashkenazim in German lands who suffered from the ravages of the Thirty Years War. More interesting than the decision itself is the entry in the minute-book justifying it:

> The natural mercy and compassion of the Jewish people [*povo de Ysrael*], and especially of those belonging to this holy community, have stirred the men of their *Mahamad* to find a remedy for the great sufferings of the poor of our Hebrew nation, especially the Ashkenazim who have been expelled from Gemany … and at the same time to bring an end to the great injury which has resulted from the desecration of the blessed name of God due to violations of His holy Torah, bring loss of honor among His people.[145]

Taking action in such a case was without doubt a religious obligation. Indeed, the solidarity expressed is couched in religious terms. The Jewish people is depicted as an ideal religious body, the collectivity of believers and observers of Torah law. The very fact that it was felt necessary to justify the decision this way seems noteworthy, and the justifications themselves are interesting: 1) the natural compassion of the "Portuguese" Jews and 2) the honor of the Torah, which could not be properly observed by homeless and hungry refugees. In the archival documents I have studied, I have not seen—and would not expect to see—a decision to aid "Portuguese" Jews accompanied by such a justification.

Closer to home, such sentiments were not to be found. Although as we have seen, in the early years *tudescos* participated in the ritual life of the "Portuguese," this situation was short-lived. In 1639, the merger agreement of the united Portuguese-Jewish community stated that *K.K. Talmud Torah* was established for "Jews of the Portuguese and Spanish Nation," and that Jews of other "nations" would require permission from the *Mahamad* to participate in its services.[146]

Thus, in everything that concerned actual contact, the communal leadership acted to maintain as great a distance as possible between the "Men of the Nation" and Jews of other ethnic background. This policy became more harsh and rigid with time. It is true that with the change in the character of Ashkeanzi immigration in the period after 1648—when larger numbers of Polish and Lithuanian refugees began arriving in Amsterdam—"Portuguese" attitudes changed somewhat. They showed higher regard for these emigres than for the earlier refugees from German lands: the *polacos* were better educated and among them were respected scholars.[147] Indeed, the Lithuanian scholar Moses Rivkes, who arrived as a refugee in the Netherlands in 1655, was given the unusual honor of being admitted to the yeshiva of the De Pinto family in Rotterdam.

Around 1660 the Polish and Lithuanian Jews were able to break away from the German-Jewish congregation and organize themselves in a separate congregation, further emphasizing their difference. But the "Portuguese" soon viewed the *polacos* as having *tudesco* qualities, and by the time the German and Polish congregations united, in 1673, the willingness of the "Portuguese" to differentiate between the two groups of Ashkenazim seems to have disappeared.[148] Still, as late as 1683, one of the very few non-"Portuguese" to participate in any aspect of the life of *K.K. Talmud Torah* was the Polish rabbi Joseph bar Eliezer, who pursued rabbinic learning at the De Pinto yeshiva.[149]

Eventually, even the time-honored custom according to which the descendents of Uri Halevi, the rabbi from Emden, were accepted as members of *K.K. Talmud Torah* was challenged. It is not clear how many persons took advantage of this privilege over the years. In adulthood, Uri Halevi's grandson (Uri Phoebus Halevi) belonged for a time to the Polish-Jewish congregation and then the German-Jewish congregation of Amsterdam; apparently it was only in 1673 that he made use of his privilege and became a paying member of *K.K. Talmud Torah*.[150] A few other members of his family also joined the Portuguese-Jewish community. But even this concession to the family of the founding rabbi of the community galled members as time passed. In a ruling of 1700, communal leaders made a strikingly harsh ruling that declared that the right to inherited membership claimed by Uri Halevi's descendants was "imaginary." True, Uri Phoebus Halevi and other members of the family had been admitted in the mistaken belief that their claim was valid, but an investigation by communal leaders showed that

> nothing is on record of any obligation on our part to extend to the ... descendants [of Uri Halevi and his son Aron] the right to membership which they claim our congregation owes them; and even if this were the case (which it clearly is not), the communal officials of that period ought to have realized that it was not appropriate that these people continue on in our congregation, for they should have recognized that these people did not harmonize with our own people, as far as their customs are concerned.[151]

Those who had already been admitted as members were allowed to remain—Uri Phoebus Halevi was buried at Ouderkerk in 1715, with a tombstone inscribed in Portuguese[152]—but the ruling stipulated that "henceforth absolutely no other be admitted under any pretext."[153]

The strong inclination of the "Portuguese" to exclusivity had multiple causes—and functions. There can be little doubt that Iberian concepts of blood were internalized and adapted by the ex-conversos in a way that permitted them to retain in the diaspora a kind of ethnic segregation that had been forced on them in the Peninsula. But the impulse was also a response to the experience of being uprooted and undergoing a self-transformation that entailed many strains. The need to maintain a distance from Ashkenazim reflected in part the need to perpetuate a self-image of social superiority, and eventually became part of a defensive posture adopted toward the gentile world.[154]

The ethnic exclusivity of the "Portuguese" in Amsterdam had no basis in Jewish law. Some of its expressions actually contradicted Jewish law. For example, the ex-conversos were reluctant to accept into the community a convert to Judaism whose father was not "Portuguese."[155] Such a person was unequivocally Jewish; the problem was his or her ethnicity. Likewise, *negros e mulatos judeos*—converted servants or illegitimate children of servants—were denied the full privileges of communal membership, though there was no rabbinic justification for such a rule.[156] There are explicit decisions of the *Mahamad* of the Amsterdam community which also glaringly contradicted basic norms of Jewish communities. In 1657, for example, it prohibited "*tudescos*, Italian Jews and mulattos" from attending the communal school.[157] It decided in 1671 that "considering the difficulties that would arise," an Ashkenazi mate of a "Portuguese" woman could not be accepted as a member of the community or buried in Ouderkerk, and the same would hold for the offspring of such a marriage.[158] In 1697, it decided that even *Portuguese Jewish males* who married Jewish women who were not of "the Nation" would lose their rights as members.[159] And in 1709, in an effort to enforce these rulings, procedures were instituted for clarifying the origins of persons applying for membership in the community, if there was any reason for doubt.[160] These criteria for acceptance in a Jewish community are deviations of the first order from Jewish practice, and reflect the particular anxieties of the "Portuguese" about loss of their precarious sense of self.

Despite the considerable material which can be marshaled to show how the "Portuguese" leadership acted to protect the boundaries of "the Nation," it is difficult to convey in twentieth-century concepts how being "Portuguese" was perceived among the emigres in relation to being Jewish. The link was fluid and ambiguous and sometimes conflicted but, as we shall see in the next chapter, immensely powerful. Members of the communal elite drew both from deep-rooted converso patterns and from consciously developed ideas about Jewish history and theology to create an ethos that accommodated both loyalties.

Abbreviations

DJH	*Dutch Jewish History*
EH	Ets Haim Collection
GAA	Gemeentelijke Archief, Amsterdam
JQR	*Jewish Quarterly Review*
JSS	*Jewish Social Studies*
REJ	*Revue des Études Juives*
SR	*Studia Rosenthaliana*
TGP	*Triumpho del govierno popular*

Notes

1. H. P. Salomon, "The 'De Pinto' Manuscript: A Seventeenth-Century Marrano Family History," *SR* 9 (1975), 59.
2. Ibid.
3. Ibid.
4. Ibid., 60.
5. Isaac Cardoso, *Las Excelencias de los Hebreos* (Amsterdam, 1679), 90–91. Cf. Yosef Hayim Yerushalmi, *From Spanish Court to Italian Ghetto* (New York and London: Columbia University Press, 1971), 380.
6. The popular converso conception of circumcision as a kind of sacramental act must have had implications for women. Given the social and economic dependence of women on men and the strongly patriarchal character of Iberian society, it is not surprising that the issue was not raised. One would like to know how women responded to the absence for them of such a differentiating act.
7. Julio Caro Baroja, *Los judíos en la España moderna y contemporánea* (Madrid, 1978), 3:361.
8. While the entire testimony is fascinating, some of it is of doubtful reliability, and there is no evidence that the witness, Esteban de Ares de Fonseca, was pressured into being circumcised in Amsterdam by being put in *herem*, as he told the Inquisition. The entire account is published in Caro Baroja, *Los judíos en la España*, 3:359–64.

9. Samuel Aboab, *Sefer ha-zikhronot* (n.p., n.d.), fol. 75. Cf. Yerushalmi, *Spanish Court*, 200. A similar position was adopted not long afterward by the "Portuguese" rabbi Moses Rafael d'Aguilar of Amsterdam, when a forged rabbinic opinion was sent to conversos in Bayonne advising them that without circumcision their observance of other precepts was useless for their salvation. "*Reposta e discurso sobre certas perguntas de Bayona e foy em nome dos Hahamim*," Ms. EH 48A11, 213v–225v. And see Yosef Kaplan, "Rabbi Moshe Rafael d'Aguilar's Role with Spanish and Portuguese Emigres in the Seventeenth Century" (Hebrew), *Procedings of the Sixth Congress of Jewish Studies* (1976), Part B, 99–100.

10. Yosef Hayim Yerushalmi, "The Re-education of the Marranos in the Seventeenth Century," *The Third Annual Rabbi Louis Feinberg Memorial Lecture in Judaic Studies* (March 26, 1980), 4–5.

11. Stephen Gilman, *The Spain of Fernando de Rojas* (Princeton: Princeton University Press, 1972), 197.

12. Elvira Cunha de Azevedo Mea, *Sentenças da Inquisicão de Coimbra em metropolitanos de D. Frei Bartolomeu dos Mártires* (Porto, 1982), 450.

13. Antonio Baião, *A Inquisição em Portugal e no Brasil* (Lisbon, 1921), 137–38.

14. Ibid., 178.

15. Ibid., 157.

16. Feliciano Sierro Malmierca, *Judíos, moriscos e Inquisición en Ciudad Rodrigo* (Salamanca, 1990), 178.

17. Baião, *A Inquisição em Portugal*, 129.

18. Ibid., 141.

19. María Antonia Bel Bravo, *El auto de fe de 1593: los conversos granadinos de origen judío* (Granada, 1988), 151.

20. I. S. Révah, "Les Marranes," *REJ* 118 (1959–60), 53–54.

21. See Isaiah Tishby, *Messianism in the Time of the Expulsion from Spain and Portugal* (Hebrew) (Jerusalem, 1985), 44 n. 111.

22. Jaime Contreras, *El Santo Oficio de la Inquisición de Galicia, 1560–1700: poder, sociedad y cultura* (Madrid, 1982), 607.

23. Cecil Roth, "The Religion of the Marranos," *JQR* 22 (1931–32), 5.

24. Cunha de Azevedo Mea, *Sentenças*, 344.

25. Ibid., 375.

26. António Borges Coelho, *Inquisição de Évora* (Lisbon, 1987), 1:223–24.

27. Ibid., 211.

28. For a discussion of some of the Christian works frequently cited by Portuguese Jews, see Daniel Swetschinski, "The Portuguese Jews of Seventeenth-Century Amsterdam: Cultural Continuity and Adaptation," in Frances Malino and Phyllis Cohen Albert, eds., *Essays in Modern Jewish History: A Tribute to Ben Halpern* (Rutherford, NJ: Fairleigh Dickinson University Press, 1982), 68.

29. Cunha de Azevedo Mea, "Orações judaicas na Inquisição Portugesa—século XVI," in Y. Kaplan, ed., *Jews and Conversos: Studies in Society and the Inquisition* (Jerusalem, 1985), 159–63.

30. "Bento tu, Adonay, nosso Deos, que com teu mandamento anoitecem as noites e com sabedoria abre as portes e com entendimento mudas as horas e ordenas as estrellas no ceo como he tua vontade e crias dia e crias noite e envolves a luz entre as escuridades..." (Cunha de Azevedo Mea, "Orações," 162).

31. Cunha de Azevedo Mea, "Orações," 166–67.
32. Cunha de Azevedo Mea, *Sentenças*, 378.
33. See Yerushalmi, *Spanish Court*, 276–99; idem, "Professing Jews in Post-Expulsion Spain and Portugal," in *Salo Wittmayer Baron Jubilee Volume* (Jerusalem, 1974), 1023–58; idem, "Conversos Returning to Judaism in the Seventeenth Century: Their Jewish Knowledge and Psychological Readiness" (Hebrew), *Proceedings of the Fifth World Congress of Jewish Studies* (1969), vol. 2 (Jerusalem 1972), Hebrew section, 201–209.
34. See I. S. Révah, *Spinoza et le Dr. Juan de Prado* (Paris/The Hague: Mouton, 1959), 24; idem, "Aux origines de la rupture spinozienne: nouvel examen des origines, du déroulement et des conséquences de l'affaire Spinoza-Prado-Ribera" (part 3), *Annuaire de Collège de France* 70 (1970), 650; Yosef Kaplan, *From Christianity to Judaism: The Story of Isaac Orobio de Castro* (Oxford and New York: Oxford University Press, 1989), 125–27.
35. Joseph Shalom ben Gallego, *Sefer imrei no'am* (Amsterdam, 1628–1630), fol. 141r.
36. Yosef Hayim Yerushalmi, "The Re-education of Marranos in the Seventeenth Century," in *The Third Annual Louis Feinberg Memorial Lecture in Judaic Studies* (March 26, 1980), 7.
37. See the discussion of this literature in Yerushalmi, "The Re-education of the Marranos," 7–12.
38. This has been suggested by Roth, "The Role of Spanish in Marrano Diaspora," in Frank Pierce, ed., *Hispanic Studies in Honour of I. González Llubera* (Oxford: Dolphin Book Co, 1959), 302–303.
39. See A. K. Offenberg, "The *Primera Parte del sedur* (Amsterdam 1612)," *SR* 15 (1981), 234–37.
40. See Meyer Kayserling, *Biblioteca Espanola-Portugueza-Judaica*, ed. Y. H. Yerushalmi (New York: Ktav, 1971), 59–64.
41. Harm den Boer and Herman Prins Salomon, "Another 'Lost' Book Found: The Melo Haggadah, Amsterdam 1622," *SR* 29 (1995), 119–34.
42. See Kayserling, *Biblioteca*, 50–52.
43. The most important published works of this kind are Immanuel Aboab's *Nomologia* (Amsterdam, 1629) and Isaac Cardoso's *Las Excelencias de los Hebreos* (Amsterdam, 1679). Worthy of note is the early translation of the polemical Karaite work *Hizzuk emunah* by Isaac Athias, *Fortificacion de la Ley de Mosse* (Hamburg, 1621). Many of the important polemical works attacking Christianity, however—among them those of Isaac Orobio de Castro—circulated in manuscript, for obvious reasons.
44. *Libro intitulado Obligacion de los coraçones, compuesto por el excelentissimo senor el grande Rabenu Moseh de Aegypco* (!) translated by David Pardo, son of Joseph Pardo (Amsterdam, 1610); *Hobat Alebabot, Obrigaçam dos coraçoes*, translated into Portuguese by the Amsterdam rabbi Samuel Abas (Amsterdam, 1670).
45. The work was translated by the Amsterdam-trained rabbi Jacob Abendana, using ibn Tibbon's translation into Hebrew of the original Judeo-Arabic work. The *Kuzari*, which pits Judaism successfully against Greek philosophy Islam, and Christianity, had obvious appeal for the "Portuguese," an appeal which may have been enhanced by Halevi's notions about the superiority of Jewish "lineage."
46. *Tratado de la Thesuvah o Contricion* (Amsterdam, 1613); *Tratado de los Articulos de la Ley Divina* (Amsterdam, 1652).

47. On the hesitations that delayed such translations, see Yerushalmi, "The Re-education of the Marranos," 8–10.

48. Menasseh ben Israel, *Thesouro dos dinim, que o povo de Israel he obrigado saber, e observar* (Amsterdam, 1645–47), dedication, n.p.

49. *TGP*, 61–76 (Keter Torah); 77–112 (Torah Or); 113–16 (Pinto Yeshiva); 117–31 (Meirat Yenaim). Cf. W. Chr. Pieterse, *Daniel Levi de Barrios als geschiedschrijver van de Potugees-Israelitische Gemeente te Amsterdam in zijn "Triumpho de Govierno popular"* (Amsterdam, 1968), 106–17.

50. See Pieterse, *Daniel Levi de Barrios*, 110.

51. Shabbetai Sheftel Horowitz, *Sefer vav ha-amudim* (Amsterdam, 1653), fol. 9v (published at the end of his father's work *Shenei luhot ha-brit*; appropriate excerpts published in Simha Assaf, *Documents on the History of Jewish Education*, 4 vols. [Hebrew] [Tel Aviv, 1925–1930], 1:70–71).

52. Jacob Katz, *Tradition and Crisis* (Syracuse, NY: Syracuse University Press, 1993), 162.

53. Clause 22 of the merger agreement, published in Pieterse, *Daniel Levi de Barrios*, 160.

54. Shabbetai Bass, *Sefer siftei yeshenim* (Amsterdam, 1680), fol. 8r–v. The passage has been published in Assaf, *Documents*, 1:155–56.

55. Daniel Swetschinski, "The Portuguese Jewish Merchants of Seventeenth-Century Amsterdam: A Social Profile" (PhD dissertation, Brandeis University, 1980), 2:388–89.

56. See Katz, *Tradition and Crisis*, 158–62.

57. There they "did not have to flatter and ingratiate themselves to anyone." And see Katz, *Tradition and Crisis*, 161–62, 163.

58. Pieterse, *Daniel Levi de Barrios*, 97.

59. GAA, PA 334, No. 19, fol. 459.

60. See Katz, *Tradition and Crisis*, 65–68.

61. The second clause of the merger agreement states that the means of enforcing the *Mahamad*'s authority would be like those exercised in Venice (*segindo ho estilo de Veneza*). See the merger agreement published in Pieterse, *Daniel Levi de Barrios*, 156.
    Unfortunately, no copy of the statutes of the Venetian community has survived, so no detailed comparison is possible. For other ways in which the Venetian community served as the model for the Amsterdam community, see Miriam Bodian, "Amsterdam, Venice, and the Converso Diaspora," *DJH* 2 (Jerusalem, 1989), 47–65.

62. See Abraham Neuman, *The Jews in Spain: Their Social, Political and Cultural Life during the Middle Ages*, 2 vols. (Philadelphia: Jewish Publication Society of America, 1948), 1:53.

63. "Que o Mahamad terá autoridade e superioridade sobre tudo" (GAA, PA 334, No. 19, 21).

64. Most importantly, it accepted the right of the *Mahamad* to impose the ban or *herem*. See Yosef Kaplan, "The Social Functions of the Herem in the Portuguese Jewish Community of Amsterdam in the Seventeenth Century," *DJH* 1 (1984), 113 n. 4. But this acceptance was not absolute. In at least two cases city authorities intervened on behalf of persons who had been placed under the band (ibid., 144, 145).

65. See Kaplan, "Social Functions of the Herem," 118–19.

66. GAA, PA 334, No. 19, 204. Cf. Kaplan, "Social Functions of the Herem," 136.

67. GAA, PA 334, No. 13, fol. 6v. Cf. Kaplan, "Social Functions of the Herem," 118. The patterns of behavior of generally uncommitted conversos living outside the Peninsula have been explored in two studies based on Venetian inquisitorial documents: Brian Pullan, "'A Ship with Two Rudders': 'Righetto Marrano' and the Inquisition in Venice," *The Historical Journal* 20 (1977), 25–58; idem, "The Inquisition and the Jews of Venice: The Case of Gaspare Ribeiro, 1580–1581," *Bulletin of the John Rylands University Library* 62 (1979), 207–31. On uncommitted or minimally attached "Portuguese" in London, see Matt Goldish, "Jews, Christians and Conversos: Rabbi Solomon Aailion's Struggles in the Portuguese Community of London," *Journal of Jewish Studies* 45 (1994), 227–57; Isaiah Tishby, "New Information on the 'Converso' Community in London According to the Letters of Sasportas from 1664/1665," in *Exile and Diaspora: Studies in the History of the Jewish People Presented to Professor Haim Beinart on the Occasion of His Seventieth Birthday* (Hebrew volume) (Jerusalem, 1988), 470–96; Yosef Kaplan, "Wayward New Christians and Stubborn New Jews: The Shaping of a Jewish Identity," in Lloyd P. Gartner and Kenneth R. Stow, eds., *The Robert Cohen Memorial Volume* (Haifa, 1994), 2741; and Yosef Kaplan, "The Jewish Profile of the Spanish and Portuguese Community of London in the Seventeenth Century," in D. Katz and Y. Kaplan, eds., *Exile and Return: Anglo-Jewry through the Ages* (Jerusalem, 1993), 133–45.
68. Rafael Meldola, *Mayim rabbim* (Amsterdam, 1737), part 2, Nos. 51 and 52. See also No. 53, Meldola's later prohibition, on more legalistic grounds.
69. GAA, PA 344, No. 10 (Bet Israel records), 60.
70. Lionel Barnett, *El libro de los Acuerdos, Being the Records and Accompts of the Spanish and Portuguese Synagogue of London from 1663 to 1681* (Oxford, 1931), 23. A year earlier, in 1665, the rabbi Jacob Sasportas had expelled from the synagogue those who refused to be circumcised (Tishby, "New Information," 478–80).
71. Two such cases are recorded in the cemetery records in the years 1617 and 1618. See W. Chr. Pieterse, *Livro de Bet Haim do Kahal Kados de Bet Yahacob* (Assen: Van Gorcum, 1970), 91 (a twelve-year-old boy "uncircumcised in life"), 93 (Baruch Senior, "who was circumcised after his death").
72. Pieterse, *Livro de Bet Haim*, 45.
73. Ibid., 102, 106, 107.
74. It is misleading both in its implication that it entailed complete expulsion and in its implication that the *herem* was imposed by ecclesiastical authorities. In fact it was imposed by the lay authorities in consultation, at most, with the rabbis. The issue has been discussed, inter alia, by Henri Méchoulan, "Le herem à Amsterdam et 'l'excommunication' de Spinoza," *Cahiers Spinoza* 3 (1979/80), 117–34.
75. For a discussion of the many infractions for which a *herem* was threatened, see Kaplan, "Social Functions of the Herem."
76. The rather pathetic story is related in Roth, *A Life of Menasseh ben Israel: Rabbi, Printer and Diplomat* (Philadelphia: Jewish Publication Society of America, 1934), 52–57.
77. GAA, PA 334, No. 19, 413. Cf. Kaplan, "Social Functions of the Herem," 118–19.
78. See Yosef Kaplan, "The Travels of Portuguese Jews from Amsterdam to the 'Lands of Idolatry' (1644–1724)," in Kaplan, ed., *Jews and Conversos: Studies in Society and the Inquisition* (Jerusalem, 1985), 27–41.

79. Punishments imposed by the *Mahamad* have been studied in detail by Kaplan, "Social Functions of the Herem."

80. *SR* 2, 124, No. 78; *SR* 3, 114, No. 124; *SR* 3, 248, No. 197 (see also *SR* 6, 242–43, Nos. 660, 661, and *SR* 7, 120, Nos. 693 and 696); *SR* 4, 255, No. 315; *SR* 7, 268, No. 743; *SR* 8, 301, No. 844 (and see *SR* 8, 304, Nos. 855, 860, and 861, also *SR* 10, 97, No. 883); *SR* 10, 213–14, No. 948; *SR* 11, 91, No. 1157; *SR* 13, 227, No. 1522; *SR* 13, 234 n. 45; *SR* 15, 146. No. 1779 (charge of rape); *SR* 24, 76, No. 2896.

81. *SR* 2, 124, No.78.

82. *SR* 20, 110–11, No. 2508; *SR* 24, 70, No. 2863.

83. *Lopes Suasso Family*, 59.

84. Kaplan, "Social Functions of the Herem," 129.

85. I. S. Révah, "Le premier règlement imprimé de la 'Santa Companhia de dotar orfans e donzelas pobres,'" *Boletim internacional de bibliografia luso-brasileira* 4 (1963), 677.

86. See Swetschinski, "Portuguese Jewish Merchants," 67–68.

87. GAA, PA 334, No. 19, 25.

88. See I. S. Révah, "Les écrivains Manuel de Pina et Miguel de Barrios et la censure de la communauté judéo-portugaise d'Amsterdam," *Tesoro de los Judíos Espanoles* 8 (1965), lxxiv–xci.

89. See Harm den Boer, "Ediciones falsificadas de Holanda en el siglo XVII: escritores sefarditas y censura judaica," *Varia Bibliographica: Homenaje a José Simón Díaz* (Kassel, 1987), 99–103.

90. Révah, "Les écrivains," lxxxv–lxxxvii.

91. Seven years earlier the *Mahamad* had prohibited the printing in Amsterdam of De Barrios's poetic work *Flor de Apolo*, partly due to criticism that in this work De Barrios attributed divinity to gentile gods—even though the critic acknowledged the purely rhetorical purposes of De Barrios in doing so. Révah, "Les écrivains," lxxxii–lxxxiii.

92. On the censorship of De Pina's work *Chanças del ingenio*, deemed indecent by the *Mahamad*, see Révah, "Les écrivains," lxxiv–lxxvii.

93. Shlomo Simonsohn, ed., *Responsa of R. Yehuda Aryeh of Modena* (Hebrew) (Jerusalem, 1956).

94. While Modena was not a Sephardi Jew, his stature and his close ties to the Sephardi congregations of Venice made him a logical figure to turn to. Ample evidence of his ties with Sephardim can be found in his autobiography *Chayye Yehuda* (Hebrew), ed. Daniel Carpi (Tel Aviv, 1985) or in the English translation with extensive notes prepared by Mark Cohen, *The Autobiography of a Seventeenth-Century Venetian Rabbi* (Princeton: Princeton University Press, 1988).

95. Modena's summary of Da Costa's arguments has been published by Carl Gebhardt, *Die Schriften des Uriel da Costa* (Amsterdam, 1922), 3–10.

96. As Révah has shown, despite his claims to the contrary Da Costa must have been familiar with some aspects of postbiblical Judaism while still a "judaizer" in the Peninsula. See I. S. Révah, "La religion d'Uriel da Costa," *Revue de l'Histoire des Religions* 161 (1962), 45–76.

97. See Modena's opening statement, *Magen ve-zinnah*, ed. A. Geiger (Breslau, 1856), fol. 1r.

98. Modena's 1616/17 letter to the Hamburg community excommunicating Da Costa was published by L. Blau, *Leo Modenas Briefe und Schriftstücke* (Budapest, 1905), No. 156, 146, and again by Gebhardt, *Schriften*, 150. That this letter refers to Da Costa

was established by N. Porges, "Leon Modena über Uriel da Costa," *Zeitschrift für Hebräische Bibliographie* 15 (1911), 80–82. The ban placed on Da Costa by the Venetian community on 23 Ab 5378 (August 14, 1618) was published in Blau, *Briefe und Schriffstücke*, 95ff., and Gebhardt, *Schriften*, 181–82. Again, it was Porges who established that the ban refers to Da Costa, in his above-cited article.

99. The Amsterdam ban was published by Gebhardt, *Schriften*, 181–82.
100. A copy of this book, *Exame das tradiçoes phariseas* (Examination of Pharisaic Traditions), has only recently been found (and republished): Uriel da Costa, *Examination of Pharisaic Traditions*, with facsimile of the original, translation, notes, and introduction by H. P. Salomon and I. S. D. Sassoon (Leiden and New York: Brill, 1993).
101. Da Costa, *Examination*, 234.
102. Ibid., 246–48.
103. Ibid., 195.
104. Meijer, "Hugo Grotius' *Remonstrantie*," *JSS* 17 (1955), 97–98.
105. Da Costa, *Examination*, 429.
106. The Remonstrant theologian Philip van Limborch published the autobiography in 1687 as an appendix to his *De Veritate Religionis Christianae Amica Collatio cum Erudito Judaeo*, titling it *Exemplar humanae vitae*. It has been published by Gebhardt, *Schriften*, 105–23.
107. See especially Révah, "La religion d'Uriel da Costa," 45–56.
108. See the sources cited by Salomon in Da Costa, *Examination*, 23. Johan Müller's report of Da Costa's death has been published by Gebhardt, *Schriften*, 202–204.
109. Alexander Altmann, "Eternality of Punishment: A Theological Controversy within the Amsterdam Rabbinate in the Thirties of the Seventeenth Century," *Proceedings of the American Academy of Jewish Research* 40 (1972), 17–20.
110. The debate has been thoroughly examined, and the relevant documents published, by Altmann, "Eternality of Punishment," 1–88.
111. Altmann, "Eternality of Punishment," 53.
112. Gerschom Scholem, *Sabbatai Sevi: The Mystical Messiah* (Princeton: Princeton University Press, 1973).
113. On the movement in Amsterdam, see Scholem, *Sabbatai Sevi*, 518–45, 749–64; also Yosef Kaplan, "The Attitude of the Leadership of the 'Portuguese' Community in Amsterdam to the Sabbatian Movement" (Hebrew), *Zion* 39 (1974), 198–216.
114. See Yerushalmi, *Spanish Court*, 303–13.
115. See Scholem, *Sabbatai Sevi*, 893–95.
116. This circle and its evolution have been studied with great skill by Révah, *Spinoza et le Juan de Prado*; idem, "Aux origines de la rupture spinozienne: nouveaux documents sur l'incroyance dans la communauté judéo-portugaise d'Amsterdam à l'époque de l'excommunication de Spinoza," *REJ* 123 (1964), 359–83; idem, "Aux origines de la rupture spinozienne: nouvel examen des origines du déroulement et des consequences de l'affaire Spinoza-Prado-Ribera," *Annuaire de Collège de France* 70 (1970), 562–68; 71 (1971), 574–89; 72 (1972), 641–53.
117. On Prado's flirtation with deism in the Peninsula, see Révah, "Aux origines," (1972), 650–51.
118. The *herem* is published in Révah, *Spinoza et Juan de Prado*, 57–58.

119. The entire deposition of the monk is published in Révah, *Spinoza et Juan de Prado*, 61–65; for the statement concerning Spinoza, see p. 64.

120. Révah, "Aux origins" (1964), 371–83.

121. On the measures (not always consistent) taken by the Dutch authorities from the 1640s to the 1670s concerning heterodox religious ideas, see Jonathan Israel, *Dutch Republic: Its Rise, Greatness, and Fall, 1477–1806* (Oxford: Clarendon Press, 1995), 889–933.

122. See Jacob Teicher, "Why Was Spinoza Banned?" *The Menorah Journal* 45 (1957), 57; Révah, *Spinoza et Juan de Prado*, 29–30; Méchoulan, "Le herem à Amsterdam," 123–24.

123. See Kaplan, *From Christianity*, 122–26, 146–47.

124. For a detailed analysis of Orobio's correspondence and the *Mahamad*, see Kaplan, *From Christianity*, 146–56.

125. On Orobio's functions as a communal leader, see Kaplan, *From Christianity*, 189–99.

126. Bringing an analogue from the discipline he shared with Prado, namely medicine, he asked what Prado would think of someone who held a medical opinion that contradicted the opinion of Galen, Avicenna, Valles, Garcia, Fernelio, "and others of this class." This was indeed clinging to tradition, in the second half of the seventeenth century!

127. Isaac Orobio de Castro, *Epístola invectiva contra Prado, un Philósopho Médico que dudava o no creía la verdad de la divina escriptura y pretendió encubrir su malicia con la afectada confessión de Dios y Ley de Naturaleza*, published in abridged form in Révah, *Spinoza et Juan de Prado*, 86–129.

128. Révah, *Spinoza et Juan de Prado*, 97.

129. Ibid., 109–10.

130. See the discussion of this in Kaplan, *From Christianity*, 167–69. On "fideistic skeptics," see Richard Popkin, "Scepticism, Theology and the Scientific Revolution in the Seventeenth Century," in I. Lakatos and A. Musgrave, eds., *Problems in the Philosophy of Science* (Amsterdam, 1968), 12–17.

131. Kaplan, *From Christianity*, 169.

132. Pieterse, *Livro de Bet Haim*, 4, No. 2.

133. Presumably due to the paucity of material from Venice, the first instance I have encountered of the use of the term *tudesco* among the Ponentine Jews dates from 1660, in a letter in Portuguese concerning the redemption of a captive: "chegou aqui Davi [*sic*] tudesco polaco" ("Copie di lettere, Resc. de Schiavi de T.T.," Archivio della Communità Israelitica, Venezia, file 7, fol. 30v; Central Archives for the History of the Jewish People, Jerusalem, HM 5221).

134. Pieterse, *Livro de Bet Haim*, 92.

135. See Yosef Kaplan, "The Portuguese Community in Seventeenth-Century Amsterdam and the Ashkenazi World," *DJH* 2 (Jerusalem, 1989), 29.

136. The *Mahamad* lent the *tudescos* 300 guilders of the 410 guilders needed to buy the land for the cemetery. GAA, PA 334, No. 19, 131.

137. M. H. Gans, *Memorbook: History of Dutch Jewry from the Renaissance to 1940* (Baarn, 1977), 29.

138. He was taxed only two guilders for the purchase of the cemetery in 1614 (Pieterse, *Livro de Bet Haim*, 150, 176).

139. GAA, PA 334, No. 1142, p. 143 (17 Adar Sheni, 1631).

140. GAA, PA 334, No. 1142, p. 88 (12 Ab, 1627).
141. On the different attitude of the *Mahamad* to "Portuguese" and Ashkenazi poor, see the revealing description of the changing roles of the *Avodat Hesed* society in Kaplan, "The Portuguese Community and the Ashkenazi World," 32–33.
142. Herbert Bloom, *The Economic Activities of the Jews of Amsterdam in the Seventeenth and Eighteenth Centuries* (Williamsport: Bayard Press, 1937), 25–26.
143. GAA, PA 334, No. 19, 242.
144. Ibid., 765.
145. Ibid., 194.
146. From the text of the merger agreement published in Pieterse, *Daniel Levi de Barrios*, 156.
147. See Kaplan, "The Portuguese Community and the Ashkenazi World," 35–36.
148. Ibid., 37–39, 42.
149. *TGP*, 114, 116.
150. L. Fuks and R. G. Fuks-Mansfeld, *Hebrew Typography in the Northern Netherlands, 1585–1815* (Leiden: Brill, 1984–87), 2:236–37.
151. GAA, PA 334, No. 20, 293.
152. Fuks and Fuks-Mansfeld, *Hebrew Typography*, 2:242.
153. English translation of ruling in H. P. Salomon, "Myth or Anti-Myth?: The Oldest Accounts Concerning the Origin of Potuguese Judaism at Amsterdam," in his *Deux études portugaises* (Braga, 1991), 297–98.
154. The best-known expression of this posture is the lengthy letter to Voltaire composed in 1762 by Isaac de Pinto (a great-grandson of a brother of the Isaac de Pinto who fled from Antwerp to Rotterdam), in which he protested Voltaire's failure in his article "Juifs" to distinguish between Ashkenazim and the culturally superior Sephardim ([Isaac de Pinto], *Apologie pour la nation juive, ou réflexions critiques sur le premier chapitre du VIIe tome des oeuvres de M. de Voltaire au sujet des juifs* [Amsterdam, 1762]). Similarly indignant is a letter of 1778 from a Portuguese Jew in Paris to the London *Mahamad*, in which, "zealous ... for the welfare and honour of my nation," the author complained of the failure of the Paris authorities to honor the special privileges of the Sephardim over the Ashkenazim (*Transactions of the Jewish Historical Society of England* 20 [1959–61], 18).
155. Yosef Kaplan, "Jewish Proselytes from Portugal in 17th Century Amsterdam—The Case of Lorenzo Escudero" (Hebrew), *Proceedings of the Seventh World Congress of Jewish Studies* (Jerusalem, 1981), 4:99–101; idem, "Political Concepts in the World of the Portuguese Jews of Amsterdam during the Seventeenth Century," in Kaplan, Méchoulan, and Popkin, eds., *Menasseh ben Israel and His World* (Leiden: Brill, 1989), 54–57.
156. A 1614 regulation set aside a separate burial plot for "slaves, servants, and Jewish girls who are not of our Nation" (Pieterse, *Livro de Bet Haim*, 4). Some modifications were made in 1647, but the principle of segregated burial was maintained (GAA, PA 334, No. 19, 224). In 1644 it was decided that a nonwhite male could not be called to the Torah or receive other synagogue honors (ibid., 173). The issue of attitudes to converted blacks or mulattos among the Portuguese Jews has yet to be explored thoroughly. Meanwhile, see the enlightening material in Robert Cohen, *Jews in Another Environment: Surinam in the Second Half of the Eighteenth Century* (Leiden and New York: Brill, 1991), 143–59.

157. Yosef Kaplan, "Relations between Spanish and Portuguese Jews and Ashkenazim in Seventeenth-Century Amsterdam," in *Transition and Change in Modern Jewish History: Essays in Honor of Shmuel Ettinger* (Hebrew) (Jerusalem, 1987), 403.

158. GAA, PA 334, No. 19, 643.

159. GAA, PA 334, No. 20, 230. And indeed in the nineteenth century the community refused to bury in its cemetery a "Portuguese" Jew who had alienated himself by marrying an Ashkenazi woman. See J. Michman, "Between Sephardim and Ashkenazim in Amsterdam," in I. Ben-Ami, ed., *The Sephardi and Oriental Jewish Heritage* (Hebrew) (Jerusalem, 1982), 136 n. 7.

160. GAA, PA 334, No. 20, 510.

JEWS AND GERMANS*

Gershom Scholem

I

To speak of Jews and Germans and their relations during the last two centuries is, in the year 1966, a melancholy enterprise. So great, even now, is the burden of emotions, that a dispassionate consideration or analysis of the matter seems almost impossible; we have all been molded too strongly by the experience of our generation to permit any such expectations of detachment. Today there are many Jews who regard the German people as a "hopeless case," or at best as a people with whom, after what has happened, they want nothing to do, for good or for evil. I do not count myself among them, for I do not believe that there ought to be such a thing as a permanent state of war among peoples. I also deem it right—what is more, I deem it important—that Jews, precisely as Jews, speak to Germans in full consciousness of what has happened and of what separates them. Upon many of us the German language, our mother tongue, has bestowed the gift of unforgettable experiences; it defined and gave expression to the landscape of our youth. Now there is a kind of appeal from the German side—both from the reaches of history and from a younger generation that is coming to the fore—and precisely because this appeal is so uncertain and irresolute, indeed, embarrassed, something inheres in it that many of us do not wish to shun.

To be sure, the difficulties of generalizing, as when we say "the Germans" and "the Jews," intimidate the observer. In times of conflict, however, such all-embracing terms prove easy to manipulate; and the fact that these general categories are vulnerable to questioning has never prevented people from using them vociferously. Many distinctions would be in order here. For not all "Germans" are Germans and not all "Jews" are Jews—with, of course, one appalling exception: when power was in the hands of those Germans who really meant all Jews when they referred to the Jews, they used that power to the best of their ability to murder all Jews. Since then, those who survived this murder, or were not exposed to it because of the accidents of history, find it somewhat difficult themselves to make the proper distinctions. The dangerous pitfalls that accompany any generalization are well known: arbitrariness, self-contradiction, and incoherence. The relationships I am discussing are too various and unique to be covered by any blanket assertion that could not be countered by a different and almost equally defensible one. And yet, fully aware as I am of these difficulties, I wish to make clear what it is that moves me about this theme—certainly one of the themes that have most agitated the Jewish world in the past one hundred and fifty years and more.

In 1948 Alfred Doeblin, a Jewish writer who had converted to Catholicism in his old age, wrote to another Jew that he should take care, when addressing a German audience, to avoid using the word Jew, for in Germany it was still a term of abuse; only anti-Semites would be pleased by its use. According to Doeblin, anti-Semitism was deep-seated among the Germans and more malicious—in the year 1948!—than prior to 1933. Indeed, I myself can testify that even in 1966 many Germans who would like to dissociate themselves from the Nazis (occasionally rather as an afterthought), to a certain extent still confirm the validity of Doeblin's remarks by their evident aversion to calling any Jew a Jew unless he absolutely insists on it. After having been murdered as Jews, the Jews have now been nominated to the status of Germans, in a kind of posthumous triumph; to emphasize their Jewishness would be a concession to anti-Semitism. What a perversion in the name of progress, to do everything possible to avoid facing the realities of the Jewish-German relationship!

But it is precisely the facing of these realities that I consider to be our task, and when we speak of the fate of the Jews among the Germans we cannot speak emphatically enough of Jews *qua* Jews. The atmosphere between Jews and Germans can be cleansed only if we seek to get to the bottom of their relationship, and only if we employ the unrestrained criticism that the case demands. And that is hard: for the Germans, because the mass murder of the Jews has become the greatest nightmare of their moral existence as a people; for the Jews, because such clarification demands a critical distance from crucial phenomena of their own history. Love, insofar as it once existed, has been drowned in blood; its place must now be taken by historical knowledge and conceptual clarity—the preconditions for a discussion that might perhaps bear fruit in the future. If it is to be serious and undemagogic, such a discussion must be approached on a level beyond that of the political and economic factors and interests that have been, or are, under negotiation between the State of Israel and the German Federal Republic. I am lacking in any competence in this area, and at no time will I refer to it. I am not even certain that it can help us at all in posing the right questions or in attempting to answer them. We have all heard a great deal about this matter and, precisely as Jews, we are not always at ease when a false connection is created.

II

Until the latter half of the eighteenth century, and to some extent even beyond that time, the Jews in Germany led essentially the same existence as did Jews everywhere. They were clearly recognizable as a nation; they possessed an unmistakable identity and a millennial history of their own, however they themselves or the peoples around them may have assessed that history. They had a finely honed awareness of themselves and participated in a religious order that forced its way with extreme intensity through their very pores and into their life and culture. To the degree that the influence of the German environment—and such influence was never entirely absent—penetrated into the *Judengasse*, it did so not because the Jews deliberately turned to it and embraced it, but in large part through a barely conscious process of osmosis. To be sure, German cultural values were frequently enough transformed into Jewish values (and, linguistically, into Yiddish). The conscious relations between the two societies were of a delicate nature, however, and especially so during the two centuries preceding the era of emancipation. The religious culture of the dominant strata of Jews was self-contained and remained wholly alien to the German world.

But the economically strongest element—as it was represented in the phenomenon of the *Hofjudentum*—Jewish management of court finances—and the group at the bottom of the social ladder that was in communication with the German underworld, maintained a kind of contact with the Germans that was in both cases perilous. They moved among the Germans in a special manner, and in so doing they were at the mercy of the slightest change in political or social conditions. Nothing would be more foolish than to speak of an intimate attachment between German Jews and Germany during that age, during which not a single precondition existed for it. Everyone knew that the Jews were in exile, and however one might view the meaning of that exile, there was no doubt as to its enduring significance for the social condition of the Jews.

The overwhelming majority of the Jews, which did not belong to these marginal groups and was relatively less affected by their vicissitudes, at that time lived completely within the mold of tradition; a mold cast by their material and spiritual history during the long ages of exile. At the same time there is no mistaking the fact that in the latter half of the eighteenth century a grave weakness at the core of their Jewishness became visible.

It was as if they had arrived at the nadir of one phase of their historical existence and were no longer certain where the road would lead. This weakness had already become evident at the time Moses Mendelssohn set out upon his career as a kind of conservative reformer of German Jewry. With him, and above all with the school he inspired, there began among Jews a conscious process of turning toward the Germans; a process subsequently graced and furthered by mighty historical forces. There began a propaganda campaign for the Jews' resolute absorption by German culture and, shortly thereafter, for their absorption by the German people itself. There also began the struggle of Jews for civil rights, a struggle which extended over three or four generations, and which was finally won because—let us not deceive ourselves—it was conducted on their behalf by a decisive and victorious stratum among the non-Jews.

With these struggles, which were furthered no less by the French Revolution than by the German Enlightenment, a momentous change commenced in German Jewry. At first the change was hesitant and most uncertain, just as the Judaism of those undergoing it was often uncertain and embarrassed. They still had a strong sense of their peoplehood as Jews, though frequently not of the meaning of this peoplehood, which had been or was in the process of becoming lost to them. But, to put the case explicitly, they also began casting those infinitely yearning and furtive glances at the realm of German history—as a possible replacement for the Jewish realm—which became so characteristic of them in their relations to the Germans for the next hundred years and more. Those elements of German Jewry that viewed this process with the greatest reservations—especially the once preponderant and still very strong circles of the traditionally pious—were marked off from their more enthusiastic fellows by nothing more distinct than an oppressed silence, broken only rarely among them by direct voices of warning; it is as if they were recoiling from their own suffering. In any event, up to about 1820, when the Jews of Germany are mentioned, it is almost exclusively as the members of the Jewish nation in Germany. In the next two generations, however, linguistic usage alters completely; terms such as *Mosaic persuasion*, and similar phrases favored by Jews and Germans alike, now begin their career.

The furtive glances cast by the Jews toward the Germans were from the very outset attended by considerable changes and dislocations, which at a later stage of the process were to lead to bitter problems. As a price of Jewish emancipation, the Germans demanded a resolute disavowal of Jewish nationality—a price the leading writers and spokesmen of the Jewish avant-garde were only too happy to pay. What had begun as furtive glances turned into a passionate involvement with the realm of German history; and the objects of enlightened toleration not infrequently became ardent prophets, prepared to speak in the name of the Germans themselves.

The attentive reader of German reactions to this process and its acrobatics soon perceives the note of astonishment and a partly amiable, partly malicious irony that recurs again and again in these expressions. With the renunciation of a crucial part of Jewish existence in Germany, the ground was prepared for what appears to many of us to have been a completely false start in the history of modern relations between Jews and Germans—even though, given the conditions of 1800, it possessed a certain immanent logic of its own. When the Western people emancipated the people of Israel, they did not, to quote Buber (1932), "accept it as Israel, but rather as a multitude of individuals." Among the non-Jews, the most stalwart fighters for the cause of the Jews were precisely those who most consciously and articulately counted on the disappearance of the Jews *qua* Jews—who indeed, like Wilhelm von Humboldt, considered the disappearance of the Jews as an ethnic group a condition for taking up their cause. The liberals hoped for a decisively progressive Jewish self-dissolution. The conservatives, however, with their sense of history, had reservations about this new phenomenon. They began to chalk up against the Jews an all-too-great facility for renouncing their ethnic consciousness. The self-abnegation of the Jews, although welcomed and indeed demanded, was often seen as evidence of their lack of moral substance. We have clear documentation to show that the disdain in which so many Germans held the Jews fed on the ease with which the upper cultural stratum of the Jews disavowed its own tradition. For what could a heritage be worth if the elite of its chosen heirs were in such a rush to disavow it?

Thus a sinister and dangerous dialectic arose. Broad circles of the German elite demanded of the Jews that they give up their heritage, and went so far as to set a premium on defection; at the same time, however, many despised the Jews for just their excessive willingness to oblige. As for the socialists, Karl Marx's grotesque and disgusting invective in *On the Jewish Question* may be taken as a sign of their total frivolity and ignorance; they were completely at a loss before the issues involved in this new turn of events, and could do no more than press for the dissolution of the Jewish people and its historical consciousness, a dissolution to be completed by the advent and victory of the Revolution. They could see no sense whatever in considering the Jews as active participants in any meaningful encounter. For them, as the slogan had it, the Jews were merely "oil for the wheels of the Revolution."

Such, then, was the dangerous dialectic of the whole process. The Jews struggled for emancipation—and this is the tragedy that moves us so much today—not for the sake of their rights as a people, but for the sake of assimilating themselves to the peoples among whom they lived. By their readiness to give up their peoplehood, by their act of disavowal, they did not put an end to their misery; they merely opened up a new source of agony. Assimilation did not, as its advocates had hoped, dispose of the Jewish question in Germany; rather it shifted the locus of the question and rendered it all the more acute. As the area of contact between the two groups widened, the possibilities of friction widened as well. The "adventure" of assimilation, into which the Jews threw themselves so passionately (it is easy to see why) necessarily increased the dangers that grew out of the heightened tension. Added to this was the fact that there was, if I may use Arnold Zweig's expression, something "disordered" about the Jews who were exposed to this new encounter with the Germans—and in a double sense: they were "disordered" by their existence under the undignified conditions they were forced to live in as well as its social and personal consequences; and they were "disordered" by the deep insecurity that began to hound them the moment they left the ghetto in order, as the formula had it, "to become Germans." This double disorder of the Jews was one of the factors that retarded, disturbed, and eventually brought to a gruesome end the process—or trial—that now began in such earnest. The refusal of so many German Jews to recognize the operation of such factors, and the dialectic to which they bear witness, is among the saddest discoveries made by today's reader of the discussions of those times. The emotional confusion of the German Jews between 1820 and 1920 is of considerable importance if one wishes to understand them as a group, a group characterized by that "German-Jewishness" (*Deutschjudentum*) many of us encountered in our own youth and which stimulated us to resistance.

At the same time, however, and in the very midst of this insecurity, something else happened: the long-buried creativity of the Jews was liberated. It is true that by entering so eagerly into a new world, the Jews relinquished the security their ancient tradition had once bestowed upon them, and would frequently continue to bestow in an impressive way upon those who held fast to it. But in recompense those Jews who threw themselves into this exciting "living experience" (*Erlebnis*) of assimilation found that it awakened something in them that under the old order had long been dormant or forgotten. These factors are deeply connected. Here it is fitting that we briefly examine and clarify those positive aspects of this process that became so meaningful precisely to the Jews, even those living far beyond the borders of Germany.

The intimate passion that the relation to things German assumed for the Jews is connected with the specific historical hour in which it was born. At the moment in time when Jews turned from their medieval state toward the new era of enlightenment and resolution, the overwhelming majority of them—80 percent—lived in Germany, Austria-Hungary, and Eastern Europe. Due to prevailing geographic, political, and linguistic conditions, therefore, it was German culture the Jews first encountered on their road to the West. Moreover—and this is decisive—the encounter occurred precisely at the moment when that culture had reached one of its most fruitful turning points. It was the zenith of Germany's bourgeois era. One can say that it was a happy hour when the newly awakened creativity of the Jews, which was to assume such impressive forms after 1780, impinged precisely on the zenith of a great creative period of the German people, a period producing an image of things German that, up to 1940, and among very broad classes of people, was to remain unshaken, even by many bitter and later most bitter experiences. For the Jews this amalgamation of a great historical hour was defined and symbolized by the names of Lessing and Schiller, and in its intensity and scope it has no parallel in the encounters of the Jews with other European peoples. Due to this encounter, the first on the Jews' way to the West, because of this new image, a high luster fell on all things German. Even today, after so much blood and so many tears, we cannot say that it was *only* a deceptive luster. It was more: it contained elements of great fruitfulness and the stimulus to significant developments.

The significance of Friedrich Schiller for the formation of Jewish attitudes toward Germany is almost incalculable and has seldom been appreciated by the Germans themselves. For to generations of Jews within Germany, and almost to a greater extent to Jews outside Germany, Schiller, spokesman for pure humanity, lofty poet of the highest ideals of mankind, represented everything they thought of, or wished to think of, as being German—even when, in the Germany of the last third of the nineteenth century, his language had already begun to sound hollow. For many Jews the encounter with Friedrich Schiller was more real than their encounter with actual

Germans. Here they found what they were most fervently seeking. German romanticism meant something to many Jews, but Schiller meant something to all of them. He was a factor in the Jewish belief in mankind. Schiller provided the most visible, most impressive, and most resounding occasion for the idealistic self-deceptions engendered by the relations of the Jews to the Germans. For the Jew who had lost his self-confidence, Schiller's program seemed to promise everything he sought; the *Jew* heard no false tones in it, for this was music that spoke to his depths. To Schiller, who never addressed them directly, the Jews did indeed respond, and the collapse of this dialogue perhaps contains one of the secrets of the general collapse of relations between Jews and Germans. After all, Schiller, to whom their love clung so passionately, was not just anybody; he was the national poet of Germany, regarded as such by the Germans themselves from 1800 to 1900. In this case, then, the Jews did not, as has happened often enough, "have the wrong address."

In this case a bridge had really been built between the Jews and the Germans, built out of the same boundless passion that induced a number of Russian Jews, who were seeking the road to humanity among the Jewish people itself, literally to adopt the name of Schiller as their own; one of the noblest figures of the Zionist movement, Solomon Schiller,[1] is a notable example of this practice. Unfortunately, however, the task of building bridges was pursued by the Jews alone. To Germans of a later day, Jewish enthusiasm for Schiller seemed merely comic or touching. Only rarely were other Germans stirred by the feeling that here, for once, there could have been much common ground.

III

The first half of the nineteenth century was a period in which Jews and Germans drew remarkably close. During this time an extraordinary amount of help came from the German side, with many individual Jews receiving cooperation in their stormy struggle for culture. There was certainly no lack of goodwill then; reading the biographies of the Jewish elite of the period, one again and again finds evidence of the understanding they encountered, even in decidedly Christian circles like the Moravians. But in keeping with the inner dynamics of the process we have been examining, things did not remain at the level of a mere struggle for culture. The Jews were at a point of radical transition from the traditional way of life, which still held sway among a majority of them, to Germanism. In the effecting of this transition, according to one contemporary source, "the German national education of the Jews and their participation in the general interests of human beings and citizens appears as the most essential task, to which everyone who expects anything of himself must be dedicated." The formulation is by Moritz Lazarus, a follower of the philosopher Johann Friedrich Herbart, and a most pristine representative of the very tendency he advocated; he himself completed the transition from pure talmudic Judaism to the new German-Jewish way of life in a mere five years! The unending Jewish demand for a home was soon transformed into the ecstatic illusion of being at home.

It is well known and easy to understand that the speed of this transformation, which even today amazes the observer, the haste of this breakup of the Jews, was not paralleled by an equally quick reciprocal act on the part of the Germans. For the Germans did not know they were dealing with such deep processes of decay in the Jewish tradition and in Jewish self-consciousness, and they recoiled from the whole procedure. As much as they would have approved of the eventual result of the process—which accorded at least with the prevailing liberal ideology and to a considerable extent with the prevailing conservative one—they were altogether unprepared for this tempo, which struck them as overheated and whose aggressiveness set them on the defensive. Sooner or later this defensiveness was to combine with those currents of opinion that from the very beginning had reacted to the whole process with antipathy and that, since the whole post-Mendelssohn generation, had never lacked for eloquent spokesmen.

It made good sense to speak of a "host people" whose guests the Jews were. Even in the best of circumstances, it was a matter of a guest being accepted into the family, but subject to dismissal if he did not live up to the requirements. This became especially clear where the liberals were concerned. The talk one occasionally hears today of a fusion that would have made excellent progress had not the advent of Nazism come between the great majority of Jews and the "citizens of a different faith" (the phrase was used in print by a Jew in the Germany of 1965!)—such talk is nothing but a retroactive wish fulfillment. Without doubt, the complete submission to the German people of so many people who in their autobiographies (which are available in abundance) characterized themselves as being "of Jewish descent"—because they no longer had any other inner ties to the Jewish tradition, let alone to the Jewish people—constitutes one of the most shocking phenomena of this whole process of estrangement. The list of Jewish losses to the Germans is infinitely long, a list of great and frequently astonishing Jewish talents and accomplishments that were offered up to the Germans. Who can read without emotion the history of those, like that of Otto Lippmann[2] from Hamburg, who to the point of suicide maintained the claim that they were better Germans than those who were driving them to their deaths?

Today, when all is over, it is no wonder that there are many who wish to recognize this claim as just. These people made their choice, and we should not contest the Germans' right to them. And yet it makes us uneasy, for our feeling points to the inner discord of even these careers. Even in their complete estrangement of their awareness from everything "Jewish," something is evident in many of them that was felt to be substantially Jewish by Jews as well as Germans—by everyone except themselves!— and that is true of a whole galaxy of illustrious minds from Karl Marx and Lassalle to Karl Kraus, Gustav Mahler, and Georg Simmel.

No one has more profoundly characterized this breaking away of the Jews from themselves than Charles Péguy, who had an insight into the Jewish condition rarely attained, let alone surpassed, by non-Jews. To him we owe the sentence: *Être ailleurs, le grand vice de cette race, la grande vertu secrète, la grande vocation de ce peuple.*[3] This "being elsewhere" combined with the desperate wish to "be at home" in a manner at once intense, fruitful, and destructive. It is the clue to the relationship of the Jews to the Germans. It is at once what makes their symbolic position so alluring and so gripping to today's observer, and what at the time caused them to appear disgusting, to be working under false pretenses, and to be deliberately provocative of opposition. No benefit redounded to the Jews of Germany from what today, under very different circumstances, invests them with positive significance for an important part of the world and brings them special consideration: I am thinking of the widespread current appreciation of Jews as classic representatives of the phenomenon of man's estrangement or alienation from society. The German Jew was held to blame for his own estrangement or alienation from the Jewish ground that had nourished him, from his own history and tradition, and was blamed even more for his alienation from the bourgeois society that was then in the process of consolidating itself. The fact that he was not really at home, however much and emphatically he might proclaim himself to be—the "homelessness" that today is sometimes accounted to his glory, in that it is taken as an image of the *condition humaine*—constituted, at a time when alienation was still a term of abuse, a powerful accusation. And it is in keeping with so distorted a state of affairs that the great majority of the Jews, and especially those who had the highest degree of awareness, concurred in this judgment of their situation; this is why, in the very teeth of the skepticism that was a part of their German environment, they aspired to or claimed a deep attachment to things German and a sense of being at home.

Thus the relations between Jews and Germans from the start contained an accumulation of seeds of discontent that was dangerous enough. The Jew's entry into German society was a most multifaceted process. It is, for instance, an important fact that during the generations of entry the Jews to a great extent lost their own elite through baptism and mixed marriages. Yet this fact also points to marked variations in the process, because not all Jews were by any means prepared to go so far. It is true that very broad segments of German Jewry were ready to liquidate their peoplehood, but they also wished—in differing degrees, to be sure—to preserve their Jewishness as a kind of heritage, as a creed, as an element unknowable and indefinable, yet clearly present in their consciousness. Although this is now often forgotten, they were not ready for that total assimilation that the majority of their elite was seeking to purchase at the price of disappearance. Their feelings may have been uncertain and confused, but the flight of their own avant-garde was more than they were willing to accept. These continuous bloodlettings, through which the Jews lost their most advanced elements to the Germans, constitute a crucial—and from a Jewish perspective, most melancholy—aspect of the so-called German-Jewish symbiosis, which is now being discussed with such pleasure and profuse carelessness. It was the petite bourgeoisie, the most ordinary citizens, who made up the main body of the German-Jewish community during the nineteenth century and from whom a wholly new class of leaders had to be brought forth in every generation. Rarely does one find any descendants among twentieth-century Jews of those families that, after 1800, led the "breakup" in favor of things German. On the other hand, the lower classes were almost entirely retained within the boundaries of Judaism, albeit a Judaism now watered down—or rather dried up and emptied—a Judaism composed of a curious mixture of the "religion of reason" with strong, frequently disavowed, strains of feeling. The attitude of these Jews toward the deserters fluctuated greatly, as is indicated by their response to the singular phenomenon of Heinrich Heine. It ranged from sensitive rejection to almost equable indifference. Heine, to be sure, was a borderline case. He could say of himself that he never returned to Judaism because he had never left it.

In all this, we must not fail to consider the inner tensions of Jewish society, which exercised no little influence on the relationship of Jews to the German environment. Germany, after all, was the scene of especially bitter arguments between the pious of the old school: the *Landjuden* and their leaders on the one hand, and the "neologians" or Reformers on the other, with the latter quickly gaining preponderance, if not numerically, then socially and politically. The term *assimilation* was first used by its defenders in the positive sense of an ideal; later the Zionists threw the word back at them in derision and as a form of abuse.

They were doubly indignant at being called "assimilationists." The tendency toward assimilation, which manifested itself in many forms, was certainly significant. Yet one cannot unequivocally say just how far the advocates of assimilation were prepared to go at the time, and not all instances of assimilation can be judged alike. In any case, however, there existed on the Jewish side a strongly critical stance toward Jews and traditional Judaism, and it is well known how often in individual cases this stance was heightened to those extreme forms we have come to recognize as Jewish anti-Semitism. It is, after all, to a German Jew who had left Judaism—though, as he wrote, he of course knew that this was impossible—that we owe what a critic once called "the most naked exposures" of the Berlin Jewish bourgeoisie that exist anywhere and will endure as a sinister document of the German-Jewish reality; I am referring to the monologues of Herr Wendriner, written by Kurt Tucholsky. The anti-Semites took pains to make the Jews look as bad as possible, but their writings are curiously overstrained and hollow. The hatred is there, but there is no knowledge of the subject and no feeling for atmosphere. Small wonder, then, that it remained for one of the most gifted, most convinced, and most offensive Jewish anti-Semites to accomplish on a definitive level what the anti-Semites themselves were unable to bring about.

We often find representatives of extreme possibilities within the same family—for example, the brothers Jacob and Michael Bernays (whose niece became the wife of Sigmund Freud). Jacob, a classical philologist of the highest rank, remained loyal to the strictest form of Jewish Orthodoxy, even to the point of neurosis; Michael left Judaism to venture on an even more illustrious career as a scholar in the field of Germanic studies and as a foremost critical interpreter of Goethe. After their split, the two brothers never spoke to each other again. A similar divergence occurred between two cousins of the Borchardt family. One of them, the writer Georg Hermann, depicted the nineteenth-century Berlin Jewish bourgeoisie in a manner never surpassed—

critically, ironically, but at the same time lovingly. The other cousin, the exorbitantly gifted Rudolf Borchardt, convinced he had annihilated everything Jewish within himself, became the most eloquent spokesman for a culturally conservative German traditionalism. He himself was the only person to read his work who was not alarmed by the paradox.

The majority, to repeat, was not prepared to "go all the way," and many searched for a middle way. Only rarely, however, did the Jews benefit from their gifted progeny. The exceptions include such significant and at the same time problematic figures as Leopold Zunz, the founder of "the science of Judaism" (*Wissenschaft vom Judentum*), Solomon Ludwig Steinheim and Hermann Cohen, the two most distinguished German-Jewish theologico-philosophical minds, and Abraham Geiger and Samson Raphael Hirsch, in their stand on tradition the great polar opposites of the German rabbinate. Most of the ablest Jewish minds, however, enhanced *German* society with an astonishingly profuse outpouring in the fields of economics, science, literature, and art.

In a famous essay, the great American sociologist Thorstein Veblen wrote of the intellectual "preeminence" of the Jews in modern Europe. It was precisely this "preeminence" that was to spell the doom of the Jews in Germany. In their economic role, the Jews had served as a progressive force in the development of nineteenth-century Germany, but long after there had ceased to be a need for that, they continued to exercise—especially in the twentieth century—a cultural function that from the very beginning had awakened unrest and resistance and that never did them any good. That the Germans did in fact need the Jews in their spiritual world is now, when they are no longer present, noticed by many, and there is mourning over the loss. But when the Jews were there, they were a source of irritation, whether they wanted to be or not, and their "preeminence" turned into disaster for them. The great majority of Germans displayed great reserve in the face of the increasing prominence of Jewish intelligence and indeed the general phenomenon of the entry of the Jews into German society. They were not prepared, as I have already said, for the turbulent tempo of this process, which struck them as uncanny.

By the middle of the nineteenth century they had at last become reconciled to the political emancipation of the Jews, but there was no corresponding readiness to accept the unrestrained movement of the Jews into the ranks of the culturally active. The Jews, of course, with their long intellectual tradition, considered themselves made to order for such an active role when they now sought to join the German people. But this is precisely what stimulated a resistance that was to become increasingly vigorous and virulent, and was finally to prevent the process of their acceptance from having any chance of fulfillment. By and large, then, the love affair of the Jews and the Germans remained one-sided and unreciprocated; at best it awakened something like compassion (as it did with Theodore Fontane, to name only one famous, but hardly unambiguous, example) or gratitude. The Jews did meet with gratitude not infrequently, but almost never did they find the love they were seeking.

There were misunderstood geniuses among the Jews, prophets without honor, men of mind who stood up for justice, and who also stood up—to an astonishing degree—for the great spirits among the Germans themselves. Thus, almost all the most important critical interpretations of Goethe were written by Jews! But among the Germans, there was never anyone who stood up for the misunderstood geniuses who were Jews. Nothing in German literature corresponds to those unforgettable pages in which Charles Péguy, the French Catholic, portrayed the Jewish anarchist Bernard Lazare as a true prophet of Israel, and this at a time when the French Jews themselves—out of embarrassment or malice, out of rancor or stupidity—knew no better than to treat one of their greatest men with deadly silence. Here a Frenchman *saw* a Jew in a way the Jews themselves were unable to see him. Nothing corresponds to this in the much-discussed German-Jewish dialogue—a dialogue that in fact never took place. At a time when no one cared a whit about them, no German stood forth to recognize the genius of Kafka, Simmel, Freud, or Walter Benjamin—to say nothing of recognizing them as Jews. The present belated concern with these great figures does nothing to change this fact.

Only very few Germans—some of their noblest spirits, to be sure—possessed that pristine open-mindedness that allowed them to see and accept the Jew as a Jew. One of them was Johann Peter Hebel, who valued the Jew for what he had to give, rather than for what he had to give up. But it was precisely among liberals that unmistakable reservations about Jews were frequently voiced. When Fritz Reuter, a typical member of the North-German liberal intelligentsia, made a speech in 1870 to celebrate the unification of Germany, he could think of nothing better than to level charges against the "miserable Jewish rascals like Heinrich Heine" who were supposedly lacking in patriotism. The feeling was widespread that the liberalism of the Jews was of a radical nature and foreshadowed subversive tendencies. And, indeed, during a century of prominence in journalism the Jews did play a highly visible role in the criticism of public affairs. The situation is completely different from their participation in the opposite direction, which was represented almost exclusively—most impressively to be sure—by converts like Julius Stahl and Rudolf Borchardt. Their main role was deeply grounded in their history as well as their social position and function.

In reaction to this role, the phenomenon of anti-Semitism—to which the Jews responded with peculiar blindness—began to send forth its malignant tendrils. Anti-Semitism now began to assume a sterilizing and destructive significance in the increasingly critical relations between the Jews and the Germans. It is unnecessary here to emphasize the specific social and political conditions under which the most radical forms of anti-Semitism eventually came to rule over Germany. But nothing is more foolish than the opinion that National Socialism came, so to speak, from out of the blue, or that it was exclusively the product of the aftermath of World War I. It belongs to the debit side of Jewish research on this aftermath that the very comfortable theory, according to which National Socialism is a historical accident, was invented by *Jews*—by Jews, to be sure, who have learned nothing and forgotten much. Anti-Semitism could not have become as virulent as it did, or have released all its murderous consequences, without a long prehistory. Not a few of the nineteenth-century tracts against the Jews read today like wholly undisguised documents of twentieth-century Nazism, and perhaps none is more sinister than Bruno Bauer's *Das Judentum in der Fremde* (*Judaism Abroad*) of 1869. Here one comes upon everything that was later preached in the Thousand-Year Reich, and in formulations no less radical. And this document came from the pen of one of the leaders of the former Hegelian Left. There was, moreover, no lack of the more "sublime" varieties of anti-Semitism—the kind that, shortly after World War I, found expression in works like Hans Blüher's *Secessio Judaica*. Such works, fluctuating between admiration and hatred, and embodying a degenerate metaphysics in the form of genteel anti-Semitism, provided a cue for the more murderous metaphysics to come. Perhaps nothing depresses us more today than the uncertain wavering of many Germans, including some of their finest minds, in the face of this dark swell.

Max Brod has spoken of the ideal of "distant love" as that which should have governed relations between Germans and Jews. The concept is a dialectical one: distance is meant to prevent an all-too-coarse intimacy, but at the same time a desire to bridge the gap. This could certainly have been a solution for the period under discussion, if only both parties would have agreed to it. Yet Brod himself admits that where there is love the feeling of distance disappears—this was true of the Jews; and where there is distance no love can arise—this was true of the main body of Germans. To the love of the Jews for Germany there corresponded the emphatic distance with which the Germans encountered them. We may grant that with "distant love" the two partners could have managed more kindness, open-mindedness, and mutual understanding. But historical subjunctives are always illegitimate. If it is true, as we now perceive, that "distant love" was the right Zionist answer to the mounting crisis in the relations between Jews and Germans, it is also true that the Zionist avant-garde hit upon it too late. For during the generations preceding the catastrophe, the German Jews—whose critical sense was as famous among Germans as it was irritating to them—distinguished themselves by an astounding lack of critical insight into their own situation. An "edifying" and apologetic attitude, a lack of critical candor, taints almost everything they wrote about the position of the Jews in the German world of ideas, literature, politics, and economics.

The readiness of many Jews to invent a theory that would justify the sacrifice of their Jewish existence is a shocking phenomenon, and there are countless variations on it. But nothing, it seems to me, surpasses in sheer self-contradiction, and a credulous demand for self-surrender that could be demanded of no one except just us Jews, the formulation produced as late as 1935 by Margarete Susman, in full awareness of the fact that the time had come of "the most fearful fate ever to strike the Jews." She wrote: "The vocation of Israel as a people is not self-realization, but self-surrender for the sake of a higher, transhistorical goal." In this case the delusion goes so far that we are asked to believe—in the name of the prophets, who indeed did not wish Israel to be a people like all other peoples—that the "original meaning of the Jewish idea is the absorption of this people by other peoples."

What is so terrible about this statement is not that it has been so devastatingly refuted by history, but that it never signified anything except a perversion whereby Christian ideas—rejected by Jews unto their dying breath—now presented themselves as the demand of the greatest Jewish minds. Such solutions have been offered to Jews again and again, and from various sources. They bespeak a great inner demoralization, an enthusiasm for self-sacrifice which has necessarily remained wholly without meaning for the Jewish community itself, and which no one ever took seriously except the anti-Semites, who found in them an especially nefarious trick of the Jews, an especially conspiratorial note. For it was precisely this desire on the part of the Jews to be absorbed by the Germans that hatred understood as a destructive maneuver against the life of the German people—a thesis repeated indefatigably by the metaphysicians of anti-Semitism between 1830 and 1930. Here the Jews are considered, to quote one of these philosophers, as "the dark power of negation which kills what it touches. Whoever yields to it falls into the hands of death."

This, in brief, is an analysis of what from the very beginning was a "false start" in the relations between Jews and Germans, one which brought the elements of crisis inherent in the process itself to an ever riper development.

IV

Where do we stand now, after the unspeakable horror of those twelve years from 1933 to 1945? Jews and Germans took very different roads after the war. The most vital segment of the Jews attempted to build up its own society in its own land. No one can say whether the attempt will succeed, but everyone knows that the cause of Israel is a matter of life and death to the Jews. The dialectic of their undertaking is obvious. They live on a volcano. The great impetus they received from the experience of the Holocaust—let us face it: the experience of the German murder of the Jews, and of the apathy and the hardheartedness of the world—has also been followed by a profound exhaustion whose signs are unmistakable. And yet the incentive, generated by their original insight into their true situation, is still operating effectively. The Germans have paid for their catastrophe with the division of their country, but, on the other hand, they have experienced a material upsurge that has placed the past years in shadow. Between these two mountains, produced by a volcanic eruption, can there now be a bridge, however shaky?

The abyss that events have flung open between the two can be neither measured nor fathomed. Unlike many in Israel, I do not believe that the only possible means of overcoming the distance is to admit the abyss into our consciousness in all its dimensions and ramifications. There is little comfort in such a prognosis: it is mere rhetoric. For in truth there is no possibility of comprehending what has happened—incomprehensibility is of its essence—no possibility of understanding it perfectly and thus of incorporating it into our consciousness. This demand by its very nature cannot be fulfilled. Whether or not we can meet in this abyss, I do not know. And whether the abyss, flung open by unspeakable, unthinkable events, can ever be bridged—who would have the presumption to say?

Abysses are flung open by events; bridges are built by goodwill. Bridges are needed to pass over abysses; they are constructed; they are the product of conscious thinking and willing. Moral bridges, I repeat, are the product of goodwill. If they are to endure, they must be firmly anchored on both sides. The people of Israel have suffered fearfully at the hands of almost all the peoples of Europe. The bridges on which we meet peoples other than Germans are shaky enough, even when they are not burdened with the memory of Auschwitz. But—is this memory not an opportunity as well? Is there not a light that burns in this darkness, the light of repentance? To put it differently: fruitful relations between Jews and Germans, relations in which a past that is both meaningful and at the same time so horrible as to cripple communication may be preserved and worked through—such relations must be prepared away from the limelight. But it is only through an effort to bring them about that we can guarantee that official contacts between the two peoples will not be poisoned by counterfeit formulas and demands. Already the worm of hypocrisy is gnawing at the delicate roots! Where love is no longer possible, a new understanding requires other ingredients: distance, respect, openness, and open-mindedness, and, above all, goodwill.

A young German recently wrote to me expressing the hope that Jews, when thinking of Germany, might keep in mind the words of Isaiah: "Remember ye not the former things, neither consider the things of old." I do not know whether the messianic age will bestow forgetfulness upon the Jews. It is a delicate point of theology. But for us, who must live without illusions in an age without a Messiah, such a hope demands the impossible. However sublime it might be to forget, we cannot. Only by remembering a past that we will never completely master can we generate hope in the resumption of communication between Germans and Jews, and in the reconciliation of those who have been separated.

Notes

* "Juden und Deutsche," a lecture delivered at plenary session, World Jewish Congress, Brussels, August 2, 1966. Published in Gershom Scholem, *Judaica 2* (Frankfurt-am-Main: Bibliothek Suhrkamp, 1970), 20–46. An adaptation, in English translation by Werner J. Dannhauser, appeared in *Commentary* (November 1966). The present translation, by Werner J. Dannhauser, is from the original lecture.

1. Solomon Schiller (1879–1925) changed his name from Blankenstein. Born in Poland, he was a member of the First Zionist Congress in 1897 and emigrated to Palestine in 1910. He was a teacher and, later, principal at Jerusalem's prestigious Rehavia Gymnasium.

2. A high official of the Senate of Hamburg who wrote an autobiography.

3. Being elsewhere, the great vice of this race, the great secret virtue, the great vocation of this people.

PART III

RE-DEFINITIONS

THE SAVAGE IN JUDAISM

Howard Eilberg-Schwartz

Savages are no more exempt from human folly than civilized men, and are no doubt equally liable to the error of thinking they…can do what in fact cannot be done. But this error is not the essence of magic, it is a perversion of magic. And we should be careful how we attribute it to the people we call savages who will one day rise up and testify against us.

Collingwood 1958

In intellectual discourse these days, the term "savage" is passé, and properly so. The term is a pejorative that implies a judgment of superiority by the person who applies the term to another group. Rather than pass judgment on others, present interpreters of culture and religion wish to understand or come to terms with the culture and religion of others. They operate on the assumption that difference does not imply inferiority. In short, the current generation of interpreters has discovered no savages. It has explored the highlands of New Guinea, the outbacks of Australia, the forests of the Congo and found that they are populated with a variety of intriguing peoples who differ from Westerners in a number of ways that are worth thinking about and exploring. But these people are not "savages" whose cultural and religious practices are inferior to those of the West.

There was a period of time, however, when savages did exist, when travelers were discovering them in many parts of the world and intellectuals were writing incessantly about them. Ironically, these travelers and writers were looking in the same places and talking about the same people as the current generation of interpreters. But what they saw were undeveloped, simple peoples who had not yet advanced up the evolutionary ladder to the point achieved by Western society. The savage, therefore, was a creation of another generation, a generation that was not only confident of the difference between its own culture and the ones it was discovering, but certain also of its own superiority. I am of course referring to the late nineteenth- and early twentieth-century students of culture and religion who routinely invoked the adjective "savage" to describe various societies.

In retrospect, we can see that the twentieth century represents a period of reaction, when the superiority of Western civilization was gradually called into question and the ethnocentric bias of scholarly discourse became a problem that had to be addressed. Numerous factors contributed to the changing tenor of discourse on culture and religion, including, among other things, the increasing problems of colonization, the growing understanding of other cultures through ethnographic study, the gradual loss of faith in the progress of science, and the paradoxical realization that the modern forms of life we have created have generated a more inhumane world than those of the so-called savages.

Whatever the reasons, as Western thinkers lost confidence in the superiority of their own culture, the "savage" gradually became extinct. As twentieth-century anthropology developed, the emphasis was on dismantling one by one the differences that previously had been relied upon to distinguish the "savage" from us. All the convenient ways of distinguishing between the societies of the West and the small face-to-face societies of New Guinea, Australia, or Africa proved to be impositions of the Western scholar.

This process is not yet complete. There are still important discourses that presuppose the category of the savage. This book is about one of those discourses, the scholarly study of Judaism. Only recently have interpreters begun to overcome the artificial and problematic opposition between Judaism and primitive or savage religions that was bequeathed to them by European thinkers of the previous three centuries (see chapters 1 and 2). This new trend, initially stimulated by the studies of Mary Douglas (1966) and Edmund Leach (1969), is now acquiring a momentum of its own.[1]

But for much of the twentieth century, interpreters avoided comparisons between Judaism and those religions that previously were considered primitive, a prejudice already pointed out by Leach (1969, 109–10), Feeley-Harnik (1982, 99), and Goldberg (1987, 7–10), among others. Since anthropology has traditionally made primitive society its domain of inquiry, few interpreters of Judaism have been willing to turn to that discipline for either a theoretical framework or substantive insight. For similar reasons, ethnographic literature and cross-cultural studies have been generally ignored. To be sure, there have been some notable exceptions, for example, the work of William Robertson Smith, James G. Frazer, Sidney Hooke, Theodor Gaster, Raphael Patai, and most recently Mary Douglas and Edmund Leach.[2] But on the whole the use of ethnographic data or anthropological theory to illuminate beliefs and practices of Judaism has been a marginal enterprise in the twentieth century until only recently.

This book argues that the suppression of the savage has had an important impact on the picture of Judaism that is created and sustained by scholarly discourse. There is, of course, no stable object called Judaism that scholars think and write about. It is a shifting, constantly changing abstraction that is created even as it is written about. It is as much a product of intellectual discourse as an object of it. Consequently, the Judaism that is talked about and examined is itself a product of certain assumptions that are taken for granted by the people doing the talking. In the past three hundred years, one of those crucial assumptions has been the presumed difference between Judaism and the religions of primitive societies.

That assumption leads to one picture of Judaism. It determines that certain kinds of questions are asked rather than others, that particular types of comparisons are considered fruitful while others are treated as uninteresting or irrelevant, and that certain methods are adopted to answer the questions interpreters deem important. It is not surprising that the picture that is created confirms the original impression, namely, that the comparison of Judaism and primitive societies is not very interesting and the subjection of Judaism to anthropological inquiry is not very important. This book questions that impression. It is my assertion that the opposition between Judaism and savage religions has become problematic and without overcoming it, a variety of interesting questions about Judaism cannot even be imagined.

There are two related reasons for the longstanding hostility toward anthropology and the comparative study of Judaism. The first of these reasons is obvious. Passing Judaism under the anthropological gaze represents a tacit admission that Judaism has important commonalities with primitive religions. Many interpreters have been unwilling to make such a concession. As I will show in some detail in chapters 1 and 2, the impulse to radically differentiate Judaism and savage religions was part of an ongoing attempt to protect the privileged status of Judaism, and by extension, Christianity. This motivation informed the work of both Jewish and Christian interpreters from the Enlightenment until the present day.

It is self-evident why Jewish interpreters would want to deny any basic similarities between Judaism and the religion of savages. But such a stance was also naturally adopted by many who wanted to protect the superior status of Christianity, since Christianity grounds its own truth claims on the Scriptures of Judaism. For example, the idea that Jesus is the Messiah is justified in terms of the prophecies of the Hebrew Bible. For the claim to be true, the authority of the prophecies must not be questioned. Since Christianity is entangled in Judaism in this way, the equation of Judaism and savage religions inevitably posed a problem for the authority and status of Christianity as well.

Consequently, those thinkers who wished to protect Christianity often sought ways of opposing Judaism and savage religions. These motivations continue to influence interpretations of Judaism throughout the twentieth century.

But this defensive posturing does not explain everything. Not all twentieth-century interpreters have felt the need to privilege Judaism. On the contrary, many viewed their scholarship as posing a challenge to the view that Judaism is unique. Nonetheless, these same interpreters have also ignored anthropology and mistrusted the comparative study of Judaism. As I shall argue below, the theoretical commitments that these interpreters inherited had been formulated, at least in part, by their predecessors who assumed a radical difference between Judaism and savage religions. Although subsequent interpreters had no stake in perpetuating a distinction between Judaism and the religion of primitives, they inadvertently did so by not questioning the received framework in which research on Judaism is carried out.

In this introduction, I show how these prejudices operate in one set of twentieth-century scholarly traditions, those that interpret Israelite religion and ancient Judaism. It is a scholarly convention to distinguish "Israelite religion" from "ancient Judaism." "Israelite religion" typically refers to the religious cultures of Israelites from at least the advent of the Israelite monarchy in the tenth century BCE to the Babylonian exile in the sixth century BCE. "Ancient Judaism" generally refers to those religious cultures that developed in the centuries following the return of Israelites (now Jews) from the Babylonian exile.[3] In this period, a variety of important changes occurred in the religion of Israel as a result, in part, of the exile and subsequent contact with Persian, Hellenistic, and then Roman cultures. As the above terminology indicates, Israelite religion is not conceptualized as part of Judaism. But that was not always the case. From the Enlightenment until well into the nineteenth century, the religion of ancient Israel was identified by a variety of interchangeable terms, including "Mosaic Legislation," "the religion of the Jews," or simply "Judaism." In what follows, I generally preserve the terminological distinction between "Israelite religion" and "ancient Judaism."

But when generalizing, as at the end of this chapter, and when referring to discourses that do not make this distinction, as in part I, I simply refer to both traditions as "Judaism."

As we shall see, the prejudice against savages contributed to the emerging hostility toward anthropology and comparative inquiry in twentieth-century interpretations of Israelite religion. This state of affairs, as I suggest in part 1, replicates strategies operating long ago in earlier discourses that equated Israelite religion with "Judaism."

Anthropology, Israelite Religion, and the Religions of Savages

The fact that interpreters of Israelite religion have generally ignored anthropology has been noted by Mendenhall (1961, 35), Gottwald (1979, 293), Feeley-Harnik (1982, 99) and R. Wilson (1984, 25).[4] As Gottwald puts it, "After W. R. Smith and J. Wellhausen studied the applicability of Bedouin tribalism to early Israelite tribalism, so headstrong was the retreat away from any further sustained anthropological and sociological studies of Israel that biblical study has been almost totally divorced from the social sciences for half a century."

I am suggesting that the retreat from anthropological studies in particular has stemmed from a desire to oppose Israelite and primitive religions. That is not to deny that certain conceptions of primitive cultures and religions have entered twentieth-century discourse on the religion of Israel (Rogerson 1978).[5] But one rarely finds interpreters of Israelite religion appealing to studies of other religions apart from those of the ancient Near East. The following quotation, taken from H. Ringgren's *Israelite Religion* (1966, 1), is symptomatic of the larger opposition between Israelite and primitive religions that has operated in biblical studies in the twentieth century:

> A different methodological problem has to do with the use of extrabiblical comparative material to explain religious phenomena in Israel… First, in many details remarkable similarities can be observed between the Israelite religion and other ancient Near Eastern religions… Israel by no means developed in a religious vacuum, but stood in close relationship to its neighbors in the religious as well as in the cultural domain. Second, our sources do not provide a complete picture of the Israelite religion. Many details that are difficult to understand on the basis of Israelite material alone can often be explained when comparative material is brought to bear on the question… Ideas only alluded to in the Old Testament appear in their proper context in the light of comparative material… What we have said shows that the comparative method is both desirable and necessary.

Ringgren insists that Israelite religion be considered in "comparative" framework. But for Ringgren, as for more interpreters of Israelite religion, "comparative" and "extrabiblical" simply mean seeing Israelite religion against the background of other religions in the same geographical area. Extrabiblical material does not include studies of the Nuer, the Dinka, the Samoans, the Plains Indians, or the Trobriand Islanders. Although Ringgren is willing to use Assyrian myths to illuminate Israelite ones, he ignores the myths of peoples who were not geographically and temporally contiguous with ancient Israel. Ringgren's work is illustrative of a general presumption in biblical studies that contextualizing Israelite religion in its ancient Near Eastern setting is more illuminating and, perhaps, less fraught with difficulties than comparing the religion of ancient Israel to religions in other parts of the world. Those writers who have situated Israelite religion in a broader context by invoking comparisons to primitive religions have been at the margins of biblical studies or have come from outside the field altogether and hence their work has been treated as less than serious.

Since comparisons between Israelite religion and non-Near Eastern religions have been unthinkable for mainstream interpreters of ancient Israel in the twentieth century, the ideas of scholars who worked on other religions, such as Durkheim, Hubert and Mauss, Malinowski, Radcliffe-Brown, Evans-Pritchard, Boas, Mead, Kroeber, and Benedict, to name only a few, rarely influenced the study of Israelite religion in any significant way. Only since the mid-sixties, when Mary Douglas (1966) compared Israelite food avoidances with the practices of "primitive" cultures and Edmund Leach (1969) applied the structuralism of Lévi-Strauss to Israelite religious narratives, has an anthropological approach emerged in the study of Israelite religion. Since their essays appeared, there has been a growing tendency to use anthropological data to illuminate aspects of Israelite religion and even to speak of anthropological approaches to the Hebrew Bible (Culley 1985). In chapter 3, I will consider the reasons for this recent interest of anthropologists in Israelite religion.

A similar resistance to anthropological inquiry has been evident in the study of ancient Judaism, particularly among interpreters of rabbinic Judaism. In discussions of these traditions, little appeal has been made to ethnographic literature or anthropological theory. Generally, the study of ancient Judaism, like the interpretation of Israelite religion, has been dominated by textual analysis or by studies which contextualize a cultural element in its historical setting. Numerous attempts have been made to see rabbinic Judaism in interaction with Greco-Roman culture or Christianity (e.g., Daube 1949; Lieberman 1950; Fischel 1977). In this case, too, there have been a few noteworthy exceptions, such as the work of Max Kadushin (1952), which relied to some extent on the anthropology of Lévy-Bruhl. More recently, under the influence of Mary Douglas, Jacob Neusner (1979) has pointed out the importance of anthropology for the study of Talmudic literature. For Neusner, anthropology primarily contributes the insight that religions are orderly and coherent systems in which "the character of the way of life and the conceptions of the world mutually illuminate and explain one another" (1979, 3). Furthermore, Neusner finds anthropology helpful because anthropologists have learned how to discern the larger issues of a culture from the minute details of a given way of life. This insight, Neusner notes, is particularly useful for the interpreter of rabbinic literature, a literature which dwells on what appear to be trivial details. Other interpreters (Eilberg-Schwartz 1986, 190–200; Hoffman 1987; Lightstone 1988) have begun to follow Neusner's lead in turning to anthropology for insight about rabbinic Judaism. But despite the importance of anthropology for his research program, Neusner has remained committed to seeing Judaism in interaction with its cultural neighbors (e.g., Neusner 1986). Indeed, Neusner has condemned cross-cultural comparisons that do not involve the comparison of cultural wholes (Neusner 1978), a position that effectively rules out cross-cultural comparisons altogether (Smith 1982).

In sum, in the study of Israelite religion and ancient Judaism there has been a strong tendency to ignore anthropological theory, ethnographic literature, and cross-cultural studies. Instead, there has been a fixation with historical contextualization, which either leads to a denigration of comparison altogether or at most seeks comparisons between contiguous religions and cultures. When comparisons are tolerated, they are almost all of the metonymic variety, that is, between cultures and religions that are in a single geographical area and hence "in contact." But there is a lack of interest in, and even hostility toward, metaphoric comparisons, comparisons that are drawn between religions and cultures that are similar in some respect but are separated in place and perhaps also in time.

The Untold Story: Why Biblical Studies Rejected Anthropology and Metaphoric Comparisons

Robert Wilson has suggested that the resistance among interpreters of ancient Israel to the use of anthropological methods and comparative data is in part a reaction against "the comparative method" of late nineteenth- and early twentieth-century interpreters of religion who, from the perspective of their successors, moved too glibly from society to society in seeking comparisons. Those who used "the comparative method" compared anything and everything in their expectation of finding a universal evolutionary scheme in the development of religion, culture, and mind. Their approach was labeled "conjectural history" since they attempted to reconstruct the specific history of a given religion on the basis of a postulated evolutionary scheme. Primitive societies provided evidence of the stages through which more advanced cultures had already moved. Since such interpreters were "armchair anthropologists" and did not examine a given cultural trait "in context," their interpretations were ludicrous from the perspective of persons who were more familiar with the societies in question. Consequently, when those using the comparative method compared items from various cultures, they were comparing one misinterpretation with another. That, at any rate, has been the judgment of subsequent interpreters of religion and culture. For interpreters of Israelite religion, these abuses were particularly evident in the works of William Robertson Smith and James G. Frazer, the most important figures to use the comparative method to understand Israelite religion. In Wilson's words,

> Like the sociologists and anthropologists whose work they used, [the late nineteenth- and early twentieth-century] Old Testament critics often wrenched the comparative material out of its social context and then embedded it in a comprehensive social theory that was frequently dominated by an evolutionary perspective. The theory and its accompanying evidence were then imposed on the Old Testament, which was interpreted so as to produce the desired results... When biblical scholars finally began to recognize these problems, they reacted by curtailing their use of anthropological and sociological material. (1984, 25)

Instead of ranging far and wide over the religions of the world, biblical scholars reacted against the comparative method by insisting on understanding Israelite religion against the backdrop of other ancient Near Eastern religions. As Sayce (1889, 357–58) puts it in his review of Robertson Smith's *Lectures on the Religion of the Semites*, "I must enter a protest against the assumption that what holds good of Kaffirs or Australians held good also for the primitive Semite. The students of language have at last learnt that what is applicable to one family of speech is not necessarily applicable to another, and it would be well if the anthropologist would learn the same lesson." If one takes this lesson seriously and treats cultures as analogous to languages, then it makes no sense to make cross-cultural comparison.[6] The only relevant comparisons are between families of cultures, cultures that have a common ancestry. Hence one must see Israelite religion in the context of neighboring religions.

Scholars of Israelite religion also noted a second advantage to seeing Israelite religion against the backdrop of other ancient Near Eastern religions. In so doing, the interpreter would have at hand empirical evidence for the historical unfolding of religions. No longer would the historian of ancient Israel have to import an a priori evolutionary framework or rely on reconstruction of the prehistory of Israelite religion, as the advocates of the comparative method had done. Now the actual history of Israelite religion was directly available from literary and archaeological remains. In the words of William Albright (1942, 77), one of the most important archaeologists of the ancient Near East and an influential historian of Israelite religion, "Archaeology makes it increasingly possible to interpret each religious phenomenon and movement of the Old Testament in the light of its *true background and real sources*, instead of forcing its interpretation into some preconceived historical mold" (emphasis supplied). Situating Israelite religion against the background of other ancient Near Eastern religions would thus avoid the perceived abuses of the comparative method, particularly as applied to Israelite religion by Robertson Smith and Frazer. The commitment to contextualization was thus reinforced by a desire to escape the evolutionary framework and speculative comparisons of late nineteenth- and early twentieth-century anthropology.

Persuasive as this argument may have been, it is not the whole story. It masks deeper, more powerful motives at work in the repudiation of the comparative method and in the subsequent obsession with the ancient Near East. One of those motives was the desire to oppose Israelite and primitive religions, a desire that permeated European thought for three centuries before our own. This is one of the reasons that the work of Frazer and Robertson Smith proved so problematic to subsequent interpreters of ancient Israelite religion. In their hands, the comparative method demonstrated provocative similarities between the religions of savages and Israelites and, consequently, threatened to undermine the privileged status of the latter. To be sure, Robertson Smith and Frazer both qualify their interpretations in various ways. In his prefatory remarks to *Folklore in the Old Testament* (1919, x), Frazer claims that "the scope of my work has obliged me to dwell chiefly on the lower side of ancient Hebrew life revealed in the OT, on the traces of savagery and superstition which are to be found in its pages ... the revelation of the baser elements which underlay the civilization of ancient Israel serves rather as a foil to enhance by contrast the glory of a people which, from such dark depths of ignorance and cruelty, could rise to such bright heights of wisdom and virtue." Robertson Smith makes similar remarks throughout his *Lectures*.

Such qualifications notwithstanding, the work of these writers could not help but impress their readers with the many similarities between Israelite and savage religions. In this respect, Robertson Smith and Frazer were more radical than their contemporaries who used the comparative method. Edward Tylor, for example, in his *Primitive Culture* (1958 [1871]), 49) mentions the Semites only three times. He neglects the "Semitic Family, which represents one of the oldest known civilizations of the world," because "this family takes in some rude tribes but none which would be classed as savages." Tylor gives the impression that the savage is temporally anterior to ancient Israel and that consequently the study of primitive religion is irrelevant to the study of ancient Judaism. But in Robertson Smith's and Frazer's works, that distance is reduced and almost eliminated. The primitive is no longer safely ensconced "behind," "before," or "under" Israelite religion but threatens to appear at its very heart and thus within striking distance of Christianity as well.[7]

That this was one of the implications of Frazer's and Robertson Smith's work is evident from their writing as well as from the reactions of critics. Robertson Smith relies heavily on information from savage societies in his *Kinship and Marriage in Early Arabia* (1903 [1885]) and *Lectures on the Religion of the Semites* (1927 [1889]). In the latter work, he argues that a large number of Hebrew practices, including rules about uncleanness and holiness, derived from a savage stage of religious development. "The fact that all the Semites have rules of uncleanness as well as rules of holiness, that the boundary between the two is often vague, and that the former as well as the latter present the most startling agreement in point of detail with savage *taboo*, leaves no reasonable doubt as to the [savage] origin and ultimate relations of the idea of holiness" (1927 [1889], 153). Robertson Smith also goes so far as to suggest that the Hebrew sacrificial institution had developed from the primitive institution of totemism, in which a kin group communed with its god by eating an animal that it thought of as one of its kin (1927 [1889], 289). As one opponent of Smith put it, his doctrine of sacrifice represented "a new theory of the essential character of the Old Testament religion," one which "cut away the basis on which the whole doctrine of salvation rests" (quoted in Black and Chrystal 1912, 417). To be sure, Robertson Smith, like Frazer, periodically reminds his readers that Hebrew religion was much more sophisticated than the primitive religions to which he was comparing it. Nonetheless, his work points to far more commonalities than most cared to admit.

It was this feature of Robertson Smith's work that Frazer highlights in his obituary for his teacher and friend. "Another important province in the history of religion which Robertson Smith was the first to explore is the religion of pastoral tribes. The conclusions which he arrived at, mainly from an analysis of Semitic sacrificial ritual, are strikingly confirmed by an induction from the facts of pastoral life as observed among rude pastoral tribes in various parts of the world, especially in Africa" (Frazer 1967 [1894], 289). Frazer also points out that Robertson Smith was one of the first to show that sacramental sacrifices

> are not confined to Christianity, but are common to it with heathen and even savage religions. Whether he was right in tracing their origin to totemism may be questioned: the evidence thus far does not enable us to pronounce decisively. But that religious ideas and observances of this type are world-wide, and that they originated, not in an advanced, but in a low stage of society and in a very crude phase of thought, is not open to question… Among the many questions which it raises, the one which will naturally interest Christians most deeply is "How are we to explain the analogy which it reveals between the Christian

Atonement and Eucharist on the one side, and the mystical or sacramental sacrifices of the heathen religions on the other." (1967 [1894], 288–89)

Similarly, Stanley Cook (1902, 413–48), in his review of the debate over Israelite totemism, notes that Robertson Smith's work implies that "the curious rite of the Ordeal of Jealousy, the superstitious fear of iron in holy places, ritual dances, scapegoats, speaking trees, and stars imbued with life, are among the indications that Israel was no different to other primitive peoples."

The same impulses were even more pronounced in the work of Frazer. In his letter to the publisher George Macmillan offering him *The Golden Bough*, Frazer writes that "the resemblance of many of the savage customs and ideas to the fundamental doctrines of Christianity is striking. But I make no reference to this parallelism leaving my readers to draw their own conclusions, one way or the other" (Downie 1970, 53). As this statement makes clear, one of Frazer's objectives was to inscribe the savage at the very heart of the "Judeo-Christian" tradition (Ackerman 1987, 164–97; Strathern 1987). Just before publishing the second edition of *The Golden Bough*, Frazer wrote to his close friend Solomon Schechter, a well-known rabbi and talmudist. "I trust," he writes, "that you will approve of the book in its new and enlarged form. There are things in it which are likely to give offence both to Jews and Christians, but especially, I think to Christians. You see I am neither the one nor the other, and don't mind knocking them impartially" (Ackerman 1987, 169–70). Most provocative is Frazer's discussion of corn spirits. Frazer notes the custom among many peoples of eating new corn as if it were the body of a corn spirit. This primitive notion of transubstantiation led Frazer to comment that "on the whole it would seem that neither the ancient Hindoos nor the ancient Mexicans [i.e., Aztecs] had much to learn from the most refined mysteries of Catholic theology" (Downie 1970, 52).

The implication of comparing primitive religions to classic traditions of the West was not lost on a number of writers. Reflecting on the impact of *The Golden Bough* on the study of classics, Stanley Casson writes,

> *The Golden Bough* marked a turning point in anthropological studies, for it forced the scholars of the literary traditions to enlarge their vision, to realize the implications of ancient Greek and Roman customs which they had failed to analyse, and to accustom themselves to the new contributions which anthropological research could make to what had hitherto been a purely literary appreciation of ancient authors. Here was the inner mind of the two great ancient civilisations being revealed intimately to scholars who had hitherto examined only the surface. Dark and mysterious rites and survivals, magic and superstition which would be normal in Polynesia or Australia, were seen to have been working in the background of the most civilised periods of the ancient world. (Downie 1970, 58)

Equally provocative was Frazer's *Folklore in the Old Testament* (1919). Custom after custom in the Old Testament became the occasion for extensive citations of parallel customs among primitive societies. Despite Frazer's disclaimers, this work created the impression that almost all aspects of Israelite religion were survivals from savagery.

Whether intentional or not, Frazer's and Robertson Smith's works collapsed the longstanding dichotomy between Israelite and savage religions. For this reason, there was a distinct advantage to be gained by rejecting the comparative method. If the method turned out to be problematic, the resemblances between Israelite and savage religions could be safely ignored. Thus while biblical scholars had some legitimate dissatisfactions with the first attempts to subject Israelite religion to anthropological inquiry, some questionable motives also contributed to the growing hostility toward anthropology and the comparative study of Israelite religion.

At least one reviewer of Frazer's work complained about his contemporaries' unwillingness to admit analogies between primitive religions and ancient Judaism. Thus in his review of Frazer's *Folklore of the Old Testament*, H. J. D. Astley (1929, 104) writes,

> Old-fashioned students of this [Old Testament] literature, hallowed by so many religious associations, are likely to be shocked by the suggestion that within its pages are contained tales and descriptions of customs that can in any way be attached to the category of folk-lore. They feel inclined to exclaim: "Hands off! Defile not the holy thing with profane touch; this is sacred ground, and must be approached only by those from whose feet the shoes have been reverently put off."

Some interpreters of Israelite religion frankly acknowledged having such sentiments. In critiquing the work of Robertson Smith and Frazer, Snaith (1944, 17) urges:

> If there are no distinctive elements in Christianity, then, in the name of whatever gods there then may be, let us be realistic and sensible. Let us dismiss the whole affair to its proper home in the limbo of the dead illusions of mankind... On the other hand, if Christianity does contain distinctive elements, both in common with Judaism and against the rest of religions ... then, in the Name of the One God, let us examine them, and let us be very sure indeed of what precisely they are. No institution, be it religious or secular, has any right to continue to exist unless it has, and can show in all the marketplaces of the world, a special and distinct reason for its separate existence.

Snaith is representative of a larger impulse within biblical studies to defend the uniqueness of Israelite religion, an impulse particularly evident in the biblical theology school (Oden 1987; Childs 1970, 47–50; Dever 1980, 1–14).

But what is so interesting and paradoxical is how the same purpose was achieved in the shift from the comparative method of Robertson Smith and Frazer to the enterprise of studying Israelite religion in the context of other ancient Near Eastern religions, a labor that has dominated twentieth-century study of Israelite religion. As noted above, this shift in emphasis is frequently thought of as a result of theoretical dissatisfactions with the comparative method. Instead of comparing elements from cultures separated in time and place, the new comparative method studied Israelite religion in the context of contiguous traditions. But the newly emerging comparative method served another purpose. It replicated the very evolutionary framework that biblical scholars found so problematic in the anthropologists' method of comparative inquiry.[8] Ironically, then, in repudiating anthropological inquiry, biblical interpreters perpetuated the old dichotomy between Israelite and savage religions.

Note, for example, how Albright (1942, 4) rejects the comparative method while at the same time reaffirming the idea of an evolutionary sequence of humankind.

> But the gap between savage mentality and the mind of modern man is too great to be easily bridged by direct observation, and the attempt [by anthropologists] to fill the gap by studying the ideas of half-savage peoples of today is nearly always vitiated by the fact that these peoples have been strongly influenced by more highly developed civilizations, virtually all of which reflect a post-Hellenic stage of progress... In such cases, we can seldom be sure about the aboriginal character of a given cultural element. The only way in which we can bridge this gap satisfactorily is by following the evolution of the human mind in the Near East itself, where we can trace it from the earliest times through successive archaeological ages to the flowering of the Greek spirit... What we have in mind is nothing less than the ultimate reconstruction, as far as possible, of the route which our cultural ancestors traversed in order to reach Judaeo-Christian heights of spiritual insight and ethical monotheism. In this book we are concerned with the religion of the Old Testament, of which the religion of the New was only the extension and the fulfillment.

Albright believed the study of religious development in the ancient Near Eastern cultures would reveal the evolutionary sequence of the human mind, by showing how the religion of the Old and New Testaments represents a superior stage of moral and spiritual insight. "In this book," he writes, "I have tried to emphasize the fact that Israelite faith was much closer to Christianity and to rabbinic Judaism than to the basically prelogical religions of the ancient Near East" (1942, 177). "No matter where we turn in the extant literature of Israel, we find sobriety and consistency beyond anything known in older cultures. Israel discarded almost all proto-logical thinking" (1964 [1940], 53).

Paradoxically, the repudiation of the comparative method within biblical studies did not involve a rejection of an evolutionary framework, as it did in anthropology. On the contrary, it enabled interpreters of Israelite religion to rejuvenate an evolutionary framework that had already been placed in jeopardy by the work of Robertson Smith and Frazer. Now biblical interpreters could produce empirical historical evidence for the fundamental antithesis between primitive religion and the religion of Israel. When Israelite religion was seen against the background of other ancient Near Eastern religions, the dichotomy between ancient Judaism and primitive religions seemed to arise "out of the data." What disturbed Albright, therefore, was not the evolutionary assumptions that informed the comparative method. What bothered him was the fact that such assumptions did not have empirical support. "No great historian or philologian is likely to construct his system in a vacuum; there must be some body of external data or some plane of reference by the aid of which he can redeem his system from pure subjectivity" (Albright 1964 [1940], 136). The way to prove an evolutionary development was not by roaming over the world as Robertson Smith and Frazer had done but by tracing the history of thought in the ancient Near East. "There is no road from primitive and savage thought to Europe which does not pass directly through the ancient Orient" (1964 [1940], 122).

This evolutionary impulse is not limited to the work of Albright. Throughout the twentieth century the emphasis on contextualizing ancient Israelite religion in the ancient Near East served similar polemical purposes for both Jewish and Christian scholars. "It is only within the setting of its environment in the ancient East that the special character of the Israelite religion emerges clearly, and only then that one can begin to understand her own distinctive place in that story" (J. Hehn quoted in Vriezen 1967, 23). Or, as Kaufmann (1972 [1937–56], 21) puts it,

> We designate as pagan all the religions of mankind from the beginnings of recorded history to the present, excepting Israelite religion and its derivatives, Christianity and Islam. This distinction assumes that, on the one hand, there is something unique about Israelite religion that sets it off from all the rest, and on the other, that there is an essential common aspect to all other religions which gives them their pagan character.

Other interpreters have shared similar sentiments (Vriezen 1967, 11; Wright 1950, 13).

Subsequent writers continued to repeat the assertion that Israelite religion reflected a fundamental development in religious mentality. "It would seem that the Hebrews, no less than the Greeks, broke with the mode of speculation which had prevailed up to their time... This conception of God represents so high a degree of abstraction that, in reaching it, the Hebrews seem to have left the realm of mythopoeic thought" (H. and H. A. Frankfort 1971 [1946], 241–44). "Long before the history of Israel began, the ancient Near East had left any stage of animism or dynamism far behind" (Wright 1950, 16). The same argument continues to find noteworthy adherents (Sarna 1970, xxviii).

Along with this fundamental rupture in religious consciousness appeared an equally significant development in moral insight. This is particularly evident when Israelite religion is compared with that of the Canaanites. "The sexual emphasis of Canaanite religion was certainly extreme and at its worst could only have appealed to the baser aspects of man. Religion as commonly practiced in Canaan, therefore, must have been a rather sordid and degrading business, when judged by our standards, and so, it seems, it appeared to religious circles of Israel" (Wright 1957, 13). When scholarship exposes the mythological and polytheistic context out of which Israelite religion emerged, "one cannot marvel enough at the power which made it possible for Israel to break away from this world of ideas and speak about the relationship of God to the world in quite a different way" (von Rad 1976, 65). Quotations such as these could be readily multiplied. What they show is how often the desire to situate Israelite religion against the background of the ancient Near East has served a defensive posturing and evolutionary agenda.

In this respect different motives operated in the rejection of the comparative method within biblical studies from the ones that operated in anthropology. To be sure, anthropologists, like interpreters of ancient Israel, also voiced doubts about wrenching items out of their cultural contexts. For this reason, American anthropology, like biblical studies, reacted against the comparative method by turning to studies of cultural diffusion among peoples in contiguous geographical areas. But the central motivation for criticizing the comparative method within anthropology was its evolutionary assumptions. For Boas and his students in the American tradition, as well as Malinowski, Radcliffe-Brown, and their students in the British school, the repudiation of the comparative method was part of an attack on evolutionary theory. In the study of Israelite religion, by contrast, an opposite impulse is evident. The emphasis on history, context, and diffusion clearly fed an evolutionary polemic. Once Israelite religion was set in its ancient Near Eastern context, a historical scheme emerged that was not altogether different from the evolutionary schemes postulated in the nineteenth century. Israelite religion appeared to arise out of and in reaction to the polytheistic religions of the Canaanites, Sumerians, Assyrians, and Babylonians. This historical orientation highlighted the unique aspects of Israelite religion, especially the development of monotheism and the repudiation of mythology. From this perspective, Israelite religion appears as a historical, rational, moral, and monotheistic religion in contrast to the mythological, irrational, ahistorical, and morally degrading religions that surrounded it. In sum, the rejection of anthropology and the comparative method and the increasing emphasis on archaeology, history, diffusion, and context had the effect, if not the intended consequence, of preserving the opposition between Israelite religion and savage religions.

This is not to deny that important theoretical issues were also at stake in the rejection of the comparative method. As noted above, critics of the comparative method raised some legitimate questions about the wisdom of taking cultural items out of their context. Moreover, not all interpreters of Israelite religion shared the biases exposed above. Indeed, some viewed the attempt to study Israelite religion in the context of other ancient Near Eastern religions as a way to challenge the ideology of Israel's uniqueness. When placed in the context of the ancient Near East, one discovered striking similarities between Israelite religion and the religious traditions of contiguous cultures. These similarities showed that Israelite religion was not a revealed religion that had dropped from the sky but a historical one that had developed out of its historical background and had absorbed many important ideas and institutions from its cultural neighbors.

Still, one wonders what would have happened in biblical studies if the impulse to differentiate Israelite and savage religions had not also been present. Clearly, these prejudices helped achieve the almost unquestioned consensus that anthropology and comparative inquiry were problematic. As often happens, a scholarly consensus once achieved turns into a foundational axiom that is passed from teacher to student. Students who did not necessarily share the prejudices of their teachers nonetheless inherited certain theoretical commitments that were shaped in part by their teachers' biases. In concentrating their efforts on situating Israelite religion against the background of other Near Eastern religions, they perpetuated an opposition that they had no stake in preserving.

Without these prejudices operating, it is conceivable that biblical studies could have responded to the comparative method differently. Interpreters of Israelite religion made the hasty judgment that since this comparative method was problematic, all cross-cultural inquiry is problematic. But as I argue in chapter 4, that conclusion is not warranted. The failure of the comparative method stemmed from its evolutionary assumptions and its disregard for the larger cultural contexts in which specific elements found their place. It would have been equally reasonable to conclude that a more judicious sort of comparative method, one that attended to elements in their cultural context and one that operated without evolutionary assumptions, would prove more compelling.

This at any rate was the conclusion within the nascent British school of anthropology, which has harbored a strong comparative thrust despite its repudiation of the comparative method as practiced by Robertson Smith and Frazer. For Radcliffe-Brown, as for many students in that tradition, the goal of fieldwork was to see whether the insights derived from studying tribe x could be generalized to tribe y. For example, Radcliffe-Brown attempted to formulate a theory of kinship that could explain kinship systems in diverse contexts. In the British tradition, the failure of the comparative method did not mean that comparisons across cultures were inherently problematic.[9]

In retrospect, it is ironic that interpreters of Israelite religion, suspicious of the comparative method, so enthusiastically took up the study of other ancient Near Eastern traditions. As subsequent reflection has shown, comparisons between religions in the same geographical area are fraught with the same kinds of theoretical problems as comparisons between religions in different geographical areas. As Fohrer puts it in his *History of Israelite Religion* (1972, 25),

> When using this comparative [Near Eastern] material, we must of course be careful to observe and maintain the unique features of Israelite religion. Something that sounds like a feature of another religion need not have the same meaning it has in the other religion. Religious concepts or customs can have different meanings and purposes in two different religions, even when these religions are close neighbors geographically and historically. The ancient Near Eastern material must therefore always be employed with caution.

Other interpreters have expressed similar reservations (Anderson 1951, 285, 291; Frankfort 1951; Sarna 1970, xxvii; Vriezen 1967, 23).

In any comparative study, the same kind of interpretive difficulties present themselves: What should be compared and why? Is the comparison of two traits valid? What are the criteria for deciding? How can one be sure that parallel traits in two contiguous cultures have the same meanings in their respective cultural systems? It is appropriate that biblical scholars referred to their new approach as "the comparative method," for it has a number of the same interpretive difficulties as "the comparative method" employed by the late nineteenth- and early twentieth-century anthropologists. Interpreters of Israelite religion were deceived in thinking they had developed a more objective method for interpreting religion. They had not.

The thrust of this argument is not to deny the importance of diffusion as a cultural process, the importance of a historical perspective, or the usefulness of seeing Israelite religion against the background of the ancient Near East. Without a doubt, our understanding of Israelite religion has been enriched by the project of comparing it to contiguous traditions. The point is simply that things could have been other than they were. The impulse to study Israelite religion in the context of the ancient Near East did not have to dominate biblical studies to the exclusion of other kinds of interests. Alongside the concern with context and diffusion, biblical studies could have nourished a tradition of cross-cultural comparison, one that attended to theoretical developments within anthropology while at the same time taking account of the results achieved by students of ancient Near Eastern cultures. At the very least, this discussion reopens the question of whether cross-cultural inquiry and anthropological theory can further our understanding of Israelite religion. This book is a wager that they can.

Judaism and Savage Religions in Anthropology

If biblical interpreters have been guilty of perpetuating an opposition between Israelite religion and primitive religions, a similar story has to be told about the discipline of anthropology. Apart from Frazer's *The Golden Bough* and *Folklore in the Old Testament*, there had been no attempt by anthropologists to make Israelite religion or ancient Judaism a serious focus of inquiry until the work of Mary Douglas (1966) and Edmund Leach (1969).[10] Thanks to Douglas's work, the Israelite dietary restrictions have entered anthropological discourse and have had an important impact on anthropological theory (e.g., Bulmer 1967; Tambiah 1969). To be sure, references to Israelite religion are found in anthropological writings before Douglas's work. But such references are episodic and generally serve as a rhetorical device. By referring to practices or conceptions of the Israelites, the anthropologist domesticated the alien practice or belief by pointing to an analogous practice that was recognizable but not too familiar. The following statement from the preface to Evans-Pritchard's *Nuer Religion* (1956, vii) is symptomatic of the role played by Israelite religion and ancient Judaism in twentieth-century anthropological writings. "When, therefore, I sometimes draw comparisons between Nuer and Hebrew conceptions, it is no mere whim but is because I myself find it helpful, and I think others may do so too, in trying to understand Nuer ideas to note this likeness to something with which we are ourselves familiar without being too intimately involved in it." Within anthropology, episodic references to Israelite religion served to illuminate primitive religions, but Israelite religion itself was not considered a legitimate object of inquiry.

The tendency among anthropologists to ignore Israelite religion and ancient Judaism, like the prejudice among biblical scholars against studies of primitive societies, was partially a reaction to the comparative method of the late nineteenth- and early twentieth-century anthropologists. Within anthropology, dissatisfactions with the comparative method and "armchair anthropology" produced an emphasis on fieldwork that involved living for an extended period of time among the people under study.[11] Ethnography seemed to avoid the abuses of the comparative method. Not only did participant-observation side-step the problem of postulating a people's history, but it enabled anthropologists to view cultural items as part of a larger cultural and social system within which they operated. As noted above, in the American tradition the retreat from the comparative method also led to an interest in the interrelationships among cultures and religions in contiguous geographical areas. Since a rejection of the comparative method produced an emphasis on intensive fieldwork and face-to-face interaction with the people under study, anthropologists lost interest in religious cultures such as Judaism that could only be investigated through historical sources. The conjectural history of the comparative method was replaced by a study of real historical and social processes. As Evans-Pritchard (1951, 74) later puts it, "Formerly the anthropologist, like the historian, regarded documents as the raw material of his study. Now the raw material was social life itself." In other words, in rejecting the nineteenth-century comparative method, twentieth-century anthropology repudiated the model of anthropologist as classicist.[12] In its place emerged another model, the anthropologist as traveler and visitor among alien peoples.

While all of these factors were no doubt at work in the diminishing interest in Judaism among anthropologists, this still is not the whole story. A strong interest in intensive studies actually predated the demise of the comparative method (Stocking 1983). For this reason, the shift from anthropologist as classicist to anthropologist as fieldworker cannot be completely attributed to growing dissatisfactions with the comparative method. The assumption of a fundamental distinction between primitive and civilized peoples also contributed to this development. Not only was this opposition already in place before anthropologists discovered the importance of fieldwork, but the very emphasis on fieldwork was in part a result of anthropology's commitment to the study of primitive society.

This opposition is evident in the work of late nineteenth-century anthropologists who ignored Israelite religion. As noted previously, Edward Tylor does not include the Semites in his *Primitive Culture* (1958 [1871], 49) because "this family takes in some rude tribes but none which would be classed as savages." Similarly, in his *Anthropology and the Classics* (1966 [1908], 3) R. R. Marett writes,

Anthropology and the Humanities—on verbal grounds one might suppose them coextensive; yet in practice they divide the domain of human cultures between them. The types of human culture are, in fact, reducible to two, a simpler and a more complex, or, as we are wont to say (valuing our own achievements, I doubt not, rightly), a lower and a higher. By established convention anthropology occupies itself solely with culture of a simpler and lower kind. The Humanities, on the other hand ... concentrates on whatever is most constitutive and characteristic of the higher life of society.

The task of anthropology as it was articulated in the late nineteenth century was to understand the origin and development of religion, culture, and the human mind. To understand the origin of these phenomena necessitated looking at primitive cultures which were thought to reflect the early history of humankind. Primitive societies were living fossils, relics of a distant past which European culture had long ago transcended. The religion and culture of higher civilizations could shed no light on the early history of religion, culture, and humanity.

An opposition between Israelite religion and primitive religions was contained in this larger distinction between primitive and civilized peoples. This is why the religion of Israel fell outside the purview of anthropological inquiry. Although it retained survivals from a primitive past, Israelite religion had largely transcended and thus obscured its primitive origins. The study of Israelite religion could not contribute to an understanding of how religion began, the issue at the center of anthropological attention.

The operation of this opposition is evident, for example, if one compares the work of Emile Durkheim and Max Weber. Durkheim, whose work provides the foundation for several traditions within anthropology, formulated his theories by studying the Australian aborigines. These societies, Durkheim assumed, were the most primitive and simplest available for study. Studying them would enable him to understand the origin and function of religion in a way that was not possible when studying religion in complex and developed societies (Durkheim 1965 [1915], 13–20; Lukes 1985, 455–57). By contrast, Weber, whose work especially influenced sociology, developed his theories through an explication of the "world religions" (*Weltreligionen*) that is, Confucianism, Buddhism, Hinduism, Judaism, Christianity, and Islam (Parsons 1968, 2:539; Lukes 1985, 457). As anthropology and sociology emerged as recognizable and distinctive disciplines, an opposition between world and primitive religions was presupposed and preserved.

That the disciplinary divisions reflected this ideological opposition was both evident and embarrassing to those working within anthropology. As early as 1931, Radcliffe-Brown (1958 [1931], 45) notes in a presidential address to the British Association for the Advancement of Science that

anthropology as now organized includes as a third field the study of the languages and cultures of non-European peoples, and particularly of those peoples who have no written history. This separation of the people of the world into two groups, one of which is studied by the anthropologist, while the other is left to historians, philologists and others, is obviously not justifiable by any logical coordination of studies, and is no longer fully justified by practical considerations, as it was when it first arose.

But anthropology did not change. Although the ideological basis of these dichotomies had long since been called in question, the disciplinary commitments had already been formed. Anthropologists would continue to study in small face-to-face societies; historians, philologists, and theologians would continue to study Israelite religion and ancient Judaism.

As is now evident, strong motives for ignoring the study of Judaism existed within anthropology before the discipline's emerging hostility toward history and growing interest in intensive fieldwork. Ironically, then, the developing emphasis on ethnography is better understood as the result rather than the cause of the lack of interest in classical traditions. Since anthropology had already designated primitive societies as its objects of inquiry, it had to develop an appropriate method for studying these societies. Since nonliterate folk seemed like "people without history," the only way to understand them was by living and talking with them.

The connection among these factors is evident in Malinowski's methodological introduction to *Argonauts of the Western Pacific*, the work often credited with articulating the theoretical justification for ethnography. "In our society," writes Malinowski (1961 [1922], 12),

> Every institution has its intelligent members, its historians, and its archives and documents, whereas in a native society there are none of these. After this is realised an expedient has to be found to overcome this difficulty. This expedient for an Ethnographer consists in collecting concrete data of evidence and drawing the general inferences for himself. This seems obvious on the face of it, but was not found out or at least practised in Ethnography till field work was taken up by men of science.

The method of study was partially determined by the choice of subject matter. Had anthropology not already repudiated the classics, fieldwork may not have become the *sine qua non* of anthropology. It is not surprising, therefore, that in the past few decades as anthropology has begun to widen its own horizon and take an interest in complex and literate societies, history has emerged once more as a valuable tool (e.g., Sahlins 1981; 1985).

As in the case of biblical studies, one wonders how anthropology might have been different had the opposition between primitive and civilized not had such a significant impact on the formation of the discipline. Without such an opposition it is possible to imagine that Israelite religion and ancient Judaism, among other classical traditions, could have remained more central in anthropology's repertoire. In ignoring these traditions, the practice of twentieth-century anthropology was paradoxically influenced by one of the assumptions that it had officially rejected, the assumption of a fundamental difference between higher and lower religions. The lack of interest among twentieth-century anthropologists in Judaism is itself a "survival" of an older attitude of the nineteenth century which viewed such religious cultures as fundamentally different from those of savages.

Given that such an opposition has been operative both among interpreters of Judaism and anthropologists, it is not surprising that that the dichotomy was eventually institutionalized in the university: the study of Judaism and the religions of "primitive" societies are housed in different departments; the former takes place in departments of religious studies, Near Eastern languages, oriental or Jewish studies, the latter in departments of anthropology. As I suggest in chapter 3, the recent interest in Judaism by anthropologists such as Douglas and Leach is the consequence of a growing dissatisfaction with this division.

As anthropology overcomes this original opposition, the anthropologist can once again become a classicist and the classicist an anthropologist. In retrospect it is clear that the difference between doing ethnography and studying a people through their textual remains is by no means as sharp as early ethnographers once thought. The metaphor of culture as text, initially formulated by Clifford Geertz, has proven invaluable for cultural analysis (see Scholte 1987). To be sure, when an ethnographer lives with a group, she or he questions informants and therefore has an experience that is unlike the activity of interpreting texts. But the operations by which that experience is turned into an ethnography are similar to those used in interpreting texts (Clifford and Marcus 1986; Clifford 1988). The ethnography that is produced is generally written after returning from the field and may take months or even years to write. In giving an account of religion or culture, the ethnographer relies on "fieldnotes" or a text that has been taken from its original context. No matter how intensive or thorough the fieldwork, the ethnographer must intervene to produce a coherent, logical account. In Geertz's (1973, 9) now classic formulation, "What we call our data are really our own constructions of other people's constructions of what they and their compatriots are up to." This recent understanding of ethnography as a form of writing requires a reevaluation of the assumed differences between doing fieldwork and studying classics and thus helps put in question the longstanding opposition between anthropology and classical studies.

The Savage Within

As the opposition between Judaism and savage religions is obliterated, one can expect to find the savage reinscribed within Judaism. By this I mean that some traits originally assumed to be characteristic of primitive peoples alone will turn out on reflection to be characteristics of Judaism itself. In saying this, I am anticipating that the same process which has already taken place within the disciplines of anthropology and philosophy will also finally occur within the study of Judaism. As anthropologists and philosophers dismantled the opposition between savagery and civilization, they began to realize that what they had originally seen in the savage was in fact a shadowy version of ourselves that we had failed to recognize.

My argument regarding the savage is similar to Hayden White's argument about the "Wild Man." White (1978, 7) suggests that the concept of "Wild Man" helped to sustain Western cultural myths by serving as a negative point of reference. As this concept and others like it were unmasked, they were interiorized.

> From biblical times to the present, the notion of the Wild Man was associated with the idea of the wilderness—the desert, forest, jungle, and mountains—those parts of the physical world that had not yet been domesticated or marked out for domestication in any significant way. As one after another of these wildernesses was brought under control, the idea of the Wild Man was progressively despatialized. This despatialization was attended by a compensatory process of psychic interiorization.

A similar process of interiorization has taken place in the case of the savage. But in contrast to the "Wild Man," the savage has undergone what might be called a cultural interiorization. Characteristics of savages have been absorbed into Western culture's understanding of its own practices.

As an example, consider the way in which qualities once ascribed to the savage mind were gradually incorporated into the characterization of the Western mind. Lévy Bruhl (1985 [1910]), for example, describes the savage mind as "impervious to experience," by which he means that natives fail to notice when experience proves certain beliefs and practices to be fallacious. According to Lévy-Bruhl, this characteristic of primitive thought explains why natives continue to perform magical rites, such as throwing grain in the air to produce rainfall, even though such rites regularly fail to produce the desired effect. The primitive mind simply does not take account of disconfirming evidence because it is based on a kind of logic different from our own, a logic rooted in emotional connections rather than logical ones. For Lévy-Bruhl, therefore, the savage is irrational, at least when compared to the scientist who takes note of disconfirming evidence. Indeed, science is the paradigmatic rational activity, because science progresses by subjecting hypotheses to empirical tests and by relinquishing them when they are refuted by evidence.

Lévy-Bruhl was not alone in this characterization of the savage mind. Tylor and Frazer, although working from different assumptions, also note the way that primitive thought protects its practices from disconfirming evidence (Evans-Pritchard 1933; 1934). It does this by elaborating secondary rationalizations and by giving ad hoc explanations that will account for the failure of a rite. For example, if throwing grain into the air does not produce rain, a native might blame the failure of the rite on the neglect of one of the proper procedures or taboos. Alternatively, a native can always blame its failure on hostile forces believed to undermine the magical act. When the weight of tradition stands behind a practice, disconfirming evidence cannot undermine the confidence that natives have in its efficacy.

Malinowski (1961 [1922]; 1954 [1925]; 1978 [1935]), among others, attempts to undo the opposition Lévy-Bruhl, Tylor, and Frazer created between the impervious savage and the rational scientist. Based on intensive fieldwork, he argues that the native is in fact sensitive to experience and understands a great deal about nature. Malinowski points to the sophisticated technology developed by the Trobriand

Islanders for coping with their environment, including their methods of cultivating and raising crops and their techniques for building and sailing boats. The success of the Trobrianders in these activities presupposes a great deal of knowledge about the environment. The Trobrianders know very well that seeds will not grow if they are not planted during the proper season and in the proper kinds of soil. Moreover, they understand certain principles of buoyancy; otherwise, it would be impossible for them to construct canoes. The presence of such technology, therefore, indicates that natives have experimented with nature and learned certain lessons. Malinowski moves beyond the opposition created by his predecessors by arguing that the savage is sensitive to experience and therefore as rational as a scientist. In Malinowski's judgment, the only difference between a native and a scientist is the respective quantity of empirical information that their cultures have each accumulated.

The collapse of any sharp dichotomy between the savage and civilized mind eventually had the consequence of allowing those qualities originally associated with primitive thought to reappear as traits of scientific thinking. Polanyi (1958), Kuhn (1970), Feyerabend (1975; 1978), and Lakatos (1970), among others, have suggested that the scientific community itself is in some sense impervious to experience and protects its own theories against disconfirmation. Opposing the view of the scientific community as continually looking for evidence to test current theories, Kuhn, for example, draws attention to the way that scientists devote themselves to the puzzles that a given paradigm has created. Normal science is the attempt to make nature fit into the box provided by the paradigm within which scientists are working. According to this view, the scientific community (at least during the activity of normal science) attempts to protect the paradigm against refuting evidence. It does this, Kuhn argues, by pushing out of sight the evidence that would undermine the paradigm with which it is currently working. In addition, scientists elaborate secondary interpretations and ad hoc answers to protect the paradigm against a seemingly recalcitrant fact. Kuhn suggests that all the puzzles on which scientists work can, from another point of view, be seen as problems that undermine the theories to which scientists are committed. Yet, most of the time those problems are treated as puzzles that test scientists' ingenuity, not facts that threaten scientific theories.

For the present purposes, it does not matter that Kuhn's understanding of science has been criticized in some quarters. What is significant is how the collapse of the distinction between the savage and scientific mind resulted in the interiorization of "savage" traits within Western self-understandings. In short, if nineteenth-century and early twentieth-century intellectuals discovered the savage in distant places, subsequent thinkers gradually learned that if savagery is to be found anywhere, it is at home among us. In this sense, the study of the savage has proved to be a learning process about ourselves.[13]

The Savage in Judaism

As the opposition between Judaism and savage religions continues to give way, a process similar to the one described above will occur. Traits once associated with the savage will be recognized as part of Judaism itself. The investigations in this book are intended to contribute to this process. They focus on some of the practices of Israelite religion and ancient Judaism that have been marginalized for being associated with primitive religions, such as circumcision and the menstrual taboo as well as more general rules governing the purity and impurity of objects. In addition, I examine a number of rules governing animal husbandry and agriculture, such as the prohibitions against boiling a kid-goat in its mother's milk, sacrificing an animal before it is eight days old, taking a mother bird and her fledglings from the nest, sacrificing an animal and its offspring on the same day, mating two different kinds of animals, eating land animals that do not chew their cud and have cloven hooves, cutting the corners of one's field, and planting two different crops in a single field. It is no accident that such practices have received scant attention by comparison with other problems, such as the idea of covenant, God, or the divine-human relationship. The denial of the savage in Judaism requires that such practices be suppressed because they invariably remind interpreters of primitive religions. The suppression of primitive elements is accomplished in two ways: either they are ignored or, when they are mentioned, they are trivialized as either "survivals" from "primitive" religious forms or as degenerated practices from an even earlier and once sophisticated form of religion. Either way the invocation of a temporal sequence effectively denies that such practices are essential to Judaism. Moreover, when such practices are discussed, their similarity to parallel practices in primitive traditions is typically denied. As our embarrassment in the face of such similarities subsides, however, practices once marginalized can be rediscovered, and their role within Judaism more fairly estimated.

The willingness to set Judaism on equal footing with "savage" religions will also further the growing rapprochement between biblical and Judaic studies on the one hand and anthropology on the other. A turn toward the anthropological tradition will provide a fresh set of questions to ask about Judaism and new ways of answering those questions. For example, since Durkheim's and Mauss's *Primitive Classification* (1963 [1903]) one of the recurring projects within anthropology has been to understand the diverse ways societies classify their world and the criteria by which they do so. In fact, some anthropologists have gone so far as to suggest that differences in cultures boil down to differences in classificatory schemes. While understanding such schemes is traditionally an anthropological concern, it does bear on the study of Israelite religion and ancient Judaism, as I have attempted to show in chapters 8 and 9. Recent ethnographies have also examined the way in which root metaphors shape social practices. The attention to this issue within anthropology alerted me to the way in which certain root metaphors provided a foundation for rituals and narratives of ancient Israel (chapter 5).

Anthropology, of course, uses numerous interpretive lenses. This book by no means exhausts the possibilities. It stems from a particular tradition, within anthropology, namely, the one that emerges from the work of Durkheim and is carried forward by the British social anthropologists, particularly Radcliffe-Brown, Evans-Pritchard, Douglas, and Turner, as well as the work of Lévi-Strauss. In appropriating this tradition, however, I have also tried to take account of the criticisms that have been leveled against it. I am aware, for example, of the problems of functionalism (Hempel 1968; Merton 1967; Penner 1971), as well as the criticisms made of the structuralist perspective of both Radcliffe-Brown and Lévi-Strauss (Harris 1968; Hayes and Hayes 1970; Moore and Olmstead 1952; Rossi 1974). While the influences of these approaches are evident in my own work, I move beyond the limitations of those traditions in various ways.

It is for this reason that numerous other voices are heard throughout this book. I have tried, for example, to take account of the increasing impact of literary criticism on the discipline of anthropology. Consequently, symbolic and cultural anthropology, as exhibited particularly in the work of Geertz and Fernandez, have influenced my conception of cultural analysis, as has work on the cultural construction of gender and sexuality (e.g., Rosaldo and Lamphere 1974; Ortner and Whitehead 1981). Finally, postfoundational discussions within philosophy (Rorty 1982; Gadamer 1975), literary criticism (Fish 1980; Johnson 1980), history (Foucault 1973; 1977; White 1978), and history and philosophy of science (Kuhn 1970; Feyerabend 1975; 1978) have all shaped my thinking in various ways. These voices by no means set the agenda for this book, but they do hover in the background and make their clearest statement in this Introduction and the first two chapters. In particular, the work of deconstructive critics (Culler 1982; Johnson 1980) and Foucault (1973) has taught me that the key to a tradition often lies in what it excludes. My reading of these writers drew my attention to the way the primitive has been marginalized in modern discourses on Judaism.

But it is the anthropologists who are my primary interlocutors. Conversations with their works have been particularly illuminating in my own quest to make some sense of particularly unusual aspects of Judaism. These writers taught me to look for certain connections that I otherwise would not have seen. From Douglas and Lévi-Strauss, I learned to attend to relationships between eating and sexual practices and to homologies between rules governing animal husbandry and those governing social relations. Durkheim and Radcliffe-Brown showed me how the structure of social relationships has an impact upon a person's experience of social life, an experience that is in turn reflected in other discursive and nondiscursive practices. Turner, Geertz, and Fernandez impressed me with the importance of symbols and metaphors in the performance of rituals.

From this tradition as a whole, I have also derived a particular understanding of what it means to interpret a social practice. According to all these writers, the interpretation of a practice emerges when its relationship to various other social activities is determined. According to this view, cooking styles, kinship rules, sexual prohibitions, bodily cleanliness, and theological assertions intersect and overlap in interesting ways. The role of the interpreter is to see how these various domains reinforce, reflect, or stand in tension with one another. While interpreters of Israelite religion and ancient Judaism have been attentive to the integrative tendencies of culture, rarely have studies been produced that attend to the relationship among the specific cultural codes that have interested anthropologists.

It is this view of culture that allows me to arrive at interpretations of given practices that would in some instances be unacceptable to the people whose practices I am interpreting. I take for granted that the connections among social practices are not always self-evident to members of a given society. While the interpreter is not omniscient, she or he may see things that people within a given culture cannot see for themselves. An anthropologist makes claims about social practices analogous to those a literary critic makes about a given work of literature. The interpreter of a text is able to see features of it that were not necessarily evident to the author. To be sure, an author always has a number of explicit goals and reasons for writing a given work in a particular way. But language also has a way of controlling the writer. Although the author may give one reason for having chosen a particular phrase or theme, the critic is perfectly entitled to come along and show additional ways that a phrase or theme links up with other parts of the work. The critic unpacks connections that an author often does not realize are there.

This view also makes sense when applied to culture and social practice. The meaning of a practice is contained in the total set of connections it makes with other discursive and nondiscursive practices that constitute the cultural system. It is this understanding of culture that allows me to say, for example, that a rule about not boiling a kid-goat in its mother's milk is parallel to the rule prohibiting incest between an Israelite boy and his mother (chapter 5). I suspect that readers who have not read widely in anthropological literature will find interpretations such as this one somewhat far-fetched. But if it does not surprise anyone that social rules are linked to certain conceptions of God, why should it seem so absurd that practices and conceptions related to food and sex are also enmeshed in one another? In one sense, adopting an anthropological perspective means learning to look for connections between such specific domains as cooking and sex.

In offering such accounts of ancient Israelite practices, I by no means intend to suggest that my interpretations are the only ones possible. Given the conception of culture just presented, I take for granted that a given practice may have more than one meaning, function, or homology. The prohibition about seething a kid-goat in its mother's milk may be interpreted otherwise than as homologous to an incest prohibition. Since a given practice is related to numerous others, the task of interpretation, which has to be shared by numerous interpreters, involves seeking all of these various connections. Indeed, in my view what gives individuals in a community a sense that a given practice is efficacious (or even ordained by God) is the fact that practices intersect with one another in numerous ways within a given culture. In other words, the more connections a given practice makes with other social activities, the more individuals experience its power.

Consider again an analogy from literature. When a writer struggles to perfect a line or verse, she eventually finds "just the right word" even though she cannot always say why that word "works" better than others. What makes that word work, as critics routinely point out, is the way that word links up in numerous ways with other words, sounds, and themes in the adjoining sentences and in the work as a whole. A similar collective process is at work in culture. The sense that one practice is better than another, that it is right, efficacious, or divinely sanctioned, often has to do with the powerful ways that this practice links up with others.

Finally, it is important to acknowledge that the kind of historical anthropology attempted here has to surmount difficulties foreign to the anthropologist in the field. Since the historical anthropologist cannot question natives about the meaning of practices, she or he is in the position of doing cultural archaeology, a mode of interpretation that involves imagining what practices meant from incomplete and partial remains. These unstated meanings can often be detected from symbolic artifacts such as metaphors, which point to larger complexes of unarticulated meaning. Cross-cultural studies are also crucial to the process of reconstructing the larger cultural system. Such studies point to meanings and functions of a practice only hinted at in the literary remains of an ancient tradition. Comparison thus emerges as a tool for imagining the unspoken meanings and correspondences that once constituted a cultural system (see chapter 4).

Having specified the agenda of this book as a whole, let me explain the strategy by which my argument unfolds. In order to make an anthropology of Judaism compelling, it is first necessary to relinquish the distinction between Judaism and savage religions. To do so necessitates understanding why that opposition has had such a grip on intellectual discourse about religion. It is to this historical question that I first turn in chapter 1. In this context, I explore the factors that produced and sustained the opposition between Judaism and savage religion in European scholarship from the seventeenth to nineteenth centuries. I then consider the impulses that have recently called that opposition into question. Once those factors are exposed, I take on the criticisms aimed at cross-cultural comparison. I argue that metonymic comparisons (those between cultures or religions in juxtaposition) are not inherently better than metaphoric comparisons (those between cultures and religions separated by time or place). Consequently, studies that place Israelite religion or ancient Judaism against the background of ancient Near East, Greco-Roman, or Christian contexts are not necessarily superior to those that move across time and space. In part 1, then, I try to overcome the opposition between Judaism and savage religions by exposing and challenging the assumptions on which it has rested.

Part 2 represents substantive contributions to an anthropology of Judaism. Here, certain practices of ancient Israel's religious cultures are examined in light of anthropological studies of "primitive" societies. As mentioned above, part 2 focuses on practices that have been marginalized in biblical studies, including circumcision, menstrual taboos, and other rules about impurity and animals. These essays join the growing number of studies that use anthropological theory and comparative ethnography to illuminate aspects of Israelite religion and ancient Judaism.[14] In addition, I explore the ways that Israelite practices are historically transformed as they are appropriated by subsequent communities that have different social structures and hence provide individuals with different experiences of the world. I am especially interested in the transformations that occur as the religious practices and conceptions of Israelite priests are inherited by other groups such as the Dead Sea community, the early rabbis, and Christians.

The Conclusion brings together the various arguments of this book, drawing particular attention to the political implications of passing Judaism under the anthropological gaze. I argue that the anthropology of Judaism is one logical and necessary conclusion of the anthropological tradition itself. One important goal of that tradition has been to dismantle the opposition between savage and civilized traditions. But that goal cannot be accomplished until the effects of that opposition are eradicated. As long as the anthropological lens is focused on some traditions and not others, the old prejudices continue to operate. The subjection of Judaism to anthropological inquiry, therefore, represents an attempt to carry the relativistic critique contained within twentieth-century anthropology to its logical conclusions. At the same time, the anthropological study of Judaism releases a savage critique of Judaism itself.

In sum, the present book is a conversation I have fabricated between a particular group of anthropologists and their heirs, on the one hand, and the religious culture of ancient Judaism, on the other. I hope that this conversation will be enlightening to some and will stimulate other colloquies of a similar kind.

Notes

1. In this book I am primarily interested in the possible use of anthropology to study Israelite religion and ancient Judaism. The following writers have appealed to anthropology for this purpose: Andriolo (1973); Carroll (1977); Davies (1977); Donaldson (1981); Feeley-Harnik (1982); Fiensy (1987); Goldberg (1987); Hendel (1988); Jay (1985; 1988); Jobling (1984); Lang (1985a; 1985b); Leach (1969; 1976, 81–97); Leach and Aycock (1983); Long (1976); Marshall (1979); Oden (1987); Pitt-Rivers (1977); Prewitt (1981); Rogerson (1970; 1978); Soler (1979); Wilson (1980; 1984). For a more detailed bibliography, see Lang (1985a, 17–20). There is also a growing trend to subject modern forms of Judaism to anthropological inquiry. See, for example, Goldberg (1987); Kirshenblatt-Gimblett (1982); Kugelmass (1986; 1988); Myerhoff (1979); Prell (1989); Zenner (1988).

2. It is interesting to note that the field of biblical studies has more readily absorbed those anthropological theories that are anticomparativist and that preserve an opposition between Israelite religions and primitive religions. This is evident, for example, in the work of Sidney Hooke and his colleagues, who relied upon Hocart's idea of a ritual and myth pattern that diffuses from a cultural center (Leach 1982). Hooke and his followers postulated that ancient Babylonian, Egyptian, and Israelite religions all conformed to a

single myth and ritual pattern. This theoretical perspective effectively ruled out all comparisons with noncontiguous cultures.

3. The history of the distinction between "Israelite religion" and "ancient Judaism" would constitute an interesting essay in its own right. It reflects historical judgments as well as theological claims. To begin with, the distinction is intended to mark the fundamental religious changes that occurred as a result of and in the wake of the Babylonian exile (sixth century BCE). The forms of Israelite religion that emerged were fundamentally different from their predecessors and had important commonalities with the forms of Judaism that emerged only later. Furthermore, the distinction draws attention to the important fact that Judaism cannot be equated with the religion of the Old Testament. Since Judaism does not receive its "classical" formulation until the emergence of the rabbis (second–sixth centuries CE), it must be understood as the religion of the Hebrew Bible as refracted through the eyes of the rabbis. The mistaken identification of Judaism with the religion of the Old Testament has been quite common since the Enlightenment, and the above distinction is in part an attempt to rectify this mistake by recognizing the historical complexity of the tradition called Judaism.

    Unfortunately, the distinction between Israelite religion and ancient Judaism has some difficulties. To begin with, it emerged from and reinforced a Christian polemic against Judaism. Christianity claims to inherit the prophetic tradition of the Hebrew Bible and to denounce "the law." The distinction between Israelite religion (which is often treated as early and identified with the "ethical monotheism" of the prophets) and Judaism (which is viewed as "late" and often identified with the priests who were concerned with law) thus encourages this Christian polemic (e.g., Wellhausen 1973 [1878]). Moreover, the claim that Judaism developed in the postexilic period was based on the assumption that the priestly writings, with their obsession with cult and law, were exilic or postexilic. But biblical scholars no longer accept a sharp dichotomy between prophetic and priestly forms of Israelite religion (G. Tucker 1985, 325–54). Moreover, there is some indication that the priestly writings may be much older (see chapter 6, note 4). If this is so, then "Judaism" is pushed back into the preexilic period and the distinction between Israelite religion (early) and ancient Judaism (late) collapses.

4. It may appear that Rogerson's work (1978) contradicts the thesis elaborated here. But that is not the case. Rogerson has focused on those biblical interpreters who have been influenced explicitly or implicitly by anthropological assumptions. I am asking a somewhat different question: Why is it that the mainstream interpreters of biblical Judaism have ignored anthropology and studies of non-Near Eastern peoples?

5. As Rogerson points out, it is generally nineteenth-century anthropological views that have entered twentieth-century discourse on Israelite religion. Twentieth-century biblical interpreters have generally ignored the work of anthropologists of their own generation. As I will suggest below, this is not accidental. Nineteenth-century anthropological views permit biblical interpreters to oppose ancient Israelite and savage religions, whereas twentieth-century anthropological theory undermines such an opposition.

6. In fact, linguistics has shown that on a formal level languages can be compared cross-culturally. This insight provides the foundation of Lévi-Strauss's structuralist perspective.

7. I fundamentally disagree with Edmund Leach (1961, 371–87; 1982, 73–93), who argues that the details Frazer considered were "not such as might be likely to arouse

passionate debate among theologians, either Jewish or Christian." That Frazer's work did create controversy is amply documented by Ackerman (1987, 164–96).

8. Childs (1970) and Dever (1980) point out the influences of Protestant theology on biblical archaeology. The purpose of the present discussion is to consider the implications of that influence for the rejection of anthropology and the comparative method within biblical studies.

9. The role of comparison within the British tradition is more complex than I am making it out to be. Evans-Pritchard, for example, had reservations about the kind of comparative method favored by Radcliffe-Brown. Nonetheless, even Evans-Pritchard did not favor abandoning the comparative enterprise altogether (Evans-Pritchard 1965).

10. I do not consider the work of Max Weber on ancient Judaism to be an exception to the claim being made here. Weber, as a sociologist, did not compare Judaism with primitive religions. In fact, Weber's own work reflects the very assumption that this essay attempts to expose. Weber focused his work on "world religions," thus assuming that Judaism could not be compared to primitive religions.

11. For a traditional account of this change see Evans-Pritchard (1951) and Harris (1968). The understanding of this transition, however, is currently under revision. See especially Stocking (1983) and Strathern (1987).

12. The relationship between early anthropology and classics is very complex. For an introduction to the subject, see Kluckholn (1961).

13. Kuhn's own understanding of scientific practice was in part inspired by Polanyi's work which also argued that scientific thought constitutes a closed system of self-validating assumptions. Polanyi was influenced in his ideas by Evans-Pritchard's treatment of Azande witchcraft beliefs.

14. See note 1.

References

Ackerman, Robert. 1987. *J. G. Frazer: His Life and Work.* Cambridge: Cambridge University Press.

Albright, W. F. 1942. *Archaeology and the Religion of Israel.* Baltimore: Johns Hopkins University Press.

_____ 1964 [1940] "How Well Can We Know the Ancient Near East?" In *History, Archaeology and Christian Humanism.* New York: McGraw-Hill.

Anderson, G. W. 1951. "Hebrew Religion." In *The Old Testament and Modern Study*, ed. H. H. Rowley. Oxford: Oxford University Press.

Andriolo, Karin. 1973. "A Structural Analysis of Genealogy and Worldview in the Old Testament." *American Anthropologist* 75: 1657–67.

Astley, H. J. D. 1929. "Biblical Folklore." In *Biblical Anthropology Compared with and Illustrated by the Folklore of Europe and the Customs of Primitive Peoples.* London: Oxford University Press.

Black, J. S., and G. W. Chrystal. 1912. *The Life of William Robertson Smith.* London: A. and C. Black.

Bulmer, R. 1967. "Why Is the Cassowary Not a Bird?" *Man* 2/1: 5–25.

Carroll, Michael P. 1977. "Leach, Genesis, and Structural Analysis: A Critical Evaluation." *American Ethnologist* 4: 633–77.

Childs, Brevard 1970. *Biblical Theology in Crisis.* Philadelphia: Westminster Press.

Clifford, James. 1988. "On Ethnographic Authority." In *The Predicament of Culture*, 21–54. Cambridge, MA: Harvard University Press.

Clifford, James, and George E. Marcus, eds. 1986. *Writing Culture: The Poetics and Politics of Ethnography.* Berkeley: University of California Press.

Collingwood, R. G. 1958. *Principles of Art.* Oxford: Oxford University Press.

Cook, Stanley. 1902. "Israel and Totemism." *The Jewish Quarterly Review* 14: 413–48.

Culler, Jonathan. 1982. *On Deconstruction: Theory and Criticism after Structuralism.* Ithaca: Cornell University Press.

Culley, Robert C. 1985. "Exploring New Directions." In *The Hebrew Bible and Its Modern Interpreters*, ed. Douglas A. Knight and Gene M. Tucker, 167–89. Philadelphia: Fortress Press.

Daube, David. 1949. "Rabbinic Methods of Interpretation and Hellenistic Rhetoric." *Hebrew Union College Annual* 22: 239–64.

Davies, Douglas. 1977. "An Interpretation of Sacrifice in Leviticus." *Zeitschrift für die alttestamentliche Wissenschaft* 89: 387–99.

Dever, William G. 1980. "Biblical Theology and Biblical Archaeology: An Appreciation of G. Ernest Wright." *Harvard Theological Review* 73/1-2: 1–14.

Donaldson, Mara E. 1981. "Kinship Theory in Patriarchal Narratives: The Case of the Barren Wife." *The Journal of the American Academy of Religion* 49/1: 77–87.

Douglas, Mary. 1966. *Purity and Danger.* London: Routledge and Kegan Paul.

Downie, R. Angus. 1970. *Frazer and The Golden Bough.* London: Victor Gollancz.

Durkheim, Emile. 1965 [1915]. *The Elementary Forms of the Religious Life.* Trans. Joseph Swain. New York: Free Press.

Durkheim, Emile, and Marcel Mauss. 1963 [1903]. *Primitive Classification.* Trans. Rodney Needham. Chicago: University of Chicago Press.

Eilberg-Schwartz, H. 1986. *The Human Will in Judaism: The Mishnah's Philosophy of Intention.* Atlanta: Scholars Press.

Evans-Pritchard, E. E. 1933. "The Intellectualist Interpretation of Magic." *Bulletin of the Faculty of Arts* 1/2: 282–311.

———— 1934. "Lévy-Bruhl's Theory of Primitive Mentality." *Bulletin of the Faculty of Arts* 2: 1–27.

———— 1951. *Social Anthropology.* London: Cohen and West.

———— 1956. *Nuer Religion.* Oxford: Oxford University Press.

———— 1965. "The Comparative Method in Social Anthropology." In *The Position of Women in Primitive Society*, 13–36. Glencoe: Free Press.

Feeley-Harnik, Gillian. 1982. "Is Historical Anthropology Possible?: The Case of the Runaway Slave." In *Humanizing America's Iconic Book*, ed. Gene M. Tucker and Douglas A. Knight, 95–126. Chico, CA: Scholars Press.

Feyerabend, Paul. 1975. *Against Method.* Norfolk: Thetford Press.

———— 1978. *Science in a Free Society.* Norfolk: Thetford Press.

Fiensy, David. 1987. "Using the Nuer Culture of Africa in Understanding the Old Testament: An Evaluation." *Journal for the Study of the Old Testament* 38: 73–83.

Fischel, Henry, ed. 1977. *Essays in Greco-Roman and Related Talmud Literature.* New York: Ktav.

Fish, Stanley. 1980. *Is There a Text in This Class?* Cambridge, MA: Harvard University Press.

Fohrer, Georg. 1972. *History of Israelite Religion.* Trans. David E. Green. Nashville: Abingdon Press.

Foucault, Michel. 1973. *Madness and Civilization: A History of Insanity in the Age of Reason.* Trans. Richard Howard. New York: Vintage.

_____ 1977. "Nietzsche, Genealogy, History." In *Language, Counter-Memory, Practice,* ed. Donald F. Bouchard, trans. Donald F. Bouchard and Sherry Simon. Ithaca: Cornell University Press.

Frankfort, H. 1951. *The Problem of Similarity in Ancient Near Eastern Religions.* Oxford: Clarendon Press.

Frankfort, H., and H. A. Frankfort. 1971 [1946]. "The Emancipation of Thought from Myth." In *Before Philosophy: The Intellectual Adventure of Ancient Man,* ed. H. Frankfort et al., 237–64. Baltimore: Penguin Books.

Frazer, J. G. 1900. *The Golden Bough.* 2nd ed. 3 vols. London: Macmillan.

_____ 1919. *Folklore in the Old Testament.* London: Macmillan.

_____ 1967 [1894]. "William Robertson Smith." In *The Gorgon's Head and Other Literary Pieces,* 278–90. Freeport: Books for Libraries Press.

Gadamer, Hans-Georg. 1975. *Truth and Method.* New York: Crossroad.

Geertz, Clifford. 1973. *The Interpretation of Cultures.* New York: Basic Books.

Goldberg, Harvey, ed. 1987. *Judaism Viewed from Within and from Without.* Albany: State University of New York Press.

Gottwald, Norman. 1979. *The Tribes of Yahweh.* Maryknoll: Orbis Books.

Harris, Marvin. 1968. *The Rise of Anthropological Theory.* New York: Harper and Row.

Hayes, E. Nelson, and Tanya Hayes, eds. 1970. *Claude Lévi-Strauss: The Anthropologist as Hero.* Cambridge, MA: MIT Press.

Hempel, Carl. 1968. "The Logic of Functional Analysis." In *Readings in the Philosophy of the Social Sciences,* ed. May Brodbeck. New York: Macmillan.

Hendel, Ronald. 1988. "The Social Origins of the Aniconic Tradition in Early Israel." *Catholic Biblical Quarterly* 50/3: 365–82.

Hoffman, Lawrence. 1987. *Beyond the Text: A Holistic Approach to Liturgy.* Bloomington: Indiana University Press.

Jay, Nancy. 1985. "Sacrifice as Remedy for Having Been Born of Woman." In *Immaculate and Powerful,* ed. C. W. Atkinson et al., 283–309. Boston: Beacon Press.

_____ 1988. "Sacrifice, Descent, and the Patriarchs." *Vetus Testamentum* 38/1: 52–70.

Jobling, D. 1984. "Lévi-Strauss and the Structural Analysis of the Hebrew Bible." In *Anthropology and the Study of Religion,* ed. R. L. Moore et al., 192–211. Chicago: University of Chicago Press.

Johnson, Barbara. 1980. *The Critical Difference: Essays in the Contemporary Rhetoric of Reading.* Baltimore: Johns Hopkins University Press.

Kadushin, Max. 1952. *The Rabbinic Mind.* New York: Bloch Publishing Company.

Kaufmann, Yehezkel. 1972 [1937–56]. *The Religion of Israel.* Trans. and abrdg. Moshe Greenberg. New York: Schocken Books.

Kirshenblatt-Gimblett, Barbara. 1982. "The Cut That Binds: The Western Ashkenazic Torah Binder as Nexus between Circumcision and Torah." In *Celebration: Studies in Festivity and Ritual,* ed. Victor Turner. Washington: Smithsonian Institute Press.

Kluckholn, Clyde. 1961. *Anthropology and the Classics.* Providence: Brown University Press.

Kugelmass, Jack. 1986. *The Miracle of Intervale Avenue: The Story of a Jewish Congregation in South Bronx*. New York: Schocken Books.

Kugelmass, Jack, ed. 1988. *Between Two Worlds: Ethnographic Essays on American Jewry*. Ithaca: Cornell University Press.

Kuhn, Thomas S. 1970. *The Structure of Scientific Revolutions*. 2nd ed. Chicago: University of Chicago Press.

Lakatos, Imre. 1970. "Falsification and the Methodology of Scientific Research Programmes." In *Criticism and the Growth of Knowledge*, ed. Imre Lakatos and Alan Musgrave. Cambridge: Cambridge University Press.

Lang, Bernhard, ed. 1985a. *Anthropological Approaches to the Old Testament*. Philadelphia: Fortress Press.

_____ 1985b. "Non-Semitic Deluge Stories and the Book of Genesis." *Anthropos* 80: 605–16.

Leach, Edmund. 1961. "Golden Bough or Gilded Twig." *Daedalus* 90/2: 371–87.

_____ 1969. *Genesis as Myth*. London: Jonathan Cape.

_____ 1976. *Culture and Communication*. Cambridge: Cambridge University Press.

_____ 1982. "Anthropological Approaches to the Study of the Bible during the Twentieth Century." In *Humanizing America's Iconic Book*, ed. Gene H. Tucker and Douglas A. Knight, 73–93. Chico, CA: Scholars Press.

Leach, Edmund, and D. Alan Aycock. 1983. *Structuralist Interpretations of Biblical Myth*. Cambridge: Cambridge University Press.

Lévy-Bruhl, Lucien. 1985 [1910]. *How Natives Think*. Princeton: Princeton University Press.

Lieberman, Saul. 1950. *Hellenism and Jewish Palestine*. New York: Jewish Theological Seminary of America.

Lightstone, Jack. 1988. *Society, the Sacred, and Scripture in Ancient Judaism*. Waterloo, ON: Wilfrid Laurier University Press.

Long, O. 1976. "Recent Field Studies in Oral Literature and their Bearing on OT Criticism." *Vetus Testamentum* 26: 187–98.

Lukes, Steven. 1985. *Emile Durkheim: His Life and Work*. Stanford: Stanford University Press.

Malinowski, B. 1954 [1925]. "Magic, Science, and Religion." In *Man, Science, and Religion*. Garden City: Doubleday.

_____ 1961 [1922]. *Argonauts of the Western Pacific*. Prospect Heights: Waveland Press.

_____ 1978 [1935]. *Coral Gardens and their Magic*. New York: Dover Publications.

Marett, R. R, ed. 1966 [1908]. *Anthropology and the Classics*. New York: Barnes and Noble.

Marshall, Robert. 1979. "Heroes and Hebrews: The Priest in the Promised Land." *American Ethnologist* 6/4: 772–90.

Mendenhall, George. 1961. "Biblical History in Transition." In *The Bible and the Ancient Near East*, ed. G. E. Wright. Garden City: Doubleday.

Merton, Robert K. 1967. "Latent and Manifest Functions." In *On Theoretical Sociology*, 73–138. New York: Free Press.

Moore, O. K., and David Olmstead. 1952. "Language and Professor Lévi-Strauss." *American Anthropologist*, 54: 116–19.

Myerhoff, Barbara. 1979. *Number Our Days*. New York: E. P. Dutton.

Neusner, Jacob. 1978. "Comparing Judaisms." *History of Religions* 18: 177–91.

_____ 1979. "Anthropology and the Study of Talmudic Literature." In *Method and Meaning in Ancient Judaism*. Missoula: Scholars Press.

_____ 1986. *The Oral Torah: The Sacred Books of Judaism.* San Francisco: Harper and Row.

Oden, Robert. 1987. *The Bible without Theology.* San Francisco: Harper and Row.

Ortner, Sherry B., and Harriet Whitehead. 1981. *Sexual Meanings: The Cultural Construction of Gender and Sexuality.* Cambridge: Cambridge University Press.

Parsons, Talcott. 1968. *The Structure of Social Action.* Vol. 2. New York: Free Press.

Penner, Hans. 1971. "The Poverty of Functionalism." *History of Religions* 11/1: 91–97.

Pitt-Rivers, Julien. 1977. *The Fate of Schechem.* Cambridge: Cambridge University Press.

Polanyi, Michael. 1958. *Personal Knowledge.* Chicago: University of Chicago Press.

Prell, Riv-Ellen. 1989. *Prayer and Community: The Havurah in American Judaism.* Detroit: Wayne State University Press.

Prewitt, Terry. 1981. "Kinship Structures and the Genesis Genealogies." *Journal of Near Eastern Studies* 40: 87–98.

Radcliffe-Brown, A. R. 1958 [1931]. "The Present Position of Anthropological Studies." In *Method in Social Anthropology*, ed. M. N. Srinivas, 45–85. Chicago: University of Chicago Press.

Ringgren, Helmer. 1966. *Israelite Religion.* Trans. David E. Green. Philadelphia: Fortress Press.

Robertson Smith, William. 1903 [1885]. *Kinship and Marriage in Early Arabia.* London: A. and C. Black.

_____ 1927 [1889]. *Lectures on the Religion of the Semites.* 3rd ed. New York: Meridian Books.

Rogerson, J. W. 1970. "Structural Anthropology and the Old Testament." *Bulletin of the School of Oriental and African Studies* 33: 490–500.

_____ 1978. *Anthropology and the Old Testament.* Atlanta: John Knox Press.

Rorty, Richard. 1982. *Consequences of Pragmatism.* Minneapolis: University of Minnesota Press.

Rosaldo, Michelle Z., and Louis Lamphere. 1974. *Woman, Culture, and Society.* Stanford: Stanford University Press.

Rossi, Ino, ed. 1974. *The Unconscious in Culture: The Structuralism of Claude Lévi-Strauss in Perspective.* New York: E. P. Dutton.

Sahlins, Marshall. 1981. *Historical Metaphors and Mythical Realities.* Ann Arbor: University of Michigan Press.

_____ 1985. *Islands of History.* Chicago: University of Chicago Press.

Sarna, Nahum. 1970. *Understanding Genesis.* New York: Schocken Books.

Sayce, A. H. 1889. "Review of William Robertson Smith's *Religion of the Semites.*" *Academy* 36 (November 30): 357–58.

Scholte, Bob. 1987. "The Literary Turn in Contemporary Anthropology." *Critical Anthropology* 7/1: 33–47.

Smith, Jonathan Z. 1982. "In Comparison a Magic Dwells." In *Imagining Religion*, 19–35. Chicago: University of Chicago Press.

Snaith, Norman H. 1944. *The Distinctive Ideas of the Old Testament.* London: Epworth Press.

Soler, Jean. 1979. "The Dietary Prohibitions of the Hebrews." Trans. Elborg Forster. *New York Review of Books* 26/10 (June 14): 24–30.

Stocking, George W. 1983. "The Ethnographer's Magic: Fieldwork in British Anthropology from Tylor to Malinowski." In *Observers Observed*, ed. George W. Stocking, 70–120. Madison: University of Wisconsin Press.

239

Strathern, Marilyn. 1987. "Out of Context." *Current Anthropology* 28/3: 251–81.

Tambiah, S. J. 1969. "Animals are Good to Think and Good to Prohibit." *Ethnology* 7/4: 423–59.

Tucker, Gene M. 1985. "Prophecy and Prophetic Literature." In *The Hebrew Bible and Its Modern Interpreters*, ed. Douglas A. Knight and Gene M. Tucker. Chico, CA: Scholars Press.

Tylor, Edward. 1958 [1871]. *Primitive Culture.* New York: Harper and Brothers.

von Rad, Gerhard. 1976. *Genesis.* Philadelphia: Westminster Press.

Vriezen, Th. C. 1967. *The Religion of Ancient Israel.* Philadelphia: Westminster Press.

Wellhausen, Julius. 1973 [1878]. *Prolegomena to the History of Ancient Israel.* Gloucester, MA: Peter Smith.

White, Hayden. 1978. *Tropics of Discourse.* Baltimore: Johns Hopkins University Press.

Wilson, Robert. 1980. *Prophesy and Society in Ancient Israel.* Philadelphia: Fortress Press.

_____ 1984. *Sociological Approaches to the Old Testament.* Philadelphia: Fortress Press.

Wright, G. E. 1950. *The Old Testament Against its Environment.* Chicago: Alec R. Allenson.

_____ 1957. *Biblical Archaeology.* Philadelphia: Westminster Press.

Zenner, Walter P. 1988. *Persistence and Flexibility: Anthropological Perspectives on the American Jewish Experience.* Albany: State University of New York Press.

Waiting for a Jew: Marginal Redemption at the Eighth Street Shul

Jonathan Boyarin

My story begins in a community, with an illusion of wholeness. I am between the age when consciousness begins and the age of ten, when my family leaves the community and my illusion is shattered. Our family lives on the edge of the Pine Barrens in Farmingdale, New Jersey, along with hundreds of other families of Jewish chicken farmers who have come from Europe and New York City in several waves, beginning just after World War I.

Among the farmers are present and former Communists, Bundists, Labor Zionists, German refugees who arrived in the 1930s, and Polish survivors of concentration camps. These, however, are not the distinctions I make among them as a child. Johannes Fabian has shown us that when we write ethnography we inevitably trap those about whom we write into a hypostatic, categorical, grammatical "present" (Fabian 1983). An autobiographer has the same power over the memory of himself and those he knew in prior times as the fieldworker who later obliterates the narrative aspect of his encounter with his subjects—the power to deny their autonomy in hindsight.[1] Those of the farming community whom I will later remember, I know therefore by their own names and places: my grandparents closer to Farmingdale proper; the Silbers off on Yellowbrook Road, with a tree nursery now instead of chickens; the Lindauers, stubbornly maintaining an egg-packing and -distribution business, while others find different ways to earn a living.

241

My child's world is not exclusively Jewish, nor am I brought up to regard it as such. Across our road and down a few hundred yards is a tiny house built by Jewish farmers when they first came to settle here. It is now, incredibly, occupied by a black family of ten. Next to them lives an equally poor and large white family. Shortly before we leave Farmingdale, the old Jew in the farm next to ours passes away, and the property passes to a Japanese businessman. The young men he hires live in the farmhouse, growing oriental vegetables on the open field and bonsai in a converted chicken coop, and they introduce me to the game of Go. The nearest Jewish household is that of my great-uncle Yisroel and his wife Helen, the third house to the right of ours.

Yet we are near the heart of Jewish life in Farmingdale. Half a mile—but no, it must be less—down Peskin's Lane (the name my grandfather Israel Boyarin gave to what was a dirt road in the 1930s) is the Farmingdale Jewish Community Center, on the next plot of land after Uncle Yisroel's house. Just past the community center is the farm that once belonged to my father's uncle Peskin, the first Jew in Farmingdale. Fifteen years after Peskin's death, the bodies of two gangsters were found buried on the farm. The local papers noted: "Mr. Peskin was not available for comment."

Our own farm consists of eleven acres. Facing the road is the house my grandfather built, with a large front lawn and an apple tree in back. Farther back, four large chicken coops mark the slope of a hill ending in our field, behind which woods conceal the tiny Manasquan River. The field, well fertilized by chickens allowed to scratch freely on it during the day, is leased each summer by a dirt farmer who grows corn. My father has joined the insurance agency begun by my mother, and they have gotten rid of the birds. The coops stand empty by my fourth birthday. One day, though, while a friend and I chase each other through the coops in play, we are startled by a pair of chickens. Their presence in the stillness and the faint smell of ancient manure is inexplicable and unforgettable. Thus, on the abandoned farm, my first memories are tinged with a sense of traces, of mystery, of loss. Do all who eventually become anthropologists have this experience in some form, at some time in their early lives?

My mother's turn to business is wise: chicken farming as the basis for the community's livelihood is quickly becoming untenable. Nor is it surprising, as she had given up a career as a chemist to come live with my father on the farm—thus taking part in the process of Jewish dispersal from the immigrants' urban centers, which in the last quarter of the century would be mirrored by a shrinking of Jewish communities in small towns and a reconsolidation of the Orthodox centers. My mother's father, an Orthodox Jew from a leading Lithuanian rabbinical family, has struggled to learn English well and has gone into the insurance business himself. After his death, my mother tells me that he had originally resisted her desire to marry the son of a Jewish socialist, but he consented when he met my father's father's father, a Lubavitcher Hasid named Mordechai.

My grandfather's concern for his daughter's future as an observant Jew was well founded. The Sabbath is marked in our family only on Friday nights: by my mother's candle-lighting, and her chicken soup in winter; by the challah; by the presence of my grandfather. We do not keep kosher, nor do we go to shul on *shabbes*.

The Jewish Community Center—with its various functions as social and meeting hall, synagogue, and school—is nevertheless a focus of our family's life. Most of the ten or so other children in these classes I see at other times during the week as well, either in public school or playing at one another's homes. I am there three times each week, first for Sunday School, and then for Hebrew school on afternoons. This odd distinction is no doubt a practical one, since some parents do not choose to send their children three times a week. But since Sunday school was first a Christian institution, it also reflects an accommodation to Christian church patterns, as evidenced by the fact that Sundays are devoted to teaching stories of the Bible. One Sunday school teacher we have in our kindergarten year captivates me with his skill in making these stories come to life, as when he imitates the distress of an Egyptian waking up to find his bed covered with frogs.

Another teacher, a young woman with a severe manner and a heavy black wig, the wife of a member of the Orthodox yeshiva in Lakewood, later causes general misery because of her inability to understand children, although I will eventually appreciate the prayers she teaches us to read. One time I come in to Hebrew school immediately after yet another in a series of martyred family dogs has been run over in front of our house. Her attempt to comfort me is like some malicious parody of Talmudic reasoning: "You shouldn't be so upset about an animal. If a chicken and a person both fell down a well, which one would you save first?"

In addition to this somewhat haphazard religious training, there is the local chapter of Habonim, the Labor Zionist Youth Organization, to which my older brother and sister belong. I tag along and am tolerated by their peers. Once I am given a minor role in a stage performance by the chapter. Though I am too young to remember quite what it is about, the phrase *komets-aleph:aw* stands out in my memory.

Later I will learn that this phrase occurs in a famous and sentimental Yiddish folksong. It is the first letter of the Hebrew alphabet, the first thing countless generations of Jewish children have been taught. Here is an unusual case in which a traditional lesson—how to pronounce the alphabet—is successfully inculcated in the secularized framework of a dramatic performance about the traditional setting. Perhaps this is because of the necessary rehearsals, in which I must have heard, as the song puts it, "once more, over and over again, *komets-aleph:aw*." The memory reinforces my later preference for this older, European pronunciation of the Hebrew vowels, my sense of the Israeli *kamets-aleph:ah* as inauthentic.

Also memorable at the Jewish Community Center is the annual barbecue run by the Young Couples' Club. Though my father will assure me in an interview years later that its association with the Fourth of July was purely a matter of convenience, the atmosphere is certainly one of festival, even including "sacrifices" and "altars": My father and his friends set up huge charcoal pits with cement blocks, and broil vast amounts of chicken; corn is boiled in aluminum garbage cans to go with it.[2] For the children, a Purim-like element of riotous excess is added: This one time each year, we are allowed to drink as much soda as we want. One year "wild," blond-haired Richie L., whose parents have a luncheonette booth for a kitchen table and an attic filled with antiques, claims to drink fourteen bottles, thus adding to the mystique he holds for me.

But it is the days when the Community Center becomes a synagogue that leave the strongest impression on my memory. There must be services every Saturday morning, but I am completely unaware of them. What I will remember are the holidays: Purim, Rosh Hashanah, Yom Kippur, Simchas Torah, and a crowd of people who just a few years later will never be there again. On the fall holidays, the shul is full of movement, impatience, noise, and warmth. Except for a few moments such as the shofar blowing, we children are free to come and go: By the steps in front, tossing the juicy, poisonous red berries of a yew that was planted, I am told, in memory of my brother Aaron, whom I never knew; inside the main doors, to look left at Walter Tenenbaum wrapped in a *tallis* that covers his head, standing at a lectern by the Ark of the Torah as he leads the service, or to look right, along the first long row of folding chairs for our fathers; thence a few rows back to where our mothers sit separately from the men, although unlike most synagogues that look and sound as traditional as this one, there is no *mekhitse*, no barrier between women and men; and finally out through the side door and down a flight of wooden steps to the monkey bars, into the ditch where one miraculous day we found and drank an intact bottle of orange soda, or into the kitchen, social room, and classroom in the basement. Once each year we children are the center of attention, as we huddle under a huge tallis in front of the Ark on Simchas Torah to be blessed.

In classic ethnographies of hunting-and-gathering groups, landscapes are described as personalized, integral elements of culture. This was true of the landscape of my childhood friendships, which today is as obliterated as any *shtetl* in Eastern Europe. Any marginal group in mass society may be subject without warning to the loss of its cultural landscape, and therefore those who are able to create portable landscapes for themselves are the most likely to endure.

The Jews have been doing so for thousands of years; the Simchas Torah tallis can stand in front of any Ark, and the original Ark, in the biblical account, was itself transported from station to station in the desert. Yet the members of a community are orphaned when the naive intimacy of a living environment is torn away from them. Such a break appears often in Jewish literature—significantly with the emphasis not forward on the beginning of adulthood, as in the European *Bildungsroman*, but rather on the end of childhood.[3]

I suddenly discover the distance between the world and myself at the end of August in 1966. When my parents pick me up from camp, they take me to a new house. For the last time, we attend high holiday services in Farmingdale. It is the only time we will ever drive there, and our family's friends no longer join us during the afternoon break on Yom Kippur for a surreptitious glass of tea and a slice of challah. Farmingdale is no longer home, and though our new house is only ten miles away, it is another world.

We live now in an almost exclusively white, middle-class suburb with many Jews, but our older, brick house is isolated on a block of working-class cubes. While neighbors my age play football in our yard, I often retreat to my room and console myself with sports books for preadolescents. My new and bewildering sense of marginality leads me to develop an exquisite self-consciousness. It is manifested in an almost constant internal dialogue, which keeps me company and will interfere with my adolescent sexuality.

Ostracism is often the fate of a new kid on the block, and it may last longer when his family is Jewish and his home better than those on either side. There is a custom in this part of New Jersey of tolerating petty vandalism on "mischief night," the night before Halloween. Pumpkins are smashed, and we, along with other unpopular families on the block, have the windows of our cars and house smeared with soap. One Halloween I wake up to see graffiti chalked in bold letters on the sidewalk in front of our house: "Jon the Jew, a real one too." My father summons the kids next door— whom we suspect of being the authors—to scrape the words off the sidewalk, as I burn with shame.

He and I never discuss the incident, but later I will compare it with a memory of Freud's: As a child, he was walking with his father, when a gentile knocked his father's hat off. Rather than confronting the man, Freud's father meekly bent over to pick up the hat, and his son's humiliation persisted into adulthood (Bakan 1958; D. Boyarin 1997). The moral is that a victim is likely to view any response as adding insult to injury. In my case, as my father asserts the American principle of equality and "teaches a lesson" to my occasional and vindictive playmates by forcing them to erase what they have written, I feel as though he is inviting them to write the words again, this time making me watch my own degradation.

The new synagogue my parents join is only a partial refuge. It exemplifies the difference between a shul and a temple. Everything in Farmingdale had faced inward: little concern was paid for praying in unison, and though the *shammes* would bang his hand on the table for silence, he was seldom heeded; even the cantor was alone with God, facing away from everyone else, rather than performing for the congregation. Calling a synagogue a temple, by contrast, is doubly revealing. On the one hand, it indicates a striving for the majesty of the ancient House in Jerusalem. On the other hand, just like the English term used to designate it, its trappings are borrowed from the Christian world, down to the black robes worn by the rabbi and cantor.

These robes lack the warm mystery of Walter Tenenbaum's tallis. The responsive readings of Psalms in English seem ridiculously artificial to me from the first. And my mother, who still comes only on the holidays though I sometimes drag my father to temple on Friday nights, complains of the rabbi's long-winded sermons and yearns aloud for the intimate conversations along the back wall of the Farmingdale Jewish Community Center. Unlike some, I do not leave the synagogue immediately after my bar mitzvah. I teach the blessings of the Haftorah to two reluctant boys a year younger than me. I briefly experience religious inspiration, and for perhaps two weeks put on *tefillin* every morning. But the atmosphere is hollow, and the emptiness breeds cynicism in me in my teens.

The coldness of the building itself is symptomatic of the lack of sustenance I sense there. The pretense and bad taste of modern American synagogues are well-known yet puzzling phenomena that deserve a sociological explanation of their own. Even the walls of the temple are dead concrete blocks, in contrast to the wood of the Farmingdale Jewish Community Center. Services are held in a "sanctuary," unlike the room at the Community Center where activities as varied as dances and political meetings were conducted when services were not being held. Aside from any question of Jewish law, there is a loss of community marked by the fact that everyone drives to the temple rather than walking. It is a place separated from the home, without the strong and patient webs spun by leisurely strolling conversations to and from a shul.

Most generally, the temple is victim to the general alienation of the suburbs. What happens or fails to happen there is dependent on what the people who come there expect from each other. Those who belong (there are vastly more "members" than regular attendees) seem bound primarily by a vague desire to have Jewish grandchildren. The poor rabbi, typical of conservative congregations, seems hired to be a stand-in Jew, to observe all the laws and contain all the knowledge they don't have the time for. They are not bound to each other by Jewish religious ways, nor do they share the common interests of everyday life—the same livelihood or language—that helped to make a complete community in Farmingdale.

I go off to college and slowly discover that my dismissal of Judaism leaves me isolated, with few resources. I had realized my individual difference on leaving Farmingdale. Now, much more removed from a Jewish environment than ever before, I become aware of my inescapable Jewishness. In the small northwestern college of my dreams, everyone around me seems "American" and different, though I have never thought of myself as anything but American. Even in the humanities curriculum on which the school prides itself, Jewish civilization is absent. It is as though Western cultural history were just a triumphant straight line from the Greeks to Augustine and Michelangelo (with his horned Moses and uncircumcised David), confusion setting in at last only with Marx and Freud.

Five years too late to benefit me, a Jewish Studies position will in fact be established at the college. Such positions are usually funded by Jewish individuals or organizations, and hence they represent the growing acculturation (not assimilation) of Jews into American academic life. The fact that they are regarded as legitimate by the academic community, however, is part of a reintegration of Jewish thought into the concept of Western humanities. Jewish ethnographers can contribute to this movement—for example, by elucidating the dialectic of tradition and change as worked out in communities facing vastly different historical challenges. We may then move beyond efforts to explain the explosive presence of Jews in post-Enlightenment intellectual life as a result of their "primitive" encounter with "civility" (Cuddihy 1974) to explore how the Jewish belief that "Creation as the (active) speech or writing of God posits first of all that the Universe is essentially intelligible" (Faur 1986: 7) provided a pathway from Torah to a restless, unifying modern impulse in the natural and social sciences.

Such notions are far beyond me as an undergraduate. At my college in the 1970s, the social scientists in their separate departments strive to separate themselves from their "objects of study"; the humanists treasure the peace of their cloisters; the artists, knowing they are intellectually suspect, cultivate a cliquish sense of superiority; and there is none of the give-and-take between learning and everyday experience that I have come to associate with the best of Jewish scholarship.

I find a friend, a Jew from Long Island, and we begin to teach each other that we need to cultivate our Jewishness. We discuss the "Jewish mentality" of modern thinkers, and paraphrasing Lenny Bruce's category of the *goyish*, sarcastically reject all that is "white." "I am not 'white,' my friend Martin proudly postures, "I am Semite." Meanwhile, reflecting on my own dismissal of suburban Judaism, I decide not to end willingly an almost endless chain of Jewish cultural transmission. I stake my future on the assumption that a tradition so old and varied must contain the seeds of a worthwhile life for me, and decide to begin to acquire them through study.

Besides, my reading as a student of anthropology leads me to reason that if I concentrate on Jewish culture, no one will accuse me of cultural imperialism (see Gough 1968). No doubt others in my generation who choose to do fieldwork with Jews are motivated by similar considerations. Jewish anthropologists as a class are privileged to belong to the world of academic discourse, and to have an entree into a variety of unique communities that maintain cultural frameworks in opposition to mass society.

Something deeper than Marxist critiques of anthropology draws me to Yiddish in particular. Before leaving Farmingdale, my best friend had been a child of survivors from Lemberg. I remember being at his house once, and asking with a sense of wonder: "Ralph, do you really know Yiddish?"

Ralph told me that although he understood the language—which his parents still spoke to him—he had never learned to speak it. Still, I was impressed that he knew this secret code. And now that I am finished with college and looking to find my own way home, Yiddish seems to be the nearest link to which I can attach myself. It is the key to a sense of the life of the shtetl, that Jewish dreamtime that I inevitably associate with my lost Farmingdale.

The Farmingdale community has, by this point, completely disintegrated: Virtually no Jews in that part of New Jersey earn their living as chicken farmers anymore. Many of those who have gone into business have moved to nearby towns like Lakewood. The Torah scrolls of the Community Center have been ceremoniously transferred to a new synagogue near housing developments on the highway between Farmingdale and Lakewood. I have never considered becoming a chicken farmer myself.

So, when I finish my college courses, without waiting for graduation, I flee back to New York. "Flee": No one chases me out of Portland, Oregon, God forbid! "Back": The city, though a magnet and a refuge, has never been my home before. Yet for three years I have shaped my identity in opposition to the "American" world around me, and I have reverted, along with my close friends, to what we imagine is an authentic New

York accent—the "deses" and "doses" that were drilled out of my parents' repertoire in the days when New York public school teachers had to pass elocution exams.

Rejecting suburban Judaism, belatedly pursuing the image of the sixties' counterculture to the Pacific Northwest, and self-consciously affecting a "New York Jew" style were all successive attempts to shape a personal identity. In each case, the identity strategy was in opposition to the prevailing conventions of the immediate social order. Similarly, opposition to their parents' perceived bourgeois complacency may underlie the involvement of young people with Judaism. Yet as Dominique Schnapper has noted (1983), for young, intellectual Jews becoming involved in Jewish religion, politics, or culture, there can be no question of canceling out prior experience and "becoming traditional." In fact, this is true even of the most seemingly Orthodox and insular Jewish communities. There is a difference between learning about great rabbis of the past through meetings with Jewish graybeards who knew them, and through reading about their merits in the Williamsburg newspaper *Der Yid.*

Of course, not only Jews are in the position of reconstituting interrupted tradition (cf. Clifford 1986: 116ff.). But since they have been in the business of reshaping tradition in a dialogue with written texts for thousands of years, Jews may benefit more directly than others from learning about what other Jews are doing with their common tradition. It is conceivable that individuals may choose to adopt traits from other communities or even join those communities based on what they read in ethnographies. Whether such cultural borrowings and recombinations are effected in an "authentic" manner will depend less on precedent than on the degree of self-confident cultural generosity that results.

Arriving in New York, I adopt a knitted yarmulke, although my hair still falls below my shoulders. I immediately begin a nine-week summer course in Yiddish at Columbia, and it seems as though the language were being brought out from deep inside me. When I go to visit my parents on weekends, my father remembers words he'd never noticed forgetting. When I take the IRT [Interborough Rapid Transit] after class back down to the Village, it seems as if everybody on the train is speaking Yiddish. Most important for my sense of identity, phrases here and there in my own internal dialogue are now in Yiddish, and I find I can reflect on myself with a gentle irony that was never available to me in English.

Then, after my first year in graduate school, I am off to Europe the following summer, courtesy of my parents. I arrive at the Gare du Nord in Paris with the address of a friend and without a word of French. I am spotted wearing my yarmulke by a young North African Jew who makes me understand, in broken English, that he studies at the Lubavitch yeshiva in Paris. He buys me a Paris guidebook and sets me on my way in the Metro. At the end of the summer, this meeting will stand as the first in a set of Parisian reactions to my yarmulke which crystallize in my memory:

- The reaction of the generous young Trotskyist with whom my friend had grown close and with whom I stayed for two weeks: She could see the yarmulke only as a symbol of Jewish nationalism. And argued bitterly that it was inherently reactionary;

- Of a young North African Jew, selling carpets at the flea market at Clignoncourt, who grabbed my arm and cried, *"Haver! Haver!* Brother Jew!"*;
- Of another young man, minding a booth outside one of the great department stores, who asked me if I were Orthodox, and interrupted my complicated response to explain that, although he was Orthodox himself, he was afraid to wear a yarmulke in the street;
- Of an old man at the American Express office who spoke to me in Yiddish and complained that the recent North African migrants dominated the Jewish communal organizations, and that there was no place for a Polish Jew to go.

Those first, fragmentary encounters are my fieldwork juvenilia. In assuming the yarmulke, I perhaps do not stop to consider that neither my actions nor my knowledge match the standards that it symbolically represents. But it works effectively, almost dangerously, as a two-way sensor, inducing Jews to present themselves to me and forcing me to try to understand how I am reflected in their eyes.

Externally, I learn many things about the situation of French Jewry. From the patent discomfort my non-Jewish Trotskyist friend feels at my display of Jewish specificity, I gain some sense of the conflicts young French Jews—coming out of the universalist, antihistorical revolutionary apogee of May 1968—must have felt years later when they first began to distinguish themselves from their comrades and view the world from the vantage point of their specific history. From the young street peddlers, I learn about how much riskier public proclamation of oneself as a Jew is perceived as being in Paris than in New York, and a concomitant depth of instant identification of one Jew with another. My meeting with the old Polish Jew at the American Express office hints at the dynamics of dominant and declining ethnic groups within the Jewish community, so vastly different from those dynamics in the United States.

Internally, I begin to understand that an identifiably Jewish head-covering places its own claims on the one who wears it. The longer it stays put, the more its power to keep him out of non-kosher restaurants grows. More important, people want to know who he is as a Jew. And if he does not know, the desire for peace of mind will spur further his effort to shape an identity.

Returning from Paris, I find an apartment at Second Avenue and Fifth Street in Manhattan. I tell people, "after three generations, my family has finally made it back to the Lower East Side." In fact, none of my grandparents lived on the East Side for a long time after immigrating, even though my mother tells me she regrets having missed the Yiddish theater on Second Avenue during her girlhood. By the time I move in, there is no Yiddish theater left. The former Ratner's dairy restaurant on Second Avenue, where, I'm told, Trotsky was a lousy tipper, is now a supermarket. Though sometimes one still sees a white newspaper truck with the word *Forverts* in lovely blue Hebrew letters on its side drive by late at night, this neighborhood has been the East Village since the sixties, and I think of it as such.

A new friend, who devotes his time to a frustrating effort to rescue Lower East Side synagogues, tells me of a shul still in use in an otherwise abandoned block east of

Tompkins Square Park. Though my friend has never been inside, he is sure that I will be welcomed, since such an isolated congregation must be looking for new blood.

The place is called the Eighth Street Shul, but its full name is Kehilas Bnei Moshe Yakov Anshei Zavichost veZosmer—Congregation Children of Moses and Jacob, People of Zavichost and Zosmer. It is owned by a *landsmanshaft* (hometown society) founded by émigrés and refugees from two towns in south central Poland. No one born in either town prays regularly at the shul now, and only one or two of the congregants are actually members of the society.

The shul is located in the center of what New York Latinos call "Loisaida"—an area bounded by Avenue A on the east, Avenue D on the west, Houston Street on the south, and Fourteenth Street on the north. Once the blocks up to Tenth Street were almost exclusively Jewish, and on nearly every one stood a synagogue or a religious school. Now two of those former synagogues stand abandoned, several more have become churches, and the rest have disappeared.

Eighth Street is a typical and not especially distinguished example of turn-of-the-century Lower East Side synagogue architecture.[4] It consists of five levels. The lowest contains a cranky and inadequate boiler. The second is the *besmedresh* or study room, which was destroyed by a suspicious fire in August 1982. The third level is the main sanctuary, long and narrow like the tenements among which it was tucked when it was built. Two rows of simple pews are separated by an aisle, which is interrupted in the center of the room by the raised table from which the weekly Torah portion is read. At the very front is the Ark, surrounded by partially destroyed wooden carvings that are the most artistic aspect of the shul. The walls are decorated with representations of the traditional Jewish signs for the zodiac; the two in front on the left have been obliterated by water damage from the leaky roof. Covering most of this level, with roughly an eight-foot opening extending toward the back, is the women's gallery. The gallery is constructed in such a way that it is easier for women sitting on opposite sides of the opening to converse with one another than to see what they are doing downstairs. Finally, upstairs from the women's gallery is an unused and cramped apartment that was once occupied by the shul's caretaker. In the roof behind it, an opening that was a skylight until there was a break-in is now covered with a solid wooden framework, allowing neither light nor vandals to enter.

Avenues B and C, which mark off the block, were once lively commercial streets with mostly Jewish storekeepers. There were also several smaller streets lined with tenements, right up to the edge of the East River. When the FDR Drive was built along the river, all the streets east of Avenue D disappeared, the tenements on the remaining available land were replaced by municipal housing, and the stores declined rapidly. During the same years, a massive middle-class housing cooperative, funded by a government mortgage, was built along Grand Street one mile to the south. Many of the remaining Jewish families moved into those houses, leaving virtually no Jews in the immediate area of the Eighth Street Shul.

Yet a minyan has continued to meet there every Saturday morning, with virtually no interruptions, throughout the years of the neighborhood's decline, while the block served as the Lower East Side's heaviest "shopping street" for hard drugs. It has lasted into the present, when buildings all around it are being speculated upon and renovated by both squatters and powerful real estate interests. It appears that until recently the main reason for this continuity was a felicitous rivalry between two men who were unwilling to abandon the synagogue because their fathers had both been presidents of it at one time. Perhaps if there had been only one, he would have given up and made peace with his conscience. Perhaps if the two men had naturally been friends they could have agreed to sell the building and officially merge their society with another still functioning further south in the neighborhood. If they had been able to agree on anything besides continuing to come to the shul, the shul might not have survived this long.

The first time I walk in, a clean-shaven, compact man in his sixties—younger than several of the congregants, who number perhaps seventeen in all—hurries forward to greet me. What's my name? Where do I live? Where am I from originally? And where do I usually go to pray on shabbes? His name is Moshe Fogel, and he sees to it that I am called to the Torah, the honor accorded any guest who comes for the first time, without asking any questions as to his level of religious observance. Later, an older member explains to me: "Once upon a time, you wouldn't get called to the Torah unless you kept kosher and observed shabbes." Now, Moish prefers simply to leave those matters undiscussed.

The history of the East Side as a place where all types of Jews have lived together reinforces his discretion. Externalities such as proper or improper clothing are not essential criteria for participation. This is true for the entire Orthodox community on the East Side and has even become part of its mystique. Rabbi Reuven Feinstein, head of the Staten Island branch of the East Broadway-based yeshiva, Tifereth Jerusalem, noted in a recent speech the common reaction in Boro Park and other thriving Orthodox centers to the nonconformist dress of East Side visitors: "It's okay, you're from the East Side." The president at Eighth Street still wears a traditional *gartl* when he prays, a belt worn over his jacket to separate the pure from the base parts of his body, and no one has suggested that such old customs are out of place today. But partly because the older members at the Eighth Street Shul walked through the East Village in the 1960s and knew there were many young Jews among the longhairs—even if they were horrified at the thought—they were willing to include in the minyan a young man in the neighborhood who, when he first came, wore dreadlocks under a Rastafarian-style knitted cap. It is also doubtless true that at that time there was no other Orthodox synagogue anywhere that he would have contemplated entering.

By contrast, it is impossible for any Jew raised in the middle of secular society (including a Jewish anthropologist) to join a traditionalist community without giving up major parts of his or her identity. The ways in which a researcher of contemporary Hasidic life "becomes a Hasid" are much more dramatic than the way in which one becomes a regular at Eighth Street—but they are probably more transient as well. In order to gain the confidence of the traditionalist communities, the fieldworker has to give the impression, whether implicitly or explicitly, that he or she is likely eventually to accept their standards in all areas of life (Belcove-Shalin 1988). All one has to do at Eighth Street is agree to come back "a little earlier next time, if possible."

Two things will draw me back to join this congregation, occasionally referred to as "those holy souls who *daven* in the middle of the jungle." The first pull is the memory of Farmingdale: the Ashkenazic accents and melodies (though here they are Polish, whereas Walter Tenenbaum had prayed in his native Lithuanian accent); the smell of herring on the old men's breath and hands; the burning sensation of whiskey, which I must have tasted surreptitiously at the conclusion of Yom Kippur one year in Farmingdale.

The second thing that draws me, though I do not come every week, is a feeling that I am needed and missed when I am absent. It's hard for me to get up early on Saturday mornings, after being out late Friday nights. It still seems like a sacrifice, as though I were stealing part of my weekend from myself. If I arrive in time for the *Shema*, about half an hour into the service, I congratulate myself on my devotion. The summer before I marry, in 1981, I hardly come at all. When I go with my brother to meet Moshe Fogel at the shul and give him the provisions for the Kiddush, I arrive "around nine-thirty," to which Moish retorts: "Even when you used to come, you didn't show up at nine-thirty!" Though he says it with a smile, a message comes through clearly: If I want to belong, I should attend regularly and arrive on time. Although I am always welcome, only if I can be counted on am I part of the minyan. The dependence of Jews on each other—a theme running through biblical and rabbinic literature—is pressingly literal at Eighth Street.

Meanwhile, my feelings about Paris coalesce into a plan. I know I want to live there for a time, but only if I will be among Jews. Since I am at the point in my graduate school career when I must find a dissertation topic, I decide to look for fieldwork situations with Jews in Paris. I make an exploratory visit with my fiancée, Elissa. Will she agree to a pause in her own career to follow me on this project? Will the organizations of Polish Jewish immigrants whom I have chosen to study be willing to have me study them?

The answer is yes to both questions. Speaking Yiddish and appearing as a nice young Jewish couple seem to be the critical elements in our success. We are invited to sit in on board meetings, negotiations aimed at the reunification of societies split by political differences for over half a century. I am struck by the fact that these immigrants seem so much more marked by their political identification than the East European Jews I've met in New York. Also, I am impressed at the number of societies remaining in a country that has suffered Nazi occupation and that historically has shown little tolerance for immigrant cultural identifications.

But I am drawn not so much by the differences between these Yiddish speakers and those I know in New York as by encountering them in an environment that is otherwise so foreign. Speaking Yiddish to people with whom I have no other common language confirms its legitimacy and reinforces the sense of a distinctive Jewish identity that is shared between generations. I go for a trial interview of one activist, who is disappointed that I didn't bring "the girl," Elissa, along with me. When he discovers to my embarrassment that I have been secretly taping the interview, he is flattered.

Just before leaving Paris, Elissa and I climb the steps of Sacré Coeur. The cathedral itself is an ungracious mass, and the city looks gray and undifferentiated below us. I experience a moment of vertigo, as if I could tumble off Montmartre and drown. Part of my dream of Paris, "capital of the nineteenth century," is an infantile fantasy of becoming a universal intellectual—to be free both of the special knowledge and of the limitations of my knowledge that follow on my personal history. Yet I know I cannot come to Paris and immediately move among its confident, cliquish intellectual elite. Even less will I ever have contact with that "quintessentially French" petite bourgeoisie typified by the stolid Inspector Maigret. My first place will be with the immigrants, whose appearance, strange language, and crowded quarters provided material for unkind portraits by Maigret's creator, Simenon, in the 1930s.[5] If I am unable to come to see Paris as they have seen it, if I cannot make out of a shared marginality a niche in the city for myself, I will be lost, as much as the "lost generation," and in a most unromantic way.

During the two years between our decision to spend a year in Paris and the beginning of that year, I attend the Eighth Street Shul more and more regularly, and Elissa occasionally joins me. Gradually, my feelings when I miss a week shift from guilt to regret. One shabbes, waking up late but not wanting to miss attending altogether, I arrive just in time for the Kiddush, to the general amusement of the entire minyan. One February morning I wake up to see snow falling and force myself to go outside against my will, knowing that on a day like this I am truly needed.

Other incidents illustrate the gap in assumptions between myself and the other congregants. I try to bring friends into the shul, partly because it makes me more comfortable, and partly to build up the congregation. A friend whose hair and demeanor reflect his love of reggae music and his connections with Jamaican Rastafarians comes along one Yom Kippur. We reach the point in the service when pious men, remembering the priests in the days of the Temple, descend to their knees and touch their foreheads to the floor. Since no one wants to soil his good pants on the dirty floor, sheets of newspaper are provided as protection. Reb Simcha Taubenfeld, the senior member of the congregation, approaches my friend with newspaper in hand and asks in his heavy Yiddish accent: "Do you fall down?" The look of bewilderment on my friend's face graphically illustrates the term "frame of reference." Another week, the same friend, failing to observe the discretion with regard to the expression of political opinions that I have learned to adopt at shul, gets into a bitter argument over the Palestinian question. Fishel Mandel, a social worker and one of the younger members of the congregation, calls me during the week to convey the message that "despite our political differences, your friend is still welcome."

After our wedding, I attend virtually every week. When Elissa comes, she is doubly welcome, since the only other woman who attends regularly is Goldie Brown, Moish Fogel's sister. Though Goldie doesn't complain about being isolated in the women's gallery one flight above the men, she seconds Elissa's suggestion that a mekhitse be set up downstairs. The suggestion gets nowhere, however: It would entail displacing one of the regular members of the congregation from his usual seat, and though there is no lack of available places (I myself usually wander from front to back during the course of the service), he refuses to consider moving.

I reason that I will have more of a voice concerning questions such as the seating of women if I formalize my relationship to the shul by becoming a member. My timid announcement that I would like to do so meets with initial confusion on the part of the older members of the society present. Then Fishel, ever the mediator and interpreter, explains to me that the shul is not organized like a suburban synagogue: "There's a *chevra*, a society, that owns the shul. In order to join, you have to be *shomer mitzves*, you have to keep kosher and strictly observe the Sabbath."

I drop my request. Shiye the president reassures me with a speech in his usual roundabout style to the effect that belonging to the chevra is a separate question from being a member of the minyan: "They send their money in from New Jersey and Long Island, but the shul couldn't exist without the people that actually come to pray here."

Meanwhile, our plans to go to Paris proceed. Our travel plans become a topic for discussion over kiddush at shul. One of the older, Polish-born members tells us for the first time that he lived in Paris for nine years after the war. We ask him why he came to America, and he answers, "*Vern a frantsoyz iz shver* [It's hard to become a Frenchman]," both to obtain citizenship and to be accepted by neighbors.

At the end of the summer, we expect to give a farewell Kiddush at the shul. A few days before shabbes, I get a phone call from Moish Fogel: "Don't get things for kiddush. We won't be able to daven at Eighth Street for a while. There's been a fire. Thank God, the Torah scrolls were rescued, but it's going to take a while to repair the damage." It is two weeks after Tisha B'Av, the fast commemorating the destruction of the Temple in Jerusalem.

Leaving New York without saying goodbye to the shul and its congregation, we fly overnight to Brussels and immediately *shlep* (the word "drag" would not do the burden justice) our seven heavy suitcases onto a Paris train. Arriving again at the Gare du Nord, I think of the thousands of Polish Jews who were greeted at the station in the twenties and thirties by fellow immigrants eager to hire workers. As soon as we get off the train, Elissa immediately "gets involved," demanding the credentials of two men who claim to be policemen and attempt to "confiscate" a carpet two Moroccan immigrants are carrying. Upon Elissa's challenge, the "policemen" demur.

We practice our French on the cab driver: I explain to him why we've come to Paris. He warns us that we shouldn't tell strangers we're Jewish. It is only a few weeks since the terrorist attack on Goldenberg's restaurant, and no one knows when the next anti-Semitic attack may come. I reply that if I hadn't said we were Jewish, we wouldn't have found out he was a Jew as well, adding that in New York the names of taxi drivers are posted inside the cabs. He says he wouldn't like that at all.

So we receive an early warning that ethnicity in Paris is not celebrated publicly as it is in New York, nor are ethnic mannerisms and phrases so prevalent as a deliberate element of personal style. This is the repressive underside of marginality. It appears wherever the individual or community think it is better not to flaunt their distinctiveness, even if they cannot fully participate in the host culture. It leads to suspicion and silence, to the taxi driver's desire for anonymity.

Arriving at our rented apartment, we meet our neighbor Isabel, who will be our only non-Jewish friend during the year in Paris, and who later explains that meeting us has helped dispel her prejudices about Jews. Over the next few days, we introduce ourselves to Jewish storekeepers in the neighborhood: Guy, the Tunisian kosher butcher; Chanah, the Polish baker's wife; Leon, the deli man from Lublin, who insists he didn't learn Yiddish until he came to Paris. We have a harder time finding a synagogue where we feel at home. For Rosh Hashanah and Yom Kippur, we have purchased tickets at one of the "official" synagogues run by the Consistoire, the recognized religious body of French Jewry set up under Napoleon. Most synagogues run by the Consistoire are named after the streets on which they're located. Meeting a Hasid on the street, I ask him whether he happens to know when Rosh Hashanah services begin at "Notre Dame de Nazareth." He grimaces and makes as if spitting: "Don't say that name, *ptu ptu ptu!*"

The synagogue is strange to us as well. Most of the crowd seems if anything more secular than most American Jews, who go to the synagogue only on the high holidays. Many teenagers wear jeans or miniskirts. Because of the fear of terrorism, everyone is frisked on entering. Inside, the synagogue is picturesque with its nineteenth-century pseudo-Moorish motifs; when it was built, Offenbach was the choirmaster. Yet it is as religiously dissatisfying as the suburban American temple I used to attend. The services seem to be conducted in a traditional manner, but it is hard to tell from among the noisy throng in back. The shammes, as a representative of the government, wears a Napoleonic hat, and the rabbi delivers his sermon from a high pulpit.

After Yom Kippur, I think idly about the need to find a more comfortable shul, and when I hear about an East European-style minyan within walking distance, I consider going on Simchas Torah. Watching television reports of terrorist attacks on Simchas Torah in other European capitals, I am consumed with shame at my own apathy, and thus I walk a kilometer or two to find the synagogue on the rue Basfroi the following shabbes.

Going in, I am first shown into a side room, where men are reciting incomprehensible prayers with strange and beautiful melodies. Eventually I realize that they are North African Jews, and I venture into the main room to ask, "Is there an Ashkenazic minyan here?"

The man I ask replies in French, "We're not racists here! We're all Jews!" at which his friend points out: "The young man spoke to you in Yiddish!" Continuing in Yiddish, he explains that while everyone is welcome in the main synagogue, the services there are in fact Ashkenazic, and so some of the North African men prefer to pray in their own style in the smaller room.

Gradually I settle in, though I have trouble following the prayers in the beginning. Remembering a particular turn in the melody for the reader's repetition of the Amidah that the president at Eighth Street uses, I listen for it from the cantor here at the rue

Basfroi, and hear a satisfying similarity in his voice. I feel like a new immigrant coming to his landsmanshaft's shul to hear the melodies from his town.

Throughout our year in Paris, I attend this synagogue about as frequently as I had gone to Eighth Street at first. Although the congregation is not unfriendly, no one invites me home for lunch, partly out of French reserve, and perhaps also because it is clear that I'm not very observant. I feel "unobservant" here in another sense: I do not register the vast store of information obviously available here about the interaction of religious Jews from different ethnic backgrounds. It escapes me, as though I were "off duty." In contrast to my feelings at Eighth Street, I am not motivated by the desire to make myself a regular here. And this is not my fieldwork situation: Nothing external moves me to push my way through socially, to find out who these people really are and to let them see me as well.

The Jews I encounter in the course of my research belong to an entirely different crowd. The landsmanshaftn to which they belong are secular organizations. If I wanted to observe the Sabbath closely, it would be difficult for me to do my fieldwork. The immigrants hold many meetings on Saturdays, including a series of *shabbes-shmuesn*, afternoon discussions at which the main focus this year is the war in Lebanon.

I mention to one of my informants that I sometimes go to the synagogue. "I admire that," he responds. "I can't go back to the synagogue now. I've been away too long; it's too late for me." Toward the end of the year, we invite an autodidact historian of the immigrant community to dinner on Friday night and ask him to recite the blessing over the challah. "I can't," he refuses, and will not explain further. Though his intellectual curiosity has led him to become friendly with us, and he is considering doing research on the resurgence of Orthodoxy among young French Jews, his critical stance vis-à-vis his own secularist movement is insufficient to allow him to accept this religious honor. Enjoying the possibilities offered by marginality is sometimes impossible for those who are neither young nor well educated and who have been deceived in their wholehearted commitments.

Throughout the year, Elissa has been growing stricter regarding *kashres*. She refuses to eat nonkosher meat and will order only in fish restaurants. She articulates our shared impression that Jewish secularism has failed to create everyday lifeways that can be transmitted from generation to generation, and that any lasting Judaism must be grounded in Jewish law and learning. Before parting for the summer—she to study Yiddish at Oxford, I to Jerusalem, to acquire the Hebrew that I will need to learn about Jewish law—we discuss the level of observance we want to adopt on our return to New York, but we come to no decision.

Elissa and I meet at the end of the summer in Los Angeles, for the bar mitzvah of her twin cousins. I am uncomfortable riding on shabbes; after spending an entire summer in Jerusalem, for the first time, it seems like a violation of myself. The roast beef sandwich I eat at the reception is the first nonkosher food I've eaten since leaving Paris.

Thus, without having made a formal declaration, I join Elissa in observing kashres (save for occasional lapses that I call my "*treyf* of the month club" and that becomes less and less frequent), and she joins me in keeping shabbes, albeit with some reluctance. Preparing to fulfill a promise made in a dream I had while in Paris, I take a further step: At the beginning of November, I begin attending daily services at another East Side shul and thus putting on tefillin again. One of my mother's cousins at the Telshe Yeshiva in Cleveland—whom I have never met—told me in my dream that I would always be welcome there, and I responded that if I got there, I would put on tefillin everyday from then on. Later in November, Elissa and I fly to Cleveland for the weekend. Though we are welcomed warmly, it is clear that the rabbis and the *rebetsins* at the yeshiva hoped for something more Jewish from me, the great grandson of the Rosh Yeshiva's second wife, Miriam.

We return to the Eighth Street Shul as well, which has been secured and repaired sufficiently to make it usable once again. There are changes. Old Mr. Klapholz, with whom I had hardly exchanged a word, has passed away. Fishel's uncle Mr. Hochbaum, a congregant for half a century, no longer attends, since he is unable to walk all the way from Grand Street. On the other hand, my long-haired friend has moved into the neighborhood and attends regularly. Two of the younger members of the congregation have small children now, and they must go to a shul where there are other children for their son and daughter to play with. In February, our oldest member passes away, and after Shavuot, another member moves to Jerusalem. Two more young men eventually begin coming regularly and bring along their infant children. Now, in June 1986, the shul has thirteen regular male attendees. I am no longer free to sleep late on Saturday mornings, and fortunately I no longer want to.

All of this, to the extent that it is of my own making, is the result of a search to realize that fragile illusion of wholeness which was destroyed when my family and almost all the others left Farmingdale. I will hazard a guess that Jewish anthropologists—perhaps anthropologists in general—are motivated by a sense of loss. Yet the seamless image of community is inevitably a child's image. We cannot regain what is lost, if only because it never existed as we remember it. Nothing in society is quite as harmonious as it seemed to me then, and I later learned about bitter political struggles that had taken place in Farmingdale, just as they had among the immigrants in Paris.

Our strategy, rather, should be to attempt to understand what it is we miss and need, which is available in still-living communities in another form. The image of wholeness which we share is foreshadowed by communities all of us stem from, however many generations back, and it can serve as a guide in the search for the reciprocal relationships of autonomous adulthood.

Anthropology is a tool for mediating between the self and the community. It has helped me to come to belong at the Eighth Street Shul: to withhold my opinions when it seems necessary, without feeling the guilt of self-compromise; to accept instruction and gentle reprimands with good humor; to believe it is worthwhile preserving something that might otherwise disappear. But belonging at Eighth Street does not mean that I have dissolved myself into an ideal Orthodox Jew. If I attempted to do so, I would be unable to continue being an anthropologist. If I fit into any category, it may be what my friend Kugelmass calls the "funky Orthodox": that is, those who participate in the community but whose interests and values are not confined to the Orthodox world. In fact, there are no ideal Orthodox Jews at Eighth Street; it is our respective quirks that provide the *raison d'être* of this haphazard but now intentional once-a-week community.

The fact that I have found a religious community that needs me because of its marginality and will tolerate me because of a generosity born of tradition is what I mean by the marginal redemption of one Jew. Likewise, if the shul survives, it will be because of its very marginality, because of the many individuals who have recognized the creative possibilities of a situation that demands that they create a new unity, while allowing each of them to retain their otherness. Isn't this the dream of anthropologists? Whether attempting to communicate knowledge between different Jewish communities, or between communities much more distant in tradition and empathy, we are messengers. We spend our own lives in moving back and forth among the worlds of others. As we do so, in order to avoid getting lost along the way we must become cultural pioneers, learning to "get hold of our *trans*cultural selves" (Wolff 1970: 40). Communities on the edge of mass society, or even on the fringes of ethnic enclaves, seem to be among the most congenial fields in which to do so.

Let me finish with a parable:

Two Jews can afford to be fastidious about the dress, comportment, and erudition of a third. It gives them something to gossip about and identify against. Ten healthy Jews can have a similar luxury; an eleventh means competition for the ritual honors. It's nine Jews who are the most tolerant, as I learned one forlorn shabbes at Eighth Street. It was almost ten o'clock, and there was no minyan. Since everyone seemed content to wait patiently, I assumed that someone else had promised to come, and asked, "Who are we waiting for?"

"A *yid*," our oldest member replied without hesitation.

Eventually a Jew came along.

Notes

1. Compare Pierre Bourdieu's critique of the structuralist theory of "reciprocal" gift exchange: "Even if reversibility [i.e., the assumption that gifts entail counter-gifts of equivalent value] is the objective truth of the discrete acts which ordinary experience knows in discrete form and calls gift exchanges, it is not the whole truth of a practice which could not exist if it were consciously perceived in accordance with the model. The temporal structure of gift exchange, which objectivism ignores, is what makes possible the coexistence of two opposing truths, which defines the full truth of the gift" (1977: 6).

   Similarly, in a narrative such as this one, because I, as author, already know the ending, it may seem as though each successive element fits into those that precede and follow it in such a way that their necessity is perfectly known. Actually my aim is to show how the background that nurtured me shaped in part my unpredictable responses to situations that in themselves were historically rather than culturally determined. See my conclusion, where I refer to one of the communities I now participate in as "haphazard but intentional."

2. Even if it was no more than a matter of convenience, this annual event demonstrates Jonathan Woocher's point that American Jewish "civil religion expects Jews to take advantage of the opportunities which America provides, and to use them to help fulfill their Jewish responsibilities" (1985: 161).

3. This may seem an outrageously loose claim, and I am quite willing to be proven wrong by literary scholars. But compare the conclusion of James Joyce's *Portrait of the Artist as a Young Man:*

> Mother is putting my new secondhand clothes in order. She prays now, she says, that I may learn in my own life and away from home and friends what the heart is and what it feels. Amen. So be it. Welcome, O life! I go to encounter for the millionth time the reality of experience and to forge in the smithy of my soul the uncreated conscience of my race. (1968: 252–53)

with the end of Moshe Szulsztein's memoir of a Polish Jewish childhood:

> When the truck was already fairly far along Warsaw Street and Kurow was barely risible, two more relatives appeared in a great rush, wanting to take their leave. These were my grandfather's pair of pigeons. The pigeons knew me, and I knew them. I loved them, and perhaps they loved me as well… But the truck is stronger than they are, it drives and drives further and further away from Kurow. My poor pigeons can't keep up, they remain behind… Before they disappear altogether from my view I still discern them within the distant evening cloud, two small flying silver dots, one a bit behind the other. That, I know, is the male, and the second, a bit in front, is the female. (1982: 352)

4. For photographs of Eighth Street and other Lower East Side shuls, both surviving and abandoned, see Fine and Wolfe (1978).

5. "In every corner, in every little patch of darkness, up the blind alleys and the corridors, one could sense the presence of a swarming mass of humanity, a sly, shameful life. Shadows slunk along the walls. The stores were selling goods unknown to French people even by name" (Simenon 1963: 45).

References

Bakan, David. 1958. *Sigmund Freud and the Jewish Mystical Tradition.* Princeton, NJ: Van Nostrand.

Belcove-Shalin, Janet. 1988. "Becoming More of an Eskimo." In *Between Two Worlds: Ethnographic Essays on American Jews*, 77–98. Ithaca, NY: Cornell University Press.

Bourdieu, Pierre. 1977. *Outline of a Theory of Practice.* Cambridge: Cambridge University Press.

Boyarin, Daniel. 1997. *Judaism as a Gender.* Berkeley and Los Angeles: University of California Press.

Clifford, James. 1986. "On Ethnographic Allegory." In *Writing Culture: The Poetics and Politics of Ethnography*, ed. James Clifford and George Marcus, 98–121. Berkeley and Los Angeles: University of California Press.

Cuddihy, John. 1974. *The Ordeal of Civility: Freud, Marx, Lévi-Strauss and the Jewish Struggle with Modernity.* New York: Basic Books.

Fabian, Johannes. 1983. *Time and the Other.* New York: Columbia University Press.

Faur, José. 1986. *Golden Doves with Silver Dots.* Bloomington: Indiana University Press.

Fine, Jo Renée, and Gerard Wolfe. 1978. *The Synagogues of New York's Lower East Side.* New York: Washington Mews Books.

Gough, Kathleen. 1968. "Anthropology and Imperialism." *Monthly Review* 19: 12–27.

Joyce, James. 1968 [1916]. *Portrait of the Artist* as *a Young Man.* New York: Viking Press.

Schnapper, Dominique. 1983. *Jewish Identities in France: An Analysis of Contemporary French Jewry*, trans. Arthur Goldhammer. Chicago: University of Chicago Press.

Simenon, Georges. 1963. *Maigret and the Enigmatic Left*, ed. Daphne Woodward. New York: Penguin Books.

Szulsztein, Moshe. 1982. *Dort vu mayn vig iz geshtanen.* Paris: Published by a Committee.

Wolff, Kurt. 1970. "The Sociology of Knowledge and Sociological Theory." In *The Sociology of Sociology*, ed. Larry T. Reynolds and Janice M. Reynolds, 31–67. New York: David McKay.

Woocher, Jonathan. 1985. "Sacred Survival." *Judaism* 34/2: 151–62.

Expanding the Canon of Jewish Philosophy: Toward an Appreciation of Genre

Aaron W. Hughes

If Alfred North Whitehead is correct and the history of Western philosophy is but a footnote to Plato, then in much of this history we encounter a struggle for the proper literary form to present philosophy. How, for example, does one portray a living, philosophical encounter in a written text? Unlike many difficult and often highly unliterary works of philosophy that would come after him, Plato's dialogues remain a testament to the portrayal of philosophy as a way of life. The fine balance that Plato strikes between the philosophical and the literary permits entry into a narrative that unfolds in front of the reader, thereby allowing him or her to struggle actively with the ideas presented within. Although the philosophical dialogue would in the centuries after Plato go in and out of vogue, the spirit illuminating it—the encounter between antagonistic views, the attempt to convince another of the incorrectness of his or her arguments, and an ultimate resolution—sought to breathe life into a written text.

What follows examines this genre in medieval and early modern Jewish philosophy. Unlike many analyses, this study does not focus on disembodied ideas or arguments, but on a particular genre, the dialogue, showing how it was deployed, geographically and temporally, by a number of different authors. My operating assumption is that a text's contents cannot be neatly separated from its form. By tracing a particular genre through time and space, locating various examples in specific contexts, I hope to pose and subsequently answer a series of questions: Why did various authors choose this genre as opposed to others? What did the dialogue allow a particular thinker to accomplish that other genres did not? How are the literary features of the dialogue used to construct a philosophical argument? What, in turn, is the nature of the relationship between Jewish philosophical dialogues and those composed by non-Jews? The answers to such questions will, I trust, contribute to our appreciation of the dynamics of Jewish philosophical writing.

The literary dialogue was but one of several genres that Jewish thinkers employed to articulate their philosophical programs. By philosophical dialogue I mean nothing more than a series of narrative exchanges between two or more distinct characters whose conversations revolve around a number of philosophical issues. These dialogues usually take place in a particular narrative setting, and through the various exchanges, we witness the development of not only a set of philosophical arguments but also the protagonists' personalities. This genre conveniently allows an author to present a particular argument, raise a number of counterarguments to it, and subsequently refute such counterarguments, thereby providing a natural venue for the philosophical enterprise.[1]

A closer examination will also reveal that Jewish philosophical dialogues tended to be composed at times when this genre was relatively popular in larger non-Jewish cultures. In the Jewish philosophical dialogue, then, we witness both a Jewish response to non-Jewish ideas, and a convenient narrative setting whereby we can get a better sense of the social and polemical production of Jewish philosophy. An analysis of this genre reveals that dialogues are not just about the ideas contained within, but that these ideas tend to constellate around a number of literary, aesthetic, and rhetorical features. These features, far from marginal, are often as important as the actual contents of the work.

Informing this study is the desire to contribute to the expansion of our understanding of Jewish philosophy—its genesis, its dissemination, its relationship to literature and literary creativity—by studying what James T. Robinson calls its "secondary forms."[2] The examination of medieval Jewish philosophy, still primarily indebted to the ideals and categories of *Wissenschaft des Judentums*, is based on a number of premises that are regarded as axiomatic. These include putting prime emphasis on ideas, often divorced from specific textual contexts. A good example of this is the *Kuzari* by Judah Halevi, in which, despite his claim at the beginning of the work that he does not necessarily agree with everything the character of the *haver* will say, the tendency is to discuss the views of this character as if he were simply Halevi's mouthpiece.[3]

Another feature of the *Wissenschaft* model is its focus on great men (e.g., Halevi, Maimonides, Gersonides) and their great texts (e.g., *Kuzari, Guide of the Perplexed, Wars of the Lord*). Yet, as great as these thinkers were and as brilliant and important as their treatises are for understanding the history of Jewish philosophy, this approach only tells part of the story.[4] Often left unanswered are questions such as the following: How did these "great works" take hold in various Jewish cultures? How did other Jewish thinkers, the so-called "epigones," react and respond to such texts?[5] An examination of secondary forms enables us to begin to answer such questions by understanding the various ways in which philosophical ideas were received and subsequently disseminated to a larger reading public.

Two caveats are in order at the beginning of this study. First, some kind of definition of what I mean by *Jewish philosophy* is in order.[6] Jewish philosophy is a modern term; none of the thinkers discussed in this study, with the possible exception of those mentioned in the epilogue, would have employed it, considered themselves to have been "Jewish philosophers," or engaged in an activity we today recognize as "Jewish philosophy." Despite this, it is nevertheless possible to identify a phenomenon for heuristic purposes regardless of whether acknowledged or mentioned by the object of study. In the present case, one can define Jewish philosophy as the reading of Jewish sources (e.g., the Bible, the Talmud, midrashim) through philosophical lenses inherited from non-Jewish cultures. The benefits of employing the term *Jewish philosophy*, it seems to me, far outweigh those of not using it. This definition, however, immediately alerts us to the fact that philosophy is not autochthonous to Judaism. It proclaims Jewish philosophy as a response, whether positive or negative, to larger non-Jewish intellectual forces. In many ways, the present study supports this thesis: when Jewish philosophers wrote dialogues they often did so to respond to dialogues written by non-Jews.

Secondly, I have no intention of denigrating studies of Jewish philosophy that focus solely on elucidating the content of texts. This approach has been too valuable and important to make into a straw man. Indeed, a quick perusal of the reference notes to the present study will reveal to just what an extent my debt is to such work. A study that focuses on secondary forms, in other words, can only take place after the elucidation of so-called "primary forms." The present work, then, naturally builds upon, expands, and hopefully will reinform such studies by showing further the richness and beauty of Jewish philosophical texts.

As I argued in my previous book, *The Texture of the Divine*, there has been a tendency in studies devoted to Jewish philosophy, especially in the medieval period, to gravitate toward the "grand" themes of the Western intellectual tradition: metaphysics, ontology, epistemology, and ethics.[7] While there is certainly nothing inherently wrong with such an approach, it tends to marginalize other features of this tradition, such as aesthetics, poetics, and rhetoric. *The Art of Dialogue in Jewish Philosophy* seeks to contribute further to these traditionally marginalized fields by examining the important nexus between philosophy and literature. Many of the thinkers discussed in this work did not consider themselves to be simply philosophers. For instance, all wrote poetry and/or other forms of literature. As poets or as litterateurs, all were surely aware of, consciously or otherwise, the literary and aesthetic conventions that governed artistic creativity in their respective cultures. I work on the assumption that these literary, artistic, and aesthetic sensibilities left traces within their philosophical compositions, and that these are retrievable.

Furthermore, dialogues, when read properly, function as windows through which we are able to examine both a specific author in addition to the broader community of which he was a part. Consequently, the various debates that arise in these dialogues are not simply theoretical, but reflect the various religious, intellectual, and social issues of the day. These issues were often extremely vitriolic, for at stake was Judaism's orientation to other cultures. For instance, what texts should Jews read? Should non-Jewish scientific sources play a role in the Jewish educational curriculum? All of the authors analyzed in this study confront and essentially attempt to mediate these various tensions. For example, when Halevi rebels against the dominant intellectual and spiritual reading of Judaism offered by his contemporaries, he does so not as an individual but as a spokesperson for what he considers to be the authentic Jewish tradition. Or, when Isaac Polleqar composes a dialogue between an astrologer and a philosopher, he does so not simply because it makes for a quaint or entertaining conversation but because he saw astrology as antagonistic to free will, one of the hallmarks of his rational understanding of religion. The astrologer, in other words, is not simply a literary character but a metonym for an ideology that Polleqar regarded as insidious, and one that, based on his vitriol, must certainly have made significant inroads in contemporaneous Jewish culture.

The dialogue thus becomes an important locus through which we are able to confront firsthand the dynamics, often nonphilosophical, behind the composition of Jewish philosophy. Yet although virtually all were written as responses, we should not however assume that the reasons behind each text's composition were necessarily the same. These responses could be subversive, as in the case of Halevi, showing how non-Jewish philosophical ideas—themselves expressed in dialogue form—threaten Jewish authenticity. His response is to overturn the rules of the genre by employing terms and categories in ways that defy contemporaneous literary expectations. Others, most notably Judah Abravanel, employed the genre because they really had no choice: the dialogue was such a popular genre in Renaissance Humanism, following the rediscovery and translation of the Platonic corpus, that it became one of the primary vehicles whereby philosophers expressed their ideas, especially those on love. In order to absorb and ultimately respond to such ideas, Abravanel had to use this genre. That he did so and that his own dialogue became a best-seller is a testament to both his literary and philosophical abilities.

A Brief History of the Dialogue in Judaism

Judaism possesses a venerable and ancient tradition of dialogue, at least broadly conceived. Indeed, one could quite easily argue that the history of the Jewish people from antiquity to the present is essentially the story of a series of dialogues and silences between God and Israel. The covenantal relationship, in other words, is one that is based on two sides communicating to each other through time. However, much like the notion of dialogue in modern Jewish philosophy, this idea of God and Israel engaged in a constant conversation is a concept or process, and not necessarily a literary encounter portrayed using a particular genre. The one real exception is the book of Job wherein we encounter a literal dialogue that revolves around a number of philosophical themes such as theodicy, freedom of will, suffering of the righteous, and so on, including often ambiguous resolutions to such issues. Not surprisingly, then, many Jewish philosophers, beginning with Saadya Gaon (882–942),[8] gravitated to the book of Job and read it as a philosophical dialogue dealing with God's providential relationship to humans.

Moreover, the phenomenon of disputation and literature plays a central role in the various sources of rabbinic Judaism (e.g., Talmud, midrashim). Many of the stories that appear in the Babylonian Talmud, as Jeffrey L. Rubenstein has well noted, gave the sages an opportunity "to ponder the tensions inherent in their culture, not an easy means of resolving them."[9] Much like the philosophical dialogues examined here, a proper understanding of rabbinic stories is contingent upon the broader literary, historical, and intellectual environments in which Jews found themselves (i.e., those of late antiquity).[10] Despite the prevalence for both disputation and stories, the existence of literal dialogues is relatively rare in this literature. One important exception, however, is the series of exchanges between Rabbi Judah the Prince and the enigmatic Antoninus, believed to be a Roman governor or emperor.[11] In these dialogues, the two characters discuss a number of issues that we could loosely label as philosophical (e.g., when life begins, the afterlife).

Despite examples such as Job and the dialogic encounters of Rabbi Judah and Antoninus, there is no evidence that when Jewish philosophers decided to compose dialogues they looked to this body of literature. For example, although Jewish philosophers wrote commentaries to Job, they rarely focused on the dialogic aspect or aspects of the work. They were, in other words, primarily interested in the contents of the work, and not its form.

A more likely candidate for the composition of Jewish philosophical dialogues would seem to be Plato. As generally acknowledged today, Plato is the true master of the philosophical dialogue. His creations are so effective precisely because they are not monologues, wherein an author expatiates at length on a single topic, but are a series of living encounters between moral agents.[12] The reader is drawn into these encounters and, much like the slave boy in *Meno*,[13] comes to the realization that he or she already possesses knowledge, only that it has yet to be articulated.[14] Socrates, in other words, helps not only his companions, but also the reader, both to clarify and to order what they already know. As literature, Platonic dialogues enable the reader to take an active role in the treatise. Plato thus succeeds in engaging, arousing, shocking, and amusing the reader,[15] thereby permitting him or her to make intellectual progress as the work unfolds.

Despite such an obvious precursor to medieval Jewish dialogues, it seems highly unlikely that Jewish or medieval thinkers had firsthand knowledge of the Platonic corpus. In a landmark essay from 1940, Franz Rosenthal argues that complete translations of Platonic dialogues, according to the information obtainable from Arabic Bibliographies, were made very rarely. Not a single one of them has come down to us, and the character of those quotations which we have before us, never seems, as far as we can now judge, to afford grounds for the slightest probability that we are concerned with the remains of a pure and complete text of a Platonic Dialogue.[16]

It would seem that the majority of Platonic texts that reached the Arabs did so by way of Galen's summaries.[17] Islamic and Jewish philosophers, then, had knowledge of the contents but not necessarily the original forms of the *Sophist, Cratylus, Euthydemus, Statesman, Timaeus, Laws*,[18] and *Parmenides*, in addition to a paraphrase of the *Republic*.[19] Another important source for knowledge of Plato came from the compilation of his sayings included in *Nawadir al-falasifa' wa al-ḥukamā'* (Anecdotes of Philosophers and Sages) by Ḥunayn ibn Isḥāq (809–893). These latter sayings, however, often had no relation to Plato's actual works. On the contrary, they became convenient ways to attach a famous name to various sayings that circulated in the Islamicate world.[20] Even though knowledge of the form of the Platonic dialogues seems to have been wanting in the medieval Islamicate world, the figure of Socrates played an important role in the literature associated with this period. This, however, was neither the Socrates of history nor the Socrates of the Platonic dialogue. To use the words of Ilai Alon,

> On the one hand the original Greek Socrates, whoever or whatever he was, as described and alluded to by Plato, Xenophon, and Aristophanes, was vaguely remembered, and on the other hand, some new traits, entirely alien to him, were added throughout the centuries of the existence of that legend. Socrates's name seems to have been known by many Arabs, and the details of his biography were often regarded as an ideal to be imitated.[21]

The Socrates of medieval Islamicate civilization was thus a pliable symbol that could be used either to uphold certain values deemed religiously significant or to show the danger of philosophy to religion. Of especial significance for understanding the former were numerous pithy sayings attributed to Socrates in which he celebrates earthly death (e.g., "Think lightly of death, for its bitterness lies in fearing it")[22] or stresses various ethical principles (e.g., "A king, seeing Socrates wearing a worn-out woolen garment during a festival, said to him, 'I wished you had adorned yourself on such a day.' Socrates said to him, 'No ornament is more beautiful than justice, for it is one of the intellect's noblest faculties'").[23] Even the anti-rationalist al-Ghazālī (d. 1111), although generally critical of Socrates as a pagan and a philosopher,[24] nonetheless favorably quotes anecdotes attributed to him about the fleeting nature of this world.[25]

So, despite the modern importance of the Platonic dialogue to Western thought, it is highly unlikely, if not outright impossible, that the Platonic method of composition would have influenced anyone in this study prior to Judah Abravanel. Before Renaissance Humanists began their translation project of the Platonic corpus, only a small number of garbled Platonic translations existed.[26] It was only in Abravanel's generation, then, that we witness the first full-scale editions and translations of Plato's dialogues. This is not to say that the character of Socrates did not play a role in the philosophical or even the popular imagination before the Renaissance, only that the ideas of Plato did not circulate in dialogue form. The result is that only those Jewish thinkers after Abravanel would have had access to the full Platonic corpus. For example, Moses Mendelssohn, early in his career, intended to translate certain of these dialogues into German. Moreover, although his *Phaedon* rewrites or updates for a German-speaking audience Plato's dialogue of the same name, in places, especially the beginning, it virtually copies its Platonic model word for word.[27]

If the origins of the Jewish philosophical dialogue can be found neither in biblical literature nor the Platonic corpus, then it would seem that we would have to look elsewhere for its origins. Yet, I argue that there really is no point of origin for Jewish philosophical dialogues because when Jews wrote them they were responding to non-Jewish dialogues written at roughly the same time. Moreover, as with the quest for "origins" generally, even if we could pinpoint with any degree of accuracy the origins of these dialogues, it would not necessarily follow that we would understand the dynamics of this genre any better.

Having said this, though, it seems likely that some of the earliest non-Jewish dialogues that Jews would have encountered originated not from the Greek-speaking world, but the Arabo-Islamic one. One of the earliest examples of an Islamic dialogue is Abū Ḥayyān al-Tawḥīdī's (ca. 930–1023) record of a debate between the grammarian Abū Saʿīd al-Sīrāfī (d. 979) and Abū Bishr Mattā b. Yūnus (d. 940).[28] Mattā b. Yūnus, one of the teachers of al-Fārābī, argues in this dialogue that logic is a universal science and thus is central to clear thinking; al-Sīrāfī, who by all accounts wins the debate, counters that logic is not universal, but a Greek linguistic habit, and consequently unnecessary for Arab speakers, who have all they need in the rules of Arabic grammar.

In addition, the first dialogue studied below—Halevi's *Kuzari*—was composed in an Arabo-Islamic environment, within which certain subcultures used the genre of the dialogue to articulate their religious, spiritual, or intellectual programs. One of the primary groups to employ the dialogue was that of the Ismaʿilis, who seem to have inherited the genre, as they did many other phenomena, from various esoteric groups of late antiquity.[29] In particular, certain treatises in the *Corpus Hermeticum* were written as dialogues, wherein gods reveal esoteric and philosophical truths to their pupils. The actual chains of transmission of this literature from late antiquity to the early Islamic world are, however, very difficult to reconstruct, primarily owing to the fact that it is virtually impossible to know what exactly the earliest Ismaʿilis were reading and, equally importantly, in what literary forms or genres.[30]

Another important and early Islamicate dialogue may be found in the debate between animals and humans in the Ismaʿili-influenced *Rasāʾil Ikhwān al-Ṣafāʾ* (Epistles of the Brethren of Purity).[31] This work, in addition to various proselytizing works composed by Ismaʿili missionaries designed to appeal to the philosophically inclined, would have circulated throughout Muslim Spain.[32] It would seem that these dialogues—and not the biblical, rabbinic, or Platonic ones—served as the immediate influence on the composition of Jewish philosophical dialogues.

Individuals such as ibn Gabirol, Bahya ibn Paquda, and Abraham ibn Ezra seem to have composed their dialogues under the sphere of influence of this Isma'ili philosophical spirituality. Judah Halevi, on the other hand, composed his dialogue as a way to subvert this sphere of influence. When Jews wrote philosophical dialogues, to reiterate, it was a response to non-Jewish dialogues. And although these non-Jewish dialogues may well have drawn inspiration from Plato, Cicero, or Augustine, until the Renaissance Jewish thinkers seem neither to have known nor to have had ready access to such texts.

A Preliminary Contextual and Literary Analysis

Most premodern philosophers do not tell us why they have chosen to write in a particular genre. Of all the dialogues examined below, only Halevi informs us of such details, although his rationale—to retell imaginatively the factors leading to the fabled existence of a Jewish kingdom somewhere in the Caucasus—is not particularly informative when it comes to answering the question of why a dialogue as opposed to some other genre (e.g., epistolary treatise). Since all of the authors are silent on this issue, let me suggest some features that dialogues present to an author, and why such features might have naturally lent themselves to the philosophical enterprise. As will become obvious in the following chapters, each dialogue was written in response to local internal and external forces, and I certainly have no intention of insinuating that these forces were identical in each text that I examine. However, it does become possible to illumine a number of features that revolve around most, if not all, of the dialogues discussed here. Before examining each of the dialogue chronologically, then, let me articulate certain features, commonalities, and issues that I will subsequently reintroduce as heuristic devices in subsequent chapters.

Although these treatises are dialogues in the sense that they deploy a series of textual interactions between two or more characters in a specific setting, it is important not to assume that all of the dialogues function in the same manner. To this end, I have given each of the chapters a subtitle that I contend accurately reflects the specific contents of each particular work. These subtitles do not so much reflect a typology of Jewish philosophical dialogues as they capture the main theme or themes of the work in question.

Having said this, though, it becomes obvious fairly quickly that the earliest dialogues are highly polemical in intent. The *Kuzari*, *Iggeret ha-Vikuah*, and *Ezer ha-Dat* all involve polemics between a character who is, at least ideologically, related to the author of the text and one or more of the characters who hold opposing positions. All of these dialogues involve the protagonist successfully convincing these antagonists that he alone holds the correct view on any given topic. Often, once the original antagonist accepts that his prior convictions are incorrect and that his protagonist's arguments are well founded, the dialogue moves from polemics to conversation. This leads to the further elucidation of key issues that were briefly touched upon in the initial polemical exchange.

The two later dialogues, the *Dialoghi d'amore* and *Phaedon*, however, lack this polemical tone. The main characters in these two works tend to interact in more friendly terms. That is, the antagonists do not hold radically different ideological perspectives, but function as characters whose dialogical interactions with the protagonist bring the intellectual encounters to completion. Ideological antagonists of the earlier dialogues thus give way to conversational partners in the later ones. Indeed, in the case of the *Dialoghi* we are not even sure who the protagonist is. Although the natural assumption is that it is Philo, as the text progresses we see that it is actually the *female* character of Sophia, someone who is unwilling to accept truth on the authority of the past, who embodies most fully the traits of a Renaissance thinker. In Mendelssohn's *Phaedon*, Socrates does not debate Sophists in order to show their ignorance and their logical inconsistencies; rather, he converses with his disciples on his deathbed, trying to convince them of the soul's immortality and providence.[33] Finally, in the epilogue we will see how the concept of dialogue is replaced by that of dialogic, a principle that no longer requires the literary genre that is the subject of this study. In modern Jewish philosophy, then, it is the spontaneity of the dialogic encounter that gives way to an authentic relationship with others and ultimately God.

All of the dialogues that appear in this study publicize, popularize, or disseminate philosophical teachings to as wide an audience as possible. They do this primarily by encoding philosophical ideas in a pleasing literary form. By giving a philosophical treatise various characters, a plot, and a setting, philosophers create texts that work on a number of different levels. A philosophically inclined reader is able to encounter in such a treatise a work of philosophy; a more literary-minded reader is able to see in the same text a work of literature. It is, however, mistaken to ignore one of these aspects at the expense of the other; for it is ultimately the intersection of philosophy and literature that is not only one of the hallmarks of these dialogues, but the main reason for their popularity. Perhaps nowhere is this more evident than in the extreme, almost uncanny, popularity that Judah Abravanel's *Dialoghi d'amore* and Mendelssohn's *Phaedon* enjoyed—not so much among Jewish audiences, but among non-Jewish ones.

The subject of chapter 2, the *Kuzari* of Judah Halevi, shows how a thinker used the dialogue to subvert treatises written by his contemporaries who, not surprisingly, articulated their own visions of Judaism in dialogues. The genre, then, enabled Halevi to portray an intellectual encounter, especially in the first book of the *Kuzari*, wherein a philosopher, a Muslim, a Christian, and a Jew put their cases before a king who sits as an independent judge.[34] The speeches that Halevi puts in the mouths of the non-Jewish characters are, unbeknownst to them, full of irony and humor, making for a highly entertaining encounter between a number of antagonists. In these encounters, the audience undoubtedly discerns the erroneous claims to monotheism made by various subcultures through Halevi's skillful use of literary terms and tropes.

It is probably no coincidence that other thinkers used such literary and often highly entertaining features of the dialogue to popularize their rationalizing agendas.

Increasingly in the thirteenth and fourteenth centuries, this genre became intertwined with the Maimonidean controversies, which witnessed a vitriolic struggle for what Jewish culture should look like.[35] Accordingly, dialogues—in addition to sermons and philosophical biblical commentaries—played a large role in disseminating Maimonidean principles to various audiences that neither understood Arabic nor were trained in the technical dimensions of philosophy. For example, Shem Tov ibn Falaquera composed at least two treatises, *Iggeret ha-Vikuaḥ* (The Epistle of the Debate) and *Sefer ha-Mevaqqesh* (The Book of the Seeker), as dialogues. The former work—a dialogue between a philosopher and a rabbinic scholar—allowed Falaquera to justify, on legal grounds, the importance of the study of philosophy.[36] The latter work, in contrast, is a series of dialogues between a student and various teachers who represent the medieval philosophical curriculum. This dialogue both popularizes the study of philosophy and functions as an encyclopedia of the various Aristotelian sciences. In like manner, Polleqar composed his highly literary *Ezer ha-Dat* in the form of a dialogue in order to defend Maimonideanism against, inter alia, astrology and kabbalah, two tools that were used by the philosophically sophisticated Abner of Burgos to justify his apostasy.[37] The dialogue became a convenient way for Polleqar to refute, point-by-point, Abner's arguments, and also to show others the philosophical principles behind this refutation.

Even a work such as Judah Abravanel's *Dialoghi* has an important pedagogical function. Here it is important to remember that Abravanel was one of the earliest Jewish thinkers to write in Italian,[38] and was also one of the first Jews to engage seriously and systematically with the main tenets of Renaissance Humanism. His *Dialoghi d'amore*, written in a highly literary and engaging style, reaches out to as broad an audience as possible, both Jewish and non-Jewish, in order to show that the rational truths associated with the Renaissance were not only the same as, but also derived from, those of the Hebrew Bible. In order to be a good Jew, then, one had to embrace Renaissance ideals, which are ultimately no different from the ideals of Judaism.

Mendelssohn's *Phaedon* also plays an important role in the popularization and dissemination of philosophical ideals. In rewriting Plato's work of the same name, Mendelssohn was able to articulate in a highly literary fashion many of the themes of eighteenth-century natural religion (e.g., the soul's immortality). This pleasing literary style, its poetic prose, and the fact that it was one of the first works of the German Enlightenment written in the form of a dialogue undoubtedly led to the general popularity of the work.

All of the authors thus saw in the dialogue a convenient mechanism to formulate and subsequently popularize philosophical principles. Moreover, all of these authors popularized such principles in response to what they considered to be pressing social issues. In other words, dialogues were not just philosophical texts, but were also convenient vehicles for articulating various forms of Jewish authenticity, whether particularistic in the case of Halevi, or universalistic in the case of the others. Yet even those emphasizing the universalistic element of Judaism nevertheless still felt compelled, as I shall show throughout this study, to stress that it was only in Judaism that one truly encountered such universalism.

Dialogues also allowed various authors to present an argument in an artificially controlled or, perhaps even better, an ideal environment. The dialogue thus enabled an author to bring together a series of opinions, arguments, ideas, or ideologies that were opposed to his own and put them in the mouth of a literary antagonist over which the author had ultimate control. Although these literary antagonists may, on occasion, surprise us with the deftness of their arguments or the quality of their responses, the victor and the ultimate outcome of polemical dialogues are never in any real doubt.

On one level, this feature makes these dialogues seem artificial. The antagonists' arguments are often too easily deflated or mocked in these textual settings, when in reality the situation was probably much more precarious or vitriolic. This is not to say that we do not get glimpses of the reality behind these textual encounters. The best example of this may be found in Falaquera's *Iggeret ha-Vikuah* when the *hasid*, the character who embodies the rabbinic-legal tradition, threatens the philosophical protagonist, the philosopher or *hakham*, with "excommunication" (*nidui*) if he does not agree with his arguments or finds them too far removed from mainstream rabbinic positions. The threat of excommunication was a central feature of the Maimonidean controversies, with adherents on opposing sides using it on their adversaries. Although this example from Falaquera is really an exception to the rule, this is not that surprising given the fact that dialogues functioned as important vehicles of dissemination. These texts, in other words, had to have clear resolutions if they were to popularize philosophical teachings. For example, there cannot be any doubt at the beginning of the Kuzari which monotheism the king will adopt. Likewise in *Ezer ha-Dat*, the strict determinism of the astrologer (a stand-in for Abner of Burgos) cannot be seen to trump the freedom of will of the philosopher (a stand-in for Polleqar).

Furthermore, Halevi makes the philosopher who appears briefly at the beginning of the Kuzari into an individual who makes a complete mockery of the king's dream.[39] Whereas the king wants to know how to improve his actions (*a'māl*) so that they may be brought into harmony with his proper intentions (*niyyāt*), the philosopher's response is completely insensitive to the king's plea:

> There is no favor or dislike in [the nature of] God, because he is above desire and will. A desire intimates a want in the person who feels it, and not until it is satisfied does he become complete… God, therefore, does not know you, much less your intentions or actions *[niyyāt wa-a'māl]*, nor does he listen to your prayers or see your movements.[40]

By putting these words into the philosopher's mouth, Halevi quickly, and one could say all too easily, dismisses the philosopher from the dialogue (in much the same way that he will do with both the Christian and the Muslim).[41]

Another clear example of how the dialogue enables an author to dispose of antagonistic positions may be found in Polleqar's highly sarcastic dismissal of astrology.

Following a lengthy and often acrimonious exchange between a philosopher and an astrologer, the latter subsequently admits that all of his instruments and predictions were meant to give him respect and a high social standing. This reversal is extreme and is essentially confined to *Ezer ha-Dat*. Not nearly as extreme is Falaquera's *Iggeret ha-Vikuaḥ*, wherein the *ḥakham* manages to convince the *ḥasid*, using a variety of legal arguments, that the study of philosophy is required for pious Jews, in addition to being legally binding.

Halevi informs us at the beginning of the *Kuzari* that we should be cautious of assuming a simple correspondence between an author of a dialogue and his main character.[42] Although we tend to equate the *ḥaver* with Halevi, the *ḥakham* with Falaquera, or the various characters who espouse philosophy in *Ezer ha-Dat* with Polleqar, there is not necessarily a one-to-one correspondence between author and main protagonist. Because of this, I spend considerable time in each chapter delineating the various characteristics and personalities that the authors give to their textual protagonists. Sometimes it seems that these characters are based loosely on actual individuals, for example, Abner of Burgos in the case of the various antagonists in Polleqar's *Ezer ha-Dat*. In a similar way, the debate between the *ḥakham* and the *ḥasid* in Falaquera's *Iggeret ha-Vikuaḥ* seems to have been based on real epistolary debates between David Kimḥi and Judah Alfakar.[43]

Other characters that we encounter in these dialogues are mythic or allegorical. Halevi's *Kuzari*, much like Mendelssohn's *Phaedon*, claims to retell past encounters, although updated for a contemporary reading public. Despite such a claim, however, Halevi primarily creates ex nihilo the mise-en-scène, debates, and subsequent conversations between the Khazar king and the various spokespeople with rival claims on monotheism. Halevi thus gives an amorphous story a firm narrative articulation, which enables him to make his case for a particular reading of Judaism. In the same manner, Mendelssohn uses Plato's dialogue of the same name to update Socrates' arguments, in addition to putting new arguments in the mouth of Socrates in order to formulate his own position on natural religion.

In like manner, it is also important to take into account the narrative settings of the dialogic encounters between characters. Rather than regard these settings as haphazard or simply a matter of convenience, I contend that they play a role in the actual contents of these works and contribute to the emergence and subsequent unfolding of the work's argument.

Although not all of the dialogues are concerned with the settings in which the encounters take place (e.g., *Iggeret ha-Vikuaḥ*), the majority are. Falaquera's other work examined here, *Sefer ha-Mevaqqesh*, for example, follows a seeker of knowledge who, in his quest, moves from teacher to teacher in the search for wisdom. This seeker spends considerable time with each teacher before moving on to the next. During each encounter, we are given brief descriptions of that teacher's workshop and place of employment, or receive an account of their duties.

In like manner, in the *Kuzari* all of the spokespeople for rival monotheisms must come to the king's court in Khazaria in order to make their case. This gives way, as others have duly noted,[44] to a situation in which the Khazar king, occupying a position of secular authority, judges presumably with equanimity between these rival religious claims. Moreover, the fact that he chooses Judaism, the "despised" religion, adds to Halevi's argument that only in rabbinic Judaism does there exist a "spiritual" authenticity deriving from the historical bond between God and Israel.

The author who spends the most detail on creating and describing various settings is Isaac Polleqar. The various dialogues recounted in *Ezer ha-Dat* take place in a number of significant venues. For instance a "young" man (*na'ar*) who is a philosopher and an "old man" (*zaqen*) opposed to philosophy acrimoniously debate the true nature of Judaism, the proper reading of Jewish sources, and the place of non-Jewish science in Jewish education. To add to the intensity of the circumstances and to show just what is at stake in their debate, all of this takes place on the cobbled streets of Jerusalem. Moreover, in a debate between an astrologer and another philosopher everything occurs in an open market where the astrologer, with his astrolabes and compasses displayed before him on a table, pitches his wares to a willing crowd. That the philosopher must debate the astrologer in front of this crowd tells the reading audience to just what an extent astrology had taken hold in Jewish society of the fourteenth century. That the philosopher ultimately triumphs before such an inhospitable crowd is certainly no coincidence and is indeed symbolic of the philosopher's place in society. Moreover, when the astrologer admits he is defeated, he joins the philosopher in debating the crowd.

Even when the setting is not described in any particular detail, it can be equally effective. Juxtaposed against the rich descriptions of Polleqar is Abravanel's virtual silence on where the dialogic encounters between Philo and Sophia take place. In particular, we are privy to a series of intimate conversations between a female, presumably unmarried, and a male, also presumably single, in some kind of private setting in which they are not interrupted.[45] The subsequent teasing and provocative dialogue that emerges out of this undefined setting adds to the erotic tensions and innuendo, in turn contributing to the philosophical discussion of love as both a cosmic and a sensual principle.

Although inherent to the genre is a certain artificiality, we must also attune ourselves to the many surprises that can and do occur in these dialogues. The author, then, does not simply manipulate the conversation between characters to move the treatise in a particular way. Indeed, one of the great surprises at the end of the *Kuzari* is that it is ultimately the rabbi who is transformed and, based on his dialogue with the king, comes to the realization that the *intention* (*niyya*) to move to Israel is not enough, but that he must *act* (*'amala*) on this intention.

In the dialogues of Falaquera and Polleqar, we encounter textual records of living debates that shook Jewish cultures of the day. Although, as noted above, the outcomes of these dialogues are never in serious doubt, the genre puts on display various characters' emotions, revealing just what was at stake in these discussions. I mentioned above the threat of the ban raised by Falaquera's *ḥasid*, a threat that was very much a part of the Maimonidean controversies of the age. Likewise the various antagonists who oppose philosophy in *Ezer ha-Dat* are not straw men, whose arguments can be easily dismissed. Although the astrologer ultimately capitulates, the strengths of some of his arguments linger. This undoubtedly is because if we scratch the surface of this astrologer we find the problematic figure of Abner of Burgos.

Similarly, the character of Sophia in the *Dialoghi* does not simply feed convenient questions to Philo to move the dialogue along; she has a personality of her own and often disagrees and debates with Philo.[46] Sophia, then, is not just a convenient textual strategy, but a character in her own right, one who significantly contributes to the philosophical discourse.[47] Indeed, the end of the *Dialoghi* has Philo still requesting from Sophia that she fulfill her "obligation" to him for his lessons on the discourse of love (*pensa di pagare tu a me li debiti che amore ragione e virtú t'obligano*).[48] The sexual tension between the characters, despite the lengthy discussions of love and desire as philosophical principles, remains.

As mentioned above, the study of dialogues enables us to get a sense of the various forces behind the composition of Jewish philosophical texts. Moreover, as will become clear in detail throughout this study, all of these dialogues were written not just for the reasons listed above, but primarily to provide a distinctly Jewish response to non-Jewish ideas, many of which were themselves written and disseminated in the form of dialogues. These non-Jewish ideas and genres—whether developed by Isma'ilis, apostates to Catholicism, Renaissance Humanists, or Enlightenment thinkers—made impressions, sometimes positively, other times negatively, on Jewish philosophers. If non-Jews had not expressed their ideas in dialogue form, then perhaps Jews would have been unlikely to have composed dialogues. This, in turn, raises larger issues for the production of Jewish philosophy, issues to which I shall return, time and again, in the following chapters.

Selection of Dialogues

I have chosen these dialogues either because I could not easily ignore them or because, it seemed to me, they had been unduly neglected in the main narrative of Jewish philosophy. The perfect example of the former is Halevi's *Kuzari*, easily one of the best-known texts in the Jewish philosophical canon, despite the fact that it mounts a sustained critique of the philosophical program of his day. Another example of a well-known dialogue that I examine is Judah Abravanel's *Dialoghi d'amore*. This work, however, is more problematic in the study of Jewish philosophy. As I shall show in detail in chapter 5, although relatively well known, its Jewish "credentials" are often questioned. How can a treatise written in Italian and that hardly mentions Jewish concerns be a work of Jewish philosophy? I contend that it is a very Jewish dialogue, and that it also enables us to witness one of the earliest Jewish responses to the "universalism" of the Renaissance. Although not interested in *explicitly* interpreting Jewish sources in the light of the Renaissance, Abravanel nevertheless mounts a Jewish response to the claims of Christian Humanism.

I have also chosen to look at a number of dialogues that are often marginalized or left out of the unofficial canon of Jewish philosophy. Probably the best example of this is the work of Isaac Polleqar. His *Ezer ha-Dat*, perhaps the most elaborate of the dialogues examined here, has for the most part been ignored in the modern study of Jewish philosophical texts. A few years ago one could have made the same case with respect to Falaquera. However, the pioneering studies of, inter alia, Steven Harvey[49] and Raphael Jospe[50] have gone a long way to making him a fairly well-known thinker. The chapter that I devote to Falaquera builds upon the work of these scholars by focusing upon his use of dialogue and the various relationships that develop between the textual protagonists.

A different example of a relatively ignored text, although for other reasons, is *Phaedon* by Moses Mendelssohn. This work, the product of his optimistic youth, is usually overlooked in favor of his more "Jewish" works such as *Jerusalem* or his preface to and German translation of Manasseh ben Israel's *Vindication of the Jews*. Even more so than Abravanel's *Dialoghi*, *Phaedon* makes no explicit reference to Judaism or Jewish sources. Indeed, if we did not know that its author was Jewish, we would *apparently* have no reason to believe that this treatise had anything whatsoever to do with Judaism. I try to make the case that it is possible to read *Phaedon* as a work of Jewish philosophy because in it we encounter, albeit in an underemphasized manner, a number of the themes and issues that will receive full attention and elaboration in Mendelssohn's later, more explicitly Jewish works.

A brief examination of the dates of all of the authors discussed in this study reveals that all lived in distinct Jewish cultures in the medieval and early modern periods. This wide geographic, temporal, and spatial framework enables me to examine the various localized contexts behind the production of such texts. I wanted to choose a set of texts with such a broad time frame and with disparate geographic environments in order to look more generally at Jewish philosophy than would be possible by examining one text or a set of texts within a particular historical moment. By examining the texts that I do, I hope both to follow a genre as it exists in various Jewish cultures and to provide meaningful generalizations about the genesis and dissemination of Jewish philosophy.

Any study that examines a particular set of texts leads almost inevitably, and perhaps justifiably, to this question: Why these texts and not others? Or, what about this additional text; surely it also contributes to the study of "x"? Let me try to offset some of this potential criticism and explain why I have examined these particular texts, and why I have opted not to include others. I should begin by saying that the scope of the present study is modest, and my greatest hope is that my contribution will encourage both new studies and a new appreciation of those dialogues not discussed here. Indeed, rather than regard this study as an end, I offer it as a point of departure for further exploration.

Dialogues proved to be a fairly popular genre among Jews of the medieval and early modern periods. This study represents an analysis of but one instance of this genre, that of Jewish philosophical dialogues. I have chosen, then, not to examine Jewish dialogues that are not philosophical. Although admittedly the line between a philosophical dialogue and a non-philosophical dialogue can be very fine or even blurred, I do not examine important dialogues such as the highly literary *Taḥkemoni* by Judah al-Ḥarizi (1165–1225)[51] or the historical *Shevet Yehudah* by Shlomo ibn Verga (1460–1554).[52]

Perhaps more provocative is my omission of a number of dialogues that have a distinct philosophical content. One text in particular that I do not examine in any detail is the *Fons Vitae* or *Meqor Ḥayyim* ("Fountain of Life") by Shlomo ibn Gabirol (1021–ca. 1058). The primary reason for this lacuna is that, despite the fact that he uses a dialogue to record a conversation between a master and a disciple, the challenge is not an integral part of the work. The disciple conveniently supplies questions to the master, who subsequently clarifies matters for the student. In fact, so contrived is the dialogue in this treatise that Shem Tov ibn Falaquera, who translated the work into Hebrew, seems to have concluded with Abraham ibn Da'ud (ca. 1110–ca. 1180) that "perhaps if [the *Meqor Ḥayyim*'s] contents were refined, [ibn Gabirol's] words could be included in [a treatise that is] less than one tenth of that treatise."[53] When Falaquera translated the work, he chose—despite the fact that he himself wrote philosophical dialogues—not to retain the dialogue form but simply to summarize the main points.

Despite the fact that I do not spend much time on ibn Gabirol's *Meqor Ḥayyim*, I do, however, examine it in the chapter devoted to Halevi's *Kuzari*. In particular, I argue that Halevi composed his magnum opus, an informed and sustained critique of the philosophical enterprise, in the form of a dialogue because many of his Jewish contemporaries who were interested in tuning Judaism in a philosophical key did so using precisely the same genre. So, whereas ibn Gabirol's provides a fairly wooden dialogic exchange, we witness in Halevi's *Kuzari*, especially in the first book and in the conclusion, a dramatic and dynamic dialogic exchange between characters. Halevi thus does on the level of genre what he does on that of content.

Perhaps the other obvious example that I have chosen not to examine in detail is *Ḥai ha-Olamim* by Yohanan Alemanno (1435–ca. 1504). This work, written just prior to Judah Abravanel's *Dialoghi*, is a dialogue between two characters, one influenced by Maimonidean philosophy and the other by some of the new trends provided by the Renaissance (e.g., rhetoric). The subsequent debate is wide-ranging and encyclopedic,[54] and its main concern is the various stages of human development, showing how the various sciences lead to human perfection. There are several reasons why I do not go into any detail with this treatise. Primary is that, from a literary perspective, Abravanel's *Dialoghi* is a much more interesting work, and therefore allows me to investigate in greater detail than Alemanno's dialogue could the intersection between philosophy and literature. Secondly, the fact that the *Dialoghi* is written in the Italian vernacular as opposed to Hebrew, the language of *Ḥai ha-Olamim*, permits me to ask important questions on the nature of Jewish philosophy—for whom was it written? What are some of its literary intentions? How was it received in a non-Hebrew-speaking world?—than would be possible if I were to examine texts written solely in Hebrew. Thirdly, and intimately related to this last point, unlike

Ḥai ha-Olamim, the subsequent afterlife of the *Dialoghi d'amore*, in both Jewish and non-Jewish cultures, makes this one of the most widely read works of Jewish philosophy in the premodern world.

Another possible lacuna in this study is that I have not chosen to examine in detail the role of dialogue and the dialogic in modern Jewish philosophy. The thought of philosophers such as Franz Rosenzweig (1886–1929) and Martin Buber (1878–1965) abounds with the concept of dialogue; in particular, how humans communicate with one another, and, through this communication, how they experience the divine presence. Indeed, Buber's entire notion of "I and Thou" (*Ich und Du*) is essentially a philosophy of dialogue.[55] The main reason that I have chosen not to analyze this phenomenon in modern Jewish philosophy is because in it the concept of dialogue tends to replace the composition of actual dialogues. The dialogic, in other words, takes precedence over the dialogue. This is not to say, however, that modern Jewish philosophers did not write dialogues. The young Buber, for example, wrote *Daniel*, a dialogue between the main character and a series of individuals, as a way to articulate his notion of authenticity. Despite the literary quality of this work, it does not seem to have played a major role in his subsequent philosophical system. In the epilogue to this study—"From Dialogue to Dialogic"—I briefly trace this metamorphosis.

Method, Aims, and Scope

Recent years have witnessed the critique of intellectual history as a study devoted solely to "great men," "great ideas," and/or "great texts" often at the expense of various marginalized groups (e.g., women, slaves, freedmen).[56] Intellectual history, according to this argument, is irrelevant at best because history is more than just the interests of elites, and at worst the perpetrator of various forms of imperialism against the disenfranchised. Increasingly, intellectual history is overlooked in favor of other disciplines within the humanities—such as social history, cultural studies, gender studies, queer theory, etc.—that seek to give voices to the traditionally voiceless. I certainly have no intention of polemicizing against such disciplines; indeed, I think that they have much to offer the study of philosophy and intellectual history. And, in the chapters that follow, I do not hesitate to embrace and use features from many of these disciplines in order to illumine, from a variety of perspectives, a set of philosophical texts. Despite this, however, intellectual history can and should play an important part in any interdisciplinary approach that seeks to understand premodern Jewish culture in all of its diversity.

Writing, be it literary or philosophical, is, to use the words of Daniel Boyarin, "one practice among many by which a culture organizes its production of meaning and values and structures itself."[57] My aim in what follows is not simply to read medieval philosophical texts as contributions to philosophy, but to connect such texts to the literary mechanisms by which specific Jewish cultures mediated (and continue to mediate) various social, cultural, and intellectual concerns. To regard such texts simply as the products of elites is to ignore the beliefs and cultural practices of Jews. As David Biale has argued,

> the intellectual elite does not exist in isolation, just as daily life does not remain in its own mute universe, unencumbered by intellectual reflection... Those who produce cultural objects, whether written, visual, or material, can never be isolated from the larger social context, the everyday world, in which they live, just as those who belong to this larger world are not immune to the ideas and symbolic meanings that may be articulated by intellectuals. The relationship between text and context ought rather to be seen as the relationship between different types of texts, rather than between the "ideas" of elites versus the "material" reality of the wider society.[58]

In many ways, the charge that intellectual history emphasizes "elite" culture at the expense of "material" or "nonelite" culture risks reifying each term at the expense of nuance. Many of the thinkers examined in this study, for example, certainly belong to "elite" culture in the sense of their education, rabbinic training, and livelihood. Despite this, however, they all had concerns that were not far removed from the so-called "nonelites." The great majority of philosophers in Jewish history wrote both for other philosophers and also for non-philosophers. Ibn Ezra, Maimonides, Gersonides, to name but a few of the biggest names of Jewish philosophy, all wrote treatises, including biblical commentaries, designed to introduce science into the traditional Jewish education curriculum.[59] In so doing, Jewish philosophers became important cultural mediators, not only between various Jewish communities and the larger cultures in which they found themselves, but also between Jewish and non-Jewish ideas.

The history of Judaism, at least until the contemporary period, is essentially the history of encounters and responses, both positive and negative, of Jews to non-Jews, non-Jewish ideas, cultures, and categories. Since Jewish philosophers essentially read Jewish sources using interpretive lenses derived from non-Jews, we are often able to witness in their writings some of these *initial* encounters and responses. Yet such ideas did not remain reified in philosophical texts, but were often filtered into nonphilosophical sources through a variety of mechanisms. One of the primary vehicles for such dissemination was through secondary forms. An in-depth study of one of these particular genres thus has the potential if not to break down the lines between "elites" and "nonelites," then at least to blunt their edges. In philosophical dialogues, we are able to apprehend the various modalities by which "elites" attempted to communicate to "nonelites," or by which traditionally conceived epigonic thinkers bridged the gap between the so-called "great" philosophers and nonphilosophers.

Even though I would be the first to admit that we encounter Judaism not just where there are Jewish texts, but also Jewish bodies, the study of premodern Judaism is, for the most part, confined to written sources (be they biblical commentaries, philosophical treatises, or tax records). The following study works on the assumption that philosophical texts are not only worthy of study, but that they also provide insights into larger social and cultural issues, ones that might otherwise be difficult to access. Yet, to analyze philosophical texts without proper consideration of their manifold cultural, gendered, and socioeconomic contexts gives us a potentially unbalanced or artificial reading. This is not to say that texts are simply the sum of their contexts, but that such texts can never be fully understood apart from them.

This study has several aims. The first is to trace a particular genre across time and space, showing various similarities, continuities, differences, and discrepancies. At the same time, however, what follows is not an explicit comparison of these dialogues but a rich contextual analysis of each one. It makes little sense to compare or contrast explicitly texts written hundreds of years apart from one another, which are produced within cultures with radically different literary, philosophical, and aesthetic sensibilities. On the contrary, I have found it much more profitable to devote a particular chapter to a specific dialogue that I regard as fundamental to the Jewish philosophical culture of that age. I subsequently describe "thickly" each dialogue, embedding it within its immediate Jewish and non-Jewish contexts. When it does seem possible to compare and/or contrast certain features among these dialogues, especially for the sake of nuance, I proceed cautiously.

Second, this study, although devoted to the genre of the dialogue, is also in many ways a comparative study of Jewish cultures.[60] Each dialogue exists within a specific cultural setting and makes use of the codes and conventions of that culture. As a result, we can envisage these texts as local sites of contention between Jewish and non-Jewish encounters. We thus witness a number of tensions, concerns, and fractures that faced a particular author, including the larger society of which that author was a part. Read in this manner, these dialogues function as part window and part mirror. As a window, they let us peer into these texts in order to apprehend a number of communal, cultural, intellectual, and religious debates, since more often than not the dialogues are between individuals with distinct ideological readings of what Judaism is or should be. As part mirror, they in many instances let us ultimately see the author's own point of view reflected in the dialogue, trying to convince us, the audience, that his reading of Judaism is the correct one.

Third, I would like to think that this examination could be read not only as a specialized study on a specific genre, but also as a new introduction to Jewish philosophy. I say "new" because most standard introductions to Jewish philosophy move rapidly from great thinker to great thinker, and from great text to great text, taking only the barest approach to larger concerns. Unlike such introductions, the present work focuses on a relatively small number of thinkers and texts, and opts to provide rich descriptions of these texts—how they interact with, struggle with, and respond to other texts, both Jewish and non-Jewish—over the course of six centuries of Jewish philosophical writing. As a result, we are able to witness the production of philosophical texts in terms of the ideas contained within, but also in relationship to a complex web of social, cultural, religious, and "nationalist"[61] features.

As should be clear from a quick glance at the table of contents, each chapter is devoted to a dialogue written at a particular moment within a distinct Jewish culture. As I mentioned above, I conceptualize each dialogue as a microcosm, one that contains any number of tensions, ideologies, or concerns that faced a particular community. In doing this I am certainly neither attempting to reduce the dynamics of an entire culture to one text nor to suggest that cultures are accessible solely through the textual or philosophical record. However, I do contend that the dialogues under discussion here permit us to conceptualize and understand, on a local level, some of the main intellectual, social, and religious sites of contention that, historically, Jews struggled with or with which they were preoccupied.

One might well object that I apply the term *dialogue* retroactively to an assortment of texts that lack any real inner cohesion.[62] Evidence here could be drawn from the fact that most of the authors did not explicitly call their works "dialogues," which raises the point that it might be artificial to employ modern terms and concepts such as *genre* to medieval texts. In addition, authors of later dialogues rarely, if ever, mention their antecedents. Although there exist a number of interesting relationships between the various authors examined here—for example, Shem Tov ibn Falaquera summarized dialogues of his predecessors; during the Renaissance there was a renewed interest in Halevi's *Kuzari*; one of Mendelssohn's teachers in Berlin, Israel Zamosc, wrote a line-by-line commentary to the *Kuzari*—one still has to ask whether or not these commonalities suffice to speak of a distinct genre of philosophical writing.

Yet, even if these authors would not have recognized their works as belonging to a specific "genre," the fact remains that all, for one reason or another, wrote treatises wherein various characters debate with one another to clarify and elaborate upon a philosophical point or argument. In what follows, I employ terms such as dialogue and genre heuristically to uncover and analyze not only the reasons behind the composition of a set of texts, but equally importantly to show the dynamics within these texts. Granted that certain of the commonalities that exist between them would not have been intended at the time of each dialogue's genesis, looking at them from the vantage point of the modern period makes it difficult to deny that they do not exist.

Although medieval conceptions of genre may well differ from modern understandings, medieval philosophers were familiar with and employed a number of distinct literary forms (e.g., allegories,[63] *summa*,[64] axiomatic works,[65] commentaries[66]) in addition to the dialogue.[67] Whether or not they actually conceived of these literary forms as genres is difficult to say. Despite this, I am comfortable in employing terms such as genre and dialogue because even if the actual terms did not exist, the conceptual and literary techniques behind them certainly did. I thus agree with Peter Heath, who, in his study of allegory in Islamic philosophical writing, argues that the

> theoretical question of the extent to which it is proper or useful to employ western critical terms for works of Islamic literatures is a general problem that can be resolved only by a comparative use of such terms in ways that are sensitive to the limits of the conceptual analogy. I use the term *allegory* here in reference to the Islamic tradition because I believe that the concept, and more important, its praxis have their own indigenous histories. My aim is not to distort our understanding of this historical tradition by indiscreetly applying concepts

borrowed from western literature but rather to employ them carefully in order to explore literary techniques and historical permutations that developed in the Islamic world.[68]

So even though the authors examined here may not have employed the term *dialogue* to describe their mode of writing, it nonetheless becomes possible to isolate a number of literary features that their works share. For this reason, I employ the term *dialogue* to speak collectively about this constellation of literary features. All the while, however, it is important to be conscious of the fact that each one of these authors uses the genre to respond to a number of external features that were not necessarily shared by either his predecessors or those who will come after him.

The chapters below replicate a similar structure. Each begins by situating a particular dialogue in its historical, social, and intellectual environments. This enables me to problematize the issues relevant to the Jewish cultures in which these texts were produced. What, for example, were the pressing intellectual and religious issues of the day? What was going on in the larger societies in which Jews found themselves? How did these societies, or perhaps more accurately their intelligentsias, conceptualize the relationship between philosophy and literature? This, in turn, permits me to set the stage for an analysis of the dialogue in question.

After examining these various contexts, I situate the author of dialogue against this backdrop. I should add, though, that for the chapters on Halevi and Mendelssohn, two of the most important philosophers in the Jewish philosophical "canon," much has been written. I have no intention of retelling their life stories here. However, with some of these thinkers—most notably Polleqar and to a lesser extent Falaquera and Judah Abravanel, who have not been subject to the same biographical studies—I have chosen to go into more detail.

The final part of each chapter moves from the global framework in which each author lived and wrote to the particular text in question. Here I am concerned with analyzing the intersection of the philosophical and the literary. As such, I go into considerable detail examining the literary dimensions of each dialogue. In particular, I focus on the nature of the characters, the way they interact with each other, and the tone of their dialogic encounters. These literary dimensions, in turn, enable me to show how the content of the work slowly emerges. This approach permits both the contextualization of each dialogue within a complex set of broader concerns, and also the conceptualization of these dialogues as a genre. I am well aware that close to six hundred years separate the dialogue in chapter 2 from that in chapter 6, with the result that these texts may resist such classification. Despite this, I persist in the attempt because even though Halevi's *Kuzari* may seem to have nothing in common with Mendelssohn's *Phaedon*, both of these texts represent literary attempts to confront a set of intellectual concerns facing Jewish communities. Even though Halevi may ultimately have responded differently than Mendelssohn to the intellectual trajectories of his day, both authors sought to articulate their visions of what Judaism was or should be, using philosophical arguments and literary techniques that they inherited from their non-Jewish contemporaries.

In this introductory chapter, I have tried to accomplish two things. First, I hope to have called attention to the importance of genre in both the creation and subsequent dissemination of Jewish philosophical writing. In so doing, I argued that a focus solely on content risks overlooking the literary and other nonphilosophical dimensions both within and behind the composition of philosophy. The content of the dialogues discussed in the coming chapters emerges not only through the ideas presented by a textual spokesperson who is often considered to be the author himself, but also through a series of dialectical encounters between characters, the exchange and interchange of ideas, literary devices that frame the encounters and various settings. Attention to these manifold details enables us to not only appreciate these literary dialogues as philosophical treatises, but also situate them in light of concerns that are not just philosophical.

Secondly, I have begun to establish a series of features around which the dialogues discussed in this study constellate. Although these dialogues were produced in distinct Jewish cultures and only make full sense when contextualized in them, these features nevertheless permit careful generalizations. Although each text invites an understanding of the intersection of the literary and the philosophical on its own terms, taken as a whole they lead to a new appreciation of a distinct genre of Jewish philosophical writings. To begin this appreciation, the following chapter examines arguably the most famous of all Jewish dialogues, philosophical or otherwise: Judah Halevi's *Kuzari*.

Notes

1. See, for example, the comments in Klaus Jacobi, "Einleitung," in *Gespräche lesen: Philosophische Dialoge im Mittelalter*, ed. K. Jacobi (Tübingen: Gunter Narr Verlag, 1999), 15–21.
2. James T. Robinson, "Secondary Forms of Transmission: Teaching and Preaching Philosophy in Thirteenth-Century Provence," in *Exchange and Interchange Across Cultural Boundaries: Philosophy, Mysticism, and Science in the Mediterranean World*, ed. H. Ben-Shammai, S. Stroumsa, and S. Shaked (Jerusalem: Magnes Press, forthcoming).
3. Although I disagree with the central premise of his analysis—that Halevi recognized that the law of reason is the ultimate truth and that this is something to which the person of faith cannot agree—one of the earliest scholars sensitive to the literary aspects of the *Kuzari* was Leo Strauss. See his comments in "The Law of Reason in the *Kuzari*," in his *Persecution and the Art of Writing* (Chicago: University of Chicago Press, 1988 [1952]).
4. I certainly do not claim to be reinventing the wheel here. Excellent examples of secondary studies that examine so-called "less important" or "epigonic" thinkers and treatises include Aviezer Ravitzky, "The Thought of Zeraḥiah ben Isaac hen She'altiel Ḥen and Maimonidean-Tibbonid Philosophy in the Thirteenth Century" (Hebrew) (PhD dissertation, Hebrew University of Jerusalem, 1979); idem, *Crescas' Sermon on the*

Passover and Studies in His Philosophy (Hebrew) (Jerusaelm: Israel Academy of Sciences and Humanities, 1988); Robert Eisen, *Gersonides, Providence, Covenant, and the Chosen People: A Study in Medieval Jewish Philosophy and Biblical Commentary* (Albany: State University of New York Press, 1995); idem, *The Book of Job in Medieval Jewish Philosophy* (Oxford: Oxford University Press, 2004); Steven Harvey, ed., *The Medieval Hebrew Encyclopedias of Science and Philosophy* (Dordrecht: Kluwer, 2000); Menachem Kellner, trans., *Gersonides' Commentary on the Song of Songs* (New Haven: Yale University Press, 1998); James T. Robinson, "Philosophy and Exegesis in Ibn Tibbon's Commentary on Ecclesiastes" (PhD dissertation, Harvard University, 2002); Carlos Fraenkel, *From Maimonides to Samuel Ibn Tibbon: The Method of the Guide of the Perplexed* (Hebrew) (Jerusalem: Magnes Press, forthcoming 2009).

5. On the importance of epigonic figures in the history of Jewish cultures, see Shlomo Berger and Irene Zweip, eds., *Epigonism and the Dynamics of Jewish Culture* (Louvain: Peeters, forthcoming 2009).

6. Requisite secondary literature on the problematics of this term may be found in Kenneth Seeskin, *Jewish Philosophy in a Secular Age* (Albany: State University of New York Press, 1990), 1–14; the collection of essays in Norbert M. Samuelson, *Studies in Jewish Philosophy* (Lanham, MD: University Press of America, 1987); Daniel H. Frank, "What is Jewish Philosophy?," in *History of Jewish Philosophy*, ed. Daniel H. Frank and Oliver Leaman (New York and London: Routledge, 1997), 1–10.

7. Aaron W. Hughes, *The Texture of the Divine: Imagination in Medieval Islamic and Jewish Thought* (Bloomington: Indiana University Press, 2004), e.g., 3–5.

8. For Saadya's reading of the Book of Job, see Eisen, *The Book of Job in Medieval Jewish Philosophy*, 17–41.

9. Jeffrey L. Rubenstein, *Talmudic Stories: Narrative Art, Composition, and Culture* (Baltimore: Johns Hopkins University Press, 1999), 3.

10. See, for example, Galit Hasan-Rokem, *The Web of Life: Folklore in Rabbinic Literature* (Hebrew) (Tel Aviv: AM Oved, 1996), 78–100; Jeffrey L. Rubenstein, *The Culture of the Babylonian Talmud* (Baltimore: Johns Hopkins University Press, 2003), 16–38.

11. E.g., *BT Sanhedrin* 91a–91b; *Avodah Zarah* 10a.

12. Dorothy Tarrant, "Style and Thought in Plato's Dialogues," *Classical Quarterly* 42 (1948): 28–30; D. Hyland, "Why Plato Wrote Dialogues," *Philosophy and Rhetoric* (1968): 38–42; Charles Kahn, *Plato and the Socratic Dialogue: The Philosophical Use of a Literary Form* (Cambridge: Cambridge University Press, 1996).

13. Plato, *Meno* 82b–85b.

14. Philip Merlan, "Form and Content in Plato's Philosophy," *Journal of the History of Philosophy* 8/4 (1947): 406–410.

15. Kenneth Seeskin, *Dialogue and Discovery: A Study in Socratic Method* (Albany: State University of New York Press, 1990), 7.

16. Franz Rosenthal, "On the Knowledge of Plato's Philosophy in the Islamic World," *Islamic Culture* 14 (1940): 393.

17. Gotthelf Bergsträsser, *Neue Materielien zu Ḥunain ibn Isḥāq's Galen-Bibliographie* (Nendeln, Liechenstein: Kraus Reprints, 1966 [1932]). This is a critical edition and translation of Ḥunayn ibn Ishḥāq's epistle documenting the translations that he had made. A convenient description of forms and genres found within the Arabic philosophical literature may be found in Dimitri Gutas, "Aspects of Literary Forms and Genre in Arabic Logical Works," in *Glosses and Commentaries on Aristotelian*

Logical Texts: The Syriac, Arabic, and Medieval Latin Texts, ed. Charles Burnett (London: The Warburg Institute, 1993), 29–76.

18. Alfarabi's (870–895) knowledge of Plato's *Laws* has been the subject of a debate between Joshua Parens and Dimitri Gutas. Parens has argued that Alfarabi in his summary to the *Laws* had access to the entire Platonic text, one that was "similar if not identical, to our own." He cites, inter alia, as "likely" evidence that Alfarabi studied in Byzantium. See Parens, *Metaphysics as Rhetoric: Alfarabi's Summary of Plato's Laws* (Albany: State University of New York Press, 1995), xxviii–xxxi. Gutas, however, argues that such evidence is highly unlikely based on (1) Alfarabi's own comments at the end of his summary, and (2) the intricacies of the Greco-Arabic translation process. Instead, Gutas argues that Alfarabi most likely used Galen's synopsis of the *Laws*. See his comments and textual evidence in "Review of *Metaphysics as Rhetoric* by Joshua Parens," *International Journal of the Classical Traditions* 4/3 (1998): 405–412. Because of its implications for my argument, I tend to side with the evidence presented by Gutas.

19. More generally, see *Plato Arabus*, ed. Richard Walzer and Paul Kraus (London: The Warburg Institute, 1951), vol. 1; Moritz Steinschneider, *Die arabischen Übersetzungen aus dem Griechischen* (Nendeln, Lichtenstein: Kraus Reprint 1968 [1902]), 54–64.

20. Perhaps not coincidentally, this is also the way that hadith literature ("Sayings" of the Prophet) was forming during this period. On the latter, see the classic study in Joseph Schacht, *The Origins of Muhammedan Jurisprudence* (Oxford: Clarendon Press, 1979).

The term "Islamicate," coined by Marshall Hodgson, refers "not directly to the religion, Islam, but to the social and cultural complex historically associated with Islam and Muslims, both among Muslims themselves and even when found among Muslims." See Marshall G. S. Hodgson, *The Venture of Islam: Conscience and History in a World Civilization* (Chicago: University of Chicago Press, 1974), vol. 1, 59.

21. Ilai Alon, *Socrates in Medieval Arabic Literature* (Leiden and Jerusalem: Brill and The Magnes Press, 1991), 29.

22. This and further examples may be found in Alon, *Socrates in Medieval Arabic Literature*, 25.

23. 'Usāma ibn Munqidh, *Lubāb al-'adab* (Cairo: n.p., 1935), 432, qtd. in Alon, *Socrates in Medieval Arabic Literature*, 131.

24. For Ghāzlī's criticisms of Socrates in particular and of Greek philosophy general, see his *Tahāfut al-falāsifa*. A convenient English translation with facing Arabic text may be found in *The Incoherence of the Philosophers*, trans. Michael E. Marmura (Provo: Brigham Young University Press, 2000).

25. E.g., Abū Ḥamid al-Ghazālī, *al-Naṣīhat al-mulūk*, ed. F. R. C. Bagley (Oxford: Oxford University Press, 1964), 139.

26. James Hankins, *Plato in the Italian Renaissance* (Leiden: Brill, 1990), vol. 1, 3–7.

27. E.g., Alexander Altmann, *Moses Mendelssohn: A Biographical Study* (University, AL: University of Alabama Press, 1973), 151–52.

28. Al-Tawḥīdī, *Al-Imtā' wa al-mu'ānasa*, vol. 1, ed. Aḥmad Amīn and Aḥmad al-Zayn (Cairo: al-Ta'lif, 1939–1944), 108–128. An English translation of this work may be found in D. S. Margoliouth, "The Merits of Logic and Grammar," *Journal of the Royal Asiatic Society* (1905): 111–29. Also see Muhsin Mahdi, "Language and Logic in Classical Islam," in *Logic in Classical Islamic Culture*, ed. G. E. von Grunebaum (Wiesbaden: O. Harassowitz, 1970), 102–113.

29. Shlomo Pines, "On the Term *Ruḥaniyyot* and Its Origin and on Judah Halevi's Doctrine" (Hebrew), *Tarbiz* 57/4 (1988): 511–40; Bernard Lewis, *The Origins of Ismailism* (Cambridge: W. Heffer and Sons, 1940), 44–54; Paul B. Fenton, "The Arabic and Hebrew Versions of the *Theology of Aristotle*," in *Pseudo-Aristotle in the Middle Ages: The "Theology" and Other Works*, ed. Jill Kraye, W. F. Ryan, and C. B. Shmitt (London: The Warburg Institute, 1986), 241–64; Steven M. Wasserstrom, *Between Muslim and Jew: The Problem of Symbiosis under Early Islam* (Princeton: University of Princeton Press, 1995), 122–35.

30. For an attempt to do this, see John Walbridge, *The Leaven of the Ancients: Suhrawardi and the Heritage of the Greeks* (Albany: State University of New York Press, 2000).

31. An English translation may be found in *The Case of the Animals Versus Man Before the King of the Jinn*, trans. Lenn E. Goodman (Boston: Twayne, 1978). On the relationship between the *Ikhwān* and the Isma'ilis, see, for example, Seyyed Hossein Nasr, *An Introduction to Islamic Cosmological Doctrines*, rev. ed. (Albany: State University of New York Press, 1993), 35–37; Majid Fakhry, *A History of Islamic Philosophy*, 2nd ed. (New York: Columbia University Press, 1983), 164. For a dissenting opinion, see Ian Richard Netton, *Muslim Neoplatonists: An Introduction to the Thought of the Brethren of Purity* (Edinburgh: Edinburgh University Press, 1991), 94–104.

32. Here it is important to note that Isma'ilis proselytized not just among Jews and Christians but primarily among other Muslims. See, for example, Farhad Daftary, *The Isma'ilis: Their History and Doctrines* (Cambridge: Cambridge University Press, 1990), 186–96; Josef van Ess, *Chiliastische Erwartungen und die Versuchung der Göttlichkeit der Kalif al-Ḥākim (386–411 A.H.)* (Heidelberg: Carl Winter Universitätsverlag, 1977).

33. Although as I will try to argue in chapter 6, we can, on one level, see in some of these companions metaphors or metonyms for, e.g., the French skeptical tradition.

34. See the comments in, e.g., Strauss, "The Law of Reason in the *Kuzari*," 118–19.

35. The classic study of these controversies remains Daniel J. Silver, *Maimonidean Criticism and the Maimonidean Controversy 1180–1240* (Leiden: Brill, 1965); a convenient selection of primary sources may be found in A. S. Halkin, ed., *After Maimonides: An Anthology of Writings by His Critics, Defenders and Commentators* (Hebrew) (Jerusalem: The Zalman Shazar Center, 1979); more recently, see the discussion in Hava Tirosh-Samuelson, *Happiness in Premodern Judaism: Virtue, Knowledge, and Well Being* (Cincinnati: Hebrew Union College Press, 2003), ch. 6.

36. E.g., Steven Harvey, "Falaquera's *Epistle of the Debate* and the Maimonidean Controversy of the 1230s," in *Torah and Wisdom: Studies in Jewish Philosophy, Kabbalah, and Honor of Arthur Hyman*, ed. Ruth Link-Salinger (New York: Shengold Publishers, 1992), 75–86; M. Herschel Levine, "Falaquera's Philosophy," in *Proceedings of the Association of Orthodox Jewish Scientists*, vol. 3–4, ed. Fred Rosner (New York: Feldheim, 1976), 577–88.

37. E.g., Shoshana Gershenzon, "A Tale of Two Midrashim: The Legacy of Abner of Burgos," in *Proceedings of the 9th World Congress of Jewish Studies, Division C: Jewish Thought and Literature* (Jerusalem: Magnes Press, 1986), 93–100.

38. Although as I shall discuss in chapter five this may be a problematic assertion.

39. Lenn E. Goodman comments that Halevi puts a lot of "thuses" and "therefores" into the philosopher's speech as a form of sarcasm. See his "Judah Halevi," in *History of Jewish Philosophy*, ed. Daniel H. Frank and Oliver Leaman (New York and London: Routledge, 1997), 197.

40. Halevi, *Kitāb al-radd wa al-dalīl fī al-din al-dhalil,* ed. David H. Baneth and Haggai Ben Shammai (Jerusalem: Magnes Press, 1977), I.1. A problematic English translation may be found in Hartwig Hirschfeld, trans., *The Kuzari: An Argument for the Faith of Israel* (New York: Schocken, 1964), 36. For the sake of convenience, future citations will be from the book and section of the Judeo-Arabic edition of Baneth and Ben-Shammai, with the page number from the translation in parentheses. Mention should also be made in this context of an excellent French translation: Judah Hallévi, *Le Kuzari: Apologie de la religion méprisée,* trans. Charles Touati (Paris: Verdier, 1994).

41. Although, as the dialogue progresses, Halevi's relationship to philosophy, especially that of Avicenna, is not so easily dismissed. In this regard, see Shlomo Pines, "Shi'ite Terms and Conceptions in Judah Halevi's *Kuzari,*" *Jerusalem Studies in Arabic and Islam* 2 (1980): 215–17.

42. See the Comments in Strauss, "The Law of Reason in the *Kuzari,*" 98–103. Another important study that is sensitive to the literary claims of the *Kuzari* is found in Eliezer Schweid, "The Literary Structure of the First Book of the *Kuzari*" (Hebrew), *Tarbiz* 30 (1961): 257–72.

43. See the evidence cited in Harvey, "Falaquera's *Epistle of the Debate* and the Maimonidean Controversy of the 1230s," 76–81; Gilbert Dahan, "Epistola Dialoghi: Une tradiuction Latine de *l'Igeret ha Vikuaḥ* de Shem Tov ibn Falaquera," *Seferad* 39/1 (1979): 56–57.

44. E.g., Schweid, "The Literary Structure of the First Book of the *Kuzari,*" 259–60; Strauss, "The Law of Reason in the *Kuzari,*" 102–103.

45. Abraham Melamed, "The Woman as Philosopher: The Image of Sophia in Judah Abravanel's *Dialoghi*" (Hebrew), *Madaei ha-Yahadut* 40 (1990): 122–23. I would like to thank Prof. Melamed for calling this article to my attention, and for sending me an offprint of it.

46. E.g., Judah Abravanel, *Dialoghi d'Amore,* III.233–34. An English translation of this may be found in F. Friedeberg-Seeley and Jean H. Barnes, trans., *The Philosophy of Love (Dialoghi d'Amore)* (London: Soncino Press, 1937), 273–77. For the sake of convenience, future citations will be from the book and page number from the English translation in parentheses. See the comments in Melamed, "The Woman as Philosopher," 113–30.

47. See Hava Tirosh-Rothschild, "Jewish Philosophy on the Eve of Modernity," in *History of Jewish Philosophy,* ed. Daniel H. Frank and Oliver Leaman (New York and London: Routledge, 1997), 557 n. 101.

48. *Dialoghi* III.391 (Friedeberg-Seeley and Barnes, 468).

49. E.g., *Falaquera's Epistle of the Debate: An Introduction to Jewish Philosophy,* ed. and trans. Steven Harvey (Cambridge: Harvard University Press, 1987).

50. E.g., Raphael Jospe, *Torah and Sophia: The Life and Thought of Shem Tov Ibn Falaquera* (Cincinnati: Hebrew Union College Press, 1988).

51. Judah al-Ḥarizi, *The Book of the Taḥkemoni: Jewish Tales from Muslim Spain,* trans. David Simha Segal (London: Littman Library of Jewish Civilization, 2001). See the comments in Ross Brann, *Power in the Portrayal: Representations of Jews and Muslims in Eleventh- and Twelfth-Century Islamic Spain* (Princeton: Princeton University Press, 2002), esp. 140–59.

52. Shlomo Ibn Verga, *Shevet Yehudah* (Jerusalem: Mekhon benei Yisakhar, 1991). For secondary literature, see Yosef Haim Yerushalmi, *The Lisbon Massacre of 1506 and*

the *Royal Image in the Shebet Yehudah* (Cincinnati: Hebrew Union College Press, 1976).

53. Abraham Ibn Da'ud, *The Exalted Faith*, trans. Norbert M. Samuelson (Rutherford, NJ: Fairleigh Dickinson University Press, 1986), 40.

54. See, e.g., Abraham Melamed, "The Hebrew Encyclopedias of the Renaissance," in *The Medieval Hebrew Encyclopedias of Science and Philosophy*, ed. Steven Harvey (Dordrecht: Kluwer, 2000), esp. 448–54; Fabrizio Lelli, "La Retorica Nell'Introduzione del Hay ha-'Olamim," in *Hay ha-'Olamim (L'immortale): Parte I: La Retorica*, ed. F. Lelli (Florence: Leo S. Olschiki, 1995).

55. E.g., Paul Mendes-Flohr, *From Mysticism to Dialogue: Martin Buber's Transformation of German Social Thought* (Detroit: Wayne State University Press, 1989), 93–126; Steven Kepnes, *The Text and Thou: Martin Buber's Dialogical Hermeneutics and Narrative Theology* (Bloomington: Indiana University Press, 1992), 19–40; Gilya Gerda Schmidt, *Martin Buber's Formative Years: From German Culture to Jewish Renewal, 1897–1909* (Tuscaloosa: University of Alabama, 1995), 21–47.

56. For instance, in an excellent local analysis of the Jewish community of Valencia at the time of the anti-Jewish riots of 1391, Mark D. Meyerson argues: "a history that privileges philosophical, theosophical, and polemical texts often overlooks crucial details of Jewish socioeconomic life and the complexities of Jewish coexistence and conflict with non-Jews." See his *A Jewish Renaissance in Fifteenth-Century Spain* (Princeton: University of Princeton Press, 2004), 7. Although on one level I agree with him—intellectual history has been traditionally unconcerned with socioeconomic life—on another, I completely disagree, as philosophical texts, when read with a different set of concerns, have the potential to tell us much about "socioeconomic" life and the relationships between Jews and non-Jews.

57. Daniel Boyarin, *Carnal Israel: Reading Sex in Talmudic Culture* (Berkeley: University of California Press, 1993), 12, qtd. in Tova Rosen, *Unveiling Eve: Reading Genre in Medieval Hebrew Literature* (Philadelphia: University of Pennsylvania Press, 2003), 26.

58. David Biale, "Preface," in *Cultures of the Jews: A New History* (New York: Schocken, 2002), xxvi.

59. See, for example, Ralph Lerner, *Maimonides' Empire of Light: Popular Enlightenment in an Age of Belief* (Chicago: University of Chicago Press, 2000), 3–13; Kenneth Seeskin, *Searching for a Distant God: The Legacy of Maimonides* (Oxford: Oxford University Press, 2000), 142–75.

60. In using the term *Jewish cultures* I am influenced by the discussion in Efraim Shmueli, *Seven Jewish Cultures: A Reinterpretation of Jewish History and Thought*, trans. Gila Shmueli (Cambridge: Cambridge University Press, 1990), who writes, for example, that "By culture I mean a set of shared symbols which represent an organized collective attempt to express the meaning, or meanings, of life and to make the world habitable by transforming its impersonal vastness and frightening dimensions into an understandable and significant order" (3). In Judaism, these "shared symbols" include God, Torah, chosenness, etc.; yet, for Shmueli, while "these concepts have endured, their meanings have changed, the inevitable result of the changes occurring in the ontologies underlying these concepts and experiences" (4). To this discussion of Jewish cultures should also be added the essays in Biale, ed., *The Cultures of the Jews*.

61. By employing the term *nationalist* here, I certainly do not refer to the modern concept of Zionism, but to a form of biblical nationalism, in which certain Jewish thinkers

appealed to the supremacy of the cultural and literary forms of ancient Israel. See, for example, the rich discussion in Ross Brann, *The Compunctious Poet: Cultural Ambiguity and Hebrew Poetry in Muslim Spain* (Baltimore: Johns Hopkins University Press, 1991), 23–58.

62. See the cautionary comments in Eisen, *The Book of Job in Medieval Jewish Philosophy*, 10.

63. See, for example, Jon Whitman, *Allegory: The Dynamics of an Ancient and Medieval Technique* (Cambridge, MA: Harvard University Press, 1987); Peter Heath, *Allegory and Philosophy in Avicenna (Ibn Sīnā)* (Philadelphia: University of Pennsylvania Press, 1992).

64. E.g., Leonard Boyle, "The Setting of the *Summa Theologiae* of St. Thomas: Revisited," in *The Ethics of Aquinas*, ed. Stephen J. Pope (Washington: Georgetown University Press, 2002); Mark D. Jordan, "The Protreptic Structure of the *Summa Contra Gentiles*," *The Thomist* 50/2 (1986): 173–209.

65. E.g., Gillian R. Evans, "Boethian and Euclidean Axiomatic Method in the Theology of the Later Twelfth Century," *Archives Internationale d'Histoire des Sciences* 30 (1980): 36–52.

66. E.g., Eisen, *Gersonides on Providence, Covenant, and the Chosen People*; idem, *The Book of Job in Medieval Jewish Philosophy.*

67. See, for example, the collection of essays in Jacobi, ed., *Gespräche lesen: Philosophische Dialogue im Mittelalter.*

68. Heath, *Allegory and Philosophy in Avicenna*, 6–7.

Index of Subjects

Index of Names

Lightning Source UK Ltd.
Milton Keynes UK
16 April 2010